TIME, SPACE, AND THE MARKET

TIME, SPACE, AND THE MARKET

RETROSCAPES RISING

STEPHEN BROWN AND
JOHN F. SHERRY JR.

EDITORS

M.E.Sharpe
Armonk, New York
London, England

Library of Congress Cataloging-in-Publication Data

Time, space, and the market : retroscapes rising / edited by Stephen Brown and John F.
Sherry, Jr.
    p. cm.
Includes bibliographical references and index.
ISBN 0-7656-1012-4 (cloth: alk. paper) — ISBN 0-7656-1013-2 (pbk.: alk. paper)
1. Marketing—Case studies. 2. Time and economic reactions—Case studies. 3.
Nostalgia—Case studies. I. Brown, Stephen, 1955– II. Sherry, John F.

HF5415 .T568 2002
380.1—dc21   2002030850

Printed in the United States of America

The paper used in this publication meets the minimum requirements of
American National Standard for Information Sciences
Permanence of Paper for Printed Library Materials,
ANSI Z 39.48-1984.

BM (c) 10 9 8 7 6 5 4 3 2 1
BM (p) 10 9 8 7 6 5 4 3 2 1

To that retroscape we all have fled and watered,
The University

Contents

Exhibits

Introduction

Boats Against the Current

1

No Then There

Of Time, Space, and the Market

Stephen Brown

When asked, in the early 1930s, to comment on the less than picturesque aesthetics of Oakland, California, Gertrude Stein famously quipped that there's "no there there." If Stein were passing judgment today, she'd probably conclude that there's no there anywhere, since "Oaklandization" has accelerated in the interim. Today's McCities come equipped with the exact same corporate chains and fast food McFranchises; our McShopping malls, airport terminals, and convention centers are cut from the same placeless cloth; and, thanks to the McNet's much trumpeted dislocation of spatial relations, our awareness of thereness has all but evaporated. Place is history. Or so it seems (Hannigan 1998; Ritzer 1999; Sorkin 1992).

Although it is often contended that areal differentiation is disappearing in our world of "non-places" (Augé 1995), closer examination reveals a countervailing commercial trend. Far from experiencing a spatial apocalypse, we are witnessing a renewed interest in place, as the recent rise of dramatic servicescapes like Niketown, ESPN Zone Chicago, and Bass Outdoor World readily attests (Sherry 1998a; Sherry et al. 2001). True, these spaces tend to be rapidly replicated in towns and cities across the globe—there are now nineteen Niketowns, for example—thereby giving with one hand what they take away with the other. But the fact of the matter is that making sense of place is back on the executive agenda. Staging time, space, and the market is a corporate priority. Generating *genius loci* is the order of the day (Sherry 2000).

One of the principal ways in which this sense of place is being reanimated is through evocations of times past. That is to say, many of today's much-lauded servicescapes are actually retroscapes (Brown 2001). Niketown, for

3

example, has been aptly described as "one part nostalgia to two parts hi tech" (Hannigan 1998, p. 92) and "a hi tech cross between a store, a museum and a media experience" (Ritzer 1999, p. 111). The Irish theme pub comprises a combination of carefully sanitized Emerald Isleisms culled from the imaginary history of that troubled land (Brown and Patterson 2000). Celebration, Disney's renowned new town in central Florida, is an evocation of 1950s Americana, an Eisenhowerian idyll that never existed outside Burbank studio back lots (Ross 1999). Las Vegas, likewise, is more than a congeries of kitsch locales—Rome, Egypt, Paris, New York, Hollywood, and so forth—but ersatz environments at a particular point in time, be it ancient Rome, predynastic Egypt, *fin de siècle* Paris, Prohibition-era New York, the Golden Age of Hollywood, or the Wild, Wild West that wasn't (Gottdiener 1997).

As these examples illustrate, retroscapes come in all shapes and sizes, from individual rooms (the Colonial "look") and retail stores (American Girl), through shopping malls (Faneuil Hall) and neighborhoods (Old Pasadena), to central business districts (Vieux Carré), "new" urban communities (Kentlands, Maryland) and, if you take the tourist brochures on trust, entire countries, or sizeable regions thereof (Merrie England). Retroscapes, furthermore, are not confined to physical places or tangible topographies. Consider the Internet. Although it is usually portrayed as the latest thing, a newfound land behind the screen, the merest glance across its virtual landscape reveals that the Net is irredeemably retro. Apart from its general sense of steam-driven sluggishness, as well as its armies of amateur genealogists and tenders of family trees, the Net is replete with retro home pages, many of which are akin to cyber Victorian parlors—overstuffed, overwhelming, overindulgent. And then, of course, there's e-commerce. The very term carries retro connotations, since "commerce" is next to "comestible," "purveyor," and "emporium" in the lexicon of ye-olde-shopping speak. Just as retro realtors, insurance agents, and auto dealers importune us with allusion to epochs untainted by crass commercialism ("faithfully serving the local community since 1954" etc.), so too their virtual equivalents adopt suitably antiquated linguistic camouflage (see Brown 2001).

Increasingly apparent though it is, this recent rapid rise of retroscapes has attracted comparatively little attention from the marketing academy. There is, as we shall see shortly, a substantial scholarly literature on servicescapes (Sherry 1998b) and retromarketing is emerging as an important area of academic endeavor (Brown 2001). But the overlap remains unexplored by marketing researchers, if not by our anthropological, sociological, and geographical brethren (though even here retroscapes *qua* retroscapes remain unstudied). However, given the latter-day profusion of retro goods and services and, moreover, given the space-time stereotyping that the imagineers of retroscapes are frequently accused of, surely it is time to ask—*pace* Stein—whether there is No Then There.

This question, to be sure, can be answered in a number of ways. Inventories of retroscapes can be assembled; classifications of retroscapes can be constructed; definitions of retroscapes can be formulated; histories of retroscapes can be written; distinguishing features of retroscapes can be identified; comparative studies of retroscapes can be conducted; questionnaire surveys of consumer attitudes to retroscaped environments can be mounted; rigorous retroproneness scales can be developed, under carefully controlled experimental conditions, and validated in a representative sample of retroenvironments. The designers, creators, and architects of retroscapes can also be investigated by marauding tribes of ethnographically minded marketing researchers, and the cultural significance of their cosmos-building beliefs reported. The designers' beliefs can be reported, too.

Although all of these approaches have merit, it is arguable that they leave something to be desired. Space is special. Geography matters. Location is not just a dot on a map or a digitized coordinate from a circling satellite. Place is more than a marketing P. Meanings, messages, memories, and motives inhere in places—marketplaces in particular (Brown 1992)—and it is our belief that *genius loci* can't be fully captured by "established" research procedures, valuable though these are. Philosophers, poets, playwrights, painters, and photographers can capture it, but conventional marketing and consumer researchers are constrained by the scientistic norms, hard-fact expectations, and self-perpetuating dispassion of the prevailing positivistic paradigm.

The present text, then, comprises a congeries of creatively written essays. Some, we believe, are works of art in themselves. But they all represent attempts to do something different, something atypical, something innovative, something imaginative, something more than run of the marketing mill. Granted, there are risks in such unorthodox approaches—ridicule, rejection, remonstration, rancor—but if they encourage marketing and consumer researchers to reflect on their own reactions to retroscaping, then this anthology will have served its purpose.

Despite its title, *Time, Space, and the Market* is not a philosophical tract. It is situated, rather, at the confluence of three streams of marketing scholarship. The first of these is the veritable cascade of publications on servicescapes. Place, as noted previously, is being recuperated by marketing and consumer researchers (Cova 1999). Recent years have seen studies of shopping centers (Csaba and Askegaard 1999), gift shops (McGrath 1989), flagship stores (Peñaloza 1999), swap meets (Belk, Sherry, and Wallendorf 1988), farmers' markets (McGrath, Sherry, and Heisley 1993), heritage parks (Goulding 2000), bridal salons (Otnes 1998), brandfests (McAlexander and Schouten 1998) and many more besides. Some of these analyses, admittedly, incorporate retroscaped components. A good example is O'Guinn and Belk's (1989) naturalistic investigation of Heritage Village USA, a religious theme park redolent with the revivalist spirit of ole-time, God-fearing, Bible-belted, Southern Baptistry. As a rule, however, the retro side of servicescapes has gone unremarked hitherto.

The second stream of scholarship surging into the present volume is the latter-day literature on nostalgia in general and retromarketing in particular. For the past ten years or so, the marketplace has been inundated with yestertat. Replicas, remakes, reissues, rereleases, relaunches, reproductions, retreads, re-creations, reinventions, and reenactments are the order of the day (Carlin 1997; Harris 2000). Marketing academicians, naturally enough, have sought to steer a course through this memory maelstrom and they've identified a range of possible causal factors: the aging of the baby boom generation, that pines for the products of yore (Holbrook and Schindler 1994, 1996); the *fin de siècle* effect, humankind's compulsion to look back at centurial transitions (Stern 1992); and attempts by time-pressed, anxiety-stricken, future-shocked consumers to cocoon themselves from the trials and tribulations of today's fast-changing world (Brown 1999). However, the spatial manifestations of this retromarketing *mentalité* have attracted comparatively little academic attention thus far.

The third scholarly tributary flows from marketing's misty methodological mountains, our scholarly Shangri-La. A postmodern putsch is underway in the land where the blinded by science lead the blinded by science, and hordes of heretical methodologists are trying to seize control (Belk 1995; Hirschman and Holbrook 1992; Sherry 1991). Or so the story goes. Be it true or false, they say that the revolutionaries have thrown open the theoretical floodgates and released a raging torrent of qualitative research techniques. Sourced in the wholesome headwaters of the humanities and liberal arts, this methodological *tsunami* has swept through the marketing floodplain and enriched the impoverished scholarly soil with its intellectual alluvium. The present book is anchored in—or, rather, floats uneasily on—these storm-tossed waters of academic inundation. It is not a Noah's Ark, admittedly, but it's not the Nautilus either. Pequod, perhaps.[1]

The confluence of these rivers of marketing research, needless to say, is sometimes stormy, occasionally threatening, and at times impassable. But, it is mostly plain sailing. A compass, nevertheless, is called for and pre-postmodern marketing matelots should note that *Time, Space, and the Market* is organized in accordance with the traditional tripartite division of geographical scale—*micro*, *meso*, and *macro*. Micro, in this case, refers to rooms, buildings, individual retail stores, and shopping centers. Enclosed retroscapes, in essence.

Meso ranges from heritage parks and beachfronts to holiday resorts and river valleys. Open yet bounded retroscapes, in other words. Macro, finally, is the most ambitious of all. Geographically, it includes nation-states, virtual worlds, ancient cultures, and, in the penultimate chapter, the basic organizing principle of the universe. The big picture, in short.

Appropriately enough, this micro/meso/macro classification is itself inherently retro, insofar as it used to be the *bête noire* of geographers and spatial scientists. Much printers' ink has been expended on verifying the classification, drawing boundaries between the individual categories, and debating whether concepts, patterns, or processes could be transferred from one tier to another (Watson 1978). No doubt geographers still engage in such stolid typological pursuits, but the latter-day emergence of chaotics, where fractals and analogous self-replicating patterns are discernible at all spatial scales (be they snowflakes or coastlines), has effectively consigned the micro/meso/macro classification to the trashcan of history (Johnson 2001). This does not mean that the present volume comprises a chaotic assemblage of chapters, out of which a semblance of sense will eventually emerge like a kind of marketing Mandlebrot Set.

Actually, that's a perfect way of describing *Time, Space, and the Market*. The conventional title, cover, and structure of the text masks the stylistic, spatial, and scholarly diversity it contains.

Take the first chapter in the first section, where John Sherry steps up to the plate, albeit a pseudo plate in the deep dark heart of ESPN Zone Chicago, a retrothemed sports emporium close to Chicago's Magnificent Mile. Comfortably ensconced in the uterine embrace of the Throne Zone, a La-Z-Boy-bedecked, giant TV screen-garlanded, Dolby Surround Sound-surrounded holodeck of holies, Sherry surfaces from the amniotic fluid of anamnesis, adjusts his metaphorical jock strap (XXL, he maintains), and strikes out across the forgotten topography of memory to provide a pungent, plangent, paronomastic paean to place marketing in all its pulchritudinous manifestations. He reflects on his extensive retro research experience, which ranges from the archetypal retroscape, Niketown, to his recent work in the birthday-besuited environs of Black Rock City, an annual assemblage of anachronistic anarchists in the Nevada desert, and comes to the conclusion that he's an inveterate internee of pseudo agoras, a cosmonaut of consumer research adrift in the multiple universes of the marketplace.

And Sherry's not the only one, as Belk shows in Chapter 3, where he takes us on a textual tour of the "dollhouse for adults" that is *The Sims*. A phenomenally successful computer game, *The Sims* requires players to start a family, oversee its development, maintain a harmonious household, and ensure that its members make their way in the wide, if pixilated, world beyond. The virtual brood has to be fed and watered, spit and polished, and lifted and laid—literally—though, in fairness to the simulants, they are required to earn their keep, engage in appropriately neighborly acts, and avoid the downward spiral to dysfunctionalism, destitution, and dipsomania. However, the irony of *The Sims* is that even though its players are building the faux future, they do so by rebuilding the phony past. The houses, furnishings, personal possessions, and moral codes contained in the computer game are deeply retrospective, a virtual throwback to an imagined 1950s of burgeoning burbs, pearly picket fences, happy-clappy nuclear families, and ever-optimistic beliefs in bright new tomorrows. It's Disney's Tomorrow-land for yester-minded baby boomers. Retrotopia is here. Retrotopia is now. It's a small world after all.

Clicks and mortar are hard to beat and *The Sims* is singularly seductive. However in Chapter 4, Goulding drags us back to the equally endearing bricks and mortar of small time retroperators, retropreneurs, and retromovers and shakers. Based partly on her personal experience as a part-time trader in 1950s sunglasses and partly from a qualitative study of retro apparel outlets, she makes an important distinction between authentic and inauthentic retrowear. The former comprise reproduction pants, corsets, bustiers, mini-skirts, stilettos, and so on, whereas the former are the real things, thrift shop throwaways gathering dust in forgotten corners of independently owned retro retail stores. Indeed, the discovery-cum-recovery of such hidden treasures is an important part of their consumer appeal, as is the social side of the retroshopping experience. Conjoined by a shared interest in retro chic, consumers use the retail stores as waystations on the road to suitably retrothemed nightclubs and restaurants. Social and subcultural considerations aside, Goulding contends that retro represents a form of consumer resistance, a refusal of the blandness and ubiquity of chain store fashions, a quixotic search for authenticity in the irredeemably inauthentic world of retrocouture.

The retro rag trade is all very well—rampant recycling, remember, has long been a characteristic feature of fashion—but surely the tavern is a haven of peace and quiet, a port in the storm of modern life, a tranquil tabernacle of comfort, constancy, conviviality, and the *craic*. Not so, according to Patterson and Brown in Chapter 5, who reflect on the rise of the Irish theme pub, a Celtic-twilighted composite of little people-peopled, faux fairyland-filigreed and peat-briquetted, begorrah-bespoken, bejabbers-bejasus, better be Beamish. No, make mine a Guinness. Yet despite the cavils of the critics, who disdain such *Erin go brach* retroscaping, and notwithstanding the mini industry that has developed around the manufacture of pseudo-shillelaghs, sham o'shanters, and plastic paddy paraphernalia, an empirical study of customer introspections reveals that retroscapes resonate. For all the almost antiques, genuine fakes, and half-timbered Hibernalia that such ersatz establishments contain, they nonetheless convey a profound sense of place to reminiscence-prone patrons. In many ways, the Emerald Isleisms inscribed in imitation imbiberies like Scruffy Murphy's and Molly Malone's are (in the words of Ireland's unofficial ambassadors, U2) even better than the real thing. Or should that be stuck in a memory you can't get out of?

The melodious motif continues in the final chapter of the first section, where Pauline Maclaran practices her scales on the piano of past times. Ostensibly a melancholic marketing tale about the decline and fall of Powerscourt Townhouse Center, a nostalgia-steeped servicescape in the central shopping area of Dublin, she extemporizes on her musical theme to compose a personal yet universal scholarly symphony. Taking the abandoned Powerscourt piano as a symbol of this once flourishing now floundering shopping complex, she introduces a contrapuntal personal narrative about a baby grand piano, a family heirloom imbued with memories of a great aunt, which was bequeathed to the author, can't be abandoned, and looms reprovingly over her everyday existence. Looming is the operative word, since the much loved piano is too big, too bulky, too unobliging in today's mobile, minimalist, MTV-mediated milieu. Parlor-sized pianos have their place, as do festival shopping malls and the concert grand pianofortes therein, but time moves on, nothing lasts forever, a change is as good as a rest, and clichés are not just for Christmas. The clarion call of new and improved is hard to resist, albeit the music of memorable marketplaces is always playing in the background and is permanently preserved in the amber of remembrance.

Maclaran's solo on the Powerscourt piano is accompanied in Chapter 7 by Troester's tom-tom beat of time-was powwows. These drums, however, are even more distant than those of Jim Reeves, a sixties country crooner who met an untimely end and is now playing twice nightly in the Grand Old Opry in the sky. Circa 1954, a big-talking backwoods booster called Anthony Wise created Historyland, an off the beaten track tourist attraction in the wilds of Wisconsin. Historyland was a cross between Disney's Frontierland and living history museums like Colonial Williamsburg, Greenfield Village, and Plimoth Plantation. It not only celebrated the traditional culture of the Chippewa, an indigenous Native American tribe, but it tapped into the locality's lucrative, if short lived, history of logging, rolling, and lumberjackscapades. Tree felling contests, authentic Indian encampments, and the relentless promotional tattoo of Tony Wise ensured that his facility flourished throughout the fifties, when the Wild West was where it was at for Hollywood filmmakers and network TV executives. Historyland, sadly, was constructed of marketing smoke and mirrors. Hopelessly underfinanced, it went under in 1989, was subsequently razed to the ground by the local fire department, and nothing is left today except a photograph-bespattered, road-side diner run by polyester-clad senior citizens.

Anthony Wise was no Kubla Kahn and Historyland no Xanadu, but his retro pleasure dome has its parallels in the sunless sea of the sunshine state. In Chapter 8, the plight of Huntington Beach is taken up by Hope Schau, a long-time resident of this small but beautifully formed settlement on the southern edge of the Los Angeles conurbation. The epicenter of the easy-living, sun-kissed, surfboard-and-lodging lifestyle, Huntington Beach shot to fame in the 1960s when it surfed the surf music wave courtesy of Jan and Dean, the Beach Boys, and similar foam-flecked, me-too musos. The wave sub-sided, the town mellowed into a low-rent, beach-bum nirvana, and everything was cool. Way cool. Until mendacious, money-grubbing marketing men spotted an opportunity to reinvent Huntington Beach as a retro resort, a silicon simulacrum of the seminal sixties surf city scene. The local council capitulated. The million dollar condos went up. A museum of surfboarding was built. A faux boardwalk, complete with faceless chain stores, cappuccino capitalists, Jan and Dean diners, pay-by-the-pound-of-flesh parking lots, and a brand new old-fashioned pier, was constructed in very short order. For some, it is paradise regained. For others, it is marketing at its most meretricious. For Hope Jensen Schau, a marketing professor who grew up in Huntington Beach, it offers an opportunity to examine the intracommunity tensions that this beachfront bonanza precipitated.

Bad as the Huntington Beach beachfront is, or appears to be, it is a veritable repository of authenticity compared to the beachfront that is featured in Chapter 9. On this occasion, the "beach" is adjacent to the Big Kahuna wave pool in Noah's Ark, a retro themed water park in Wisconsin Dells, a retro themed holiday resort in the sclerotic heart of cream cheese country. Worse, our guide to this polypropylene paradise is a Genuine Gaelic Griswold, a bumbling Irish academic who grumbles, gripes, and generally makes life hell for his patient, much-put-upon family. He complains about his kids' retro musical preferences; makes an exhibition of himself in the retro hotel lobby; disdains the retro ridiculousness of the Wisconsin Dells experience; and, after encountering the acme of retro in a Classic Denny's Diner, eventually comes to realize that families matter, holidays can be fun, and plastic retroscapes aren't so bad after all. Retro, *pace* Congreve, has charms to soothe a savage breast.

From the breast to the Brule. A seventy-mile river valley in northern Wisconsin (our retro state of choice), the Brule is renowned for its excellent fishing, hunting, and get-away-from-it-all-ness. It is the veritable Happy Valley of outdoor types and backwoodspersons, a sacred river in a secret setting, known only to the piscatorial cognoscenti. However, it is much more than that to the one and only Morris B. Holbrook, doyen of the introspective essay and sometime chronicler of Manhattan's concrete canyons. According to our retroprospector non-pareil, it is a yesterspace of the first water, a place where childhood memories, ancestral pastimes, consumer behavior, and an unexpected inheritance coalesce into a personal retroscape that is almost superrealist in its intensity. When a collection of his grandfather's carefully catalogued photographs falls into Holbrook's hands, it serves as a celluloid equivalent of Proust's Madeleine, a mode of involuntary transportation to the sights, sounds, and smells of times past. Combined with the entries in his grandfather's evocatively written log, our contemporary time traveler conjures up the consumption rich yet marketing poor milieu of his childhood vacations, as well as the ghost of a much-admired raconteur and multitalented photoessayist, Arthur Tenney Holbrook.

Memories are not only involuntary, as Marcel Proust found with his dunkin-driven, nibble-nourished reveries, but they are impermanent. They fade. They falter. They fuse. They leave only the faintest Freudian trace on the mystic writing pad of remembrance. The same is true of retroscapes. To some extent at least. As Robert Kozinets shows in his excursus on Burning Man, an annual, seven-day festival held in the Nevada badlands, retroscapes can appear and disappear in quick succession, like familiar landmarks in a desert sandstorm. Black Rock City is a temporary encampment of 25,000 people, which springs up overnight, engages in an aestheticized orgy of potlatch-like practices, immolates itself in a frenzy of profligate pyromania, and rises Phoenix-like from the ashes the following year. It is an ephemeral conglomeration of communitas and the carnivalesque, a cupidity-free zone where marketing in all its money-first forms is resisted and reviled. Black Rock City is also a site of postmodern primitivism, a liminal space where Silicon Valley Girls (and Guys) attempt to get back to nature, get in touch with the inner aesthete, and find utopia in nearly noble savagery. Unlike our hunting and gathering ancestors, however, who slashed and burned and left an exhausted environment in their wake, Burning Man is nothing if not ecoconscious, a nu-hippy happy valley, an impermanent monument to old style new agery and neo-neolithic nostalgia.

Equally nostalgic, if rather more firmly established, is the fabulous fiftieth state. For Borgerson and Schroeder, in fact, Hawaii is the archetypal retroscape, a paradisal apotheosis of the happily unspoilt past with gratifyingly modern amenities. Almost. In the first chapter of the third section, they show how this arcadian image of Hawaii was constructed—retrofitted, rather—in the 1950s, thanks to the market-building, move-the-merchandise, monochrome-is-history, color-film-finagling activities of the imperious Kodak corporation. It was furthered by the fifties fad for all things aloha, popular music in particular. A meditation on the authors' compendious collection of Hawaiian records reveals that the album cover artwork unfailingly draws upon and contributes to Hawaii's paradisal sense of place. Meanwhile the music is a milieu where country and western meets Tin Pan Alley in an admittedly melodious mishmash of musical traditions, none of which are native to the islands, though they are regarded as indigenous in retrospect. Retrospection, indeed, is the essence of Hawaii. It is a primitive paradise only a plane flight away. It is an invented tradition that keeps reinventing itself, as the recent luau revival by latter-day leis-lubbers and tiki-baristas bears eloquent witness. It is a retroescape from the trials and tribulations of today's high-pressure workplace, nonstop rat race, headless chicken steeplechase.

Talk of headless chickens can mean only one thing. Gastronomy alert! In Chapter 13, Patrick Hetzel chows down on the retroscape of French cuisine. It is a milieu where antiquity is all, vintage is vital, tradition is ever on tap, and old-and-improved is the order of the day. True, the Gallic gastroscape is seasoned with a soupcon of contemporaneity—fresh ingredients, innovative recipes, nouvelle cuisine, and the seasonal flux of gustatory fashion—but the past is a platter that is perpetually piled high, a piping hot dish that never goes cold, a yesterbuffet for backward-glancing bon viveurs and tipsy trufflers of time was. For Hetzel, this epochal epicureanism is epitomized by the establishments of Alain Ducasse, a two-time, three Michelin star holder, who stands on the shoulders of prior gastro giants such as Alain Chapel, Alexandre Dumaine, and Fernand Point. His restaurants are located in Grand Hotels, they are redolent of *la belle époque*, their design adopts a Louis XIV aesthetic, the ambience alludes to *le grand siècle*, the service is to die for, and the menu comes straight from Heaven, where past and present coalesce and time shall be no more.

Now, time may be no more in the heavenly hereafter, but in the here-and-now and the then-and-there it is still alive and well. What's more, it always has been and will continue to be so for the foreseeable future, according to Costa and Bamossy in Chapter 14. Taking the latter-day rise of retroscapes as their point of departure, they argue that time, space, and the market have long been with us, late and soon. It is an integral part of human history and culturally ubiquitous to boot. Despite appearances to the contrary, humankind's chronotopophilia didn't start with the Hard Rock Café in 1971, or Main Street USA in 1955, or Coney's Island's Luna Park in 1904. With this in mind, they identify four types of retroscape: spectacular hyperrealities constructed for profit-making purposes (Las Vegas, etc.); itinerant stage sets, complete with costumed performance artistes and their props (e.g., medicine shows); ritual reenactments of salient—often supernatural—events in a society's past (bonfire nights et al.); and natural scenery, prospects, panoramas, and the like, which are regarded as retroscapes by human observers (the American West, for example). These various forms are found in all societies, though the precise character of the preferred retroscape differs from culture to culture and time to time. These preferences, what is more, are explicable in terms of consumer wants, needs, and behaviors, as well as the historical and economic circumstances of the societies concerned.

Societies change, however, as do the retroscapes that characterize or typify extant societal arrangements. This is nowhere better illustrated than in the recent rise of e-commerce in general and commercial Web sites in particular. In Chapter 15, Venkatesh contends that Web sites represent a postmodern return to the printed catalogues of yore, the "Big Books" of Sears, J.C. Penney, Montgomery Ward, and analogous universal providers. After an historical overview of the printing industry and concomitant commercial revolution, he argues that whereas traditional catalogues are constrained by their physical bulk, semi-immutability, and static representation of the commodities concerned, today's no less compendious Web sites are virtual, changeable, and inherently interactive. Yet despite important differences in ethos, aesthetics, and consumer use patterns—Web sites are visited, printed catalogues are visitors—most marketing and consumer researchers continue to make direct comparisons between the two, using identical metrics and assessment criteria (visual appeal, entertainment value, escapism, enjoyment, efficiency, excellence, economic value, etc.). Such approaches have their merits, but Venkatesh brings an alternative perspective to bear on the issue, inasmuch as his chapter combines personal introspection, philosophical speculation, empirical analysis, and historical context into a remarkable retro mode of postmodern marketing discourse. In so doing, he offers a contemporary version of William Blake's poetic apothegm concerning the world in a grain of sand. The silicon-chipped World Wide Web, he contends, can best be comprehended in poetic prose, compelling narratives, and imaginative bon mots.

When it comes to poetic prose, compelling narratives, and imaginative bon mots, few consumer researchers are better equipped than John Sherry. Before we get to Sherry's concluding chapter, however, the barrier of Brown's reflexive ruminations on retromarketing research has to be overcome. Commencing with an encounter between the author and Professor Philip Kotler, the peerless pedagogue, Chapter 16 takes us on a journey into Stephen's murky marketing past. More specifically, it dredges up deeply painful memories of a memory-based research project that went disastrously wrong. True, this abandoned study of time, space, and the market eventually led to *Time, Space, and the Market*, albeit by a circuitous route, but that doesn't make the memories any less distressing. Ironically, and appropriately, the lessons learned from Brown's aborted exercise chime with the recent reflexive turn in memory research and, moreover, with Turner's (1999) thesis that reflexivity is the fundamental organizing principle of the universe.

Now, reflexivity may or may not be of cosmological significance, but it is central to our understanding of retroscapes. The *locus classicus* of retroscape research, John Sherry's (1998a) seminal essay on Niketown Chicago was the original inspiration for the present volume, and it is entirely appropriate that he should bring this book to a close with a few reflexive words on time, space, and the market. Writing in the aftermath of the 9/11 tragedy, which further reinforced Western society's (re)turn to the comforts and security of an imagined past, he summarizes the retrofuturistic mind-set that currently prevails in the United States, whether it be the retrogladiatorial contest that was Super Bowl XXXVI or the retrospectacular opening ceremony of the Winter Olympic Games in Salt Lake City. In this regard, it is perhaps entirely appropriate that Sherry's imperishable essay on Niketown—I'm almost tempted to call his signature research method *Being-in-the-John*—has lasted longer than the retroscape it evokes and encapsulates. Whereas Sherry's wonderful article has recently been republished in a geographical textbook (Wrigley and Lowe 2002), Niketown Chicago itself has been completely remodeled, extensively refurbished, and generally consigned to the trashcan of store design history. Anyone expecting to find the monumental mountain bikes, tropical fish tanks, and two-story mural of Michael Jordan that John so eloquently describes, will be sorely disappointed. The pen, as Bulwer-Lytton nearly said, is mightier than the swoosh.

Note

1. There is, of course, a fourth and final estuary that flows into *Time, Space, and the Market.* And that is our contributors' streams of thought. This volume could not have set sail without its peerless scholarly complement, who set aside the time and created the space to write evocatively about the marketplace. They responded instantly to the lightest touch of the editorial tiller and, a few mutinous mutterings notwithstanding, they were as good a cerebral crew as we could ever hope to assemble. The lash proved unnecessary, much to the disappointment of one or two contributors, let alone the malevolent editors! This book, moreover, would never have made it safely into port were it not for the skillful piloting of Harry Briggs and his collegial coastguards at M.E. Sharpe, for which we are very grateful. Anchors aweigh. . . .

References

Augé, Marc (1995), *Non-Places: Introduction to an Anthropology of Supermodernity,* London: Verso.
Belk, Russell W. (1995), "Studies in the New Consumer Behaviour," in *Acknowledging Consumption,* ed. Daniel Miller, London: Routledge, pp. 58–95.

Belk, Russell W., John F. Sherry, Jr., and Melanie Wallendorf (1988), "A Naturalistic Inquiry into Buyer and Seller Behavior at a Swap Meet," *Journal of Consumer Research,* 14 (March): 449–70.

Brown, Stephen (1992), *Retail Location: A Micro-scale Perspective,* Aldershot: Avebury.

——— (1999), "Retromarketing: Yesterday's Tomorrows, Today!" *Marketing Intelligence and Planning,* 17 (7): 363–76.

——— (2001), *Marketing—The Retro Revolution,* London: Sage.

Brown, Stephen and Anthony Patterson (2000), "Knick-knack Paddy-whack, Give a Pub a Theme," *Journal of Marketing Management,* 16 (6): 647–62.

Carlin, George (1997), *Brain Droppings,* New York: Hyperion.

Cova, Bernard (1999), "Servicescapes: From Modern Non-Places to Postmodern Common Places," *Journal of Business Research,* 44 (1): 37–45.

Csaba, Fabian F. and Søren Askegaard (1999), "Malls and the Orchestration of the Shopping Experience in a Historical Perspective," in *Advances in Consumer Research,* vol. 26, ed. Eric J. Arnould and Linda M. Scott, Provo, UT: Association for Consumer Research, pp. 34–40.

Gottdiener, Mark (1997), *The Theming of America: Dreams, Visions and Commercial Spaces,* Boulder, CO: Westview.

Goulding, Christina (2000), "The Commodification of the Past, Postmodern Pastiche, and the Search for Authentic Experiences at Contemporary Heritage Attractions," *European Journal of Marketing,* 34 (7): 835–53.

Hannigan, John (1998), *Fantasy City: Pleasure and Profit in the Postmodern Metropolis,* New York: Routledge.

Harris, Daniel (2000), *Cute, Quaint, Hungry and Romantic: The Aesthetics of Consumerism,* New York: Basic Books.

Hirschman, Elizabeth C. and Morris B. Holbrook (1992), *Postmodern Consumer Research: The Study of Consumption as Text,* Newbury Park: Sage.

Holbrook, Morris B. and Robert M. Schindler (1994), "Age, Sex and Attitude Toward the Past as Predictors of Consumers' Aesthetic Tastes for Cultural Products," *Journal of Marketing Research,* 31 (August): 412–22.

——— (1996), "Market Segmentation Based on Age and Attitude Toward the Past: Concepts, Methods and Findings Concerning Nostalgic Influences on Consumer Tastes," *Journal of Business Research,* 37 (June): 27–39.

Johnson, Steven (2001), *Emergence: The Connected Lives of Ants, Brains, Cities and Software,* London: Allen Lane.

McAlexander, James H. and John W. Schouten (1998), "Brandfests: Servicescapes for the Cultivation of Brand Equity," in *Servicescapes: The Concept of Place in Contemporary Markets,* ed. John F. Sherry, Jr., Chicago: NTC Business Books, pp. 377–401.

McGrath, Mary Ann (1989), "An Ethnography of a Gift Store: Trappings, Wrappings, and Rapture," *Journal of Retailing,* 65 (4): 421–49.

McGrath, Mary Ann, John F. Sherry, Jr., and Deborah Heisley (1993), "An Ethnographic Study of an Urban Periodic Marketplace: Lessons from the Midville Farmers' Market," *Journal of Retailing,* 69 (3): 280–319.

O'Guinn, Tom C. and Russell W. Belk (1989), "Heaven on Earth: Consumption at Heritage Village, USA," *Journal of Consumer Research,* 16 (September): 227–38.

Otnes, Cele (1998), " 'Friend of the Bride'—and Then Some: Roles of the Bridal Salon During Wedding Planning," in *Servicescapes: The Concept of Place in*

Contemporary Markets, ed. John F. Sherry, Jr., Chicago: NTC Business Books, pp. 229–58.

Peñaloza, Lisa (1999), "Just Doing It: Consumer Agency and Institutional Politics at Niketown," *Consumption, Markets, Culture,* 2 (Spring): 337–400.

Ritzer, George (1999), *Enchanting a Disenchanted World: Revolutionizing the Means of Consumption,* Thousand Oaks: Pine Forge Press.

Ross, Andrew (1999), *The Celebration Chronicles: Life, Liberty and the Pursuit of Property Values,* New York: Ballantine.

Sherry, John F., Jr. (1991), "Postmodern Alternatives: The Interpretive Turn in Consumer Research," in *Handbook of Consumer Research,* ed. Thomas S. Robertson and Harold H. Kassarjian, Englewood Cliffs: Prentice Hall, pp. 548–91.

—— (1998a), "The Soul of the Company Store: Niketown Chicago and the Emplaced Brandscape," in *Servicescapes: The Concept of Place in Contemporary Markets,* ed. John F. Sherry, Jr., Chicago: NTC Books, pp. 109–46.

—— (ed.) (1998b), *Servicescapes: The Concept of Place in Contemporary Markets,* Chicago: NTC Books.

—— (2000), "Place, Technology and Representation," *Journal of Consumer Research,* 27 (September): 273–78.

—— et al. (2001), "Being in the Zone: Staging Retail Theater at ESPN Zone Chicago," *Journal of Contemporary Ethnography,* 30 (4): 465–510.

Sorkin, Michael (ed.) (1992), *Variations on a Theme Park: The New American City and the End of Public Space,* New York: Hill and Wang.

Stern, Barbara B. (1992), "Historical and Personal Nostalgia in Advertising Text: The *fin de siècle* Effect," *Journal of Advertising* 21 (4): 11–22.

Turner, Frederick (1999), "An Ecopoetics of Beauty and Meaning," in *Biopoetics: Evolutionary Explorations in the Arts,* ed. Brett Cooke and Frederick Turner, Lexington: ICUS, pp. 119–37.

Watson, Mary, K. (1978), "The Scale Problem in Human Geography," *Geografiska Annaler,* 60B (1): 38–47.

Wrigley, Neil and Michelle Lowe (2002), *Reading Retail: A Geographical Perspective,* London: Arnold.

Part I

Micro Retroscapes

2

Bespectacled and Bespoken

Gazing from Throne Zone to Five O'Clock and Head

John F. Sherry, Jr.

Look on my works ye Mighty and despair!

—Shelley, *Ozymandias*

Apologia

Like that traveler from an antique land, bone-weary yet vaguely energized from a set of recent journeys I've allowed to interfere with the writing of this essay until the eleventh hour, I find myself alone late at night, in an empty quarter of the world's busiest airport, sharing space with vigilant armed soldiers younger than my children, who patrol the corridors of O'Hare in defense of my privilege to inhabit the much-maligned and misnamed no-place of this lonely terminal. As I watch the pair prowl past the banks of ambient television screens, oblivious both to the sonorous soundbites of the airport newschannel and the schizo-frenetic badinage of color commentators across the cornucopia of contests blaring from the concourse sports bar, the inspiration for my essay finally dawns. The image of the callow warrior, the antiflâneur impervious to the potion poured in his ear and the spectacles poised over his eyes, strikes me as the funhouse mirror image of my sensuous self, a doppelgänger through the glass darkly, whose ghostly presence merits meditation even in my languorous state. For sadly, no matter how tired I feel, the siren song of the marketplace has always been the swansong of sensible self-regard. As I am drawn inexorably to the flickering cathode

19

beacons of the Fox Sports Skybox, I muse, like Homer Simpson, that I've turned out TV, and trust I've found the hook upon which to hang my story.

I'm the only soul in the Skybox, the hour so slow that even the bartender has deserted his station. *Being-in-the-Skybox* invites reverie, if less eloquently than Proust's Madeleine. The Skybox is a dense metaphor, playing off of its literal emplacement in an airport, its passing resemblance to the luxurious glass palaces perched atop arenas and stadiums, and the surround of television monitors engulfing its patrons. I'm boxed in on a number of levels, packaged effectively as part of the consumption spectacle. I smile in recollection of the masterful intertextual cross-promotion that Fox Sports always manages to wage during the male bonding ritual of its Sunday NFL pregame show, and for a fleeting moment I'm *in-the-television*, branded as effectively as the network. I struggle to follow the Duke–Kentucky ball game on a number of monitors, as a host of other sports vies for my attention, which seems to wander back hypnotically to a vérité account of soccer hooliganism, the twist being that the actual players themselves are engaged in wanton acts of violence. Vintage sports photos adorn the walls of the Skybox, and autographed framed jerseys of Michael Jordan and Sammy Sosa remind me of the city's graces. The girdered ceiling of the Skybox evokes a sense of theatrical props, warehouse space and satellite struts, giving the interior a retrofuturistic feel. A faux al fresca patio, complete with flagstone flooring and bistro seating comprises a vestibule of sorts to the Skybox proper. I'm outside even as I'm inside. I'm bucolic even as I'm high tech. I've got one foot in the future and one in the past, the present evanescent as my vision treks across the tubes. The fourth wall of the Skybox, the real if not virtual window into spectacle, abuts the concourse itself, casting passersby as unwitting actors in a reality series, the comic relief that is the foil to athletic drama, the distraction from commercials distracting viewers from the games. Only tonight, I alone am both the viewer and the viewed, the subject and the object.

With this realization, this essay is born. A native account from deep within the heart of spectacle seems a doable proposition. Immersion in spectacle characterizes much of our experience, yet we lack an introspective chronicle of our suspension in that medium. Yet, wait. It's not just spectacle that's monopolized my recent research efforts. I've also been quite captivated by antispectacle as well, although there seems to be no adequate term to capture this phenomenon arising from the temporary autonomous zones of populist playfulness (although Mark Dery's notion of a pyrotechnic insanitarium comes close). When consumers produce such a mindscape, unfettered by the marketer's intention, and released from the hegemony of the gaze, we are blessed with something akin to a communal sensorium, part holistic sensation and part oceanic merger, that roots us in the present no matter how time is invoked in the process. A noncommercial Erehwon of immediacy, consumed in its creation and created in its consumption. A groundbox rather than a Skybox. Breaking back into this box is a noble pursuit. It is also appropriately playful.

What follows, then, is a thick inscription of a personal odyssey through the precincts of spectacle and sensorium, a subjective personal introspection on the playgrounds of my most recent scholary inquiry. A kind of multisite autoethnography merging emic and etic, stopping I trust, just short of emetic. I contrast my experience of retail theatre in themed flagship brand stores with my participation in the comedy of the commons at the Burning Man Project. I bookend my chronicle with another place-based reverie rather than offer a programmatic conclusion, which more befits the eccentricity of this essay. My account resembles more an ethnographer's journal than field notebook, and unfolds more kaleidoscopically than I would prefer. I seek to provide the reader a sense of what it is like to be me as I inhabit retroscapes that appeal to my multiphrenic self, in the hope that such idiography may illuminate the affecting presence—both reassuring and disconcerting—of consumption sites. My own reaction to being in these places has considerable range: hypervigilance, overstimulation, suspension of disbelief, tranquility, comfort, nostalgia, romanticism, anger, exultation, sheepishness, and abiding rightness contend with one another and ramify to still other dimensions. The "no then there" quality of retroscapes that fixes us in the amber of a past eternally present, and gives us that bittersweet back to the future feeling I imagine to be a contemplative chronogasm, I find difficult to capture in prose. Herewith is my attempt.

> Even instant replay is a form of nostalgia: a brief visit to the immediate past for reexamination, before slapping it onto a highlight video for further review and re-review on into the indefinite future.

> —George Carlin, *Brain Droppings*

Throne Zone: The Eternal Return

I've spent a good portion of my professional life these last few years immersed in the flagship brand stores of marketers whose livelihood is linked directly to sports. I gravitate to this category for a number of reasons, chief among them being my lifelong involvement in sport as both a participant and spectator. I find sport to be a cultural focus of the United States, and a source of root metaphors for understanding the dynamics of everyday life. Sport is a social cynosure for us. It is widely observed that sport is the nearest we come to a civil religion in our country, and is a secular ritual without parallel in contemporary society. Sport affords individuals the opportunity, at a minimum, to experience personal mastery and a sense of flow; it is also a vehicle of hierophany and kratophany, permitting us the occasional experience of transcendence. Perhaps of greatest relevance to this essay is the inherent conservatism, indeed the essentially reactionary essence, of sport, as we experience it in the United States.

Because it is equal parts paleolithic procurement and liturgical license, hedged about by rules frequently honored more often in the breach, sport is among our preeminent venues of retail theatre. Agon and agora collide in spectacular fashion in the precincts of Niketown, ESPN Zone, Galyans, Bass Outdoor World, REI and similar servicescapes that have comprised my recent fieldsites. As much as it directs consumer behavior, the *mise-en-scène* of merchandising seems always to encourage improvisational (if not guerrilla) theatre as well. When consumers are invited to indulge the ludic impulse, coproduction or cocreation of consumption is an inevitable outcome. Sport is a retroritual, and play is a regressive mechanism. Regression to glory days real or imagined is a flagship staple. Regression to childhood is a consumption quest. A back to the future, modern primitive utopian fantasy is the themed promise, whether exalted in the guise of pantheon, museum, or gallery (as at Nike Town) or democratized on field and screen (as at ESPN Zone). Sport binds us back to the source, and demands a retroscape that will return us semiotically and technologically to primal urges.

To achieve their world-building aims, these stores must hybridize other cultural venues high and low, exotic and familiar. They must bring the outside in, encompassing landscapes within their marketspace. Inside these stores, I can climb rocks, rappel, shoot weapons, fish and paddle, and toss and kick balls IRL; virtually, I can skydive, race motorcycles and stockcars, golf, and bowl. I can study exhibits and venerate shrines at my leisure or frantically scan images of current and past contests or commercials as they pulse across endless banks of monitors. (I am reminded of the re-exteriorization of sportsworld I observed on a recent neighborhood excursion that took me past a frontyard birthday party of young boys scrambling around a rock-climbing tower erected on a flat Midwestern lawn, the real virtual rockface allowing the kids to simulate the indoor climbing that simulates the outdoor climbing their impoverished topography denies them. Marketers will always bring the mountain to Mohammed.) I can observe traditional gender-based behavior unfold, and spontaneous communitas emerge around games. I can domesticate this public space, converting hermetic to hestial place. ESPN Zone is a classic encapsulization of this multiphrenic, fragmented, kaleidoscopic, spectacular experience, and its retroscape provides an opportunity to reconsider my own practices of inhabitation, which I've neglected in other published accounts.

Exhibit 2.1 **Ultimate viewing area**

   The focus of participative contest—of the most physical although not necessarily most active sort—at this eatertainment venue is the Arena, a megaplex of virtual reality-, video- and actual games that allows players to compete and perform on a communal stage. The Arena is reminiscent both of an arcade and of a carnival midway; the miniature courts, rinks, alleys, fields, and tracks enshrined within its ersatz stadium give something of a *wunderkammer* feel to the area as well. Ubiquitous television monitors apprise patrons of the progress of contests in a host of sports around the globe, punctuating the flow of flâneurs around the space. Hyperstimulation and sensory overload are the order of the day, the feeling of being overwhelmed dominating the experience of most visitors.
   The focus of the spectatorial gaze—a far from passive enterprise—is the Screening Room, a virtual fortress of solitude walled off from the open air ambience of the rest of the servicescape. This marked enclosure is the inner sanctum of the site, and is effectively restricted to paying adults. It is home to a working broadcast booth, an ornate bar, an eating area decorated with nostalgic art and memorabilia, a terraced-and-tiered arrangement of dining and drinking booths whose table tops sport individual monitors, a pair of "Skyboxes" devoted to private parties, an "ultimate viewing area" whose "Throne Zone" consists of a bank of leather reclining chairs outfitted with state of the art audio systems and remote controls, and, on the focal wall, a battery of twelve large screen monitors flanking an enormous center monitor whose screen measures twelve by sixteen feet. The screens broadcast a wide variety of sporting events, and a message board above the screens scrolls crawlers laden with advertising, contest updates, and sports trivia across the entire visual field.

To dwell in this inner sanctum, to inhabit a throne, is to agree with informants who describe the experience as a sports fan's wet dream, a player's players' club, the zone within the Zone. True fanatics dream of the day they will be able to purchase a personal seat license (like the ones NFL stadium season ticket holders possess) granting them instant access to reclinerworld. While the Screening Room may serve as cultural forum for the public channeling of our ADD syndrome—the sensory overload-induced hyperactivity of the Arena being replaced by the information overload-induced caroming of the glance—the retro aura of the seat is almost sedative hypnotic in its effect. The dweller moves through several realms at once. The ultimate viewing area is a dimly lighted space. Its galleried seating is reminiscent of a theatre, perhaps even a drive-in. The dweller is immersed in a cinematic dreamworld of images, a semisomnolent state interrupted by the occasional big play or its acknowledgment by the cheers of anonymous seatmates. The electronic hearth on each tabletop discourages conversation, inviting instead a kind of Homeric basking between bites of pub grub (Mmm . . . Open faced club, sand wedge).

For those ensconced in the recliners, the throne is a constant reminder that it is good to be king. The dweller reclines splendidly, in regal isolation, enveloped in plush leather, wrapped in surround sound, and taxed only to manipulate the armrest handset that controls choice of audio feed. Serving women bearing food and drink cater to the dweller's carnal desire, replenishing stores on a regular basis. The transfer of nourishment from hand to mouth is most often accomplished without lifting the gaze from the screens, as if the dweller were in a trance. Short of administration via IV-drip, the dweller is lost in a primal retrograde male fantasy. Constant feeding by a vigilant nurturing woman while bathed in the glow of the Ur-boob tube, entranced by alpha-masculine images of monumental inconsequentiality. . . . This into-body experience of altered consciousness is disrupted every so often by the high fidelity verisimilitude of a cracking bat or a bone jarring tackle, jolting the dweller from an oneiric utopia to a physical dystopia, often causing flinching, head-ducking, or other startle reflexes in transit. And sometimes not, as overserved dwellers occasionally doze in the recliners, where they are allowed to sleep off their surfeit. This caretaking is not merely postprandial, but postcoital, if informants' constant allusions to the correlation of screen size and masculinity are properly credited. Grappling with phallic lack and indulging delusions of grandeur are by-products of the polymorphous perversity of play in the ultimate viewing area. In the throne, the dweller becomes the apotheosis of the couch potato, the ultimate lazy boy. As I inhabit the recliner, I return not merely to my living room or den, the domestic locus of my patriarchal bliss. I return to the womb, enfolded in the embrace of a cybernetic medium, a culture of remediation.

Exhibit 2.2 **Throne zone**

But wait, there's more. Beyond the womb. Beyond the den. Ripped untimely from the tacking fantasies of the glance, the dweller multitasks from screens to digital script, assimilating crawler lines into overall awareness. The Screening Room bears strong resemblance to a Las Vegas book. Fantasy leaguers track the performance of their dream teams as a welter of statistics ticks across the banner. Gambling, that universal game of first resort, while not permitted on the premises, is impossible to prevent. When storied rivalries unfold in images and numbers, partisan fans may form a communitas of contest, engaging each other from the totemic comfort of their clustered clan, challenging, taunting, pledging, and sending drinks across the gulf of allegiance binding them as a spectacle. Sometimes it's carnival in the inner sanctum.

And sometimes the inner sanctum warps to meet the outer limits. The timeless, folkloric aura of the chair emanates from the recliners in the Throne Zone. The privilege of infallibility as the cleric speaks *ex cathedra*, the sense of absolute authority as the executioner flips the switch on Ol' Sparky, and the patriarchal eminence of Louis on the throne or Archie in the Barcalounger® (from pater pathos to bunker bathos) as each tends to his own all rest squarely on the chair. More than one informant has spoken to me of the Enterprise fantasy that the smart recliner engenders in the technophile. Like Kirk on the bridge, the dweller in the chair commands technology enabling one to boldly go where no man has gone before: the idiosyncratic mindscape of sportopia. Better still, like Robojock on the Holodek, the dweller realizes his cybernetic self, and becomes a *gundun*, or perhaps a postmodern centaur: a Chiron of the gridiron, a Hawking of hockey, a *tel-athlete* beyond the pale. The captain's chair is a magic carpet, a miracle of techgnosis, and the best seat in the house for an armchair theorist of the retroscape.

> The desert is a sublime form that banishes
> all sociality, all sentimentality, all sexuality.

—Jean Baudrillard, *America*

Five O'Clock and Head: A Welcome Home

Of all the tears in the fabric of space and time it's been my good fortune to wander through, my recent sojourn in Black Rock City (BRC) is among the most memorable. I live with the dust of this journey a full year later, the alkaline grit in my notebooks and camping gear a grounding reminder of my life among nomads of the temporary autonomous zone created by the Burning Man project (BMP). Burning Man is an annual postmodern pilgrimage to the remote Black Rock desert of Nevada, a week long gathering of creative refugees bent upon escaping the late capitalist strictures of everyday life, who transform a desolate lunar landscape into an ephemeral city of art. This nomadic gathering achieves a critical mass of 25,000 souls over the course of a week, before congregants decamp and disburse to the four quarters, leaving no physical trace of the technoasis they have imagineered in the wilderness. Citizens of BRC create a luminous, tented technopolis of aesthetic activity, an antistructural Disneyworld—Coney Island—Las Vegas pastiche that renounces marketplace norms in favor of a gift economy, that serves as a liturgical and theatrical stage for the performance of myriad enlightened interaction rituals aimed at reviving the sense of community, the kind of organic solidarity believed to characterize an earlier, simpler age. With its emphasis on radical self-expression, universal participation, and egalitarian relationships, the BMP fosters an aura of immediacy and presence, authenticity and earnestness, and an urgent and abiding sense of nowness, sustainable only in a liminal space far removed from conventional temporal concerns. Newcomers are frequently hailed with the cordial greeting, "welcome home," by more seasoned dwellers. That home comprises metaphysical space as well, which BRC citizens carry back with them when they return to the world.

My home at BRC is Five O'Clock and Head, a campsite whose coordinates designate my position on the embodied metropolis. The city plan is the figure of the Man, a literal grounding of the focal icon of the BMP and an architectural embodying of the theme of this year's gathering, which, as my luck would have it, is the body. My perspective of the BMP is grounded in

Exhibit 2.3 **Playa installations**

my desert address. Like some weird permutation of my Myers-Briggs typing (a typing I find fluctuates wildly with my context, although not wildly enough, I fear), the address defines me, or maybe better, describes me, for the hundreds of pilgrims I invite back for interviews, or redirect to other quarters of the city. I am mildly annoyed I'm not squatting at a more exotic and intriguing locale—an intersection of midnight and genitals might make for more interesting encounters and analysis—but elated at my strategic field position on the esplanade, in full view of both the ceaseless procession of nomads, and the altar on the playa, the towering effigy of the Man, the lodestar my fellow pilgrims have steered by to gift me with their presence.

Five O'Clock and Head is home to a number of theme camps, those nominally private domestic spaces whose residents transform to public places of entertainment and personal transcendence, that, ramifying down every avenue of BRC, collectively give the BMP its dramaturgical character. These camps are the sites of performance, seats of small craft production, and sets of encounters that impart a sense of continuous artistic activity to the residents of BRC. The emergent and visible character of aesthetic process is everywhere palpable, and not merely in the creation of art. Perhaps even more in its disbursement is the lived immediacy of art experienced in this community. For the art of BRC is evanescent, made to be given away or sacrificed in conflagration. Part potlatch, part holocaust, the essence of this art resides in the moment, and must always circulate if it is to achieve its end.

Five O'Clock and Head is my window onto the playa, the Pleistocene lake bed that is the staging ground for the focal shrines and rituals of the BMP. The playa is the playground of the pilgrims, a latter-day causeway of carnivalesque, upon which the megainstallations and spectacular performances are celebrated and the millions of microencounters and mutual meanderings of nomads are consummated. The playa is at once the most public of spaces and the place of most intensely private personal experience. I recount three of my own such experiences in the following paragraphs.

The desert is a world of extreme contrasts. I have sweltered in one hundred degree-plus days of scorching sunlight, and shivered in near-freezing nighttime temperatures despite my layering of Polartec®. (In my own mind, the prime directive of the gathering that warns of the danger of dehydration and heat stroke—"Piss Clear"—is confounded with the cold, posted leave-no-trace recycling admonition "Sort Your Shit" to produce a kind of liminal scatalogic of survival, a karmic ecophysics of propriety attuned to the event.) The optics of the site is remarkable as well; as I comprehend bodily for the first time Milton's conceits of the fiery lake and darkness visible. When the rain comes, the welcome relief it provides is negated by the sea of mud it creates, immobilizing nomads in their tracks. The harmattan of BRC is an awesome force as well. The inconstant wind can be ferocious, driving the desert dust ahead of it like a screen of microscopic nettles, stinging, blinding, and parching all those in its path.

Pedalling back across the playa one afternoon from a distant fieldsite, I am aware of a gathering storm that may prevent me from reaching home away from home any time soon. The dust swirls around me, and my vision is quickly obscured. As my visibility declines to zero, I slow my bicycle to a coast, and then dismount, fearful of crashing into a fellow pilgrim, or an immovable art installation. Soon I am effectively disoriented, existing only in the immediate chaos of the windstorm. Despite the nagging concern of impending collision with other disorienteers, I embrace this existential envelope of temporary isolation (as I might a Chicago blizzard or a northwoods fogbank) for its novelty and evocation. Cinematic images of Lawrence of Arabia and Mad Max contend for share of mindscape with those imagined installation landmarks that I hope will restore my bearings. In my pleasant detachment, as the wind storm swirls about me, I register a brief break in the dustcloud up ahead of me. Blinking in the direction of the gap, I glimpse the bare outline of the Man itself. Just as quickly, the curtain is pulled closed, and then yanked open once again. As I draw closer, the Man emerges from the ghostly eddying of the alkali dust, a postapocalyptic vision of gigantic proportion, beckoning all survivors to its shadow. I make out other pilgrims

Exhibit 2.4 **Man emerging from storm**

in the haze, slouching as I am, *ad astra per aspera*, toward bedlam to be borne back to the source. Like Kubrick's monkeys around the monolith, or Heston's astronaut confronting Lady Liberty laid low, we converge upon the Man as if in some technoshamanic dream, suffused with an awe so terrific we are dumbstruck, thankful to know where we are while wondering where that might be. Lost and found in trackless time, and feeling sheepish from the rocketing from sublime to ridiculous the event has afforded me, I make furtive eye contact with these other orphans of the storm, then head home in the settling calm to swap visions with my campmate.

Late one night on my rounds through BRC, I gravitate toward the playa where sculptors continue to hammer and weld on installations that would be considered enormous by gallery or museum standards, but which are dwarfed by the panoramic desertscape of their current studio space. I draw close to one piece in particular, an outsized casting of the human heart. Authentically detailed, the heart is a hollow vessel built to contain a fiery essence. It is now a radiant furnace, incandescent in the frigid desert night. Pilgrims gather around the sculpture, suffused with the warmth of its vermillion glow. I snake my way through the circle, seeking the innermost ring, there to thaw out my writing hand and thence to probe the pericardium of venerators.

My progress is arrested by another pilgrim, whom I later discover to have been the artist of this telltale heart. Placing his hand upon my chest, above my own heart cloaked in Polartec® against the desert chill, he intones the BMP artists' mantra "I made this just for you," before slipping back into the anonymity of the crowd. During this invocation and laying on of hand, I feel a deep heat spread through my chest, as if my heart were thawing. The intimate immediacy of the experience is palpable, and for a moment, the blazing sculptured heart and my own are one. I feel simultaneously touched and beguiled, exalted and fooled. I want to accept this extraordinary experience even as I deny it, to pay homage to the huckster who has used sympathetic magic to warm my heart. Did he conceal a heating element, a mechanical or chemical handwarmer, in his palm? Did he read gullibility or longing in my researcher's gaze? Could he know the anthropologist was seeking a shaman in this secular ceremony? Or do I just hope for a Barnum door to close after my horse sense has escaped? Reluctantly, but gratefully, I accept the gift, and wander to another venue, wondering if extraordinary experience or madness of crowds awaits me yet again.

Too tired to sleep, and too cold to converse, I collapse on the ground in front of the fire barrel of my camp site, in the darkest hours of the early morning, and space out for awhile. My consciousness is altered by sleep deprivation, excessive work, and sensory overload. The fire throws images against the nearby tents, and until the technothrob of electronic music delivers me back to the present, I am lost in Plato's cave, refiguring the flickering shadows as they dance against thin nylon walls. A steady procession of costumed pilgrims files by my fireside, en route to more hermetic spaces than my hestial flop. Disjointed images of my odyssey flit across the theatre of my mind as I stare into the fire: camels stroll past the vestibule of my tent; I'm hijacked by the Captain of a fifties era livingroom ensemble floating across the desert; I dodge the phallic and vulval artcars tooling about BRC; fire twirlers dance on the outskirts of consciousness; a ululating horde of feminists bike rides naked on the esplanade; a monumental lingam and yoni sway to the touch of pilgrims that climb on and through them. A Freudian nightmare in other circumstances, this vision is a pleasant companion to the physical exhaustion that numbers my bones.

My fireside draws visitors. Other residents of the theme camp drift home and take up seats next to the barrel. Nonresident pilgrims drop by to warm their hands, request directions, or solely to visit before resuming their journey. We all still wear our playa personae, some outfits more outrageous than others, some simply reflective of our secret selves. I'm still tricked out as a fool, although my fellow travelers are kind enough to see a jester. Many of us are ringed with glow sticks, thin luminescent plastic cylinders we wear both to glorify the night and to encourage high-speed revellers not to run us down in the dark with whatever vehicles they nominally control.

A young man saunters up fireside, and plunks himself down in our midst. High on a psychopharmacopia he boastfully details for us, he announces that he's been jones-ing for some glow sticks. Seeing our well-equipped entourage, he's come to beg, borrow, or steal. In the spirit of our no-vending economy and in light of our mendicant's enthusiasm, we ask him what he's got to barter in exchange for our magic light. Over time, we decline his offer of various drugs, and accept instead a handful of unremarkable bric-a-brac, the trade relationship rather that the goods the object of our negotiation. Once in possession of a ring of glow sticks, our visitor chews open a cylinder, and dribbles chemiluminescence down his tongue, teeth, and chin, looking for all the world like he's just bitten the jugular of one of the dragon vehicles that cruises the playa. Over our shouted protests, and against medical advice, he stumbles off into the night, hoping to catch the next rave before the effect wears off. This flower child unstuck in time is a discordant collage of images in my tired imagination. A Merry Prankster on walkabout. Venkman exorcised of Slimer. Samson strung out on g.m. honey, slaying himself with the jawbone of an ass. Here walks a powerful argument opposing fire in the belly. This mendicant is a retroscape.

> More matter with less art.
>
> —Shakespeare, *Hamlet*

Coda

On the day this essay is scheduled to be completed, I've managed to think through its principal currents without having actually committed them to paper. Rather than braid together the strands I've jotted in my commonplace book, I opt instead for a trip to the Art Institute, a long anticipated date I'd hoped to enjoy with a clear conscience. As fate would have it, the day surpasses my fondest expectations, and presents me with a perversely postmodern wraparound revelatory incident that spurs this chapter to completion. Predictably enough, the event returns me inexorably, in the fashion of a Mobius strip, to familiar research preoccupations, reminding me yet again how the gift must circulate. The circuits I wander seem always to deliver me to servicescapes and presents.

In the company of an unbearably beautiful guide, who succeeds from time to time in jolting me back to the immediate here and now, I snake my way along as part of a sinuous queue wending its way as a single organism (if not ourouboros, at least some slyly segmented centipede) through an exhibit entitled "Studio of the South." Suspended in an audiobubble that the curators' voices create and sustain through my headphones, propelled by their commentary (to which I am compelled to respond, in their absence, to the void in my own bubble), and the group's momentum, I float through the meticulously constructed corridors of time that chronicle the migration of the painters Van Gogh and Gauguin from metropole to countryside, from an intensely public world to intensely private ones. Old paintings and old photographs conspire to tell the story of a partnership devolving into a kind of old married couplehood, and thence to irreconcilable rift. The curators situate the waxing and waning of the collaboration in the careful context of the events and images of the day, helping consumers to appreciate the artworks in historico-cultural perspective. A partial mock-up of the Yellow House, the painters' southern residence, is created in the museum, complete with a gauzy backlit staging of the studio and a floor plan of the building stencilled on the ground. As my gaze wanders from photo timeline to vignettes, from posted aphorisms to their contemplators, and, ultimately, to the legend on the floor, I find that I have strayed into the imagined kitchen of the mock-up. Wishing only that I could smell the morning coffee and sausages that might have inspired such awesome art, lost in a virtual taste of Arles, caught up in an emplaced embrace of embodied mastery, I float through the curated kitchen down a short corridor, hand in hand with the muse that guides me.

Not toward a bright light does this rebirth canal ascend, however. With little warning, and even that little repressed in the suspension of my disbelief, I am delivered directly into the gift shop module that surmounts the exhibit. What ectopic poignancy! *Quel vernissage!* The electronic hum of a battery of concordant registers announces the conclusion of the carefully choreographed chronology of the partnership, dissolving the dynamic duo in the frentic franchising of everything most Gogh Gauguin gouging. Stunned by both the abruptness and inevitability of the marketplace I neglected to anticipate, torn by the conflicting desire to ridicule crusaders after Starry Night mouse pads and to score a more obscure Sower tchotchke for my partner, I suppress the urge to cry out, "Lend me your ear!" and attend instead to my inner one, the seat of conscience as well as balance. This need of "something with sunflowers on it" that I hear voiced around me and within me is the fate of the epicure in the postmodern era, as I understand it in the seventh moment. The aura with which we (re)charge the world, no matter how mechanically reproduced, seems an organic requirement for life. And still, I am always surprised to (re)experience that epiphany in the marketplace, to hear the chant of commodities Victor Hugo detected, to feel the amorous glances Freud found commodities to cast at us. As fetish and totem, the primal appeal of the artifact is undeniable, no matter how clinically I dissect it. (The refrigerator magnet of Vincent's bedroom chair brought back by friends Janeen and Gary from their pilgrimage to Arles and disbursed to illustrate a presentation that they made at ACR, reminds me of this appeal, as I regard it fastened to the lampstand on my desk as I pen these thoughts, those friends now incorporated into my museum reverie.) The marketplace itself—and the gift shop par excellence —is every bit as much a retroscape as is, by nature, the museum.

Acknowledgments

The author thanks Mary Ann West of the Bose Corporation for the loan of the high-tech, sound-dampening headphones that allowed him to log three hours of sound sleep per night during his weeklong stint at Black Rock City, an achievement that would otherwise have been impossible. He thanks his fieldmate Rob Kozinets for a steady stream of multisite insight over a host of projects. He thanks his students Krittinee Nuttavuthisit and Benét DeBarry Spence, whose Throne Zone photographs accompany this chapter, and Adam Duhachek and Diana Storm for the field observations that enlarge his understanding of sportsworld.

Still Curious? Some Sources

Dery, Mark (1999), *The Pyrotechnic Insanitarium: American Culture on the Brink,* New York: Grove.

Kozinets, Robert (2002), "Can Consumers Escape the Market?: Emancipating Illuminations from Burning Man," *Journal of Consumer Research,* 29 (June): 20–38.

Kozinets, Robert, John F. Sherry, Jr., Diana Storm, Adam Duhachek, Krittinee Nuttavuthisit, and Benét DeBarry-Spence (2002), "Themed Flagship Brandstores in the New Millennium: Theory, Practice, Prospects," *Journal of Retailing,* 78: 17–29.

McCarthy, Anna (2001), *Ambient Television: Visual Culture and Public Space,* Durham, NC: Duke University Press.

McMurtry, Larry (1999), *Walter Benjamin at the Dairy Queen: Reflections at Sixty and Beyond,* New York, NY: Touchstone.

Peñaloza, Lisa (1999), "Just Doing It: A Visual Ethnographic Study of Spectacular Consumption Behavior at Nike Town," *Consumption, Markets and Culture,* 2 (4): 337–400.

Sherry, John F., Jr. (1998), "The Soul of the Company Store: Nike Town Chicago and the Emplaced Brandscape," in *Servicescapes: The Concept of Place in Contemporary Markets,* ed. John F. Sherry, Jr., Lincolnwood, IL: NTC Business Books, pp. 109–46.

————— (2000), "Place, Technology and Representation," *Journal of Consumer Research,* 27 (December): 273–78.

Sherry, John F., Jr. and Robert Kozinets (in press), "Sacred Iconography in Secular Space: Altars, Alters and Alterity at the Burning Man Project," in *Contemporary Consumption Rituals: A Research Anthology,* ed. Cele Otnes and Tina Lowrey, Mahwah, NJ: Lawrence Erlbaum.

Sherry, John F., Jr., Robert Kozinets, Diana Storm, Adam Duhachek, Krittinee Nuttavuthisit, and Benét DeBarry-Spence (2001), "Being in the Zone: Staging Retail Theatre at ESPN Zone Chicago," *Journal of Contemporary Ethnography,* 30 (August): 465–510.

Sherry, John F., Jr. and John Schouten (2002), "A Role for Poetry in Consumer Research," *Journal of Consumer Research,* 29 (September): 218–34.

Stratton, Jon (2001), *The Desirable Body: Cultural Fetishism and the Erotics of Consumption,* Urbana: University of Illinois Press.

3

The Sims and the Retro Future

Russell W. Belk

In the introduction to his magnum opus, historian David Lowenthal (1985) quotes the famous opening of *The Go-Between* by L.P. Hartley (1953): "The past is a foreign country: they do things differently there." Lowenthal took the title for his own book from this opening and went on to observe that unlike most of history when people scarcely distinguished the past from the present, we now feel deeply nostalgic about the past and seek to visit it just as we visit different places. As tourists we go to heritage sites, reconstructed villages, and history museums. We read histories, historical novels, and autobiographies, and watch documentaries, feature films, and television series about our past. And we visit the historical re-creations of Disney, Williamsburg, Jarvick as well as numerous historic castles, battlefields, bridges, trails, and homes. As Stephen Brown (2001) points out, advertising is pillaging its own historical offerings in order to re-present romantically rendered retro images. And fashions, furniture, music, restaurants, retailers, and architects also direct us to a romantically re-created misty realm of past times dripping with nostalgia. We even eagerly visit homes associated with historical fictional characters like Sherlock Holmes who have never walked the face of the earth (Grayson and Martinec 2001). With all this colonization of the present by the past, it will perhaps come as no surprise that the past has also begun to colonize the future.

I do not mean by this that we should look to 1950s science fiction films to learn what the future holds for us, or that Leonardo Da Vinci, H.G. Wells, or Nostradamus offered true visions of what lies ahead. Nor do I mean that those who forget the past are doomed to repeat it, that everything old is new again, or that we have entered the dead horse latitudes of postmodernism wherein true creativity is impossible. I mean rather that despite our best intentions as avowed individualists to actively claim agency in shaping our personal futures, we are constrained from within and without to do little more than patch together a Frankenstein monster of a future made out of bits and pieces of the past and present.

Ah, but you might object that we are entering the brave new world of the Internet, computer simulations, and virtual reality, where there is far more to cyberspace and earth than our philosophies have yet dreamt of (e.g., Lee 1996). As if to counter these protestations, I have chosen to focus this retro future analysis on what may well be the most popular simulation of all time: the computer game called *The Sims*, along with its spinoffs, extensions, or follow-ups, which to date include, *The Sims: Livin' Large*, *The Sims: House Party*, and *The Sims: Hot Date*. By focusing on these games' scenarios as well as how they are consumed, I hope to demonstrate just how and why the future is, perhaps unavoidably, envisioned as a blast from the past.

In addition to informing how we simulate and consume our futures in the context of these computer games, there may be a larger lesson to be learned from this examination, involving the limitations of marketing research for new product and service development. We may even be forced to accept that our holy of holies, the Marketing Concept, is dead wrong. Beyond this, I would like to encourage marketing and consumer scholars and researchers to begin taking such games seriously. So while the topic of this chapter may be fun and games, my intent is not, sorry to say, to leave the reader laughing, smiling, or blissful. Hopefully I will also not leave you weeping, cursing, or angry either. I would be delighted, however, if you were a bit more quizzical, perplexed, or pensive about computer games generally, and *The Sims* in particular.

The Game

In the world of personal computer games, only rarely does a game reach the million mark in sales. A few months after it was introduced in early 2000, *The Sims* had already surpassed this mark (Shachtman 2001). By the end of 2000 *The Sims* had sold 1.8 million copies and was the top selling computer game in the United States (Howell 2001). By April of 2001, sales had topped four million, the *Livin' Large* expansion pack for the game had sold more than two million units, and the just released *House Party* expansion pack had already sold half a million units (Vance 2001). Created by Will Wright who seven years earlier had introduced the highly popular *SimCity*, *The Sims* and related products have remained top sellers since their introduction. They have spawned more than 200 personal Web sites, online interest groups, chat rooms, and online bulletin boards (Wright 2001). *The Sims* game has been referred to in reviews as "the Skinner box that is the home" (Coffey n.d.), "a dollhouse for adults" (Folkers 1999), "a soap opera" (MSNBC 1999), and "Part doll-house, part *The Truman Show* . . . Bob Vila meets *Melrose Place*" (Howell 2001). Playing *The Sims* has been called "playing God" (C. Taylor 1999), "[being] the script writer for a soap opera" (Udell n.d.), "social Darwinism made easy" (Coffey n.d.), and "keeping up with the Simses" (Scanlon 1999). The last characterization reflects the strong consumer theme in *The Sims*. The game has three modes: build, buy, and live. The player must, in part, keep Sims characters happy by building or buying them a house and purchasing things for them to enjoy in their house. In order to acquire these things, the player must also get his or her Sims jobs, partners, food, and clothing.

Playing *The Sims* has no real end, unless you manage to kill all of your Sims by starvation or fire. And even then you can bulldoze their house and start again. There are also no set objectives in the game. This is instead, as the name implies, a simulation. Simulations grew out of war simulations, and a number of the popular games like Quake are still largely pretend strategy and warfare. The same is true of a number of business school management simulations, although rather than annihilating the enemy firms, financial dominance suffices. But *The Sims* is more about trying out various occupations, personal relationships, living arrangements, decor, clothing, friends, and lifestyles. In this respect, a closer forerunner may be the MOOs (multi-user dimensions, object-oriented) or MUDs (multi-user domains) that were popular in the early and mid-1990s (Turkle 1995). In a number of these MOOs, like the Lambda MOO run by Digital Equipment Corporation, online users could visit the site and explore (through text rather than graphics) various rooms, where they could meet (through messages rather than appearance) the various people currently visiting the MOO. Like many chat rooms, those at the MOO could assume names, genders, and identities that might be quite different from their offline lives.

The Sims is played within the graphically simulated home and neighborhood of the player's characters. In the current version of the game it is also played by a single player and there is neither a sense of competition nor winning. Players have nearly total autonomy in deciding how to play. They become their Sims character and live his or her life. They can impose their own personal preferences, values, ethics, and goals onto the characters. The 107-page instruction manual for the game begins with this (truncated) introduction:

> Romance. Jealousy. Destruction. Intrigue. You might think it's just a typical day in our nation's capital. No, it's much more interesting than that. It's another world entirely, and quite a vivid one. Welcome to the world of

> *The Sims.* . . . These Sims are creatures of moods, of urges, of soaring desires—even if those desires are for pizza. In short, your Sims can be a lot like you. Or your parents. Or the President's parents. You get to design them that way. . . . It's a world of your own handiwork: if you're more interested in home electronics than houseplants, your Sims household can be gizmo heaven. If you want to fill your houses with Sims who would rather samba than scour sinks, so be it. But once you set it up, a Sim household will make some demands upon you.

As with the *SimCity* game from Maxis (producer of *The Sims* and a division of EA—Entertainment Arts), this game continues to evolve. I focus primarily on the core game, *The Sims*, with occasional reference to the expansion packs.

In the build mode the player can build or expand a house, including such details as style, wall coverings, landscaping, doors, and windows. In the buy mode, the player can choose from any of 150 objects (with many more in the expansion packs and available as downloads from official and unofficial game Web sites). In the live mode, after creating the sex, personality, skin color, and appearance of Sims characters, these named people are allowed to act with varying degrees of player-independent autonomy. They may, at least with player control, make friends, joke, flirt, dance, eat, shower, relieve their bladders, go to work, sleep, play, date, fall in love, marry, have children, clean house, play games, throw parties, and more. To furnish a home, buy food, enlarge a house, learn new skills, entertain, and most other facets of living, the Sims must have jobs and earn money. They do not drive or own cars, but a carpool picks them up for their jobs at a set hour in the morning. They go on dates downtown (in *Hot Date*) via taxi. They find out about jobs in the newspaper or on the Internet if they own a computer. The game features ten career tracks: business, entertainment, law enforcement, crime, medicine, military, politics, professional athletics, science, and xtreme sports, with ten levels of advancement in each. The *Livin' Large* expansion pack adds five more careers: musician, slacker, paranormal, journalist, and hacker. If they have or learn the requisite skills and personality traits and have enough social contacts, Sims can advance in their jobs and their salaries increase accordingly. On the other hand, if they are too tired, hungry, in too bad a mood, or miss work two days in a row they will fail to advance and can be fired. In caring for the Sims, including feeding them, being certain they bathe and use the toilet, and keeping them entertained and happy, the game is like a highly evolved Tamagotchi pet.

The player must monitor nine different motives for each of his or her Sims: bladder, comfort, energy, fun, hunger, hygiene, mood, room (home environment), and social. If any of these motives get dangerously low, the

Sim will perform badly, get depressed, urinate on itself, be unsociable, or even die. Different motives are satisfied in different ways including consuming, eating, urinating, bathing, dancing, drinking, painting, sleeping, cooking, and cleaning up. If Sims without cooking skills try to cook a meal they may start a fire, possibly burn down their house, and perhaps die a fiery death in the process. Sims can also starve to death or drown. They can read books to gain new skills and magazines to gain new interests. When Sims die there is a nonobligatory funeral, an urn of ashes, and (for a price) a tombstone. Various service people can be hired, including pizza delivery, repair people, maids, gardeners, newspaper delivery, a robot (in *Livin' Large*), restaurant and bar personnel (in *Hot Date*), and a caterer and bands (in *House Party*). Sims can give back rubs, tell jokes, tickle, kiss, and give gifts in order to make others like them better. When two people like each other, they can move in together and (if different sexes) marry. A married couple can have children. Care of these perpetual children then becomes an additional responsibility. As they get older the children go to school and get grades. Poor moods, hunger, and sleepiness can result in crying or poor school performance. This in turn will result in a social worker taking away the crying babies and older children with bad grades being shipped off to military school. While children go to school, adults go to work. Neighbors come over to socialize or party. In the basic Sims game and the first two expansion packs, the player only sees them in the home and yard. In *Hot Date* they can go downtown, to the beach, or to parks and shops. In a forthcoming expansion pack called *Simsville*, players will reportedly be able to go to other homes and perhaps other locations like a shopping mall.

Existing expansion packs offer more building styles, more consumer goods, more looks ("skins") and clothing, more neighborhoods, and such features as ghosts, love potions, and even a partying and pool-playing Drew Carey. While Sims never explicitly make love and are covered by a discrete mosaic pattern when naked, in *Livin' Large*, a Vibromatic Heart Bed can be purchased that allows Sims to "play in bed." *Hot Date* allows a progressive series of intimacies that go as far as petting. Using an industry self-rating system, *The Sims* and their expansion packs are rated as "teen, comic mischief, mature sexual themes, and mild animated violence." Premarital and extramarital affairs, same sex relationships, polygamy, and multiple partners are allowed, although jealousies may result in fights.

At any given point in playing, the players can go into a photo mode and take pictures of their houses and Sims that can then be uploaded to the game Web site. Any player can then go to this Web site and download other Sims families and houses into their own neighborhood. A neighborhood can have ten homes and the *Livin' Large* expansion pack adds four new neighborhoods to the original one. By frequenting user Web sites or chat rooms, players may become aware of various "cheats" available to add money, change landscaping, and adopt various shortcuts in the game (see also Barba 2000; Chong and Cohen 2001; Cohen 2001).

Machiavellian players can kill off Sims, provoke fights, bulldoze houses, create "slave" families employed to earn money, and engage in other hostile or exploitative tactics. Or a player can be achievement-motivated, nurturing, family oriented, adventurous, acquisitive, or a party animal. Time passes quickly as each second is a Sims minute, and in accelerated mode the speed of play is still faster. Consuming various goods satisfies many of the Sims' basic needs including those of hunger, fun, social, energy, mood, hygiene, room, and comfort. Certain purchasable objects "advertise" themselves as fulfilling various motives. Generally speaking, more expensive objects satisfy motives better than lower priced objects. For instance, a Mission Bed costing §3000 (SIMoleans—the currency of the Sims) provides more comfort than a §300 cot, allowing your Sim to get by with less sleep and also contribute to the room motive. However, some false advertising also exists, in which the advertised motives are not really satisfied by the object. Furthermore, user personality makes certain products differentially satisfying. Many of the relationships between actions while playing Sims and outcomes bearing on personal and interpersonal well-being are probabilistic rather than deterministic. For instance, "playing" on the Vibromatic bed (which is only possible if Sims' attraction scores are sufficiently high) has a one-in-eight chance of producing a baby.

In *The Sims*, as with some other fantasy simulations, there is a chance to try out different identities. As Ball (1967) discerns, "[These games] may be invested with social meanings which have their own consequences for socialization, especially as regards roles, identity, situational definition, or more generally, the social construction of reality itself" (p. 449). To a far greater degree than the MOOs and MUDs investigated by Turkle (1995), *The Sims* allows the user to take on different appearances, personalities, clothing, jobs, ages, races, and genders. Sexual preferences, families, food choices, decor, friends, and interests can also be changed with ease. If an identity is no longer amusing or otherwise engaging, it is easy to create another. Possessions also are not an identity straitjacket, as they have depreciated values at which they can be disposed of in order to acquire new things. If a house grows too small it can be expanded, bulldozed, and rebuilt, or abandoned in order to move into another (in which case creating new Sims is obligatory). Or a player can download entirely new households and Sims from the Web and then occupy them.

This chapter's opening descriptions of *The Sims* as a dollhouse for adults, a soap opera, the Truman Show, and a Skinner box, may have become more apparent by now. But is this really new? No doubt children have for many years played out fantasies and toyed with identities using comic books, dolls, and other toys. In this regard, simulations like this are only more elaborate and automated. One further thing that has changed, however, is that much of the Sims identity that can be created by the player comes from consumer goods. A part of the appeal of the expansion packs for *The Sims* as well as from a number of Web sites like "Mall of the Sims," is the expanded consumption choices they provide. Furthermore, total immersion in and extended play of these games often means that they may take on a pseudo-realistic, dreamlike, archetypal quality for the player. As Erik Davis (1998, p. 204) reports, many hard-core computer gamers report that these games seep into their REM sleep.

The Sims and other simulation games like *SimCity* and *Black and White* have been called "God games" by *Wired* editor Kevin Kelly (1994). Power is part of the appeal in such games—the power to create the world as one wishes it to be (Fine 1983). While players get to play God in such games, in *The Sims* God still throws dice in the sense that control is not so perfect that outcomes are fully determined. Even if the player is aware of the nature of the probabilistic algorithms of *The Sims* and takes advantage of all cheats to take more control, there are still uncertainties about outcomes, especially when the Sims are allowed to act autonomously. Cheats are reportedly expected in fantasy games such that players don't see them as undermining their sense of accomplishment and fun (Fine 1983; Sanger et al. 1997). But if the cheats were to remove all uncertainty, the game would lose interest. Thus it is not surprising that one of the pieces of advice offered on Sims Web sites is to not take advantage of all possible cheats.

The Retro Elements

So what's so retro about *The Sims*? The first, and most superficial, retrograde, retrofitted, retroactive elements are many of the houses, furnishings, outfits, and characters. About a third of the furnishings that can be bought are retro, including such items as a Sioux City wicker chair, a mission end table, a reproduction bust of Athena, a grandfather clock, an Andersonville pedestal sink, a lava lamp, a Josephine sleigh bed, an English garden swing, an antique terrestrial globe, a Pall Mall gas lamp, an Old Thyme restored oven, and a Piazza Amoretto fountain. House styles and clothes/appearances are also frequently retro repro. There are fan Web sites for *The Sims* that specialize in historical categories, so users can download famous people, places, and periods, like Roman times, complete with costumes, props, and architecture. In the *House Party* pack, party types include Western (with country music and a mechanical bull) and Luau (with Hawaiian music and leis), while party outfits also include disco, medieval, and Roman. In *Livin' Large* there is also a genie, the Grim Reaper, a tragic clown, Frankenstein's monster, and cat burglars, while *Hot Date* adds an Old Prude who is likely to show up and start wailing with her purse on Sims who have chosen to kiss or otherwise show affections in public.

As the presence of the Old Prude suggests, the moral tone of *The Sims* is also retro. While her presence adds humor and highlights the generation gap (Sims players are assumed to be adolescents projecting their young adult fantasies onto their characters), the Old Prude and many other elements in this game represent a morality that is centered in the suburban America of the 1950s. Characters must get a job, get up early to catch their car pool (no telecommuting allowed), advance through a career path, earn more money, buy more things, clean house, and practice good personal hygiene. The Sims manual recommends having one spouse in a family stay at home and keep house. If possessions are bought on credit and the credit bills go unpaid, they are repossessed. The dating model of *Hot Date* is also retro in this age of hanging out and hooking up. Among the ways to impress a date (with greater intimacy being the payoff) are to bring flowers, go shopping together, give gifts, and take the date to more expensive bars and restaurants. The one who asks the other out does all the paying, and those with more money have a distinct advantage. There are no divorces for Sims and "all the Sims, even the poorest, live in a pleasant suburb with well-kept streets and good public schools" (Segan 2000). Children must get enough sleep and food so that when they go to school they don't get picked up by the welfare worker or sent to military school. Maids and gardeners are also throwbacks to an earlier era when such pseudo-slavery was more democratized.

Along the various career paths there are also moral dilemmas to be faced. For instance, law enforcement officers must decide whether to take a bribe, criminals must decide whether to join in a crime that is tempting but may be a police sting, doctors can try to settle a malpractice suit out of court or risk losing the case, and politicians can get financing from the estate of a young attractive intern in exchange for "private consultations." Connections are important as well. Career advancement in upper levels requires having lots of friends.

Playing the Game

At the same time, the Sims is also an amoral game. None of the "right" actions are prescribed as they are in earlier board and computer games about careers and living, like *The Game of Life*. But from hanging out in Sims chat rooms and monitoring Sims bulletin boards, it is clear that sadists who intentionally kill their characters or delight in having them pee in their pants are the exception rather than the rule.

Creator Will Wright reports that the modal age of Sims players is in the twenties (Wright 2001). Based on online users who reveal their ages, there are two main age groups of Sims players. One group ranges in age from nine to fifteen with a mode of twelve (at least based on revealed ages). A second group ranges in age from nineteen to forty and consists of college students, young adults, and parents who may have bought the game for their children, but play just as much or more themselves. One woman in the latter group, on the December day I am typing this, went online in a Yahoo group for the "Sims Obsessed" to apologize that she would not be online for a while because her husband suffered a heart attack yesterday and his life was more important than the game. Others who were online offered sympathy and said to let them know how he was doing. Another forty-six-year-old woman just diagnosed with colon cancer asked others in the group to pray for her and received many assurances that they would. Other users, besides talking about how to decorate their Sims Christmas tree and Sims house for each of the twelve days of Christmas, talked about RW (real world) topics like how to toilet train a Yorkshire terrier. These groups have obviously become lifelines linking the VR (virtual reality) world of the Sims with the RW of Sims players.

Unlike with most computer games, at least one-fourth of Sims players are women (Weise 2001), and it appears they make up nearly half of Sims Web site/interest group participants. Will Wright (2001) says that 30 percent of registered owners are women, but that the real number is likely more than 40 percent. This is remarkable in the computer game field where males are generally more than 95 percent of game players. From the comments of online user/reviewers, many see *The Sims* as a gender-neutral game. For instance, Victoria from Atlanta observes:

> The gaming industry has often been criticized for being male-oriented in its shoot-'em-up type games. What a relief to have an excellent passive game on the market [*The Sims*] that appeals to both men and women.

Since the game itself largely avoids imposing sex role stereotypes (although there is a female maid service), it allows the user to impose whatever sex roles they desire. Characters can be loving, caring, and helpful or they can be selfish, aggressive, and mean. Some males who were used to more violent games were surprised to learn how much they liked playing with a "dollhouse." Others found that they couldn't make the adjustment. Danny of Port Angeles, Washington, wrote:

> This game stinks on ice. This game is not fun. There is not really that much to do. It is boring, well at least to me it is, but if you like other sim games such as sim farm, sim ant, sim city or sim copter, you will probly [sic] like this game. The only problem with me is I don't like these other sim games and so I don't like this one. I like games like Starcraft age of empires and other war games.

Just as some males were surprised to learn they could like playing dolls, some females were surprised to learn they could like computer games at all. For instance, a woman from Tampa noticed the parallel to playing dolls as an attractive feature of the game:

> My boyfriend has been a hard core gamer for a few years now and I've had a hard time relating to his obsession. Well, that is no longer a problem! I bought *The Sims* about a month ago and I love it. It's like a [sic] interactive Doll house with electronic paper dolls.

Players commonly give their Sims characters their own names, making extended self expressly evident. As Kozinets (2001) notes:

> Entertainment products (commercial popular culture) affords both some of the key conceptual spaces available in contemporary society for constructing identity and a sense of what matters in life. (p. 78)

The Sims is most likely to be played alone, although many players report showing their friends and letting them play for a while. An online interactive version of the game is reported by some sources to be a pending future addition to the Sims line. The most commonly reported manner of Sims game play is that of obsession. While early posters to online bulletin boards tend to influence later posters, the most frequently offered descriptor of the game is "addictive." Like collectors who often use this term to describe themselves (Belk 1995), it seems meant to make compulsive-appearing behavior appear slightly humorous, but not truly abnormal.

One motivation for devoted play of *The Sims* is the feeling of control and power in "playing God." One man took this as the ultimate challenge:

> "The Sims" has managed to allow the ordinary gamer, to become some person's fate. Scary as it is, it is also intoxicating, to have someone's life in our hands. You will be tempted to ruin some lives and start others; all of this is possible with "The Sims." . . . Or maybe you can't handle being a god?

Control and playing God on the computer seems to be especially attractive to males, a group that is only slowly losing its predominance among computer game players (Levy 1984).

Perhaps the ultimate retro element of *The Sims* is the regression into infancy that may result from identifying with Sims characters who can't even feed, bathe, or relieve themselves, and who are in constant danger of starvation or immolation without help of the player-god. If this is a case of ontogeny recapitulating phylogeny, then it would seem that the human race is infantalizing. This is in fact how Belk (2001) described the Las Vegas experience and how Kinsella (1995) accounts for the Cuties phenomenon in Japan. In the case of Las Vegas, we find middle-age adults wandering through fantasy-themed casinos in pajama-like jogging suits, with coins clasped tightly in their hot little hands and plastic cups, behaving in totally nonrational ways by putting their coins in glittering gonging machines. They play games, besides gambling, like dress up, pig out, and shopping spree. In the case of the Japanese Cuties fad, Japanese adolescents adopted comics, clothing, music, baby talk, and baby writing, and a variety of merchandise, such as *Hello Kitty* items, all aimed at embracing a cute, loveable, small, vulnerable, and pitiable image.

The Retro Future

If Las Vegas visitors pursue a recess-like suspension of adulthood in order to become guiltlessly self-indulgent (Belk 2001), and Japanese Cuties, alienated by the role straitjackets of Japanese postindustrial society, embark on a romanticized journey back to an idealized childhood, as Kinsella (1995) suggests, what should be made of the Sims retro journey back to infancy? Speaking of toys and board games of a precomputer games era, Sutton-Smith (1986) suggested:

> As achievement and success become increasingly important for children, so toys themselves became increasingly associated with such achievement and success. Toys now signify that the child is an owner, a consumer, and an achiever. (p. 127)

The Sims continue to socialize children (as well as some adults) into a materialistic consumer culture, but they do not provide the sorts of achievement motivation represented in the winner-take-all strategy and race gameboards popular during most of the twentieth century (Andrews 1972; Dixon 1990; Mergen 1980; Parlett 1999). So something more is needed to account for willing self-infantalization by players projecting themselves onto their Sims characters.

In part, our fascination with games involving actors, models, dolls, soldiers, and other imaginary persons is due to the appeal of fantasy and role playing (Fine 1983). Here the toy offers a means of rehearsing adult and other fantasy identities, and a way of learning about gender, age, expression, interaction, control, agency, and a variety of other aspects of life. While dolls have long served the child's need for mimicking adult behavior (Callois 1962), dollhouses first emerged among adults in sixteenth-and seventeenth-century Germany and the Netherlands as ways for the adults in wealthy merchant families to comprehend the luxuriousness of their lives (Cross 1997). Only at the end of the eighteenth century did dollhouses come to be built for children, specifically girls, to teach them housekeeping (Wilckens 1980). The miniature scale of dolls and many other toys allows creative exploration or routine practice of imagined lifestyles and possibilities. Such objects are not merely anthropomorphized by the child, but are projections of the user's self (Belk 1988). While there is also identification with characters in films and on television, with computer simulated games there is a difference. Rich Hillerman, an executive at *The Sims* parent company, Electronic Arts, explained that:

> If we give users options, they don't choose the unsuccessful outcome. . . . You go to a movie, you're willing to see something tragic happen to the hero because you can separate yourself. In a game, you've got too much ego involved. (Weise 2001)

Childhood itself, as a special privileged state, is largely an invention of the eighteenth and nineteenth centuries (Aries 1962; Sutton-Smith 1986; Cross 1997). Prior to this time, children were thought of merely as miniature adults. Even in the early twentieth century, toys and games were not seen as mere playthings and often had to carry a burden of religious or moral instruction to be pursued without guilt. These lessons were incorporated in nineteenth-century board games (Andrews 1972). The *Mansion of Happiness* is thought to be the first American board game and was developed in 1843 by the daughter of a Massachusetts clergyman. In the game virtues such as prudence, truth, industry, humility, and charity brought advancement, while vices such as drunkenness, breaking the Sabbath, cheating, cruelty, and perjury led away from the mansion of happiness (a euphemism for heaven) and often to punishments such as the whipping post, the stocks, poverty, and prison. In the *Checkered Game of Life* (1860), which helped found the Milton Bradley company, there were also nonreligious moral virtues of honor, truth, bravery, education, ambition, industry, perseverance, and honesty, as well as the vices of gambling, intemperance, idleness, and crime. Parents recognized the modeling and shaping aspects of toys and sought to assure that toys teach "good" or educational lessons, even to the point of forgetting that the child's chief rationale for playing is to have fun (Huizinga 1970). But when the Milton Bradley company introduced *The Game of Life* in 1960 on the one-hundredth anniversary of the *Checkered Game of Life*, the pertinent virtues were truncated to competing and earning money (Burns 1978; Canary 1968). These were still moral lessons, but the game involved a much more individualistic morality. Today, any such moral lessons are a thing of the past. As we have seen, *The Sims* is an amoral game, which caters to the desire for mimicry identified by Callois (1962), but without the instructional overtones of moral board games or educational toys and games. It is instead more of a vehicle for projective role-playing and consumer indulgence.

But still more is needed to explain the fascination with the infantalized Sims. Another part of their attraction may lie in our fear of the future. Nothing represents the future today as much as the personal computer. Computer and video games arose, Sutton-Smith (1986) suggests, in response to our fear of the computer and its control of our lives:

> The Computer then has become a Force in ourselves, not a physical force (to be countered by games of physical skill), not a random force (to be countered by games of chance), nor a deceptive force (to be countered by games of strategy), but an entirely logical and mnemonic force, to be countered by, of all things, video games. (p. 65)

Similarly, Turkle (1984) argues that:

> For the child for whom little seems under total control, toys and simple machines are reassuring exceptions. Dolls, soldiers, wind-up toys—all of these "come alive," but only at the child's command. Computer toys that talk, cheat, and win are not so compliant. Yet they have a "holding power." In part it is the holding power of the feared. . . . We are drawn to what frightens us, we play with what disturbs us, in part to try to reassert our control over it. (p. 34)

We fear the computer, according to one argument, because:

> We attribute God-like qualities to computers, assuming them to be all-knowing and all-powerful. We feel diminished by their powers, frightened and out of control. We confer great honor and wealth on the priesthood that understands and uses them. This techno-worship verges on the ancient sin of idolatry. (Cobb 1998, p. 44)

In the context of the traditional computer game, Sutton-Smith (1986) argues, the adaptive strategy is to beat the computer using physical skill, hand-eye coordination, strategy, and luck. The successful player thereby demonstrates that he or she is in control and that the computer is not to be feared after all. While we may no longer regard the computer as a god (Park-Curry and Jiobu 1982; Davis 1998) nor see machines as Cartesian embodiments of an orderly universe (Sutton-Smith 1986), the idea of mastery is no doubt still an underlying reason for much video game playing (Gilmore 1971). Just as the legendary John Henry pitted himself against the steel driving machine, some of us seem compelled to pit ourselves against many computer video games in a valiant effort not to be bested by technology. To beat the computer in the case of *The Sims* is to have one's Sims characters survive and prosper. Furthermore, users are proud of going beyond the limits of the game by downloading software patches to allow such things as seeing the Sims nude (without the pixelation that otherwise covers them as they shower, use the toilet, or go swimming or hot-tubbing sans clothing) and having Sims children grow up and become fully playable characters (rather than remaining in a perpetual state of childhood).

Although mimicry and overcoming fear of the computer by exerting control seem to be part of the attraction of *The Sims*, something more is still needed to account for the fascination with Victorian houses, retro clothes and furnishings, tired plots, and the invocation of yesterday's models of dating, marriage, child rearing, and death. The missing something seems to be a widespread inability to imagine a future that is not composed of a rehashing of the past and present. Both the available props and characters draw inevitably on the past. Even seemingly futuristic elements like Servo the robot (only §15,000), draw more on fifty-year-old science fiction than they do on current technology, much less innovative visions of the future. Like Disney's Tomorrowland and Epcot Center, those who play *The Sims* are most apt to construct what Brown (2001) called "a pre-postmodern relic of what the future used to hold" (p. 140). Not just the props, houses, clothing, and furnishings, but the entire scenario of *The Sims* and the lives dreamed up by its players is strikingly bankrupt in terms of creativity and originality. A look at the homes and people uploaded by players onto *The Sims'* Web site (www.thesims.com) will show much that mimics what is and has been and little or nothing that anticipates what might be. In trying to act as visionaries, artists, engineers, novelists, musicians, choreographers, and inventors, most consumers (Sims players and others) show they are hopelessly inept. They may be able to rehash, remix, replay, and regurgitate, but they seldom seem capable of a truly original thought, much less an original lifestyle, philosophy, or even a design for a new car, coat, or computer program.

Therein lies a key weakness of the so-called marketing concept. Giving consumers what they want is a fine humanistic (if profit-driven) ideal, but only so long as consumers know what they want and can articulate it. Given all the creative tools of *The Sims* (e.g., HomeCrafter home design tools, FaceLift personal appearance designer, Art Studio paint and photo subprogram), little is produced that is not a minor variation on a theme from the past. For the many product areas where we welcome innovation (including music, education, film, fictional writing, computers, electronics, fashions, and design of goods and services), the consumer may well be the least appropriate and least useful person to ask what is wanted. Besides being hopelessly uncreative, consumers are also very social creatures whose desire for mimicry seems to overpower any personal sense of taste. Thus, even as simple an object as a new shoe design cannot be readily judged by the mass of consumers until they see whether other people are wearing it. We may get some heuristics, like the Sim heuristic that more costly is more desirable, but we seldom are apt to get originality, creativity, or vision. Therefore, design is probably best left to the designers, art to the artists, music to the musicians, education to the educators, and invention to the inventors. For most others, whether they are living simulated (VR) lives or real (RW) lives, reworked versions and retro re-creations are about all we can expect. If Sims players and other consumers think they have seen the future, they must also think that it looks an awfully lot like the past.

Back to a Better Future?

Lest I come off as the Old Prude in *Hot Date* castigating the retrogressive unoriginality of Sims players and the inability of consumers to know what they want in fields like art, music, entertainment, and technology, there is another more liberatory (Firat and Venkatesh 1995) take on *The Sims* that should be acknowledged. Speaking of simulation games generally, Pesce (2000) says:

> The "make pretend" worlds of computer simulation bring us opportunities that reality doesn't easily offer. We are at the threshold of a revolution in human experience. Computer simulation is starting to be used as an engine of the imagination, bringing to light some of the most intangible aspects of our being. Just as music, dance, and poetry have helped us articulate the quiet parts of ourselves, simulation will become a new aesthetic, an art form with its own power to illuminate the depths of our being. (p. 248)

To Heim (1993) and others (e.g., Cobb 1998; Davis 1998; Noble 1999; M. Taylor 1999; Taylor and Miles 1997; Wertheim 1999) our play with computers and hyperspace is nothing less than a search for God and paradise.

Considering *The Sims* in particular, Henry Jenkins, comparative media studies director at MIT, argues that:

> The real lesson of "The Sims" is [in the] unharnessing [of] the creative power of grassroots citizens to contribute to the design and development of a game. They thought of it from the very beginning as a tool set for people to tell their own stories, to set their own goals, not a kind of rigidly railed interactive experiences, but a participatory culture (Vance 2001).

Jenkins (2002) notes that in June 2000, Yahoo's Web directory listed more than 33,000 fan Web sites, with 1,200 for Star Trek alone. He argues that such sites, including those for *The Sims*, allow geographically dispersed participants to feel a sense of virtual community centered around their brand loyalty to a game, star, team, or other focus of their fandom. As the second paragraph of the "Playing the Game" section above suggests, there is little doubt that such a sense of community exists for *The Sims*. In an interview by Jenkins (forthcoming) with Will Wright, *The Sims* creator forecast that in the future two-thirds of Sims content will come from consumers, shared freely on their Sims Web sites. Will Wright has said that these more active players take a leadership role, actively drive storytelling, and are essentially unpaid software developers (Wright 2001).

But what is the nature of these stories? Weise (2001) asks:

> What do *The Illiad*, *Beowulf* and *Hamlet* have that *Doom*, *Quake*, and *Tomb Raider* don't? After all each involves bloodshed, revenge and people armed with nasty weapons running amok.

The answer, she suggests, is that they have plot, character development, and narrative tension, which the shoot-'em-up games distinctly lack. What of the simulation games like *The Sims* then? According to Will Wright (2001) there are now 16,000 stories that have been uploaded by Sims players onto the Sims Web site. And while most of these stories are not very compelling, a few hundred are pretty good. Good here may mean that they are technically compelling (e.g., building a Sims ski lift and getting characters to ski), creative (e.g., the Grim Reaper falls in love and it fails to work out for obvious reasons), moralistic (e.g, "Starbucks Sucks" in which the small Turkish coffee shop owner is hero and Starbucks the villain), or humanistic (e.g., cathartic stories about abusive relationships). Just as not everyone can be a great author or playwright, not everyone is going to be a great Sims storyteller. But no doubt some true works of art will be produced in this and other simulation games and they will emerge from 16,000 or 16 million stories and survive to become our new literature. And if the story is a story of our past, can't we say the same for the stories of Homer and Shakespeare?

Finally, we might ask, does all this really matter? I think it does. The computer game industry already generates more money than the film industry (Pesce 2000). Henry Jenkins (2001) calls computer games the art form of the twenty-first century and compares their impact on culture to that of jazz or movies on culture of the twentieth century (although he suggests that such games are now at a stage comparable to the silent movie). But for game fans, this is not a passing entertainment like seeing a movie. It is instead a hobby; an avocation; an addiction. As Gelbner (1999) argues, rather than being a break from work, hobbies reproduce values of the workplace. But in this case, with the addictive hobby being that of participation in simulated storytelling about individuals, families, and neighborhoods, perhaps a much broader set of values is being reflected. Videogames in general, and *The Sims* in particular, may tell us something about ourselves and our world. Whether this is a retro tale, a futuristic tale, or some hybrid or other alternative remains to be seen. Ultimately what makes these tales significant is that they tell us something about ourselves and the human condition.

References

Andrews, Peter (1972), "Games People Played," *American Heritage*, 23 (4): 64–79, 104–5.

Aries, Phillipp (1962), *Centuries of Childhood*, trans. Robert Baldick, London: Jonathon Cape.

Ball, Donald (1967), "Toward a Sociology of Toys: Inanimate Objects, Socialization, and the Demography of the Doll World," *Sociological Quarterly*, 8 (4): 447–58.

Barba, Rick (2000), *The Sims Livin' Large Expansion Pack: Prima's Official Strategy Guide*, Roseville, CA: Prima Games.

Belk, Russell W. (1988), "Possessions and the Extended Self," *Journal of Consumer Research*, 15 (September): 139–68.

——— (1995), *Collecting in a Consumer Society*, London: Routledge.

——— (2001), "May the Farce Be With You: On Las Vegas and Consumer Infantalization," *Consumption, Markets, & Culture*, 4 (2): 101–23.

Brown, Stephen (2001), *Marketing—The Retro Revolution*, London: Sage.

Burns, Thomas A. (1978), "*The Game of Life*: Idealism, Reality and Fantasy in the Nineteenth- and Twentieth-Century Versions of a Milton Bradley Game," *Canadian Review of American Studies*, 9 (Spring): 50–83.

Callois, Roger (1962), *Man, Play and Games*, trans. Meyer Barash, New York: Free Press.

Canary, Robert H. (1968), "Playing the Game of Life," *Journal of Popular Culture*, 1 (Spring): 427–32.

Chong, David and Mark Cohen (2001), *The Sims Hot Date Expansion Pack: Prima's Official Strategy Guide*, Roseville, CA: Prima Games.

Cobb, Jennifer (1998), *Cybergrace: The Search for God in the Digital World*, New York: Crown.

Coffey, Robert (n.d.), "The Sims," www.gamespot.com/features/game_evol_p4/index.html.

Cohen, Mark (2001), *The Sims House Party Expansion Pack: Prima's Official Strategy Guide*, Roseville, CA: Prima Games.

Cross, Gary (1997), *Kid's Stuff: Toys and the Changing World of American Childhood*, Cambridge, MA: Harvard University Press.

Davis, Erik (1998), *Techgnosis: Myth, Magic + Mysticism in the Age of Information*, New York: Three Rivers Press.

Dixon, Bob (1990), *Playing Them False: A Study of Children's Toys, Games, and Puzzles*, Stoke-on-Trent, UK: Trentham Books.

Fine, Gary Alan (1983), *Shared Fantasy: Role-Playing Games as Social Worlds*, Chicago: University of Chicago Press.

Firat, A. Fuat and Alladi Venkatesh (1995), "Liberatory Postmodernism and the Reenchantment of Consumption," *Journal of Consumer Research*, 22 (June): 239–67.

Folkers, Richard (1999), "The New Sims on the Block," *U.S. News Online*, May 3.

Gelbner, Steven M. (1999), *Hobbies: Leisure and the Culture of Work in America*, New York: Columbia University Press.

Gilmore, J. Bernard (1971), "Play: A Special Behavior," in *Child's Play*, ed. R.E. Herron and Brian Sutton-Smith, New York: John Wiley, pp. 311–25.

Grayson, Kent and Radan Martinec (2001), "Fact or Fiction? The 'Authentic' Homes of Shakespeare and Sherlock Holmes," paper presented at Association for Consumer Research Conference, October, Austin, Texas.

Hartley, L.P. (1953), *The Go-Between*, London: Hamish Hamilton.

Heim, Michael (1993), *The Metaphysics of Virtual Reality*, New York: Oxford University Press.

Howell, David (2001), "Sims Teach Kids Game of Life," *Edmonton Journal*, February 26.

Huizinga, Johan (1970), *Homo Ludens: A Study in the Play Element in Culture*, New York: Harper and Row.

Jenkins, Henry (2002), "Interactive Audiences?: The 'Collective Intelligence' of Media Fans" in *The New Media Book*, ed. Dan Harries, London: British Film Institute, see web.mit.edu/21fms/www/faculty/henry3/collective%20intelligence.html.
——— (2001), paper delivered at "Educating Game Designers" session, Entertainment in the Interactive Age Conference, Los Angeles: Annenberg Center, see: www.annenberg.edu/interactive-age/program.html#, January 30.

Kelly, Kevin (1994), *Out of Control: The Rise of Neo-biological Civilization*, Reading, MA: Addison-Wesley.

Kinsella, Sharon (1995), "Cuties in Japan," in *Women, Media, and Consumption in Japan*, ed. Lise Szkov and Brian Moeran, Honolulu: University of Hawaii Press, pp. 220–54.

Kozinets, Robert V. (2001), "Utopian Enterprise: Articulating the Meanings of *Star Trek's* Culture of Consumption," *Journal of Consumer Research*, 28 (June): 67–88.

Lee, Iara (director) (1996), *Synthetic Pleasures*, video, 83 minutes, ASIN: 1572521031.

Levy, Steven (1984), *Hackers: Heroes of the Computer Revolution*, New York: Anchor.

Lowenthal, David (1985), *The Past Is a Foreign Country*, Cambridge, UK: Cambridge University Press.

Mergen, Bernard (1980), "Games and Toys," in *Handbook of Popular Culture*, ed. M. Thomas Inge, Westport, CT: Greenwood Press, pp. 163–90.

MSNBC (1999), "Next in Sim Series: A Soap Opera Sims Game Is Set to Bring Family Life to the Computer Screen," MSNBC Online, May 14.

Noble, David F. (1999), *The Religion of Technology: The Divinity of Man and the Spirit of Invention*, New York: Penguin.

Park-Curry, Pamela and Robert M. Jiobu (1982), "The Computer as Fetish: Electronic Pop God," in *Objects of Special Devotion: Fetishism in Popular Culture*, ed. Ray B. Browne, Bowling Green, OH: Bowling Green University Popular Press, pp. 328–35.

Parlett, David (1999), *The Oxford History of Board Games*, Oxford: Oxford University Press.

Pesce, Mark (2000), *How Technology Is Transforming Our Imagination: The Playful World*, New York: Ballantine Books.

Sanger, Jack, Jane Wilson, Bryn Davies, and Roger Whitakker (1997), *Young Children, Videos and Computer Games: Issues for Teachers and Parents*, London: Falmer Press.

Scanlon, Jessie (1999), "Keeping Up with the Simses," *Wired Magazine*, June: 62.

Segan, Sascha (2000), "A World of Their Own: Online Game Lets You Play God," *ABCNEWS.com*, abcnews.go.com/sections/tech/DailyNews/sims000322.html, March 22.

Shachtman, Noah (2001), "Suburban Fantasy in Your PC," *Wired News* (www.wired.com), April 8.

Sutton-Smith, Brian (1986), *Toys as Culture*, New York: Gardner Press.

Taylor, Chris (1999), "Playing God," *Time*, March 1.

Taylor, Mark C. (1999), *About Religion: Economies of Faith in Virtual Culture (Religion and Postmodernism)*, Chicago: University of Chicago Press.

Taylor, Mark C. and Jack Miles (1997), *Hiding (Religion and Postmodernism)*, Chicago: University of Chicago Press.

Turkle, Sherry (1984), *The Second Self: Computers and the Human Spirit*, New York: Simon and Schuster.

——— (1995), *Life on the Screen: Identity in the Age of the Internet*, New York: Simon and Schuster.

Udell, Scott (n.d.), "The Sims: From the Creator of Sim City Comes a Really Different Kind of Game," *Computer Games Online*, www.cdmag.com/articles/020010/sim_e3.html

Vance, Ryan (2001), "The Cult of the Sims," TechTV, TechLive, May 4, www.techtv.com/news/story/0,24105,3325507,00.html.

Weise, Elizabeth (2001), "Game Developers Turn to Classics for Inspiration," *USA Today* online (www.usatoday.com), June 15.

Wertheim, Margaret (1999), *The Pearly Gates of Cyberspace: A History of Space from Dante to the Internet*, New York: W.W. Norton.

Wilckens, Leonie von (1980), *The Dolls' House*, London: Bell and Kyman.

Wright, Will (2001), keynote speech, Entertainment in the Interactive Age Conference, Los Angeles: Annenberg Center, www.annenberg.edu/interactive-age/program.html#, January 29.

4

Corsets, Silk Stockings, and Evening Suits

Retro Shops and Retro Junkies

Christina Goulding

Retroscapes, retro shopping, retro film, and retro fashion have all become constant, almost taken for granted, features of everyday life. Love it or hate it, it would appear retro is here to stay, although it has not had an easy time of it. For the lone voice crying in the wilderness, retro represents a revolutionary turn in marketing thought, a harbinger for change, and the opportunity to apply a new twist on old ideas (Brown 2001). Nevertheless, not all share this view and it is probably fair to say that the majority of scholars are more willing to scorn the rise of retro than to welcome its ascendancy. Vociferous excoriations have been launched by the "purists," particularly in the realm of culture, and especially with regard to the popularization of such sacred institutions as museums (Hewison 1987). These retroscapes, embodied in the form of the living museum and championed by Colonial Williamsburg in the United States, a reconstructed eighteenth-century town, funded to the tune of $79 million by John D. Rockefeller, (which incidentally involved the destruction of 700 post-1790 buildings) are partly responsible, if we are to believe what we read, for such monumental events as the end of history, the death of innovation, and the compression of time and space (Walsh 1992). Salacious theory indeed.

Retro, however, is not confined to the realm of the museum, but exerts an almost subliminal influence on our shopping experiences. This is exemplified in the fusion of past and present in the "utopian" shopping malls epitomized by Powerscourt, Dublin (Maclaran and Brown 2001), and the more blatantly nostalgic design of shops such as "Past Times" and "Laura Ashley." Here potpourri ambience, Edwardian cotton, and lace Helena Bonham Carter

English Rose merchandise, reign supreme. And it does not stop there. The retrorevolution has even dared to breach the hitherto sanctuary of the British pub. Over the past two decades we have witnessed a veritable explosion of themed pubs, offering every type of drinking environment from remade, remodeled interiors dripping in plush Victorian velvet and gold (Norman 1990), to the ersatz setting of the "real" Irish public house, painstakingly cloned by chains such as O'Neills and the Greenall's Group (Brown and Patterson 2000). More often than not, the result of this "pastization" is a synthetic, sanitized, cornucopia of copper kettles, dried herbs, and commodified nostalgia, making them an easy target for the critics of the "Disneyfication" syndrome.

However, retro goes beyond the realm of mere imitation. A fundamental feature of retro is that, like nostalgia, it selects aspects from the past, always positive, and mixes them with the modern to create a new hybrid form that appeals to contemporary expectations. Palpable illustrations of this can be seen in Hollywood blockbusters. Take for example the film *Braveheart*, with its blend of historical fact and historical inaccuracies. Allegedly, the postrelease merchandising, such as statues of Braveheart, had to be withdrawn and refashioned, because they did not bear Mel Gibson's face. A more recent example is *Moulin Rouge*, a remake of John Houston's 1952 film of the same name, which has been hailed as a modern version of the Judy Garland–Mickey Rooney "hey gang let's put on a show" film (Landesman 2001). *Moulin Rouge* may be described as a postmodern, heterochronic mix of parody and pastiche, of old and new, and a merging of styles, eras, and genres. Supposedly set at the dawn of the twentieth century, one scene features Nicole Kidman, in character as Satine, dressed as Marlene Dietrich in *The Blue Angel*, singing "diamonds are a girl's best friend" before breaking into Madonna's "material girl." This blurring of the boundaries between history and contemporary popular culture and the accompanying hype has had further implications for the world of retro consumption, most notably, the realm of fashion. Even before the film's release, Gaultier, Galliano, McQueen, McCartney, and Versace were all showing corsets and bustiers ranging from boned, zipped, laced, flesh colored, satin, leather, denim, feathered, and bejeweled, to distressed. Even the corsetieres to the Queen, Rigby and Peller, are offering variations described as "feats of engineering" (McCord 2001) which promise to bone, hone, and tightly tone even the most curvaceous figure. This in itself is nothing new. History has long influenced filmmakers, whose products have in turn influenced the fashion industry. Furthermore, over the past twenty years, fashion has become increasingly cyclical, caught in a constant process of reinvention and recycling. We have had the return of the miniskirt (several times), as well as, horror of horrors, the flares of the 1970s, which are currently in vogue. The late 1990s saw contemporary versions of the soft, flowing lines of lace and velvet of the flower power generation, while designer collections in 2001 predicted the revival of the 1950s Doris Day look. Conversely, for those who do not care for the twee girlie, soft and cuddly image, the vamp is the alternative with stilettos the shoes to be seen in. Crucially, however, these clothes are not direct copies of the original; rather, they are updated versions with a modern twist. The miniskirt worn with Doc Marten boots is probably a far cry from Mary Quant's revolutionary vision. Nevertheless, it is this fusion of old and new that distinguishes retro from the historical or the authentic. Yet despite this explosion of retro into so many spheres of consumption, for a significant group of consumers dedicated to the style of past eras, reproduction and remodeling are not enough. What they want is "the real thing," and there are retro shops that purport to offer this, which brings me on to the actual subject of this chapter. The aim of the previous, albeit brief, trip around the retro maze, was to locate a phenomenon that has attracted little attention from retro commentators— the retro shop. Not the retro of Laura Ashley, but the independently owned specialist shops that have proliferated and flourished in every British city since the 1960s. These shops are dedicated to selling "authentic" clothes and the paraphernalia of bygone decades. Nevertheless, though interesting in themselves, any understanding of their enduring appeal must be seen as a two-sided story; of selling and consuming. What follows is an attempt to tell this story by incorporating reflective commentary and visual illustrations, and hopefully, through the process, to present a case that the retro experience may not be quite the superficial inauthentic parody it has been painted.

Retro Is Not New!

One way to conceptualize retro consumption is to locate it in relation to the postmodern experience, which may be seen as a desire on the part of an alienated group of consumers, faced with nothing but ersatz reconditioned style, to return to a golden age of creativity, romance, and beauty—a time when men were men and women were glamorous. Indeed the current vogue for retro has been described as part of the nostalgia craze for bringing history into an ahistorical present (McRobbie 1994). However, while we might talk about "the death of innovation" as characteristic of this so-called soulless society, it is important to recognize that retro is not necessarily new. Over a century ago the aesthetes and pre-Raphaelites, faced with the dark invasion of the industrial revolution, retreated backward to a time of Arthurian chivalry. Rejecting the symbols of progress, they escaped through nostalgic fantasy, which became a common theme of many paintings and the subject of poetic verse (Gaunt 1975). Artists unsympathetic to the political economists' view of history rebelled by evoking superficial nostalgic impressions, manifest in the romantic paintings of, for example, Alma Tadema, who reconstructed the world of the ancients with a new modern realism (Hunter 1981). However, things really took off with the birth of the teenager, an American concept imported into postwar Britain, which saw the creation of what we might term contemporary youth subcultures. The first of these were the "Teddy Boys," characterized by their deadpan expressions, "aggressive sideboards, masses of hair at the back and a fuzzy shock of it at the brow" (Fyvel 1997, p. 389). Nevertheless, the style did not develop from the street. On the contrary, the full Edwardian dress of curled bowlers worn over long hair, tailored knee-length Edwardian coats, and ultra-tight trousers, from which it evolved, was first worn by the affluent young male "Sloane Rangers" of the early postwar period, and bought at shops on Savile Row in Mayfair. However, while this class merely flirted with the style, it was soon adopted by young unskilled males from the tough working-class riverside areas of the East End of London, as a symbol of revolt against society (Fyvel 1997). Continuing this line of resistance, later subcultures, such as the Beats of the 1950s, followed the trend of mix-and-match by engaging in rummage sales in search of satin dresses and sheer blouses from the 1930s that, worn in the 1950s, "offered a strong sexual challenge to the gingham-clad domesticity of the moment" (McRobbie 1994).

The retro experience of today, however, is more firmly rooted in the hippy counterculture of the late 1960s. Hippies, with their taste for old fur coats, crepe dresses, antique lace petticoats, velvet skirts, and army coats, reflected an interest in authenticity and pure natural fabrics. Naturally enough, in order to meet market demand, the late 1960s saw the proliferation of "alternative" secondhand shops. These shops were opened and managed by hippies themselves, reflecting an entrepreneurial turn in the antimaterialistic counterculture, which is often overlooked in the literature on subcultures. These alternative entrepreneurs stocked their shops with leather flying jackets, 1920s flapper dresses, and the popular peasant ethnic look. Nonetheless, nothing lasts forever and by the 1970s the hippy movement had started to fade (McRobbie 1994). Commercially, these now established business men and women, in order to survive, were forced to turn their attention to contemporary nostalgia and the new generation of retro customers; young people who, bored with the exaggerated extremes of the "glam rock" decade, were looking to the past for creative inspiration.

Close Encounters of the Pastmodern Kind

Consequently, it is possible to conceptualize retro as a form of consumer resistance. Certainly my own initial experiences with retro confirms this to a degree. This encounter occurred in the late 1970s, the era of glam rock, six button waistbands, ski-jumpers, ribbed platform shoes, and the mullet hair cut. Who could resist resisting? It was the time when punk was in its infancy and being different involved the creative use of bin-liners, safety-pin jewelry, gelled and solidified spiked hair, and the adoption of an "I'm of the street" anarchic attitude. Punk, in its early days, is often described as style of the street, from the street but it was no more of the street than the original Teddy Boy look, or the middle-class hippy movement. Punk originated in the art colleges and trendy London bars, and was essentially about marketing, although this fact is denied by many subcultural commentators, especially those emanating from the Birmingham Center for Contemporary Cultural Studies, which was established in the 1970s. The notion of street culture resistance is a prominent theme that permeates the work of, for example, Hall and Jefferson (1996) and Gelder and Thornton (1997) whose influential compilations adopt the position that youth subcultures are situated in the dialectic between a "hegemonic dominant" culture and the subordinate working-class "parent culture" of which youth is a fraction (Clarke et al. 1997). Consider, however, the role of Malcolm McLaren, manager of the original punk bad boys The Sex Pistols. Apart from knowing how to manipulate media attention for all the shock value he could muster, together with Vivienne Westwood, a fashion designer, he opened the shop "Sex" on Kings Road, London. Here, poorly made bondage trousers sold for around £50 a pair, a considerable and not streetly sum in the 1970s. Johnny Rotten, the lead singer of The Sex Pistols was also quoted on a recent radio program as saying that the band marketed themselves on hate, which in itself is a unique selling proposition, and one that proved to be very lucrative. Nonetheless, there is no denying that for anyone with the slightest aesthetic pretensions, the choice between multibuttoned waistbands and punk had little appeal, unless, that is, one looked backward for inspiration.

My first experience with retro came when I stumbled across a shop called Bill and Belle, named after the proprietors, Bill (I never knew his second name) and Patti Belle, the wife of Steve Gibbons, a well-known rock musician at the time. Both, in their mid to late thirties, were certainly not about to conform to the stereotypical ideal of mature and sensible thirtysomethings. On the contrary, Bill's countenance was that of an aging and slightly receding James Dean in *Rebel Without a Cause*, while Patti sported pink hair, full net-layered ballet skirt, and ballet pumps. Their fascination with masquerade and fancy dress possibly did not lend itself easily to more mainstream professions, so the shop was as much an outlet for their exhibitionism as it was a business. Bill and Belle was situated on the edge of Birmingham city center in the theater district, later to become Birmingham's Chinatown. The building itself was old but interesting, the type that one cannot pass without pausing to peer through the window, which was filled to overflowing with an erratic assortment of 1940s and 1950s paraphernalia. This paraphernalia ranged from pill-box hats on plastic heads to full-scale dummies complete with makeup and dressed from head to toe in coordinating period clothes. Scattered around these mannequins lay antique perfume sprays, cigarette holders, jewelry, and film posters from the era.

Inside the shop the effect was that of a treasure chest. The lighting was always dim in that Dickensian "old curiosity shop" way that never fails to incite curiosity and invite exploration. Clothes rails held layers of garments ranging from full-length velvet and taffeta evening gowns to floral silk, pinched at the waist, day dresses that somehow reflected the faded elegance and sophistication of a bygone era. Other rails played host to fox-fur capes and wraps, jackets, and three-quarter and full-length fur coats. Mirrors on the walls were draped in jet necklaces, imitation pearls, and diamante chokers, while racks held row upon row of shoes; sling-backs, suede platform ankle straps, and round-toed stilettos. In effect, to describe the layout as cramped would definitely be an understatement. However, despite any evidence of carefully positioned products or attention to retail psychology, the attraction was seductive and the urge to stay and explore, irresistible. Worn leather chairs provided an invitation to pause and rest, not to rush the experience, while old chests and traveling trunks lay half open, hugging the walls. These were filled with a discarded array of Audrey Hepburn headscarves, elbow-length satin gloves, seamed nylons, silk stockings still in their original packaging, and tortoiseshell-rimmed sunglasses. Indeed it was sunglasses that led me into my first entrepreneurial venture. This stemmed from my accidental discovery of an old, dilapidated shop that was due for demolition, outside of which hung a sign declaring "Sunglasses for sale—10 pence a pair." On inquiring about them, I was amazed to be shown boxes filled with original 1950s "cat" glasses which the owners were desperate to get rid of and were about to throw out with the rubbish. Needless to say, I bought the lot and sold them to a variety of retro stores for a very healthy profit. These were in turn sold to customers and other retro outlets such as those in Camden in London, for an even healthier return. The market for retro, even then, while not mainstream was significant, and demand for authentic objects was high. However, while the authenticity of the products, the eclectic and seemingly haphazard display that evoked feelings from childhood, such as the sense of adventure and excitement when let loose in a toy store, were important, they were not necessarily the core of the shopping experience. This centered largely around the relationships formed, both with the owners of Bill and Belle and with other customers. This was similar to the experience described by

McRobbie (1994) in her analysis of "rag alley" shopping and secondhand stores, which she views as an extension of the open-air street markets of urban city areas that functioned as daytime social meeting places as much as places of transaction. So too, the retro shops with their emphasis "on individual service, shared interest and opposition to the sterile formality of designer shops and department stores" (McRobbie 1994, p. 141) adopted a personal side to the shopping experience that relationship marketers could learn lessons from.

With regard to selling there was never any pressure. Interaction took the form of conversations centered around mutual interests, which could sometimes last for hours, and customers often used the shop as a meeting place. The air was one of informality. However, despite this, few left empty-handed or failed to return. The result: customer loyalty and word of mouth recommendations. The retro experience, nonetheless, seldom stopped with the act of purchasing. These same customers and the proprietors often met up later in bars before going on to clubs that catered to their narcissistic behavior, captured in the experience of dressing up, looking different, and escaping into a world of fantasy and glamour. One such club, "King Tuts," was adopted as a regular venue. Here the style was 1940s. Women dressed in strapless dresses, net-covered pillbox hats, silk stockings, and high platform ankle-strap shoes. Red lipstick was the norm, and for those who smoked, a long cigarette holder was almost obligatory. As for the men, Brian Ferry epitomized the look in his publicity photographs for his version of "these foolish things"; slicked back, jet-black hair, white dinner jacket, bow tie casually undone, hands in pockets—the picture of classic, but taken-for-granted elegance.

Nevertheless, the experience was never just about nostalgia or any real desire to relive the days of the Glen Miller big-band sound. On the contrary, in these clubs retro blended with the contemporary in order to fit the mood, create an atmosphere, and define something unique that was in direct opposition to the frenetic pastiche of the "glam rock" era. Consequently, the music was a conglobation of the crooning of Sinatra with the New York underground street anthems of Patti Smith and Jefferson Airplane's hauntingly eerie "White Rabbit." Other artists included Iggy Pop and Lou Reed, who were sufficiently egregious as to be recognized as part of the scene, while Roxy Music's nostalgic renditions and David Bowie's space-aged melodies were probably the closest to popular music that was played at these venues. Consequently, the retro experience cannot be explained away simply in terms of nostalgia, but must be seen in the light of contemporary aesthetics in relation to style, fashion, music, and social groupings, all of which are as relevant today as they were over twenty years ago.

Exhibit 4.1 **Stephen poses for the camera dressed in the style of 1950s Hollywood**

The New Wave Retro Revolution

The desire for retro has not, in fact, diminished. On the contrary, retro has become much more a part of mainstream culture than ever before. Moreover, contemporary retro is not about a particular era. It would appear that younger retro consumers need to be able to identify in some way with a period that is not too far removed from living memory (Goulding 2001). So the retro consumers in their thirties tend to feel nostalgic for the 1940s and 1950s, while those in

Exhibit 4.2 **Winston struts his stuff for his themed retro Elvis wedding**

their twenties relate more to the style and music of the 1960s and even the 1970s. Thus we have seen a proliferation of retro nights dedicated to the fashion and music of Abba, the 1970s Swedish singing sensation, and Gary Glitter, the king of "glam," best remembered for his posturing on six-inch-high platform boots, skin tight, diamante-covered jackets opened to the waist to reveal a lupine-like chest, with hair styled in an exaggerated parody of the Teddy Boy quiff. Additionally, posters for *Boogie Nights, Disco Fever*, and of course that 1970s icon, John Travolta and the *Saturday Night Fever* experience, reflect a widespread interest in the music and style of the 1970s. The era that was seen as vulgar when lived through is today reflected upon as fun, a chance to masquerade and escape the pressures of the working week. Alternatively, the more committed retro junkie may engage in Northern Soul weekends, which offer the opportunity for modern day "mods" and "modettes" to escape on their Vespas and Lambrettas to venues that aim to re-create the "Wigan scene" of the late 1960s, the decade that saw the popularization of Motown music and "ska," a form of reggae imported into Britain from Jamaica in the 1950s.

Retro Fashion and Authenticity

As one might expect, the fashion industry has not been slow to jump on to the retromania bandwagon. However, while fashion currently capitalizes on the

Exhibit 4.3 **Caroline, a modern day "Modette," poses in original 1960s outfit, complete with bobbed hair, pale pink lipstick and dramatic eye make-up. Next to her is twenty-nine-year-old Andrew, a contemporary hippy who admits to being locked into the 1960s**

nostalgia boom, it is less concerned with authenticity and more focused on recycling styles in a form of bricolage that will appeal to a wider market than the purists who scour rag alleys and retro shops for the real thing, whether it be original silk or nylon stockings from the 1940s and 1950s or flower-adorned plastic macs from the 1960s. A recent quote from the London *Sunday Times Style Magazine* illustrates this trend in a section titled "Flash back to the 40s," where designers happily admit to raiding the archives for autumn's key looks. "From cat walk to High Street we show you the most glamorous ways to go back to the future. Dress code; prim, not too proper and fully accessorized with handbag, peep toe shoes, leather gloves, fur tippet, Bette Davis broaches and true red lippy. Prada spearheaded the revival, but MaxMara and Dolce and Gabbana also sent the 1940s look down their runways" (Ricky 2000).

This in itself raises questions regarding innovation and whether we really have come to the end of the road. If we think back over the past hundred years, it is possible to identify a clear style for every decade, from the flappers of the 1920s, the Jean Harlow vamp of the 1930s, Bette Davis's classically cut, tailored style that characterized the 1940s, the tightly belted flared skirts and American rock look of the 1950s, the Mary Quant and Biba dominated 1960s and the rise and rise of the miniskirt, the glitter-riddled glam rock 1970s, and the *Dynasty* shoulder pads of the power dressing 1980s. But, what has really happened in terms of defining style since then? Apart from the minimalist or baggy casual look sported by the chemical rave generation, we can only identify an accelerated process of remixing and recycling of former trends. However, "true" retro is different, it is less about recycling and more about authenticity. Today, retro shops can be found in every major city, many with the emphasis on 1950s American "rockabilly" style, bearing names such as "The Depot," "Route 66," and "Retromania." Most retain the essential features of the original retro shops, namely, an air of informality, shared interest, and personal service. What is offered for sale remains a rather arbitrary ensemble of men's and women's clothes; original Levi jeans, jackets, and shirts; cigarette lighters; dresses; hats; and even comics from the decade. One such shop is Houghtons, a retro shop specializing in 1940s and 1950s paraphernalia, which is located in a bohemian district in central England. Like Bill and Belle, the ambience is unmistakingly inviting. The ground floor offers an array of clothes, jewelry, film posters, books, records, furniture, ornaments, and objects for the home. People still continue to use these shops as places to meet, and Houghtons provides the perfect setting for such assignations. On the first floor is a 1950s-style coffee bar complete with Wurlitzer jukebox where people can interrupt their browsing and enjoy freshly ground coffee served from an original 1950s coffee maker. However, while the earlier retro shops tended to collect their stock from jumble sales and rag alleys, today's stock is bought by the ton from American warehouses, much of which is discarded, but carefully sorted for the occasional gem. This process is consistent with McRobbie's (1994, p. 140) description of rag alley shopping where

> for every single piece that is rescued and restored a thousand are consigned to oblivion. The sources which are raided for "new" second hand ideas are frequently old films, old art, photographs, "great" novels, documentary footage and textual material.

She goes on to make a very important and relevant point that "second hand style continually emphasizes its distance from second-hand clothing."

The emphasis here should most definitely be on the word style, which is at the core of the often frenetic searching of charity shops, retro outlets, and rag alleys, in the quest for that elusive, authentic piece of clothing or jewelry that can be added to the individual's collection. However, despite the aesthetic appeal, the question remains: Why is the past exerting such a strong, magnetic attraction in the present?

Time-Space Compression: The Nostalgic Turn in Consumer Behavior

This appears to be a question that has provided scholars with some food for thought, the result of which is a rich body of theory focusing largely on the nature of contemporary, or postmodern, consumer society. One characteristic of postmodern society is the notion of time-space compression, or an ongoing struggle to maintain a sense of place and time in an increasingly changing and volatile world. Coupled with this is the idea that "innovation is dead" and all we can do today is exploit images and styles from bygone eras (Jameson 1983). If one adopts the dystopian view of postmodern or late capitalist societies, the argument that we exist in a world of total eclecticism and pastiche where all that remains is a parody of what went before (Jameson 1983), might be applied to explain the current retro phenomenon. Coupled with this is the idea of space, which unlike the modernist experience, has nothing to do with any overarching social objective, "save perhaps the achievement of timeless and 'disinterested' beauty as an objective in itself" (Harvey 1989, p. 240). Within this gloom-ridden view lies the idea that today we have seen the disappearance of a sense of history, which has led to a pervasive depthlessness (Jameson 1983). Essentially the "time-space compression," characteristic of the post-Fordist era where technologies have altered the speed and pace of life, "have so revolutionized the objective qualities of space and time that we are forced to alter, sometimes in quite radical ways, how we represent the world to ourselves" (Harvey 1989, p. 240). Taken together with the demise of community, the fragmentation of daily life, and the sense of self, which, some would argue, typify the postmodern condition, it might appear that conditions for nostalgia and retrospection are ripe. But what exactly is nostalgia? Essentially, nostalgia is memory with the pain removed. It is a positive orientation to the past that reflects a negative appraisal of self in the present. Its rise has been ascribed to feelings of alienation and fragmentation in the present, resulting from social and moral decline and feelings of loss of a golden age (Davis 1979).

Nonetheless, with regard to retro, there is little evidence to support this nihilistic and dysfunctional view of the alienated individual, miserable in the present, confused over time and space, with nothing to look forward to except an ersatz and commodified re-creation of history. Consequently, while acknowledging the sophistication of the arguments and the brilliant cultural analyses of such writers as Fredric Jameson, David Harvey, and Jean Baudrillard, I have one simple question: Where is the evidence? Furthermore, I accept that there may be disillusionment with contemporary style, there may be boredom in the workplace, and new technology can sometimes feel invasive, but let's face it, the past was not exactly Utopia either. Nostalgia, whether vicarious or firsthand allows us to filter out the realities of sexual and racial discrimination, worker exploitation, and societal inequalities. Hollywood always liked a happy ending and it is their lingering legacies that reinforce the "it's a wonderful life" image of a lost age of innocence. That is not to deny that nostalgia is part of the experience. It is, but it is not necessarily a reaction against current-day malaise, rather it is a preference for former styles and outward expressions of beauty. In the context of retro consumption, nostalgia is used creatively to give new meanings and definitions to experiences, similar to those described by Firat and Venkatesh (1995) in their analysis of the liberated postmodern individual who can accept paradoxes and play with the multitude of potential identities available to them. In keeping with this position, the pastiche associated with retro may be seen as celebratory, as averse to reflective of a sterile and depthless mainstream culture. Retro allows the individual to play with the norms, conventions, and expectations of style and even gender, largely through the manipulation and personalization of fashion. This device is not, of course, exclusive to retro consumers, but it is one that allows consumers to use fashion as a means of self-definition, a way of constructing narratives of personal history, and an instrument for interpreting the dynamics of their social sphere. Fashion may also serve as a method for contesting and transforming conventional social categories, especially those that have strong gender associations (Thompson and Haykto 1997).

Strong Women in Sharp Suits: Questioning Gendered Fashion Through Retro Consumption

In line with the pastiche, convention-defying dress associated with the creative liberated postmodern consumer comes a questioning of gender appearance and meaning. One might argue that while marketing has always been about consumption, gender has always been about difference (Kacen 2000). However, the embracing of retro from the 1970s onward has involved significant flirting with the idea of androgyny, while masculinity and femininity are conceived as a coadunation of scattered meanings and shifting significance. In other words, gender identity is no longer merely a natural fact, but a pastiche of possibilities (Kacen 2000). Indeed, it has been suggested that the female body uses simulation strategically in ways that challenge the stable notion of gender in the edifice of sexual difference. This is most manifest in the ways in which the female body can be refashioned in the flux of identities that speak in plural styles (Schwichtenberg 1990). An interesting example of this is provided by McRobbie who discusses the dress of the singer Patti Smith on her first album cover. Smith, dressed casual, free of makeup, with a jacket slung over her shoulder and a tie loosened at the neck, was unmistakenly from the New York underground: "pale, faded, dark, undernourished, intense and committed" (McRobbie 1994, p. 149). This look, however, was never fully adopted by female retros. Nonetheless, the wearing of men's suits did become, and remains, part of the dressing up game, but with a more subtle aesthetic, the effect being more Dietrich or Garbo than Smith. The style reflects a soft focus, with beautifully cut men's suits, silk ties, hats, berets, and diamante jewelry—masculine clothes, made unequivocally feminine. Humphrey Bogart trench coats are worn with the belt pulled tightly over pencil skirts, seamed stockings, and black suede stilettos, all designed to emphasize the female body.

However, this sexuality is not just confined to women. On the contrary, men's construction of who they are is accomplished as much through style, clothing, and body image as it is for women (Kacen 2000). While men do not adopt the clothes of the opposite sex, there is a heavy emphasis on style, on authenticity, and on sexual attractiveness whether it is the retro experience of the 1940s where the men wear carefully tailored loose suits, hats, and silk ties (think a more classic version of Kid Creole) or the reinvented "Mod" in his mohair suit, complete with just the right number of buttons, and of course hand stitching. At the core, it is about stylized images of beauty and a nostalgic remembrance of the days when "men were men and women were women."

Taken at face value, this might appear to be a sexist and overly simplistic evaluation of the situation. Nonetheless, it is not about women being subservient and men being dominant; quite the reverse in fact. It is about strong role models, both female and male, which incorporate images of femininity and masculinity at their most powerful. Undeniably, Hollywood's finest were beautiful, they were feminine, but they were also in control. Nobody could ever accuse Bette Davis or Joan Crawford of being shrinking violets. They were women on top who could be ruthless, beguiling, down but never out. Even off screen they made their own rules and flew in the face of convention. One only has to consider Dietrich's gender-bending "bring me another lover" reputation which defied all the codes of "respectable" society; a true rebel with a cause. Men also had their charms. Gable's lop-sided grin, wit, and

Exhibit 4.4 **Debra juxtaposes feminine attire with a manly pint of beer**

lovable rogue persona exuded sexuality, while Cary Grant's boyish vulnerability projected a warm and sensitive side to the male ego.

In this respect, retro consumption also depends on a form of socialization into the images, aesthetics, and self-expression. The adoption of retro style is often influenced by how the past is portrayed by the media with benchmarks for dress and appearance readily available in the plethora of material such as biographies, histories of Hollywood, and films from the era, all harking back to the time when Hollywood cinema helped to create new standards of appearance and bodily presentation (Featherstone 1991). Seen in this context, dress becomes a luxury of the body, a release from linear, chronological time, where an imaginative time is possible in which the body changes, or to be more precise, is changed, in relation to the moment. This may also be seen as part of the struggle to empower difference between the alternative social group and the mainstream (Calefato 1997). Retro consumption in relation to style and fashion may well be described as a culture of narcissism. And, undeniably, within this culture there is a greater emphasis on the performing self where the focus is on appearance, display, and the management of impressions (Featherstone 1991).

Exhibit 4.5 **Thomas and Grace display their take on 1950s style**

On this last point, it is important to note that retro behavior is not necessarily an individual act, but must be seen in the context of the group. Indeed,
one might go as far as to suggest that "the cult of the body and other forms of
appearance have value only in so much as they are part of a larger stage in
which everyone is both actor and spectator" (Maffesoli 1996, p. 77).

Retro and the Rise of the "Neotribal" Consumer

Today it is generally held that modern consumption sites are spaces of social-
ity, where the status of the individual is encoded in favor of the group. They are
places where personas are unfurled and mutually adjusted. The performance
orientation toward "the Other" in these sites is such that "tribe-like but temporary groups and circles condense out of the homogeneity of the mass" (Shields
1992, p. 108). On a conceptual note Maffesoli (1996) talks about the rise in
what he terms "neo-tribes" or the transitory group, which is neither fixed nor
permanent, but involves a constant back and forth movement between the tribe
and the masses. Indeed it is this tribal affiliation which serves as the backdrop
to the many contemporary movements we are witnessing today, especially where
the development of new lifestyles based on acts of pure creation are concerned.
Accordingly, these "neo-tribes" may be

Exhibit 4.6 **A group of retrophiles get together for a night out. The girl holds up a flyer for "MegaActive," a retro shop specializing in 1950s memorabilia**

effervescent, ascetic, oriented toward the past or the future; they have as their common characteristic on the one hand, a breaking with the commonly held wisdom and, on the other, an enhancing of the organic aspect of the social aggregation. (Maffesoli 1996, p. 96)

These groups are held together by a certain ambience and a state of mind. Solidarity is expressed through lifestyles that favor appearance and form, and nowhere is this more evident than in the retro club or venue, whether conjuring up the sophistication of the 1940s or re-creating the excitement of the 1960s. However, within these groups there are unspoken codes of acceptance.

Reworking Bourdieu's (1984) idea of economic, social, and cultural capital, Sarah Thornton (1995) introduces the term subcultural capital, which bestows status upon its owners. Accordingly, buying, creating, or wearing the right clothes; having the appropriate accessories; and knowing the correct dance steps are all ways of increasing an individual's subcultural capital. Of course, the existence and importance of these will vary depending on the degree of commitment to the group. For those who use retro as an occasional release, as in the case of the 1970s "weekender," subcultural capital has little relevance outside of the immediate environment. For the committed retro consumer, for whom retro is virtually part of a general lifestyle, it is an entirely different story. Take for example the contemporary "Northern Soul" movement, which is linked to the "Mod" scene of the 1960s. At least once a month, literally thousands of individuals congregate at different venues held throughout the country that aim to re-create the atmosphere and music of the early days. In the context of this retro event, there are strict codes of belonging: a form of subcultural capital which defines membership. This capital includes knowing and understanding the right music and dance steps, sporting the appropriate hairstyles, and of course wearing the right clothes, which must be retro and not repro. These in turn are read for their authenticity. In this case even having the right kind of transport is a code of membership, with the Vespa or Lambretta as much a defining symbol of belonging as the Harley Davidson is for bikers (Schouten and McAlexander 1995). Furthermore, these retro experiences have an enduring appeal, or as Brown (2001) points out, some revivals have outlived their original movements. Since the 1970s, 1940s and 1950s retro has been popular reincarnated northern soul has flourished since the early 1980s, and possibly before, while the latest retro craze is the return of punk, although how long it will last second time around is yet to be determined. With regard to punk paraphernalia, a growing number of Web sites are devoting themselves to auctions, where the highest bidder can walk away with an original pair of bondage trousers for around £80. Additionally, punk shops modeled on McLaren and Westwood's "Sex" are starting to spring up across the country to cater to these new retro arrivals.

Interestingly, some of the original punk superstars are still around, touring Britain and Europe with their geriatric, but *authentic* brand of punk. For example, Charlie Harper of the 1970s punk band the UK Subs is approaching the grand old age of sixty, but is still going strong. Venues are filled to capacity with new wave "new wavers" flocking to see the likes of The Dammed, still headed by David Vanian, the original vampiric lead singer. Vanian, despite acquiring several excess pounds of middle-age spread and a Nosferatu countenance, which today owes more to nature than makeup, is hailed as a demigod by this new generation of fashion anarchists. Moreover, The Dammed are not alone. Other punk icons such as the UK Subs, the Vibrators, Slaughter and the Dogs, Cockney Rejects, and GBH, all original 1970s punks, are suddenly finding their musical careers revived. Lucrative record deals are being cut and tours arranged to spread the revitalized message of the punk ethos. New groups are also on the ascendancy with Rancid, Offspring, and Green Day originating from the United States importing American interpretations of ska, reggae, and "hard-core" punk, in true eclectic retro style. To provide a showcase for these punk evangelists, three-day punk revival festivals, such as "Holiday in the Sun," are planned for London, Berlin, and Tokyo, while The Sex Pistols, the true kings of punk, played a

Exhibit 4.7 **Batman and Catwoman: two neopunks**

jubilee gig to celebrate the Queen's Silver Jubilee in June 2002. This date, coincidentally, also marked the twenty-fifth anniversary of their controversial single "God Save the Queen." And thus the retro cycle goes on!

Retro and Marketing: Some Concluding Remarks

So, in summary, what is the retro experience all about, and why should this group of consumers, diverse as they undoubtedly are, be of interest to marketers? They are not, after all, the typical targets or respondents of the "repro" retro marketers. However, they can tell us something about retailing experiences and the importance of personal service, genuine customer interest, and relationship building. Possibly the retro shop is one of the few remaining bastions of retailing that offer this in its truest sense. Moreover, while maintenance is high in terms of customer interaction, the result is low expenditure on advertising, widespread word of mouth recommendations, and enduring customer loyalty.

This group of consumers also highlights the importance of authenticity in contemporary or postmodern society, and a desire for experiences that transcend pastiche and parody. There is a world of difference between the 1970s, "boogie night" experience of polyester flares and platform boots, and the re-created northern soul night, or even the new wave punk revival, that goes beyond a sentimental, schmaltzy nostalgia for a rose-tinted past. Rather it is based on genuine style preferences and positive acts of consumer creativity. However, as creative acts of consumption are rarely expressed in isolation, this forces us to consider the nature of the group and outlets for these neotribal expressions of subcultural capital. In fact, it is virtually impossible to separate the various threads, which brings me to the final question: How do we capture the essence of retro consumption in the contexts described? Schouten and McAlexander (1995), in their account of biker subcultural activity, describe consumption in terms of product constellations emanating from the Harley Davidson. However, it possibly makes more sense to describe subcultural consumption, and I use the term subculture with a certain degree of artistic license, as "experiential and product" constellations, at the heart of which is the shop and the experience of relationship building and purchasing. We also need to account for the meaning or meanings derived from the product itself—the condition, the age, the label, its scarcity value, and of course its authenticity. There is also an assembly process, of putting the "look" together, and then there is the display or performance element which takes place within the social context. One might also consider general lifestyle characteristics in order to gain a truly holistic picture, but that is the subject of another essay.

References

Bourdieu, Pierre (1984), *Distinction: A Social Critique of the Judgment of Taste,* London: Routledge.

Brown, Stephen (2001), *Marketing—The Retro Revolution,* London: Sage.

Brown, Stephen and Anthony Patterson (2000), "Knick-Knack Paddy-whack, Give a Pub a Theme," *Journal of Marketing Management,* 16 (6): 647–62.

Calefato, Patrizia (1997), "Fashion and Worldliness: Language and Imagery of the Clothed Body," *Fashion Theory,* 1 (1): 69–90.

Clarke, John, Stuart Hall, Tony Jefferson, and Brian Roberts (1997 [1975]), "Subculture, Cultures and Class," in *The Subcultures Reader,* ed. Ken Gelder and Sarah Thornton, London: Routledge, pp. 100–11.

Davis, Fred (1979), *A Yearning for Yesterday: A Sociology of Nostalgia,* London: MacMillan.

Featherstone, Mike (1991), "The Body in Consumer Culture," in *The Body: Social Process and Cultural Theory,* ed. Mike Featherstone and Bryan Turner, London: Sage, pp. 170–96.

Firat, A. Fuat, and Alladi Venkatesh (1995), "Liberatory Postmodernism and the Reenchantment of Consumption," *Journal of Consumer Research,* 22 (3): 239–67.

Fyvel, Tosco (1997[1963]), "Fashion and Revolt," in *The Subcultures Reader,* ed. Ken Gelder and Sarah Thornton, London: Routledge, pp. 388–92.

Gaunt, Anthony (1975), *The Aesthetic Adventure,* London: Sphere.

Gelder, Ken and Sarah Thronton (eds.) (1997), *The Subcultures Reader,* London; Routledge.

Goulding, Christina (2001), "An Exploratory Study of Age Related Nostalgia and Contemporary Consumption," Special Session, Reconceptualizing Age, *Association for Consumer Research,* Austin: Texas, October 8–11.

Hall, Stuart and Tony Jefferson (1996), *Resistance Through Ritual: Youth Subcultures in Postwar Britain,* London: Routledge.

Harvey, David (1989), *The Condition of Postmodernity: An Enquiry into the Origins of Cultural Change,* Oxford: Blackwell.

Hebdidge, Dick (1997 [1983]), "Posing Threats, Striking Poses," in *The Subcultures Reader,* ed. Ken Gelder and Sarah Thornton, London: Routledge, pp. 393–405.

Hewison, Robert (1987), *The Heritage Industry: Britain in a Climate of Decline,* London: Methuen.

Hunter, Michael (1981), "The Preconditions of Preservation: Historical Perspective," in *Our Past Before Us: Why Do We Save It?,* ed. Michael Binney and David Lowenthal, London: Temple Smith.

Jameson, Fredric (1983), "Postmodernism and Consumer Society," in *The Anti-Aesthetic: Essays in Postmodern Culture,* ed. Hal Foster, Port Townsend, WA: Bay Press, pp. 111–25.

Kacen, Jaqueline (2000), "Girrrl Power and Boyyy Nature: The Past, Present and Paradisal Future of Consumer Gender Identity," *Marketing Intelligence and Planning,* 18 (6/7): 345–55.

Landesman, Christina (2001), "Give 'em the New Razzle Dazzle," *Sunday Times Culture Magazine,* September 9.

Maclaran, Pauline and Stephen Brown (2001), "The Future Perfect Declined: Utopian Studies and Consumer Research," *Journal of Marketing Management,* 17 (3/4): 367–90.

Maffesoli, Michael (1996), *The Time of the Tribes: The Decline of Individualism in Mass Society,* London: Sage.

McCord, Sarah (2001), "What a Waist," *Sunday Times Style Magazine,* September 9.

McRobbie, Angela (1994), "Second-Hand Dresses and the Role of the Rag-Market," in *Postmodernism and Popular Culture,* ed. Angela McRobbie, London: Routledge, pp. 135–54.

Normon, Philip (1990), *The Age of Parody,* London: Hamish Hamilton.

Rickey, Melanie (2000), "Flash Back," *Sunday Times Style Magazine,* September 3.

Schouten, John and James McAlexander (1995), "Subcultures of Consumption: An Ethnography of the New Bikers," *Journal of Consumer Research,* 22 (1): 43–52.

Schwichtenberg, Cathy (1990), "Postmodern Feminism and Madonna: Towards an Erotic Politics of the Female Body," National Conference on Rewriting the (Post) Modern, (Post) Colonialism/Feminism/Late Capitalism, University of Utah, March 30.

Shields, Rob (1992), "The Individual, Consumption and the Fate of Community," in *Lifestyle Shopping: The Subject of Consumption,* ed. Rob Shields, London: Routledge, pp. 99–113.

Thompson, Craig and Diana Haykto (1997), "Speaking of Fashion: Consumers' Uses of Fashion Discourses and the Appropriation of Countervailing Cultural Meanings," *Journal of Consumer Research,* 24 (June): 15–42.

Thornton, Sarah (1995), *Club Cultures: Music, Media, and Subcultural Capital,* Cambridge: Polity Press.

Walsh, Kevin (1992), *The Representation of the Past: Museums and Heritage in the Postmodern World,* London: Routledge.

5

Comeback for the *Craic*

A Literary Pub Crawl

Anthony Patterson and Stephen Brown

These days, every self-respecting travel writer feels obligated to serve a tour of duty in Ireland (Belfrage 1988; McCrum 1999; O'Rourke 1989; Theroux 1985). This Irish literary pilgrimage has become so jaded that recently one inspired scribbler sought to rejuvenate the genre by hitchhiking *Around Ireland with a Fridge* (Hawks 1999). Typically, these Eire-trotters are so astounded by the breath-taking scenery, so perplexed by the perpetual political divide, and so shocked by the changed country they encounter, that they are driven to ponder this "commotion of culture" (McCracken 1998) over a pint of Guinness in one of the island's pervasive, popular, and peculiar pubs. The esteemed literary pilgrimage becomes a steaming literary pub-crawl.

Given his proclivity for the Irish pub retroscape, Pete McCarthy (2000, p. 109), Englishman and self-confessed "heritage-obsessed saddo," is no different from those in whose footsteps he totters. Motivated by a desire to escape "the depressingly corporate environment offered by pubs in the English countryside," his journey in search of "idiosyncratic, family-owned hovels with no food, or décor, that remain temples to hospitality, conversation and drink" (p. 55), led him to formulate guidance for tourists traveling around Ireland. First, "Never Pass a Bar That Has Your Name On It"; second, "The More Bright Primary Colours and Ancient Celtic Symbols Outside the Pub, the More Phoney the Interior." McCarthy is patently aware that Irish pub retroscapes, indeed the entire gamut of Irish culture, is an invention, based on what he calls the marketing of a "sentimental Irishness" (2000, p. 335). Much as he baulks at the "unspeakable indignities in the name of heritage" (2000, p. 201), much as he tries his best "to disapprove of all this populist stuff," he fails, quite simply because "everyone's clearly having a good time" (2000, p. 255).

This understanding that authenticity is on the wane (West 2001) and that the creation of "simulations" has to a large extent replaced the real (Ritzer 1999) has been a fairly accepted point of academic discourse for nearly thirty years (Fisher and Murray 2001). While there have been attempts to capture "living history," that is, the *exact* re-creation of a particular place or event from the past, it is increasingly the case that many designs evocative of the past are simulations that rely to a large extent on pseudo-history or pure invention (Handler and Saxton 1998; Sack 1992). The purpose of this "heritage industry" (Hewison 1989) is not to replicate the past, but to improve it, to remove all contradictions, ambiguities, and inconsistencies from an era—thereby purifying its essence (Hobsbawn and Ranger 1992). Consider the creation of the olde-time toiletries and quality food shoppe, Crabtree and Evelyn, in 1972 (Woodham 1997); the reenactment of historical battles by heritage sites for the entertainment of tourists; and even the success of mock 'n' roll performed by Elvis Presley lookalikes, and tribute bands like the Rolling Clones, The Bootleg Beatles, and Björn Again (Ruthven 2001).

Irish theme pubs are particularly indicative of this "let's-invent-a-tradition" tradition. McCarthy is correct; the typical Irish theme pub, with its garish green décor, pseudo-Gaelic invocations, "thousand welcomes" doormats, shamrock-inscribed fittings, peat-burning fireplace, freshly brewed stout, wide range of whiskeys, conspiratorial hints of under-the-counter-poteen, and general air of pseudo-hiberno bonhomie, cannot be considered indicative of today's Ireland, yesterday's Ireland, or any other Ireland this side of *The Quiet Man*. Irish theme pubs, in point of fact, are commercially motivated commodifications of the Celtic revival of the late nineteenth century, which was itself a politically motivated commodification—an invented tradition—of half-baked Irish prehistory (Patterson et al. 1998). In this context, the Irish have also been charged with perpetuating a "stage Irish identity"— itself a creation derived from colonial archetypes—as a deliberate form of economic survival designed to engage the custom of a pub community (Scully 1997). This tendency to create an "imagined community" (Anderson 1983) based on "place myths" (Shields 1991) has accelerated over recent years now that most of Dublin's pubs have cast off their once sedate and modest decor and been redecorated to provide tourists with the only authenticity they recognize. Soon perhaps we will be left with only the simulated pub version—a copy without an original.

Thus the seriously sentimental styling and worldwide success of the Irish theme pub (Brown and Patterson 2000; Lego et al. 2002), coupled with its very public denigration as a fictional "quaintspace" (Dear and Flusty 1988), makes it a particularly noteworthy case study to place under the "tourist gaze" (Urry 1989). Our purpose in this chapter is simply to offer some insight into how consumers behave, what they feel, and what they think when they visit these places of retromania. As is true of almost every academic endeavor today, these questions have to a limited extent already been theorized upon by academics, in disciplines as diverse as Cultural Studies, Geography, Heritage Studies, and Sociology. Using an eclectic selection of methods and perspectives they have scrutinized a variety of commercial-scapes: general themed places (Sorkin 1992; Gottdiener 1997), themed restaurants (Stenger 1997; Wright 1989), shopping malls (Backes 1997; Goss 1999), theme parks (Wallace 1985), and other Disneyfied districts (Malamud 1998; Chang 2000). Irrespective of their value, for the most part these studies adopt disparate approaches to the study of retroscapes (but see Brown 2000)[1]; are confined mostly to the realm of the conceptual; offer little in the way of empirical findings; neglect commercial considerations; and tend to focus on the "politics of meaning." Whereas our concern, here at least, is simply to develop a deeper understanding of how consumers consume retro design (Franklin 2002).

In the tradition of the "pluralists" (Sherry 2000) we begin this interpretive and naturalistic study by delving into the textually represented *etic* of consumer voices by way of Holbrook's (1995) now infamous methodology—subjective personal introspection (SPI)—where the aim is to discover "personal experience unknowable to anyone else" (Stern 2000, p. 72). While McCarthy's introspective travelogue offers us an excellent starting point for this chapter, its empiricism would be found wanting by SPI's fiercest critics, since it represents a sample of one (Wallendorf and Brooks 1993). Although this strategy has been followed "successfully" by other prominent consumer behavior researchers (Holbrook 1994; Reid and Brown 1996), we aim to sidestep the criticism by producing a polyphonic text.

We thus embark, Pete McCarthy style, on a literary pub-crawl in search of the quintessential Irish theme pub experience. Nor is it necessary to travel to Ireland to find this hyper-real pub, so ubiquitous has the simulation become. In fact, if anything, it is preferable that we experience the pub simulacrum in its purest state, uncorrupted by any lingering vestiges of reality that might remain in Ireland. Luckily, the practicalities of work conspired to bring us to an appropriate city, Sheffield, U.K. Situated in the heart of England, Sheffield boasts many Irish theme pubs but the principal attraction was an eager assembly of thirsty MBA students, ninety-two of them in all, thirsty to experience all that an Irish pub can offer. Each was asked to submit a narrative recounting their personal experiences of visiting Irish theme pubs. These

MBA students represented a fair sprinkling of countries from around the world: China, India, Cameroon, Mexico, Morocco, Spain, Greece, and England. We thought that it would be appropriate to solicit the observations of these "outsiders" since they would be highly sensitized to the subtle nuances and peculiarities of an Irish retroscape in a way that locals could never be. They were unfettered by constraints of any kind; they were not asked to take a trip down memory lane nor were they asked to comment on their perception of the pub's authenticity. The only stipulation was that there were no stipulations; they could be as free and easy with their thoughts as they liked. Thankfully, despite the fact that English is a second language for many of them, they managed to produce remarkably insightful essays about their experiences in an Irish pub retroscape.

So what did we discover while perusing these essays? The one truly surprising discovery was the astonishing amount of retroactivity. The depth to which consumers can become immersed in the panoramic detail of a retroenvironment is all too apparent, as are the key corollaries of reminiscence that operate on a number of different levels within an Irish pub setting. We contemplate the clarion calling of Guinness, the evocative aura of a commodified antiquity, the rhythm of Irish folk music, Ireland's cultural rapport with other nations, the communion of communication, the demon drink, and the ephemeral nature of that seemingly uncommodifiable essence dubbed *craic*, all of which act independently, yet simultaneously, to create a powerful nostalgic urge. Stripping this urge down to its constituent components is always a problematic process—given the dynamic nature of each—but for the purpose of explication, we proceed thus.

A major theme that resides in many essays is the desire on arrival at the chosen public house to sample a pint of Guinness. There is an unspoken assumption that it is *proper order* to order what must surely be the *proper order*. When in Rome and all that. The descriptions below should bring cheer to Guinness's board of directors:

> I went to the counter and asked for a big glass of Guinness. I had to wait for a while. Now my Guinness was ready. It was a hot chocolate color, with a creamy white foam head. It was interesting that there was a three-petal flower in the middle of the cream, made by the cream, of course. It was so cute! I peered at it and didn't want to break it. Several minutes later, the flower disappeared and the whole glass of beer turned dark black. I sipped it—oh, quite bitter! But it had looked so gentle just a minute before. I thought of the unnamed wine I saw just now. It had a similar nature to the Guinness. Was this the common nature of all Ireland—gentle looks outside but strong volition inside?
>
> (Spanish female, 26)

"A pint of Guinness, please" I said. The bartender took a cup, filled it part way with Guinness. Slowly the cup filled with light yellow beery bubbles. He placed the cup on the counter. Why not give it to me? I was wondering. He handed it to me with a friendly smile. I took the cup. I looked to the wall where several words were written, "Good things come to those who . . . wait." Then as I watched the yellow beery bubbles gradually change to black and the creamy white head form I realized. It was fantastic. You need to be patient to get Guinness. It was stronger than any other beer I had ever tasted. When I drank it, at first it tasted so bitter, but after I while, I felt good and began to linger over the taste. This is so exciting. My goodness, my Guinness!

(Chinese female, 30)

Trying to find a suitable drink for me from the feast on the menu, ranging from beer—Guinness, Murphy's, Caffrey's, Beamish—to whiskey— Jameson's and Bushmills. I decided to imitate the guests around me and ordered a small bottle of Guinness. This was my first time tasting this kind of beer and the feeling is really beyond description! Although the drink is cold, a warm stream went through my body after sipping it. It's bitter and strong, yet I am fond of the taste.

(Moroccan male, 28)

Then I realized that on most of these big-dark tables, that I was observing, there were glasses of dark-colored beer which many of the visitors of the pub were enjoying and the more I looked around the more of these glasses of beer I saw, which reminded me that it was time for me to order something to drink and of course the drink should be an Irish one. I noticed then that on the glasses the word GUINNESS was written and then I really opened my eyes and saw this word everywhere. . . .

(Chinese female, 32)

Guinness's seamless integration into the pub décor and culture makes it a quintessential aspect of the Irish pub experience. Whether purchased through a desire to fit in, a familiarity with the beer, or simply the influence of Guinness's compelling heritage, most students easily manage to hurdle this self-imposed rite of initiation with ease and are soon able to relax and reflect upon the immediate surroundings.

It is said that the single most intense pleasure of visiting a pub is the nonaesthetic one of escapism (Tuan 1998). Yet it is in precisely these conditions, in the dim light of the pub where little is really asked of us, that liberation from duty and constraint could conceivably render it possible to develop a personal aesthetic response to the surrounding commercial habitat. Consequently, the students offer some startlingly vivid vignettes of the leprechaunalia, shamrockovia, and assorted paddywhackery that are liberally scattered around these retro pubs. Predominant in their descriptions is an implicit, occasionally explicit, awareness of the pub designer's retrofication objectives:

> The shelves were stuffed with Irish antiques, works of the great Irish writers, household things and farm tools mounted on the wall. The design also incorporates a stained metal fireplace, a combination of wood and ceramic tile flooring. The furniture, allegedly imported from Ireland directly, consists of prime wood tables and chairs. Throughout the design antiques are incorporated to add realism and timelessness. Metal lamps, an Irish harp on the wall, a pipe organ sitting in a corner and even a streetlight outside the door all play their part. All these things grant you a touch of the old country and reminiscence.
>
> (Chinese male, 27)

> This was my first time going to an Irish pub, I was curious about it. I opened the heavy thick wood door, with curiosity. I looked around. I could feel the difference immediately between O'Neill's and other pubs I had visited. This was not a modern place; instead there was a taste of tradition. The lighting was dim and soft, and gave people a feeling of relaxation and comfort. Tables, chairs and stairs were all made of wood, dark brown, devoid of decoration, plain and simple.
>
> (Chinese female, 29)

> Where do I begin? The Irish is really strange. I have never seen a design like this before. The design of the pub is based on the pursuit of an antiquated style. The large spaces are divided with partitions and screens. The furniture is dark brown and big jet-black wine barrels are used as tables. Wooden paneling features heavily. Huge girders cross the empty ceiling. The walls are printed with faded red or blue with all kinds of advertising, slogans painted on them, "My goodness, my Guinness" and "Come back for the *Craic*." Many old frames are hanging on the wall. The light is so dim. Some electric lights are shaped like candles. All of them attempt a throwback to a vague past. These sensations I have only seen in films.
>
> (Spanish male, 28)

Modern Guinness signs are rejected in favor of any tin plate Guinness sign pre-1950, and providing they sport the screwdriver marks from where they were wrenched from a small-town Irish proprietor's shop front, they are worthy of display. The propensity to hark back to Ireland's modest farming past is also overwhelming. Leather tankards drip from the beamed ceiling, a scythe balanced precariously on two (rusty) nails threatens to guillotine you at any second and a well-used mangle is sitting in the corner, cheerfully inviting you to rest your pint on it. It all fits wonderfully into the heavy oak-timbered, dark-cornered, tinted-window surrounding. It took me a while when I first visited to even notice that amongst the wall-to-wall, ceiling-to-floor bric-à-brac there is a bike (sans wheels—rubber is presumably considered too modern) hanging upside down from the ceiling above the bar. The only common theme seems to be that everything is weathered, and I could happily believe that all the artifacts must have been used to plough furrows in a field, or to tend to a family of fifteen hundred years ago in deepest, darkest Ireland.

(English female, 28)

Interestingly, some of the students genuinely believe that the objects d'art are originals. They revel in the simple thought that these items might have once furnished some humble hovel long ago in Ireland's past.[2] In a not unrelated way, it has recently been contended that Andy Warhol, far from constructing a devastating critique of consumerism in his famous paintings of Campbell's soup and other items of pop kitsch, was merely painting them because they reminded him of the early life he once lived in Pennsylvania with his mother (Morrison 2002). This simple recourse to the comfort of memory is undeniably a powerful impulse. The pub retroscape with its vocabulary of detail, its amalgam of vaguely familiar, if not immediately recognizable, Irish referents induced the students to indulge in times past:

In a way this evening seemed like a stroll down memory lane, of times when one had no cares in the world and when one experienced total freedom. To a great extent, I felt affinity with the whole experience, mainly because it was reminiscent of my youth. It's kind of strange, how sitting in a pub in Sheffield so far away from home, something in my mind triggered memories from young days, making me remember all those friends who were with me at the University at that time. Today I don't even have a clue about their whereabouts and how life is treating them. Suddenly I wished for them to be with me, to be part of the evening, just to relive the times and moments we spent together. I really missed all my friends from those days.

(Indian female, 43)

Suddenly, something crossed my mind—I recalled the eve of the day I was leaving home for the UK. It seemed all the same. My "send-off" (leaving do) party was happening to me again. Having been one of my most exciting nights, (the send-party) I could recall all the events as they'd unfolded that night. However, I had taken more alcohol than my system could contain; and knowing that I couldn't cheat nature, I made up my mind to leave, the fun not withstanding. Thereafter, it seemed I had a blackout. Luckily, it was the weekend, so I slept considerably well.

(Cameroonian male, 28)

The pub provides a heaven of memory for me. That is the reason why I have been feeling relaxed since entering the pub. Everything in the pub, from photographs to bric-a-brac and furniture, indicate the information what it must be like in Irish hometowns and make me recall the feeling in my own hometown. Even though the atmosphere in my own hometown is definitely different from an Irish town, from the ornaments to the color of people's hair and eyes, I think the feeling of hometown is the same for the owner of the Irish pub and I. I understand his feeling, and he, mine.

(Chinese female 36)

This inclination toward retrospection and recollection is itself reminiscent of that age-old Hollywood image of a maudlin expatriate, attended to by a sympathetic barman, downing shot after shot of whiskey in some olde-time speakeasy. His thoughts incurably and increasingly fixed on nostalgia for the old country and all that he holds close to his heart. Among our essayists, there are certainly a few latent James Stewarts and Betty Grables just waiting to be discovered:

On the walls many pictures featuring life from the countryside; a guy who rides his horse, a woman who milks her cow. It is funny, I have a strong sense of déjà vu. I have felt this sense before. Oh yeah, every tavern in Greece that wants to display its family heritage has pictures like this hanging on its walls. I am thinking of Greece again. I miss it a lot. And this place increases the feeling. Who would have thought that there is a place that reminds me of Greece and all that I hold precious, here in the UK?

(Greek female, 27)

The low ceiling made me feel close to other people and delirious to talk to them. The old oak tables, with the same dark red color as that of traditional Chinese furniture, stirred a pang of homesickness. Ah, I remembered the old furniture in my grandmother's bedroom was dark red. A well-known Chinese poem perfectly expressed my feeling at that moment. "Nostalgia is a shallow trait, I'm on this side, motherland is on that side." Now I am far away from my parents, my grandparents and my friends.

(Chinese male, 30)

We began to talk about the family—the forever topic of men. We could not help expressing the yearning for our sweet families. George had a very lovely son who was only four months old. When he told me how deeply he missed his son and his wife there were tears in his eyes, which affected me deeply. To cheer George up, I told him how my wife and I first met. At that time I was a cardiology doctor, we met in the hospital where I was in charge of the treatment of my wife's father. When her father, thankfully, recovered, my wife and I fell in love. . . . When George heard this he was very surprised and said to me, "Chi, you are a really romantic doctor!" After we had stopped laughing and had a gulp of beer, I asked George why we had talked like this. He thought for several seconds—because of the hot atmosphere and the strong beer. We both agreed that this Irish was a really good place for people to find something in their mind, which could not be felt in normal time.

(Chinese male, 34)

As these examples illustrate, the pub retroscape can provoke deeply touching and personal memories that can be triggered either internally (in one's own head) or externally (through conversation and conviviality). It is this latter trigger that Irish pubs use to market themselves. It's what *craic*, that holistic word so often used to distill the essence of an Irish shindig, has at its core—a communication-communion, comprised of banter, barney, and blarney. Patterson (1999) makes this people component plain:

The instant I turned the key I felt myself . . . expand, is the only word I can think of to describe it—forgetting for the moment that twelve hours previously I had turned the key in the opposite direction and prayed never to clap eyes on another customer so long as I lived. It was always the way. In fact, the worse the night before, the greater, perversely, was the anticipation. I liked to think of the entire building holding its breath; we might have been at the bottom of the pile, architecturally speaking, but to me The International was never truly itself without people in its bars.

Nor is this point lost on the student imbibers:

A while later, at the stage of drunkenness that descends before the singing begins, the wonderful philosophizing that can only be indulged in at a pub like Flanagan's started. I don't know why the environment in there seemed to be conducive to putting the world to right—maybe we were all influenced by the old men at the bar so that the lads didn't feel they could restrict their conversation to football and birds in an Irish pub; but out of the blue we all began ardently debating matters of extreme importance. Suddenly everyone had an opinion and couldn't wait to express it, frequently delivering their thoughts and beliefs in the manner of a sermon, complete with finger-pointing. My friends all fell over their words trying to impart their nuggets of wisdom, interrupting and out-shouting each other at the time of night when they would normally be checking out the talent or thrashing one another at pool. If only we could all have remembered what was so important the next morning.

(English female, 29)

As we were waiting for our drink an old gentleman seated on one of the stools attached to the counter, stands up drains his beer mug and bangs it on the counter and puts his smoking pipe in between his wrinkled lips. My eyes again fall on the attractive barmaid, with a well-conditioned reflex smile. A middle-aged person, smartly dressed diverts my looks and we end up conversing with him. This one very surprisingly knows a lot about my country, seems to have visited on a number of occasions and really felt at home when he was trying to recollect some of his experiences about our country. This is another peculiar feature of this place; it is quiet enough to converse with other customers. It's quite easy to mingle with other customers too. It creates an atmosphere where people are friendly and homely. Getting to know people, having conversations such a good atmosphere is created. Aristotle's words that the "human being is a social animal" are truly evident.

(Indian male, 33)

Connecting with each other is only part of the story, for the introspectees are often able to make a connection with Irish culture. Despite the fact that the heritage in these retroscapes is unfamiliar to many of them, they are able to attain cross-cultural cognizance by relating Irish referents to their own ethnic background, thereby making a personal and meaningful connection with the Irish milieus:

In my mind, the Chinese teahouse is similar to the Irish pub. Nowadays in China there a lot of Chinese tea houses which could be divided into the modern and traditional teahouse. Of them, I prefer the latter. Generally, the traditional is decorated with Chinese water-ink painting and Chinese calligraphy. Throughout teahouses, there are a lot of wooden bamboo tables and chairs. You can listen to some traditional Chinese music or play Go and Chinese chess with a friend. Of course, compared with the Irish pub, the atmosphere is fairly calm. Usually, in the weekend, we could invite some friends to have a meal, and then go to a teahouse to drink tea and chat. Actually, it is a good way to improve friendship and release stress.

(Chinese female, 29)

The typical Celtic knot work could be found everywhere in the pub. It was painted on the wall, printed on the menu and appeared on the sofa, which somehow gave me a tribal feeling. The knot work interlace was said to be the most commonly identified kind of Celtic design. It looked like woven strands or braided strips that bend and wove among themselves. According to romantic interpretations of some archaeologists and anthropologists, the knot work interlace indicated the interconnection of life and humankind's place within the universe. I knew very little about Celtic design, but it really reminded me of Chinese knots and Greek maze pattern. Chinese knots possess a similar interlacing feature but have a different meaning. It expressed the Chinese's wishes to be happy and avoidance from mishap. While the Greek maze pattern, which I came across so much when I made a visit to Aegean island last autumn, looked almost like angular spirals and might range from a few simple turns to complex labyrinth type design. The tourism guide said the design indicated permanence.

(Chinese female, 30)

Since Ireland is blessed with a historical repository of sweet-sounding lyrical music, it is hardly surprising to discover that the essayists are often awed by the alluring fiddle-dee-dee that is piped into the pub background, or a definite preference this, performed by a live band in the pub foreground.

The most prominent feature of the day that will forever stick in my memory was undoubtedly the music; the unanimous attitude is "to hell with the English songs, bring on the Penny whistles and the bodrans." In the afternoon, the pub was a haven of sweet, lilting versions of Irish folk, the "Seamus O'Donnell from Donegal" or "My Lass Ran off with a Potato Farmer" songs. These were clearly a firm favorite amongst the Scouse-Irish locals who, like me, conveniently forget that the past three hundred years since their ancestors first set foot on England's green pastures ever happened.

(English female, 30)

Certainly in Dublin I had found the live music to be essential to the pub experience; you couldn't help but be drawn into the whole atmosphere of the occasion, finding it difficult to keep any concept of time or any consciousness of the amount of Guinness you were consuming. I fondly remember being in a pub in Temple Bar on a Monday afternoon; there was a live band playing to a packed establishment, all deep in conversation and downing their pints, the music blaring over the top, cutting out all awareness of the world outside (I remember imagining what it must be like on a Saturday evening!). There had been so much to look at in that place, so much take in that it wouldn't have been difficult to stay there all day, merrily drinking-in the atmosphere.

(Indian female, 36)

Irish music sounds quite exotic and antique. But I can tell it reflects a history and tradition, just like the music played by a Chinese ancient Zither, which can be dated to a time hundreds and even thousands of years ago. People are likely to be attracted to songs and music that can bring them back to where they were born and where they grew-up. Traditional Irish music and our Chinese traditional music resonate to all for they stir something in the soul.

(Chinese female, 30)

Maybe it's the soothing music, the conversational glut, or even the drink talking—we're not entirely sure—but one thing is for certain: these experiences certainly inspired some potent expression and imaginative flights of fancy, each of which was enveloped in the loose fricassee of fact and fiction that constitutes the respondent's own shifting, ever-changing construction of Irish history, which itself is in a state of flux:

Sitting there I meet two Irish presidents, one present and one past, the *Taoiseach*, four members of the provisional IRA (who stop me on the way to the airport), Bono (he was eating at the time), shakes the hands of The Edge (can never remember the other two's names), have afternoon tea at the American Ambassador's residency in Phoenix park, attend the "wrap" party for The Commitments, see Chris De Burgh carrying a carrier bag down Baggot Street, watch several nations get beaten in the 1990 world cup finals but only one that celebrates (Ireland), stay in a thatched cottage out on the west coast and awake to find cows chewing on the roof, attend a wake that is longer and noisier than the life of the deceased, eat boxty pancakes on Temple Bar, drink right through the night at a barge moored on a canal somewhere in Dublin, am driven through the streets by a mad colleen swigging from a bottle of Powers whiskey, drive to Belfast down both the Falls Road and Shankill Road, (graffiti apart— can't tell the difference), drive across the Wicklow mountains taking some peat as a souvenir, walk the long beach at Brittas Bay and catch the salt of the sea in my hair and in my mouth, kiss the Blarney stone (twice for good measure), go to a party at the originator of Ballygowan's mineral water and take out my peat souvenir and show it to a girl asking her if she has met my friend "Pete" before receive a signed book from Seamus Heaney dedicated to my daughter (though he gets her name all wrong on the flyleaf), attend a benefit gig for Brian Keenan (poor soul having to spend all that time with Terry Waite), entertain delegates at the Fianna Fail Ardeish, and now we are off to the next pub.

(English male, 34)

I close my eyes and dream of Ireland. Brown earth, fresh air, clear blue sky—yes that must be Ireland. Sheep lying on the grass, black and white cows standing in the rolling fields. Clouds slid by. A rural-looking stream wound slightly, with real fish living in it, just as a mirror, everything could be seen in it, the sky, cloud, and trees. . . . Autumn comes, dotted trees with red, purple and yellow, painting mountains and hills into a colorful picture. What sound do I hear? Not so clear, but like the sound of a violin, from a long distance, flowing gently sometimes high, sometimes low. It comes when you least expect, then disappears when you want to catch it. That is Ireland, with myth and magic. A land for many that is their true home. A land for many that is their ideal holiday destination. You should go to her, touch her and feel her, hence you can recognize her and get to know her. Ireland is a land for all. A breath of cold air therefore the mirror is broken. I returned to O'Neill's again.

(Indian male, 29)

These eloquent, dreamy, breathless passages illustrate that "pubbing"[3] like "shopping" is an ideal opportunity for nostalgia, daydream, and desire (Frith and Horne 1987). Yet, never too far away from such a sugarcoated view of a consumption experience you can be sure that a few cynics are sneering. Cries of dissension can be heard, but these nearly always came from the English essayists who, being more familiar with the "Irish-heritage-is-destroying-Irish-history" thesis extolled in the British press, are reflexively conditioned to express concern. While they rarely castigate the Irish retroscape in its entirety, they often prefer a more retrograde retroscape, such as Fagan's in Sheffield, to its hyper-real counterpart, best embodied by O'Neill's, the Irish chain of theme pubs, that has a franchise not three hundred meters from the door of Fagan's.

However, the picture was a lot different in the second pub, which I visited, which was Dog and Partridge. When I entered the pub I felt right from the beginning that this place was less popular and less commercial than O'Neill's, but at the same time it looked more original. The place was also divided into chambers like O'Neill's, but they were smaller and generally the whole place was smaller and the ceiling was quite low, which made the place look warm and cozy. It looked more like a house that was converted into a pub and this cozy environment makes it easy for customers to like the place.

(English male, 35)

I tried several times to find such an atmosphere in an O'Neill's pub, and every time found it sadly wanting. I had a particular idea of "Irishness" in my head; of an evening of conviviality, dancing, banter and copious amounts of alcohol, and every time I went to O'Neill's I was determined that this would be the time that I would find this atmosphere, but it never happened.

(Scottish female, 32)

Nonetheless, to those essayists unencumbered by any actual experience of Ireland, it seems that there is little, aside from the influence of their English colleagues, that can detract them from buying the sentimental brand of Irishness that Ireland has commodified and packaged so successfully. Indeed, some of the non-Irish deliberators who participated in this study, apart from those who merely browse Irish bookshops, surf the Celtic Web, and talk with passing Irish folk, activities that in any case could be dismissed as research for this project, are going to extraordinary lengths to imbibe the Irish tradition. Some, after visiting the Irish retroscapes, are booking flights to Ireland, arranging places to stay, buying guidebooks. Some are checking their family trees, with the energy of U.S. presidential wannabees—surely there is a McCarthy there somewhere?—others claim Irish roots regardless. There are now five Irish-Chinese MBA students who will only answer to the name Paddy. We exaggerate slightly, but the point still stands—the vast majority of the pensive pen-pushers are smitten. This strategy, not dissimilar to Oswald's (1999, p. 303) notion of "culture swapping," where consumers "borrow or buy the cultural trappings of other groups to form an identity" is clearly evident:

Sitting in the pub, surrounded by things related to Ireland, for the first time, I felt that Ireland was not just a single word or the name of a country to me. I began to have a more concrete concept of Ireland in my mind. Although I have never visited Ireland, in this theme pub I could feel something that I could not describe clearly in any language. It is a sense and you can only feel it. It seemed that I was touching the spirit of Ireland through the pub—O'Neill's. The bartender told me a few minutes ago that they wanted to bring everything about Ireland to this country and to their customers. In some degrees, I think, they achieved their goal to some extent. To foreigners such as I, who have never been to Ireland, the theme pub was a window that could take me there.

(Chinese male, 32)

I became very infatuated by the Irish pub and Irishness that evening. I know in my mind that in the coming year I will be visiting the Irish pub many times. I have also made it a point that no matter where I am, I will be in an Irish pub, if not in Ireland, on St. Patrick's Day, which is celebrated on 17th March. These days anyone can become Irish when the mood takes them. I will end by saying: Oh mother dear, I'm over here and I'm never coming back. What keeps me here is the Beer, the women and the *Craic*!

(Chinese female, 29)

What makes an Irish pub so special to me is what they call the *craic*, that intangible quality that comes from a host of features such as humor, bluffing, flirting, chatting and music all stuck together with the Devil's buttermilk! It is mesmerizing. The pub is also a handy place for a bite to eat, a leisurely morning brunch and a read of papers, a meeting place before the local match, the ideal location to watch a sporting event, the neutral zone to patch up with girlfriend/boyfriend or the perfect battle zone for a game of Chess!! It is in short, whatever you want it to be. All you need to become a member of this institution is a relaxed attitude, a good sense of humor and a few pounds for the barman now and again.

(Indian male, 31)

The authenticity of the Irish pubs stands up to scrutiny—the deeper I dig, the more interesting and attractive it becomes. Many, including me, are ready to buy into the myth coz it is successful the world over and I should tell you it is worth the buy. I have had some wonderful memories of this Irish pub called the Dubliners.

(Chinese female, 28)

This chapter proves that contrary to popular parlance, drinkers can recount in astonishing detail where they were, and what they did, the night before the morning after, especially in an Irish pub in Sheffield when they've each been cajoled with course accreditation marks. So aside from the nostalgia-is-a-good-marketing-tool conclusion[4]; aside from the consumers-feed-on-stories conclusion; aside from the consumers-make-their-own-meaning conclusion; aside from the need-for-more-research conclusion; aside from the Irish-pubs-have-a-long-way-to-go-especially-in-foreign-markets conclusion; aside from the universal appeal of a long-gone Irishness; aside from the retrograde retroscape idea which contrasts sharply with Ritzer's (1999) call for extra extravagance; aside from the polyglot sample; and aside from how Guinness has managed to integrate its eponymous product into the experience—what conclusions can we draw?

The cumulative empirical insights highlight that retro-consumption produces retro-flection. Perhaps this is not surprising given the retrospective nature of SPI but it can hardly account for the tremendous outpouring of nostalgia that we have sketched. It would seem that the combined pub ingredients of the Guinness commodity, the evocative aura of commodified antiquity, the folk music, Ireland's universality, social intercourse, and alcohol elixir perceived as a whole do create a powerful nostalgic urge that consumers enjoy. Respectfully, therefore, we would dispute the usual surmise that as consumers we've been *drinking to forget for as long as we can remember*. Our alternative, and much more heartening stance, is that actually we've been *drinking to remember what we never want to forget*.

Levy's (1996) point that it is difficult to summarize total impressions of a commercial environment was also underscored by our research. As consumers we perceive as a whole without being able to name the tangible elements that surround and encourage us in combination. This is especially the case in an Irish theme pub where the intimate, visceral experiences of eating, drinking, dancing, and socializing predominate. Consequently, perhaps experiences such as these will always remain subjective and private, inaccessible and incommunicable. This admission should come as no surprise to the readers and writers of eternally produced journal articles that purport to shed new light on the esoterics of a given subject. The particular of anything will always slip through the clumsy net of general impressions that researchers distill in the brewery of their minds. The language expressed in a hundred SPI transcripts—or for that matter any other research source—is always inadequate. So too is the language used to analyze and categorize general themes within such transcripts.

Still, this has been a worthwhile exercise into the peculiar dynamics of retro-consumption in Irish theme pubs. While some essayists either were unaware of the "tensions of commodities" or dwelt on the negative side of these tensions, the vast majority saw the juxtaposition of the Irish pub context as invigorating, entertaining, and liberating (Sack 1992). It has been argued that to such people "many modern things and places can be out of place, but that is itself the modern context and to be applauded" (Sack 1992, p. 172). The last remaining shard of introspective data makes this point in eloquent fashion:

> Maybe I am inclined to romanticize a past that never happened, but I still want to be part of it. And so, for me, Flanagan's is Irish in its truest form. Forget the Marks-and-Spencer bedecked high streets of Dublin, the lack of leprechauns bouncing merrily round the pavements, the shortage of old men waiting on street corners to shake your hand, the shores of the Liffey that disturbingly resemble the banks of the Thames, the local pubs in Belfast that play English music, and the locals who wear suits and work in office blocks, give me the "Irishness" of Flanagan's any day. I choose to believe that the Irish people are denying their roots, and trying to be like us! In fact, we do Irish better! We could teach them a thing or two about their heritage. Feckin' eejits!
>
> (English female, 30)

Time, gentlemen, please! You can always *come back for the craic* another time.

Notes

1. The actual tag *retroscape* is rarely mentioned. More often they are labeled as but one possible variation on a theme. Gottdiener (1997), for instance, according to his theme classifications, positions retroscapes in the *nostalgia* category, separate and distinct from a welter of competing themes, such as: *Status, Tropical Paradise, The Wild West, Classical Civilization, The Arabian Fantasy, The Urban Motif,* and *Fortress Architecture.* While helpful in a didactic sense, this reductive taxonomy is misleading, since retro themes are synonymous with many of the above-mentioned themes plus a few that are excluded from Gottdiener's analysis. The Irish theme pub, for instance, combines a retro motif with an Irish country motif. Surprisingly, Gottdiener's *The Theming of America* doesn't mention this ethnic variation despite the staggering popularity of the Irish pubs in America, such as the Guinness supported thirteen-strong chain of Irish pubs, called *Fadó*—Irish for "long ago."

2. Little do they know that there is a very serious dearth of these genuine articles. Street signs—"Kilkenny six miles," tin advertising hoardings—"Guinness is good for you," and all kinds of ornamental pub fittings are in very short supply. So much so that in order to satisfy spiraling demand from Irish theme pubs the world over, firms manufacturing ready-made modern-day antiques, such as the Dublin based Interiors Trading Company, are now common (Fracassini 2000).

3. Why does such a gerund not exist? We have clubbing but not pubbing, yet pubbing is much more common.

4. For example, Burger King announced that it has begun to convert its existing outlets in the United Kingdom and across Europe into retro-style 1950s diners (Mason 2001).

References

Anderson, Benedict (1983), *Imagined Communities*, London: Verso.

Backes, Nancy (1997), "Reading the Shopping Mall City," *Journal of Popular Culture*, 31 (Winter): 1–17.

Belfrage, Sally (1998), *The Crack: A Belfast Year*, London: Grafton.

Brown, Stephen (2000), *Marketing: The Retro Revolution*, London: Sage.

Brown, Stephen and Anthony Patterson (2000), "Knick-knack Paddy-whack, Give a Pub a Theme," *Journal of Marketing Management*, 16 (6): 647–62.

Chang, T.C. (2000), "Theming Cities, Taming Places: Insights from Singapore," *Geografiska Annaler*, 82 (1): 35–54.

Dear Michael J. and Steven Flusty (1988), "Postmodern Urbanism," *Annals of the Association of American Geographers*, 88: 50–72.

Firth Simon and Howard Horne (1987), *Art into Pop*, London: Methuen.

Fisher Eileen and Jeff B. Murray (2001), "The Real Thing: Conceptualizing Authenticity in a Commodity Culture," *Advances in Consumer Research*, 28: 137–42.

Fracassini, Camillo (2000), "Theme Pubs Turn to a Bit of Blarney as Their Source of Antiques Dries Up," *Scotland on Sunday*, September 3: 10.

Franklin Adrian (2002), "Consuming Design: Consuming Retro," in *The Changing Consumer: Markets and Meanings*, ed. Stephen Miles, Alison Anderson, and Kevin Meethan, London: Routledge, pp. 90–103.

Goss, Jon (1999), "Once-upon-a-Time in the Commodity World: An Unofficial Guide to Mall of America," *Annals of the Association of American Geographers*, 89 (1): 45–75.

Gottdeiner, Mark (1997), *The Theming of America: Dreams, Visions and Commercial Spaces*, Boulder, CO: Westview.

Handler, Richard and William Saxton (1998), "Dyssimulation: Reflexivity, Narrative and the Quest for Authenticity in 'Living History,'" *Cultural Anthropology*, 3: 242–60.

Hawks, Tony (1999), *Round Ireland with a Fridge*, London: Ebury Press.

Hewison, Robert (1989), *The Heritage Industry*, London: Methuen.

Hobsbawn, Eric and Trevor Ranger (eds.) (1992), *The Invention of Tradition*, Cambridge, UK: Cambridge University Press.

Holbrook, Morris B. (1994), "Loving and Hating New York: Some Reflections on the Big Apple," *International Journal of Research in Marketing*, 11 (September): 381–85.

——— (1995), *Consumer Research: Introspective Essays on the Study of Consumption*, Thousand Oaks, CA: Sage.

Lego, Caroline, Natalie Wood, Stephanie McFee, and Michael Solomon, (2002), "A Thirst for the Real Thing in Themed Retail Environments: Consuming Authenticity in Irish Pubs," *Journal of Food Service Business Research*, in press.

Levy, Sidney (1996), "Stalking the Amphisbaena," *Journal of Consumer Research*, 23 (December): 163–76.

Malamud, Margaret (1998), "As the Romans Did? Theming Ancient Rome in Contemporary Las Vegas," *Arion-Austin Then Boston*, 6 (2): 11–40.

Mason, Thomas (2001), "Burger King Introduces Retro Style Diners to UK," *Marketing*, January 11: 74.

McCarthy, Pete (2000), *McCarthy's Bar: A Journey of Discovery in Ireland*, London: Hodder & Stoughton.

McCracken, Grant (1998), *Plenitude: Culture by Commotion*, www.cultureby.com/

McCrum, Mark (1999), *The Craic*, London: Onion Paperback.

Morrison, James (2002), "Revealed: The Secret of Warhol's Obsession with Campbell's Soup," *The Independent*, January 20, news.independent.co.uk/world/americas/story.jsp?story=115437

O'Rourke, P.J. (1989), *Holidays in Hell*, London: Picador.

Oswald, Laura R. (1999) "Culture Swapping: Consumption and the Ethnogenesis of Middle-Class Haitian Immigrants," *Journal of Consumer Research*, 25 (March): 303–18.

Patterson, Anthony, Stephen Brown, Lorna Stevens, and Pauline Maclaran (1998), "Casting a Critical 'I' Over Caffrey's Irish Ale: Soft Words, Strongly Spoken," *Journal of Marketing Management* 14 (7): 733–48.

Patterson, Glenn (1999), *The International*, London: Transworld Publishers.

Reid, Rhona and Stephen Brown (1996), "I Hate Shopping! An Introspective Perspective," *International Journal of Retail & Distribution Management*, 24 (4): 4–16.

Ritzer, George (1999), *Enchanting a Disenchanted World: Revolutionizing the Means of Consumption*, Thousand Oaks, CA: Pine Forge Press.

Ruthven, Ken K. (2001), *Faking Literature*, Cambridge, UK: Cambridge University Press.

Sack, Robert D. (1992), *Place, Modernity and the Consumer's World: A Relational Framework for Geographical Analysis*, London: Johns Hopkins University Press.

Scully, Judy (1997), " 'A Stage Irish Identity'—An Example of Symbolic Power," *New Community*, 23 (3): 385–98.

Sherry, John F., Jr., (2000), "Place, Technology, and Representation," *Journal of Consumer Research*, 27 (September): 273–78.

Shields, R (ed.) (1991), *Places on the Margin: Alternative Geographies of Modernity*, London: Routledge.

Sorkin, Michael (ed.) (1992), *Variations on a Theme Park: The New American City and the End of Public Space*, New York: Hill and Wang.

Stenger, Josh (1997), "Consuming the Planet: Planet Hollywood, Stars, and the Global Consumer Culture," *The Velvet Light Trap*, 40 (Fall): 42–55.

Stern, Barbara B. (2000), "Narratological Analysis of Consumer Voices," in *Representing Consumers: Voices, Views and Visions*, ed. Barbara B. Stern, London: Routledge, pp. 55–82.

Theroux, Paul (1985), *The Kingdom by the Sea*, London: Penguin Books.

Tuan, Yi-Fu (1998), *Escapism*, London: Johns Hopkins University Press.

Urry, John (1989), *Tourist Gaze: Leisure and Travel in Contemporary Societies*, London: Sage.

Wallace, Mike (1985), "Mickey Mouse History: Portraying the Past at Disney World," *Radical History Review*, 32: 33–57.

Wallendorf, Melanie and Merrie Brooks (1993), "Introspection in Consumer Research: Implementation and Implications," *Journal of Consumer Research*, 20 (3): 339–59.

West, Patrick (2001), "Last Orders Down at MacFoney's," *New Statesman*, 130 (4552): 14.

Woodham, Jonathan M. (1997), *Twentieth-Century Design*, New York: Oxford University Press.

Wright, Talmadge (1989), "Marketing Culture: Spectacles and Simulation," in *Marketing Theory and Practice*, ed. Terry L. Childers et al., Chicago: American Marketing Association, pp. 326–28.

6

Allegorizing the Demise of a Utopian Retroscape

Every Piano Tells a Story

Pauline Maclaran

Through melancholy moods in smoky bar rooms and the sparkling splendor of grand opera houses, the piano has long evoked emotive and imaginative associations. Many feelings and sensations, many memories and celebrations, many hopes and longings, and many, many melodious tunes have soared from its keyboards over the ages. From the sonorous sounds of a Beethoven sonata to the rolling rhythms of a Scott Joplin ragtime, the piano has played its way into people's hearts throughout the centuries, throughout the world.

(Maclaran, Stevens, and Catterall 1998)

Almost everyone has a story to tell about a piano. Of course, this is scarcely surprising whenever we recall that this ubiquitous instrument epitomized the successful development of mass-marketing techniques in the nineteenth century, an era when the piano was at the forefront of an emerging consumer culture. It symbolized perfectly the aspirational dreams embodied in that culture, a "Golden Age" of consumerism when every household had a piano (Erlich 1975). Transcending sociocultural boundaries, no Victorian parlor was complete, or indeed respectable, without "its household orchestra" (p. 4). The piano's economic accessibility (largely due to the evolution of consumer credit)[1] is poignantly illustrated by a railway worker who, reminiscing over his childhood in working-class England, writes of his hometown:

They used to say Wolverton was "piano and herrings"—that's what they used to live on. Of course nearly everybody had a piano, I've got one, but we've never lived on herrings. (Elliott 1975, p. 3)

And so it is today that many of us still carry memories of a piano in our hearts, memories that not only tie us to past times but also to past places. For the piano, more than any other musical instrument, is rooted in place. Unlike a violin, a saxophone, or a penny whistle, you cannot conveniently carry it around or tuck it neatly into your pocket. Nor can you easily move it from place to place—even a small upright piano weighs some 560 pounds! Accordingly, whenever we remember a particular piano we will also tend to associate it with a specific locale. Whether a grandparent's drawing room on cozy Sunday afternoons or a school assembly hall on bleary Monday mornings, we are very likely to evoke an image in our minds that contextualizes the piano in its everyday setting. Who can forget Rick's Bar in the film *Casablanca*?

Allegory as a mode of representation also brings time and place together, synthesizing and storing temporal experiences in symbolic, imaginary places or spaces (Yermolenko 2001). I've chosen to tell an allegorical tale about a piano, partly to better convey the sensory and emotional experiences behind the rise and fall of a utopian shopping space,[2] but also to portray the interrelationships between time, place, and memory. In keeping with the notion of multilayered allegory, this tale will have different levels of interpretation, interweaving existential, cultural, social, political, and personal meanings (Bays 2001). Appropriately then, many voices contribute to this allegorical tale: my own as I take an autoethnographic approach to my understanding of a festival marketplace in Dublin[3]; and those of my informants from whom I collected numerous introspective essays about their own experiences there.[4] Many voices with many memories link time and place to tell a tale that addresses the overarching question of this book: Is there "no then there"? Through writing this chapter I hope to show that there are many "thens" there, as we each infuse our interpretations of retroscapes with our own lives, our own aspirations, and our own memories.

Striking A Chord: Rose-Tinted Memories of a Piano in Powerscourt

"I remember the piano was the first thing that struck me," writes Sean, a young Irishman describing for me his early memories of the Powerscourt Townhouse Center, the Dublin residence for Lord Powerscourt built in 1774 and converted into a festival marketplace in 1981. I have been researching the utopian aspects of shopping in the center for two and a half years, passing many hours with consumers, retailers, and management. As this tale will reveal in more detail later, during my time in the center a radical, and highly unpopular, refurbishment has taken place. Prior to this modernization three levels of retail outlets were grouped around an atrium-enclosed courtyard. The majority of shops in the center were specialist, with antique shops, exclusive ladies fashion, specialist jewelers, and restaurants and cafés predominating. Rising up from the courtyard was a stage for cultural events with a grand piano to provide special recitals and enhance the center's ambience. It is to this that Sean is now referring.

Reading Sean's moving description of his enchantment with such a "strange and unique find" in a shopping center, I cast my own mind back to another time, a time when I too discovered the Powerscourt Townhouse Center in the late 1980s. The experience still resonates, deeply embedded in my psyche, just as it is also engraved in the minds of many of my informants, who so vividly describe their first impressions of visiting the center. A sense of discovery pervades their writings as they remember how unusual it all seemed: the historic setting; its imposing Georgian courtyard and façade; the ancient nooks and crannies; its sweeping mahogany staircases; and the grand piano taking center stage, a focal point to lead the eye around the buzzing courtyard and upwards to the lofty atrium.

Thinking back, I too can vividly recollect that I had a similar sense of discovery as I stumbled across Powerscourt, having lost my way around Dublin's bustling streets. I was making a weekend visit to this cultural haven in the South, a refuge from drab and dreary Belfast days in the troubled "black North" as it is often referred to by southerners. The blaze of flowers and plants spilling out onto the street immediately attracted my attention. Their myriad shapes and textures lured me across the road to touch, to smell, to explore. Captivated, I strolled inside, through this cascade of blossoms and foliage to find myself surrounded by small market stalls that offered further visual delights. Plump green olives glistened in a smooth oaken vat; long strings of smoked garlic clusters dangled from on high, nestling alongside heavy bundles of shallots. A huge mound of deep red cranberries caught the attention of several passing shoppers, and I was no exception. We jostled closely together, enjoying the abundance of the displays before us.

It was then that I heard the sound of a piano playing in the distance. Intrigued, I searched for the source, wandering on through the narrow, dimly lit passageway, to come out into an immense space that was full of bustle, and people, and light. Tiered balconies surrounded the covered Georgian courtyard on three levels. They blazed with colorful signs and canopies. Behind their ornate white balustrades people were walking, or sitting and talking in the many restaurant areas. Others watched silently, leaning over the railings to better study the crowds below. Before me, in the central space, a stage rose high to one side of the Marie Rose Café. I could just see the nodding head of the piano player. Eagerly I climbed the main stairway to have a clearer view. From a vantage point on the first floor I stood for a long time, gazing at the magnificent grand piano before me, and listening to the gentle classical music. The piano player was lost in his own melodious world, oblivious to the busy throngs of shoppers around him as his fingers moved rhythmically over the ringing keys. I was engrossed in my find, absorbing the atmosphere and the many proffered pleasures that abounded all around. We had nothing like this in the North. Everything seemed so elegant, so original, and bursting with creativity.

Now as Dubliners relate their stories for me, I understand that the center made a similar impact on them. Dublin too had never seen anything like this before. In these early years, Powerscourt was the place to be seen, a place to while away a few hours browsing leisurely around the many antiques shops, picture galleries, designer goods, and small market stalls. And as their stories unfold the piano is always there too, its presence encapsulating Powerscourt's unique ambience and sophisticated environs:

> Really, first impressions of it are the piano playing in the center. The most impressive thing is the atmosphere.
>
> It is extremely strange and unique to see someone playing the piano in a shopping center, usually the only time you will see someone playing the piano is either through watching the television or through attending a concert.

Their memories richly convey how the piano enhanced their overall feelings of elsewhereness, of being somewhere that was a little more exclusive and culturally superior to other shopping centers. Tucked away from the hurley-burley of the busy Dublin streets, shielded from the hustle and bustle, Powerscourt was a refuge, an "oasis," and a "haven" from the main rush of shoppers on nearby Grafton Street. Striking a resonant, yet relaxing chord in many a harassed shopper's breast, the piano accentuated this difference, this sense of having entered a better place. Its gentle strains soothed and calmed, transporting its listeners far away from everyday cares and worries to a place of "rest and serenity," a place that relaxed and calmed the mind. Although several years have passed, Michael, a Dubliner in his late twenties, still remembers the impact of his first visit and his feelings of surprise on seeing such a large piano there:

> I remember my first time with my girlfriend. She brought me there. We would have met every Saturday. There were a lot of young people there drinking coffee and I thought it was a great place because it was somewhere that everyone used—the wealth surprised me. There were a lot of

Exhibit 6.1 **The Powerscourt piano: holding the eyes and hearts of shoppers within the reverberating chords**

people in nice clothes—this impressed me. There was also a grand piano and I had never seen one as big as that before. I was looking down on the people; you could drink coffee and observe.

Not only did the piano play a crucial role in contributing to Powerscourt's unique atmosphere, but it also epitomized the nostalgic quality to the shopping therein; the grandeur of bygone days evoked through this historic retroscape. And, as I read my informants' stories that are so full of evocative memories, this is where I find utopia: in their rose-tinted stories of a past that has now become woven into their own heritage[5]; and in a sense of tradition that now questions and undermines the present.[6]

Although most confess that they now only visit the center infrequently, it is part of their history, a place they still venerate, a place that they proudly show to visitors. The center has become a cultural icon, representing a part of the Dublin townscape that has remained untarnished by what many refer to as "The British High Street Syndrome." Joe's story is a very typical one. He no longer visits Powerscourt regularly but takes great pride in showing visitors the center. For him Powerscourt symbolizes the best of the old and new Ireland, and the piano is an important part of this symbolism, lending an air of traditional authenticity in an otherwise commercialized environment:

> I always felt a certain glow of pride when I introduced, which I invariably did, foreign visitors to Powerscourt. Through the late 80s and 90s, I felt that it represented accurately some significant aspects of the modern Ireland. A level of prosperity, a certain level, indeed, of chic, but still retaining both the sense of history and the casual informality that seemed to suggest it was possible for us to have the best of both worlds. Perhaps most enjoyable of all in Powerscourt was to sit in the balcony restaurant and watch my guests, charmed by the pianist at the grand piano on its raised stage beneath them in the central court. That was truly civilized—the music wasn't piped!

Much to my surprise, however, it is the nostalgic recollections of young students that are particularly full of moving reminiscences about the piano. Although the center holds little allure for them now at their age—after all, there is no longer any "coolness" to be gained from a visit there—they have many strong memories from their childhood. Gemma and Mary both relate for me how they remember accompanying their mothers on tedious shopping trips and how the piano music lifted their spirits as it permeated throughout the center. For them, in so many ways, the piano, its player, and its music represented the pulse of Powerscourt, an important part of their childhood that left them with lasting memories:

Exhibit 6.2 **Lending an air of traditional authenticity**

These tables also had the best view of the piano player that was there every week. The sound of it could be heard from all over the center and I think this is what I liked about it because I had always wanted to play the piano as well as the pianist that was there. . . . The music that came from the stage gave the center its heartbeat.

The sound that I can distinctively remember is the piano being played. The piano stage was situated upstairs above the Marie Rose Cafe in the middle of the center, and every Saturday the man would play the piano oblivious to all the hustle and bustle around him. He was in his own little world. I remember the piano player added so much atmosphere and character to the center, that no matter how much everyone around him rushed about or chatted to friends, every so often they would stop what they were doing and listen and quietly glimpse up. He was almost angel-like.

The Lost Chord: Childhood Memories of a Boudoir Grand

My own childhood contained a different piano, in another time, another place. The place was Belfast, not Dublin, in a house called "Upwey," a rambling Victorian house where my great-aunt played her piano in a corner of the spacious drawing room. Just as Gemma and Mary listened with rapt attention to the Powerscourt pianist, so did I listen, entranced, to my great-aunt's piano music. As a young child, I used to gaze intently as her hands moved effortlessly across the keyboard. I was always fascinated by her oblivion to the long curl of ash that developed along the cigarette that invariably dangled from one side of her mouth. Every so often the ash would break off, settling in dusty gray flakes amid the gleaming ivory keys. With a deft flick of her wrist she would brush the ash aside, at the same time ensuring that there was no noticeable pause in her playing. I could never quite work out how she managed this. Her attentive look always remained calmly fixed on the music sheet in front of her, while the cigarette remained precariously in place, quietly glowing in preparation for its next drop of ash.

Her piano was a boudoir grand, which meant that it was several feet shorter in length than the Powerscourt concert grand. However, to me as a child, it seemed enormous, and certainly in relation to my great-aunt it was. A tiny, birdlike woman, with short dark hair, she was only four feet, ten inches in height and by the age of ten I towered above her. Indeed, as she sat on her plush maroon-velvet piano stool with her feet barely reaching the big brass piano pedals, I was never quite sure how she kept herself balanced as she pushed these pedals in time to the music. One of the stories she used to tell me was how, as a teenager in the early 1900s, she had persuaded the postman to lift her onto her brother's motorbike because her feet could not touch the ground. Unbeknownst to her brother, she then drove off on his machine, heading for Newcastle, a favorite seaside resort some thirty miles away from Belfast. In those days there was little traffic and for the first twenty miles or so she roared smoothly along the road. Then she reached the Panther Bend, a notorious sharp corkscrew on the road, where she and the motor parted company. Undaunted, and luckily unhurt, she calmly waited for a car to come along, flagged it down, and requested that the gentleman lift her onto the motorbike again!

I loved the stories that she told me endlessly about her life, her adventures, and her disappointments. As a young lady she had gone to finishing school in Germany where she excelled at piano playing and had been asked to remain as a piano teacher. Yet she gave up this wonderful opportunity (as did so many other women of her time)[7] to return home to nurse her elderly parents. The only daughter in a family of four children, no less was expected of her, and she dutifully complied. So, putting her own dreams behind her, she absorbed herself in caring unconditionally for others and in playing her piano whenever time allowed. She never married and lived at Upwey with my grandfather (her brother) who had been widowed early, looking after his family (my mother and her two brothers). Then in turn, she looked after me, my parent's eldest child, as they quickly produced a succession of siblings for me. We lived at Upwey until I was twelve and my great-aunt was a constant companion, taking me for long walks, showing me the trees she loved, and allowing me to pore through her vast collection of books. She was both grandmother and mother to me during these early years. My earliest memories are full of her reading to me or snuggling me into a chair beside her as she wove lengthy fantasies which kept me amused for hours at a time; and, of course, my memory of her playing the piano.

I loved everything about my childhood at Upwey: sliding down the thick mahogany banisters that wound up the staircase to the third floor landing; hiding in the secret places that my brothers and I found throughout the house or in the dense tangle of purple and red rhododendron bushes that bordered the garden; building a treehouse in the huge sycamore tree. There was so much space everywhere, so many places for children to roam. We moved when I was twelve to a much smaller, more modest, modern house. My mother found it too stressful to live any longer with my cantankerous grandfather. She needed to get away from Upwey, but I did not. I was heartbroken and resentful. The day that I first discovered the piano in Powerscourt, I thought of my great-aunt playing her piano and of my childhood in Upwey.

Playing Out of Tune: A Note of Disc(h)ord Occurs

It was with considerable unease that I listened to the Powerscourt management's plans to carry out a major refurbishment to the center. After all, I was several months into my research and I had not anticipated this event that would impact significantly on my research process. My major unease, however, was over the management's new vision of Powerscourt. This included a modern, minimalist design approach throughout the center, and the introduction of certain chain stores that would be accommodated in larger units. Many small shops and all the market stalls scattered around the ground floor would disappear to "keep the sightlines free" and to allow more space for these larger units. The central stage that housed the piano was to go. The fate of the piano was unclear and the manager of the center was reluctant to engage in any discussion over its future. Having little wish to irritate him, I pursued the topic no further. Any initial fears were quickly dispelled, however, when I sensed the overriding optimism among retailers and consumers alike that Powerscourt would be restored to its former glory and its vibrant atmosphere re-created once again.

Although I knew it was imminent, nothing prepared me for the day that I walked into Powerscourt to find that the refurbishment had commenced. Scaffolding surrounded the courtyard and the central area was completely boarded up. The piano, the stage, the Marie Rose Café, all were gone from view. High hoardings covered in voluminous plastic sheeting blocked out the light from the atrium. The stark "business as usual" signs, hung at regular intervals around these hoardings, only served to increase the depression that I was feeling and the severe misgivings that I was already experiencing. Dirt and dust were in the air everywhere. I could feel the dust in my hair, in my nostrils, and deep down in my lungs, choking me as I tried to breathe. No one knew the whereabouts of the piano. The crashings and bangings coming from the other side of the hoardings sounded ominous, especially those of splintering wood. Joe, describing his own impressions at the same time, conveys similar feelings in a more emotive way than I can:

> My visits to the Powerscourt Townhouse tend to come in spurts, sometimes missing out for months at a time. After one such absence, I was horrified to find the heart had been torn out of the building. The central court had been more or less cleared of life. The raised stage also seemed to be facing demolition. The shops that remained open were shielded from the carnage, and the dust, by great walls of plastic. Hidden away on the top floor, like difficult tenants who refused to leave, the staff of Blazing Salads struggled, through dust and the constant noise of construction, to pretend that life could go on as before. But what of the future? All was obviously changing but just how utterly? Nobody seemed to know.

Over many months I heard this uncertainty grow, expressed by many voices as the refurbishment dragged on, and the thick dust together with the desecrated surroundings alienated the remaining small, but loyal, core of customers. Once optimistic retailers became increasingly angry. Many smaller shops closed altogether. Several retailers talked to me about the piano. Where was it? Would it be coming back? They looked to me for answers, but I had none. Management was increasingly evasive, and speculation buzzed around the topic of the piano. Then, toward the end of the refurbishment, a rumor spread quickly around the center. Yes, they said, the piano would be returning, but in a different form, and on a new stage. I think one retailer who had made the following comment to me must have started the rumor:

> A lot of people were very worried that the piano wasn't going to return. . . . Probably they will get a contemporary piano. Maybe a Yamaha, more of the Elton John type.

Slowly, but surely, I saw glimmers of a new Powerscourt begin to emerge. The chic glass-fronted Karen Millen designer clothes chain unveiled its new store, running all the way down one side of the courtyard. Gleaming white uplighters on long chrome stems replaced the soft glowing Victorian street

Exhibit 6.3 **A beleagured and dust-covered piano emerges from the rubble**

lamps that once adorned the middle balcony. Surviving floor stalls were discretely tucked away into tidy, self-contained units, leaving the aisles free and Karen Millen's pristine looks uncluttered. Piped muzak flooded the center. Finally, the central hoardings came down to reveal a wide expanse of clinical looking white tiling that awaited the arrival of fixtures and fittings to kit out a new pub-styled restaurant. And there to one side of this expanse stood a beleaguered and dust-covered piano, surrounded by bags of builders' grouting and heavy packs of tiles. Underneath it was a wheelbarrow and on top of it, the builders' coffee flasks.

I could not quite believe my eyes. It had obviously remained in the midst of all the renovation work, providing a handy shelf and storage space for the workmen. Surely it could never play again? Yet, hope springs eternal, especially where the utopian imagination is concerned.[8]

As work commenced on the central restaurant area, the piano was relegated to a corner along with other discarded items. Even in this state, its lid scratched and dirty and its keys choked with plaster dust, it attracted the attention of many shoppers, who on seeing it imagined it playing and adding to the atmosphere:

It's a pity that the center was refurbishing and I did not listen to the piano.

Exhibit 6.4 **The piano is relegated to a corner along with other discarded items**

The music playing when I visited was not live. I was unlucky on my choice of days and also with the issue of the renovation.

The piano in the corner now remains in disuse, yet you can imagine the melancholic playing of the keys and the effect it would have on the people nearby.

The piano adds something magical to the place. Nobody was playing when I was there, but it must be wonderful listening to the piano during shopping or lunch. Maybe customers do not come for the shops but only for listening to the music and relaxing themselves.

But hope was not sufficient to stop the arrival of the new flagship store, French Connection UK. Dominating the old entrance, the steely glare from its glass-fitted shop windows replaced the welcoming profusion of flowers and vegetables that live on now only in my memory and the memories of other consumers. In a streamlined and minimalist foyer, a potted palm was all of nature's charms that was left to beckon to the casual passerby. Most consumers and retailers are now agreed that the original Powerscourt aura has been lost, that it has become "like any other shopping center." Thinking back to the piano, the piped modern music proves too discordant for many and an operatic version of Michael Jackson's *Thriller* strikes the wrong note in the ear of many browsers. For some the new music is too loud and to others it seems out of place, it "jars with the surroundings." Stephen, a young Dubliner, confides his deeper worries to me at this time, worries that most other informants regardless of age, seem to share:

> The music being played now is the Corrs, which is a pity as though these are likeable and a nice symbol of success, they are a bland replacement for any piano player. This was my initial and greatest fear on first noticing this modernization—that the modern purpose would soon override with no wasting of space where commercialism is concerned.

When finally I plucked up the courage to mention the piano, the manager confessed to me that he was trying to find someone to take it away, but could not find anyone. Nowadays, few people want to shelter a concert grand. "Out with the old and in with the new," he said, somewhat defensively, at the end of our conversation. In ironic reinforcement of his words, the new French Connection sign is now emblazoned above the main entrance. "FCUK" proclaims the neon-surrounded logo to shoppers as they approach the center from Grafton Street.

Facing the Music: Letting Go of a Piano, Holding on to a Memory

In a strange and surprising way, I experienced a certain empathy with the manager as I listened to his words. I understood too well the heavy responsibility of having a piano to look after, a piano that evoked so many memories for others as well as myself. For many years I was the custodian of my great-aunt's piano. I had received it as a wedding gift from my parents, my mother having inherited it on my great-aunt's death. In some ways I was delighted, in others I was not. Restored and French-polished, it looked as magnificent as it must have done on the day my great-aunt received it some eighty years previously. Yet, while proud to be the keeper of such a grand family heirloom, I found it difficult to think of a space for it in the Georgian terrace where we lived. Somewhat fittingly for a boudoir grand, the only place of sufficient size to accommodate it was our bedroom. Bringing it there was another matter, however, for the piano was too large to be carried up the narrow staircase. Although, ostensibly, a much lesser struggle than Ada's in *The Piano*, when she transported her piano from Scotland to a beach in New Zealand, it was still to prove no mean feat. Eventually, five men and a small crane were required to maneuver the piano through the bedroom window, which had to be completely removed (frame included) to complete this operation.

And there it stayed for several years, at the expense of wardrobes, dressing tables and most other common items of bedroom furniture. For there was only room for the piano and the bed. Still, I was happy to give it a home. Occasionally I would play it, although I had never acquired my great-aunt's wonderful dexterity on the keyboard. Sometimes I would prop open the heavy mahogany lid to better hear the deep bass tones reverberate around the room. Having been easily defeated by the tedium of scale practice as a child, I had always intended to learn to play the piano with more accomplishment (although I have yet to achieve this ambition).

When we moved again some years later the piano came too. More heavy lifting gear and a team of men brought the window out again and then the piano. Now it took pride of place in the drawing room of a Victorian house that reminded me a little of Upwey but much smaller. Here the piano dominated, allowing little room for comfortable seating or other furnishings. Consequently, the room was rarely used.

More years passed and my husband and I divorced, both moving to much smaller houses. Neither of us had room for a piano. For a while the piano languished, stored on its side in my new garage and exposed to the cold and damp elements with only a thin protective wrapping and some blankets to shield it. The decorative mahogany beading around its rim had been partially destroyed when it was accidentally dropped during the move and there were bad scratch marks down one side. I had foolishly sought to avoid the high costs of professional movers and bitterly regretted that I had not taken more care. I felt guilty and I was evasive with my family when they asked what was to become of the piano.

Learning of my difficulties, a close friend volunteered her garden room. Its elegance once again regained, the piano reigned in a prime position beside huge ivy clad windows that looked out onto a tumbling mass of flowers, shrubbery, and trees. This was the first time since my great-aunt's drawing room that I had seen its proportions suit a room. For a while the piano had a home again but it was not to last. Circumstances forced my friend to move and my piano had nowhere to go. In vain I sought a home for it among family, friends, and acquaintances, but to no avail. Nobody had the inclination, much less the space, to house a boudoir grand. I decided that the time had come to let go. With a heavy heart, I decided to sell it.

I hope by now that my great-aunt's piano is playing an important role in another family's memories. Yet, this will not alter its role in my memories, memories that will live on in my imagination forever. And I have many other things that remind me of my great-aunt: her dark mahogany music cabinet, still containing many of her music sheets; her gold-bound volumes of Shakespeare's *Complete Works*; the Hoffman *Tales of Struwwelpeter* that she used to read to me; and my most precious possession, her copy of *The Rubáiyát of Omar Khayyám*. Bound in dark green leather with gold-embossed lettering on the spine, inside thin tissue paper protects the twelve black-and-white photogravures that depict scenes from the poem that so evocatively captures the ephemeral nature of our lives. "The moving finger writes; and having writ moves on." No, we can never really go back in time, only forward into the future, but as we move on we can take the past with us by holding it in our memories.

A Final Thoughtful Note

So, rather than fading as the past recedes behind us, happy memories often grow stronger, becoming imbued with a utopian aura that blurs fantasy and reality. This is what happened to the lost ambience of Powerscourt and my own childhood in Upwey. And it seems to me, then, that this is what retroscapes such as Powerscourt are about: simultaneously evoking and creating memories both of the past and for the past. As they do so these memories will bring time and space together, in many and varied ways, for each of us. This is what I have sought to convey with my allegorical tale of the piano and its many layers of meaning.

At an existential level the piano illustrates a utopianism that springs from deep within the human psyche to give expression to the human need for rootedness as well as transcendence (Richter 1975). The piano symbolizes these dual needs. Being the only musical instrument that is tied to place, it holds a special significance in terms of its location as well as signifying the transcendent effects of music and the arts.

At a cultural level the piano epitomizes the utopian nature of postmodern consumer culture, and the search for the future in the past. The central space in which the piano sat resplendent on its raised platform was not simply a "conspicuous and scandalous waste of space" (Ferguson 1992, p. 31), but an integral part of the shopping experience in Powerscourt. It was at the center of a space that was literally and symbolically devoted to our imaginations, a powerful and emotive symbol containing a multiplicity of meanings, meanings that far outweighed narrow, economic calculations and considerations. Even when unplayed it created an air of expectancy and anticipation, a hyper-real ambience that reminded consumers of the theatre, the concert hall, and the opera house, thereby simulating a more cultured environment, an environment normally very much removed from the more mundane world of shopping.

At a social level the rise and fall of the piano in Powerscourt mirrors the rise and fall of utopianism in the center. For Dublin consumers, the piano in Powerscourt represented a corner that remained unsullied by the modern environment. It lent a sense of continuity and security in terms of the tradition it was able to evoke for them. Yet, in that very tradition, in its association with past grandeur and nobler aspirations, it was able to transcend the immediate present and act as a symbol for critiquing the present, namely, the overcommercialization of the rest of Dublin. Consumers associated the loss of the piano with a capitulation to wider market forces.

Herein lay also the tale's political significance, its fourth level of meaning. These wider market forces were associated in turn with an impending loss of Irish identity in the face of increasing globalization and the encroachment of the British High Street with its uniformly bland chain stores. Ironically, when it first opened as a festival marketplace, Powerscourt had been perceived as part of an Anglo-Irish heritage that was now freely accessible to the Irish people (Maclaran and Brown 2000). Given its history, a piano in this context was a particularly appropriate symbol to denote this mass accessibility to a previously elitist culture. With the domination of a British chain store, FCUK, signified so boldly over its entrance, Powerscourt is now perceived as having regressed.

Finally, the story of the Powerscourt piano is echoed in my own parallel and personal tale that I have included to illustrate the interweaving of the past with the present, and the overlapping intersections of time and space in our lives that retroscapes such as Powerscourt may evoke.

When I last visited the Powerscourt Center, some two months ago, the piano was still there, standing unplayed and forlorn under the main stairwell. Although two years have elapsed since I completed my research, clearly no new home has yet been found for the piano. Looking tired and tarnished, it sits uncomfortably in the midst of the new minimalist décor, a poignant reminder of its former glory. What's the use of clinging to the past, I asked myself, if there's no place for it in the future? Yet, even as I pondered this notion, I saw a young couple approach the piano. Their furtive glances attracted my attention. Then, laughing into each other's eyes, she lifted up the lid of the keyboard and he played the opening notes of "Für Elise." For a few brief moments the piano's dulcet tones echoed through the courtyard once more. The melody stayed in my head for the rest of the day. Perhaps, after all, the Powerscourt piano will indeed play again . . . but that will be another story.

Notes

1. For more background on the early marketing of the piano and its influence on consumer society see also Roell (1989) and Hollis (1975).

2. For more detailed studies on the concept of utopia in relation to marketing and consumer behavior see Brown, Maclaran, and Stevens (1996), Maclaran and Stevens (1998), Maclaran, Brown, and Stevens (1999).

3. A good overview of autoethnography is given by Ellis and Bochner (2000).

4. For the use of subjective personal introspection in consumer research see Holbrook (1995); for criticism of the technique see Wallendorf and Brucks (1993); for a good defence of the technique see Brown (1998).

5. The role of cultural memory in the construction of the American West as a "utopian sanctuary of freedom" is discussed in Peñaloza (2001).

6. According to Bloch (1988), antiques perform a utopian function because, like tradition itself, they transcend the immediate present and act as a form of critique.

7. It should be recalled that in these days women had little opportunity to shape their lives. The expectations associated with a woman's role excluded them from almost any autonomous development. For a good discussion of this see Beck and Bech-Gernsheim (2002, p. 56).

8. Bloch (2000) sees hope as the essence of utopia.

References

Bays, Carol A. (2001), "Self-relexive Allegory Intersection of Time and Space in Kobo Abe's *The Woman in the Dunes*," in *Proceedings of the American Comparative Literature Association Conference:Topos/Chronos: Aesthetics for a New Millenium,* April 20–22, University of Colorado. www3.sympatico.ca/knight.sinding/acla/bays.htm.

Beck, Ulrich and Elizabeth Bech-Gernsheim (2002), *Individualization: Institutionalized Individualism and Its Social and Political Consequences,* London: Sage.

Bloch, Ernst (1988), *The Utopian Function of Art and Literature: Selected Essays,* trans. Jack Zipes and Frank Mecklenburg, Cambridge, MA: MIT Press.

Brown, Stephen (1998), "The Wind in the Wallows: Literary Theory, Autobiographical Criticism and Subjective Personal Introspection," in *Advances in Consumer Research,* vol. 25, ed. Joseph W. Alba and J. Wesley Hutchinson, Provo, UT: Association for Consumer Research, pp. 25–30.

Brown, Stephen, Pauline Maclaran, and Lorna Stevens (1996), "Marcadia Postponed: Marketing, Utopia and the Millennium," *Journal of Marketing Management,* 17(7): 671–83.

Ehrlich, C. (1975), "Social Emulation and Industrial Progress—The Victorian Piano," An Inaugural Lecture Delivered before the Queen's University of Belfast, February 5.

Elliott, Bill (1975), *Piano and Herrings,* Milton Keynes, UK: The Peoples Press of Milton Keynes.

Ellis, Carolyn and Arthur P. Bochner (2000), "Autoethnography, Personal Narrative, Reflexivity," in *Handbook of Qualitative Research,* ed. Norman K. Denzin and Yvonna S. Lincoln, Thousand Oaks, CA: Sage, pp. 733–68.

Ferguson, Harvey (1992), "Watching the World Go Round: Atrium Culture and the Psychology of Shopping," in *Lifestyle Shopping: The Subject of Consumption,* ed. Rob Shields, London: Routledge, pp. 21–38.

Holbrook, Morris B. (1995), *Consumer Research,* New York: Sage.

Hollis, Helen R. (1975), *The Piano: A Pictorial Account of Its Ancestry and Develop-ment,* Newton Abbot, UK: David & Charles.

Maclaran, Pauline and Stephen Brown (2000), "The Future Perfect Declined: Uto-pian Studies and Consumer Research," *Journal of Marketing Management,* 17 (3–4): 367–90.

Maclaran, Pauline and Lorna Stevens (1998), "Illuminating the Utopian Marketplace: Dallying with Bakhtin in the Powerscourt Townhouse Centre," in *Romancing the Market,* ed. Stephen Brown, Anne-Marie Doherty and Bill Clarke, London: Routledge, pp. 172–86.

Maclaran, Pauline, Lorna Stevens, and Miriam Catterall (1998), "Play It Again Sam: Postmodern Paradise as a Piano in Powerscourt," *Proceedings of the Marketing Paradiso Conference,* ed. Stephen Brown and Anthony Patterson, Belfast: Univer-sity of Ulster, pp. 60–71.

Maclaran, Pauline, Stephen Brown, and Lorna Stevens (1999), "The Utopian Imagi-nation: Spatial Play in a Utopian Marketplace," in *European Advances in Con-sumer Research,* vol. 4, ed. Bernard Dubois, Tina M. Lowrey, L. J. Schrum, and Marc Vanhuele, Provo, UT: Association for Consumer Research, pp. 304–9.

Peñaloza, Lisa (2001), "Consuming the American West: Animating Cultural Meaning and Memory at a Stock Show and Rodeo," *Journal of Consumer Research,* 28 (December): 369–98.

Richter, Peyton E. (1975), "Utopia/Dystopia? Threats of Hell or Hopes of Paradise," in *Utopia/Dsytopia?,* ed. Peyton E. Richter, Cambridge, MA: Schenkman Pub-lishing, pp. 1–28.

Roell, Craig H. (1989), *The Piano in America, 1890–1940,* Chapel Hill: University of North Carolina Press.

Wallendorf, Melanie and Merrie Brucks, (1993), "Introspection in Consumer Research: Implementation and Implications," *Journal of Consumer Research,* 20 (Decem-ber): 339–59.

Yermolenko, Galina (2001), "Allegory, Time, and Memory in *The Faerie Queene II. ix–x,*" *Proceedings of the American Comparative Literature Association Conference:Topos/Chronos: Aesthetics for a New Millenium,* April 20–22, Uni-versity of Colorado, www3.sympatico.ca/knight.sinding/acla/yermolenko.htm.

Part II

Meso Retroscapes

7

Roadside Retroscape

History and the Marketing of Tourism in the Middle of Nowhere

Maura Troester

In 1965, the remote American town of Hayward, Wisconsin was home to a booming tourist attraction called Historyland—seven themed restaurants, an ice cream parlor in an old train depot, paddleboat and canoe trips down the Namakagon River, live music, an Indian village with Indian powwows and craft demonstrations, a logging camp with logging shows and equipment demonstrations, and Old Hayward, a restored logging boomtown with a saloon, hotel, and over a dozen shops. The place was hopping. It was so hip that at one point Davy Jones, the heartthrob teen idol of the late 1960s, visited with the rest of The Monkees and, in the ultimate confluence of conferring cool, kissed a local girl on the cheek. The *New York Times* wrote about Historyland, calling it "more than a commercialized imitation of an old-time village." It was a "slightly less than spectacular leisure time place" according to the *St. Paul Pioneer Press*, and (according to the State Historical Society of Wisconsin), "the most constructive and useful historical work which any private individual in the Midwest has tried to undertake."

I wish I could tell you why, then, in 1989, the Hayward volunteer fire department burned the majority of this once-famous historical tourist attraction to the ground in what one volunteer fireman called "the best fire drill we ever had." I wish I could, but all I can do is offer conjecture. When I visited a decade later, I saw only remnants: one languishing restaurant called the Logging Camp Cook Shanty with a huge, empty parking lot, a rubble-strewn field, public restrooms overgrown with brush, and a burnt-out TV set lying in the grass next to a rotting nineteenth-century log loader. There was a disconcertingly understocked "souvenir shop," with plastic Indian tom-toms that still had Historyland price tags on them, next to a treasure chest filled with fluorescent-haired trolls, next to a bin of secondhand garage sale jewelry, next to a handmade bird house selling for $150.

And this: after lunch at the virtually empty Cook Shanty Restaurant (where I *swear* they served warmed-over fried chicken from the KFC down the road), an elderly woman in a polyester dress, with a quest like mine, walked around the room, peering intently into the historical photos on the wall. The weird thing is that, although most of the photos were of the lumberjacks that worked the land 100 years ago, interspersed among them were photos that weren't of the lumbering era, but they were still historical photos. These photos were of Historyland in its heyday: the Cook Shanty Restaurant in the late 1950s staffed with cooks dressed as lumberjacks; clean-cut kids watching a lumberjack balance on his head atop a 100-foot-tall pole; cheerful old men demonstrating logging equipment.

We were standing in a weak shadow of the original Logging Camp Cook Shanty Restaurant. We were looking at photos from the 1950s of the once vibrant, proud, original Logging Camp Cook Shanty Restaurant—a fake reconstruction of a *real* logging camp cook shanty built around 1890. Photos of a real logging camp cook shanty hung on the wall of a fake logging camp cook shanty next to photos of the same fake logging camp cook shanty.

Strange.

Maybe Baudrillard (1988) was right. American culture is nothing more than images secreting images secreting images secreting images. So much that you can't even find the "original," even if it was built 100 years earlier on the exact same land as the fake one.

But I didn't think of that then. I felt kind of sad that this once cool, hopping tourist attraction was less than even a shadow of its former self.

De Certeau (1988) claimed that by writing history, we "deny death and almost defy it." Maybe I'm trying to do that in the pages that follow—but that gives historians a pitiful job. The death of the past is impossible to defy. And anyway, I thought all this deterioration was also cool. For a real history buff, the leftovers are better than the real thing. Freed from the constraints of context, they leave more room for the imagination—sort of.

I say sort of because my imagination wanted the kitsch, the plastic, the fake, the phony, the hyperreal simulacrum that Baudrillard loves to deride. I didn't get that. I wanted Historyland to be the emblem of 1950s, atomic-era tourism, the family vacation in the station wagon, "Gee Butch, isn't this great," a cheap version of Disneyland, the pencil drawings filled in with unnaturally bright colors. I didn't get much of that either.

What I got was a story that feels dangerously difficult to tell. If I tell it wrong, people will get angry. Because, despite the fact that all of Historyland's documents and photos are archived at the State Historical Society, most of the people who knew Historyland are still alive, having coffee at the local co-op grocery store restaurant, operating the local chapter of the Sawyer County Historical Society, selling crafts at small souvenir shops. Not everybody is happy that Historyland burned to the ground, but saving it was too expensive for anyone to undertake at that time. Allegedly, the new owner, a man from Illinois, wanted the land in order to build a lakeside resort—but I'm getting ahead of myself.

I didn't get what I wanted because there were two problems with my quest. One: behind this particular kitschy representation of history stood a serious human being with a passion. Two: when you are living in a hyperreal world (as much of the American built environment is said to be), life itself doesn't become any less real.

This is a tale of the real and the hyperreal and the power of both to impart economic and symbolic change on a small community in the middle of nowhere.

Tourism in the Middle of Nowhere

Unbeknownst to me, my relationship with Hayward, home of Historyland, happened to be deeper and more multifaceted than I could have ever imagined, due entirely to the marketing activities of a man named Anthony Wise. For example, I'm indebted to my uncle for convincing me (way back in 1986), that Hayward is indeed in the middle of nowhere. He had just returned to Michigan from a trip to Hayward to see my cousin and her fiancé compete in the World Lumberjack Championship. I can still hear his voice as he complained about the *hours* it took to get Hayward—so many that you couldn't even drive there from Detroit. You had to fly to Minneapolis and *then* drive for *hours*. Years later, another cousin made the same journey to compete in the American Bierkebiner, a cross-country ski competition that attracts skiers from around the world. After that, my sister and her husband went camping near Hayward, came home to Chicago, and announced that, although the North Woods were beautiful, the town was nothing to write home about.

The amazing thing is that few people from Michigan have any reason to visit Wisconsin, let alone Hayward. But, by the time I trekked there to investigate Historyland, nine people in my family had been there before me, primarily to see the World Lumberjack Championship and the American Bierkebiner. Oddly enough, Historyland, the World Lumberjack Competition, and the American Bierkebiner were all founded by Anthony Wise.

When I first stumbled on the Historyland archives, my professor told me to stay away from the "Great Man Myth." (I neglected to tell him that, being raised on a strict discourse of Cold War feminism, I probably couldn't write a Great Man Myth if I tried.) But I wasn't interested in Great Men (at least not the dead ones). I was interested in Great Discourses. And Tony Wise, like all good marketers, was a purveyor of powerful discourses.

When Historyland was built in 1954, it was a "fully activated," "living" museum, staffed by real lumberjacks dressed in period clothing. Wise's dream, as he put it, was to arrange historical artifacts in such a way that, when tourists stepped into Historyland, they "felt like they were stepping back in time." The task was hard, because the past didn't present itself simply in Historyland, sprouting from the shores of the Namakagon River as if its seeds had been planted there many years before. For years, the remnants of the "great roaring logging camps" (quirky things like bucksaws, Wannigans, Go-Devils, and Drays) were neglected, left to rot, thrown in the dump, or scattered here and there around the state. They slipped into a crack between the past and the future until they became only memories, and not always good ones at that.

So before any tourists could "live the past in the present," as one Historyland brochure promised, dozens of local historians had to ferret out old logging camp stories as well as the artifacts used to tell them. Photos had to be matched with descriptions; old tools and machines had to be cleaned up and put into motion. This meant that the idea of a historical tourist attraction had to be marketed to locals willing to donate effort and energy well before it could be marketed to any tourist. And this created a problem. Hayward's past wasn't always highly valued by its residents. They simply didn't think it would sell.

This is the big-theory reason why. The famous tourism theorist Dean MacCannell wrote a book in 1973 that explained the structure of tourism in the United States. One of his most basic contributions was the idea of tourism markers: To be recognized as a worthy tourist destination, a place must be physically marked as such. The marker can be as simple as a plaque saying, "George Washington slept here," or it can be something complex, like an image of Times Square standing for New York City.

Interestingly, MacCannell seems to have stated what the good people of northern Wisconsin and Minnesota knew intuitively. In the 1950s, tourism was increasing at a rate of 10 percent annually (Wilson 1992) as postwar, baby boom families hit the open road on the new highway system in search of tourist attractions. To attract this growing market of tourists, residents of small northern towns erected giant, colorful fiberglass statues (see Exhibit 7.1): a gorilla above an appliance store; a giant ear of corn atop a picnic pavilion; Paul Bunyan, the giant lumberjack and Babe, his blue ox; even a two-story replica of muskellunge fish (a large game fish with teeth capable of severing a swimmer's toe), built two doors down from Historyland (Marling 1984). "Anything to draw people into this town is good for everybody," was

Exhibit 7.1 **Statue of Paul Bunyon and Babe, his blue ox** (*Wisconsin Historical Society, WHi-3123. Printed with permission.*)

the belief. As the creator of a giant mallard said, "People maybe won't remember Wheaton, Minnesota, but they'll remember, 'Oh yeah! That's where they saw the duck!'" (Marling 1984).

In the 1950s cultural producers (e.g., film makers, novelists, journalists, musicians) had little to say about northern Wisconsin. The popular imagination was focused on the suburbs, on the American West, on sites that produced or symbolized the nation's wealth (Wilson 1992). Hayward was considered to be in the middle of nowhere, not because there is such as place as nowhere, but because "somewhere" was someplace else—the Grand Canyon, Yellowstone Park, Hollywood, New England, Mount Vernon, Monticello, the Empire State Building. These were the places that had great history, that provided important information that "organized people's knowledge of themselves and of the social world" (Urry 1995). Hayward and the rest of northern Wisconsin and Minnesota didn't have that kind of power.

Worse, Hayward had a dicey reputation completely unsuitable for family vacationers. "Hurley, Hayward, and Hell" was the expression used by many Wisconsinites to organize their knowledge of Hayward, themselves, and the social world. The understanding implicit in the expression was this: if a man visited Hurley, he was two steps away from Hell. Going to Hayward brought him one step closer. Despite the cultural cachet of trout fishing on the nearby Brule River (Holbrook 2001), Hayward and Hurley were known for hunting, fishing, whoring, boozing, and gambling.

Unfortunately for Tony Wise, this seedy reputation grew out of Hurley and Hayward's early history. Hayward and Hurley are former logging towns. During the peak of the lumbering era in northern Wisconsin, which lasted from approximately 1880 to 1910 (Fries 1951), thousands of men migrated to Hayward every winter to work the logging camps and mills. It was a tough life: ticks and lice and cold. Food consisted of a "monotonous and unpalatable" fare of pork and beans with coffee in the morning and the "poorest grade of tea" for the other two meals. At times it was so bad that the laborers who built Hayward's first sawmill literally tipped the tables over and rioted. Lodging was nasty too: straw-filled bunkers with fleas and lice, stacked three feet above the other, stretched along the uninsulated walls of a long log cabin, heated only by a potbelly stove in the middle of the hall. On payday, when the men went into town to spend their cash in the bars and whorehouses, many townspeople chose to stay indoors.

It took a little over fifty years for the lumber companies to cut down virtually every profitable tree in Wisconsin. Then they moved south and west to greener lands. The cash that flowed through Hayward dried up. Wildfires raged through the region, consuming the brittle branches left behind after the timber was felled. The original economic plan for northern Wisconsin had been that the lumber companies would clear the land of trees and make it suitable for farming (as happened in southern Wisconsin and Michigan), but the soil near Hayward was too sandy to support farming and the region too remote to support industry (Loden 1997).

Hayward was so poor that, as one resident told me, they "didn't notice when the Great Depression came and didn't notice when it left either!" Given the region's numerous lakes well stocked with fish, and its well-developed "vice" industry, Hayward pursued one of its few economic options. Tourists to Hurley and Hayward were men. They represented a significant market for "resorts": a collection of small, private cabins each with its own fishing boat. They also represented a significant market for alcohol, prostitution, and gambling (Divine 1965).

In the early 1950s, however, Hayward's and Hurley's paths diverged. Hoping to capitalize on the nation's growing passion for summer vacations, Hayward's mayor (Tony Wise) began to reposition the town as a family vacation destination. Having already founded a ski resort just north of Hayward, his goal was to reinvigorate the town's lagging economy. His unlikely tool of choice was history.

Rebuilding the Land of History

Wise felt that Hayward was a pale shadow of its former self. He feared that it was becoming a ghost town and he believed that History, with a capital H, could help prevent this. In 1951, he founded the Sawyer County Historical Society, "an organization to train and operate as amateur historians." A year later, Wise spoke to a group of local Wisconsin historical societies. In this speech, he gives the study of local history an almost mythical power to transform people, places, and economies: "Sawyer County has been sick economically ever since the big timber and saw mills disappeared," he declared:

> It is declining in population a little each year. Young people are leaving because they feel there are no opportunities for them. A pride in past accomplishments will give a person determination, inspiration, and hope for the future. It is the job of the local [historical] societies to dig out these accomplishments and show that every generation has had to fight hard for its existence and a better life. I am sure that if our youth would realize these facts they would not so glibly give up the fight and lose all the pleasantness of small town life for the hustle and bustle of the city.

To Wise, local history had the power to stimulate a particular kind of social and economic exchange: history would lead to improved morale, which would in turn inspire the community to embark on economic initiatives such as new industry, transportation, and communication networks. Missing from this particular narrative (although perhaps not absent from Wise's understanding) are the larger social and economic forces—the structure of the logging industry and its relations to westward expansion—that put Hayward on the American "map" in the late nineteenth century and removed it by 1910. Wise argued that

an economically healthy community depended not on financial or natural resources (for Hayward had very few), it depended on hard work and pride in
one's past—not just lumbering history but fur trade and Native American history as well. The community could pull itself up by its collective bootstraps,
fueled only by hard work and an understanding of past accomplishments.

Wise also had a well-developed understanding of the importance of tourism markers. In 1953, the organization published the *Sawyer County Historical Review*, a monthly addition to the local paper. Wise wrote one of the
first editorials:

> Anybody who lives here knows that many of our summer guests are look-
> ing for other forms of recreation besides just fishing. This is especially true
> of the person who loves to go sightseeing when he is away from home. Our
> county at present offers very little to this type of individual.
>
> One of the main projects of the Sawyer County Historical Society will
> be to carry out an historic site program that will appeal to the sightseer.
> This sort of tourist attraction has been very successful in New England and
> the eastern seaboard states. We in this section of the country can do the
> same if we will get over our inferiority complex regarding local history.

Although historical museums were growing in popularity (by as much as
80 percent during the 1950s in New York State alone [Clay 1960]), most of
these museums were located in regions where the historical value of the place
had already been established.

In 1954, Wise combined his ideas about history and tourism and built
the North Wisconsin Logging Camp and Museum and the Cook Shanty
Restaurant (a.k.a. "Lumberjackland" and "Historyland") on a thin strip of
land between a county highway and the shores of the Namakagon River
(see Exhibit 7.2).

Historyland was underfinanced and couldn't afford the expertise of a
good marketer. Part museum, part business enterprise, its success depended
heavily on the goodwill and efforts of others: people willing to "urge some
of the press to visit the museum," people willing to donate artifacts, to
locate machinery, and to underwrite the cost of transporting it to Hayward.
For this to happen, people had to believe that a history museum was a
worthwhile effort.

Tricky, but Wise convinced people. He did so by wedding history (and by
extension Historyland) to the promise of future prosperity. Nobody could
argue that Hayward was not poor. All they had to do was look around. Wise
argued, however, that all people had to do to get rich was work hard, and he
told an abridged story of the past to prove it. Essentially, he said, "The lumberjacks worked hard and look at how much money flowed through Hay-

ward then." If nobody believed how hard people worked back then, all they had to do was visit Historyland. And if people did believe him and wanted a place to start working hard, Historyland provided the opportunity.

Lumberjackland was a humble thing, the first of seven attractions that ultimately became Historyland. The Logging Camp had a parking lot in the front and was an open-air museum in the back, with a blacksmith's shop, and a reconstructed long, low, log bunkhouse in between. Scattered around the back yard were logs and tools where former lumberjacks, now in their sixties and seventies, demonstrated how to cut, haul, and load logs. The bunkhouse was meticulously patterned after the original, with real straw beds, old boots, and an authentic potbelly stove. It was true to form, down to the last detail. The only things missing were the ticks, lice, and the smell of men who wore the same long underwear for five months solid. Thank God for the hyperreal.

The first brochure advertising this new tourist attraction wasn't much to write home about. It emphasized two things: education and hard work. For example, it promised that "Lumberjacks will demonstrate for you the use of many different kinds of axes, saws and other tools used in the operations that brought about the historic cry 'Timberrrr!'" It also promised to educate youngsters and their parents about felling trees, and the work necessary to get the trees downriver to the lumber mills. These were framed as "exciting deepwoods activities." To support the educational value of the attraction, the demonstrations were presented as genuine historical records, as indicated by the proper use of logging jargon: "Getting the big logs out of the woods was the job of the skidders. The trick was done using the Big Wheel, Go-Devil, Dray and Skidding Tongs. You'll see these authentic pieces of equipment demonstrated at this stop." Headlines were gerunds: "swamping," "skidding," "loading," "hauling," "driving," and "cooking." It is interesting to note that despite the precise reconstruction of the bunkhouse and cook shanty, "eating" and "sleeping" were not among the gerunds used. Lumberjackland, it seems, was a place where men worked hard.

One of the first of many journalists to write about Historyland worked for a Wisconsin historical magazine. It is worthwhile to explore this article in detail because its basic structure of logic underlay many future articles on Historyland:

> Halfway down the trail to Fable, yet still lingering on the fringes of fact, rests Wisconsin's memory of the days of the great, roaring logging camps.
>
> Lumberjacks were a blend of strength, agility and stamina. They worked unbelievably hard. From dawn to dusk, their axes rang sharply in the winter's air. And when the spring thaw set in, they danced agilely from log to log on the great down-river drives. A slip of an ax or a log was crippling; sometimes it was death.

They played just as hard. With a season's pay in their pockets they
swarmed to nearby towns, taking over with heavyhanded humor.

Combining folklore (Paul Bunyan, the giant lumberjack, and Babe, his
blue ox "measuring forty-two ax-handles and plug of tobacco between the
eyes") with patriotism ("Came the Civil War, the huge post industrial expansion and the cries [for lumber] became even louder. Wisconsin responded."),
the article situates Wise's work within a poignant discourse of destruction/
resurrection:

> Thereafter came the reckoning. By 1910, the state was importing timber,
> and by the 1920's once-prosperous, teaming lumbering communities were
> fading into ghost towns. All around lay wasteland. What the ax did not
> touch, fire all bit finished.
>
> Into this spectral past, a few years ago, stepped Anthony Wise.

Wise is framed as a messiah, the bearer of history and future prosperity:
"Young, aggressive, a man with a mission. . . . Wise marshals his historians as
he does troops. . . ." The logging camp itself receives scant description. It's the
process of building Historyland that counts, the hard work of digging up the
past and bringing it back to life. Like Wise, the author links this process with
an innate economic power, concluding the article by stating, "If Wise & Company has its way, Hayward will need the services of Paul Bunyan's old bookkeeper, Johnny Inkslinger, to record its newfound prosperity."

History only exists as simulacra. It's a symbolic act, a representation that
can never do justice to the real thing. Most economists, on the other hand,
would argue that economic prosperity is not simulacra. Economic growth is
quantifiable, measured through tangible, fungible inputs and outputs. So how
are we to draw the connection between a historical theme park and future
prosperity? The author never explained how it would happen, yet argued
with certainty that prosperity was just around the corner.

By weaving Historyland into an almost magical web of nostalgia, poetry,
and history, the author frames Historyland itself as the link between a prosperous past and a prosperous future. In this article, three concepts dominate
this representation of Historyland: Hayward's "great, roaring" past, Historyland's
reconstruction of that past, and the promise of prosperous future. Missing most
from this article are information about Hayward's current economic situation and exactly how to build this prosperous future. But that doesn't matter.
In this narrative, history as presented in Historyland was not dedicated to the
task of economic problem solving. Instead Historyland was the embodiment
of the solution.

Exhibit 7.2 **Historyland's bunkhouse, circa 1958** (*Wisconsin Historical Society, WHi-3125. Printed with permission.*)

It's the discursive act of linking past prosperity to future wealth that holds the real power here. Hayward's prosperity had died forty years earlier but, as we know, "To speak of the dead means to deny death and almost defy it" (de Certeau 1988). This is the common assumption about history (and by extensions, historical reenactments). Defying death is the goal. It was my implicit goal in writing this essay and it was Wise's explicit goal: he wanted people to feel as if they were actually reliving history.

Unfortunately, as de Certeau (1988) argues, this goal is a decoy, a front for something else. History cannot bring anything back to life. From an economic perspective, however, it seems history can do something even better. In trying to resurrect a dead past, history becomes a semireal thing—an "object of knowledge," a simulacrum. As such, it can stimulate exchange (de Certeau 1988). It can convince locals that a historical tourist attraction is good for the economy and good for the community.

When Historyland was built, history served as an advertisement of sorts, a complex and subtle structure of meaning that promoted the exchange of new ideas. These ideas concerned not only Hayward, its history, and its economy, they concerned the people who lived and worked in Hayward as well as their relationships with each other and with the people who visited.

Populating the Imaginary Space between Now and Oblivion

Given that even during the postwar economic boom, Hayward offered few jobs, one of the first things Wise set out to do was provide employment. He gave old lumberjacks well into retirement "new" lumberjack jobs. They didn't have to cut down trees anymore, or haul them away, or float them down the river to the sawmills. But they had a very similar job—it was just symbolic, a reenactment of what they did before. In 1959, Wise did the same for the Chippewa who lived near Hayward—sort of. He gave them jobs dancing and singing, jobs where they could make birch bark canoes, bead moccasins, and tan deer hides. These jobs were also symbolic reenactments, but there is a subtle and slippery difference. The people hired to perform them had never before been paid to make birch bark canoes or tan hides. These weren't the jobs of their youth, they were the jobs of their grandparents' youth.

The Chippewa hired to demonstrate old canoe production had to do a lot more symbolic work than their lumberjack pals across the way. Sure, they demonstrated the arts of beading and tanning, but just as important for Historyland's audience of mostly white visitors, these people demonstrated "Indianness." This was a tough role to play straight. In the 1950s, Indians were ever-present in the popular imagination. Dude ranches, roadside attractions like Historyland, and larger theme parks like Knott's Berry Farm and Disneyland all offered some representation of Native Americans. When Indians weren't enshrined in tourist attractions, they appeared larger than life on both television and films. In 1959, seven of the top ten television programs were Westerns; during one week in October 1959, eighty-one Western programs were aired on Minnesota television (McDonald 1987, p. 57). To build a historical tourist attraction without Indians would have been simply un-American.

This is all fine and good, but in the popular imagination supported by television and the mass media, Indians existed only within narrowly proscribed contexts. Nobody ever presented images of freshly scrubbed Native Americans wearing pearls and twin sets or driving Chevrolets to the supermarket. Instead, images of Indians were frozen in time, at a date no later than 1890, when the American frontier was officially "closed" via government census. In these images Indians were constantly presented as "the semi-nomadic hunter, occasionally squatting in a tepee or making pottery, picking berries before taking off, pronto, alternating between canoe and horse, wearing feathers, ribbons, beads and of course, giving off his masterful grunt of a doomed race" (Kaufmann 1980, p. 24).

When the media did cover Native American affairs, they most often covered the "Indian Problem." Poverty, alcoholism, refusal to assimilate into white culture—these were perceived to be the core of the problem. Historyland, however, sought to present a historical image of Native Americans different from this, different from the screaming warriors seen on TV and different form the "Ugh! We-smokum peace-pipe" images once presented at Knott's Berry Farms.

As an "object of knowledge," the Indian Village at Historyland offered different content for symbolic exchange. When tourists entered Historyland's Indian Village, they found a past that was not full of Indians ready to kidnap a child or scalp a pioneer (as in Hollywood westerns). Rather it was full of industrious, smiling people. The Chippewa who worked there demonstrated work performed long ago—just as in the logging camp. The village was orderly, peaceful, and welcoming. Framed as an education in the cultural history of the Chippewa, the Indian Village presented a form of Indianness that had forgiven recent history, the federal government's bad debts, broken promises, and economic oppression (Wilson 1996). Historyland allowed forgiveness and reparation on a symbolic level; it cleansed history of its sins in the name of tourism.

Another way of saying this is that in Historyland, when Native Americans discussed their history, a lot of it went unsaid. It couldn't have been said at a tourist attraction where money was to be made. Instead, Historyland's promotional materials for the Indian Village and weekly powwows carefully

negotiated an alternative image of Native Americans. Commonalities between white Americans and Native Americans were constantly stressed, supported by more subtle aspects of Chippewa culture such as the ingenuity of
wigwam design, or the beauty of Chippewa music.

In 1959, Wise hired a professional publicist to create *Historyland News*, a
summer newsletter distributed to all the resorts and information centers in
the region. A four-page affair, the newsletter covered everything from the
opening of the new Wannigan restaurant to the thrills of learning about felling and swamping. Most of the articles in this inaugural edition, however,
focused on the Indian Village and the weekly powwows. "The Historyland
dancers include many famous names from Indian ancestry," begins one pow-
wow promotion: "The Belilles are descendents of an Indian woman who
married the first white settler in Sawyer county way back in 1850. You'll
recognize 6-foot Charlie who wears traditional pigtails and his wife Helma,
who is as beautiful as she is happy." This narrative works to humanize the
exotic otherness of Indians as presented in the mass media. Charlie and Helma
Belille aren't just "Indians" like those portrayed in Western movies; they are
real people with European ancestors, "just like you and me."

Through its friendly tone and detailed descriptions, Historyland's promotional materials de-exoticized Indian culture. Historyland itself created a space
where Chippewa could explain their culture to a primarily middle-class,
European-American audience. The promotional materials continuously sought
to ensure that this exchange of knowledge occurred within a safe, friendly
place. For example, after inviting visitors to "Come often to Pow-wows,"
Historyland News described some Chippewa dances and prodded visitors to
"Be sure to ask them any questions you may have when they are through.
Just as you enjoy describing your hobby to an audience, so these Indians at
Historyland are glad to tell you about themselves and their dances."

The connections between Native American and white American culture
are further emphasized in a discussion of the dances performed during
Historyland's thrice-weekly powwows: "The serious and beautiful '49 dance
originated during World War I, when 50 Indians volunteered to fight the
Germans. Only 49 came back and in memory of their missing comrade, they
continue to dance this haunting and commemorative tribute to his bravery."
Here the Indian is not the enemy, he is a comrade, who, like all good Americans, was willing to sacrifice his life in the fight against the Germans.

Wise developed strong, enduring bonds with members of the Court Oreille
band; by the time of his death in the late 1980s, he was considered an elder of
the tribe. He collected and catalogued Chippewa songs and dances and ultimately built a hall for the Court Oreilles to display historical artifacts as they
wished. The point is this: Wise treated Native American history with the

same respect that he gave logging history. This point would not be worth making, except that it was at the core of every newspaper article written about Chippewa history at Historyland over a five-year period. In other words, the object of exchange between these journalists and Historyland's promoters was not Chippewa history, it was Wise's efforts to promote Chippewa history. "White Man Helps Indians" was the message, not "Chippewa Wigwam Construction Prevents Common Cold."

When Wise decided to construct an Indian village at Historyland, the event received some major regional publicity. Throughout these articles, Wise was portrayed as a "One-Man Peace Corps," valiantly giving Indians what they could not give themselves. Even the fact that Wise chose to hire "real" Indians to work at Historyland is noteworthy. This, I realized, is the Great Man Myth my professor had warned me about.

Consider this *Minneapolis Tribune* article written in 1959 by an anonymous author. Photos show a group of people dressed in woolen shirts, baseball caps, and jackets canoeing down a placid river. "Prodded by White Man," the headline reads, "Indians Explore Ancestors' Route." The text begins:

> Although they've traded birch bark for aluminum, a band of Chippewa Indians from the Hayward region of northwestern Wisconsin has returned to the canoe and the historic routes their ancestors used many years ago. They take to the river like otters and paddle all day with the riffle of rapids in their heart. They're Indians once more and they love it.
>
> Hayward's Indians are grateful to a white man for their weekend canoe adventures. Tony Wise, realtor and director of the Wisconsin Historical Society takes great interest in Chippewa customs and their present welfare. Under the guidance of Wise, who speaks the Chippewa language, the Indians began to relearn their lost art with short practice trips down the Namakagon River.

It's not worthwhile to ask whether or not these people actually became "Indians Once More" by canoeing down the Namakagon. Nor should we ask whether a white man really *taught* them to canoe and whether they were grateful for the newfound Indian status that the ability to canoe brought them. Instead we need to ask what made this particular statement possible. Vestiges of their former selves, these Chippewa could only be resurrected, could only be Indian (once more) by reenacting specific "Indian" activities. Canoeing signified that the Chippewa of northwestern Wisconsin were moving back to that mythical time before white settlers won the battle for land. To no longer canoe, to do things like eat a chili dog at the A&W, was to be no longer "Indian." In 1959, there was little discursive space for Indians to exist outside the reconstructed simulacra of their own history. Native American history took a specific form: it was framed as constantly vanishing, on the verge of being lost for good. Wise was popular among journalists because they believed he could capture this history. He could bring it back to life just before it slipped into oblivion.

Social Progress and the Quest for Historical Authenticity

By 1959, Historyland offered seven separate attractions: a traditional Chippewa village, weekly powwows, canoe trips down the Namakagon River, the Logging Camp, the Cook Shanty Restaurant, a bakery, and a new souvenir shop. Over 100,000 visitors had toured the museum at a price of 50 cents per adult and 25 cents per child. At the tour's end—after families had been immersed in historical reenactments from the making of flint arrows to the hauling of logs from the forest—a man wearing a white paper cap and white apron would exit the Cook Shanty Restaurant and blow on a four-foot long brass horn. According to Historyland promotional materials, in the logging camps "of old," the horn signaled that dinner was being served, and it functioned likewise in Historyland, inviting visitors to "eat all you can hold" of food "cooked on wood stoves and served 'lumberjack style' just as it was in the old camp days." The price of a meal was $2.50 for adults and $1.25 for children under ten.

In addition, tourists could browse Historyland's souvenir shop, built "to represent the old horse barn of logging days," said *Historyland News*. "One look in any of the attractive stalls will be enough to convince you that its barn days are over and in the place of 'Bill,' 'Pete' and 'Nellie' you'll find a fabulous variety of gifts. You're literally surrounded by stunning articles from every corner of the globe, starting right off with authentic Indian hand-crafts and ending up with Swedish Pancake mix in Historyland's Country Pantry." In addition, the souvenir shop offered things like Mexican hammocks, Navajo turquoise jewelry, squaw costumes, and old-fashioned candy.

If one primary activity of tourists is to gaze on certain meaningful objects, on tourism markets, then another primary activity must definitely be to buy. Like the bumper sticker says: *Veni, Viti, Venti.* I came. I saw. I bought. But most theories of tourism (e.g., MacCannell 1976; Urry 1995) argue that tourists buy souvenirs in order to own miniature site markers. Possessing something unique to a particular place is the ultimate souvenir. It links the place and the person and the tourism experience in one beautiful, portable package. Thus a Mexican hammock bought by a tourist in Mexico is a good souvenir. A Mexican hammock bought by tourists at a northern Wisconsin logging museum should be considered, well, cheesy (no pun intended). It should be less appropriate. Inauthentic.

Historyland was a commercial enterprise, yet it assumed the guise of a heritage museum, with the expressed purpose of "collecting, preserving and disseminating Indian, fur trade and lumbering history." All of Historyland— its Indian powwows, bakery, bunk house, logging demonstrations, old photos, birch bark canoes, wigwams, you name it—provided a rich, colorful narrative that tourists could use (if they wanted) to impart deeper meaning to their purchase of souvenirs and all-you-can-eat meals. For this reason, Historyland had the potential to be ethically suspect in the minds of those who knew better.

In 1961, the American Daniel Boorstin called staged enactments like Historyland's demonstrations "pseudo-events," and argued that they cheapened the experience of tourists everywhere. This is the kind of thing Baudrillard (1988) was talking when he coined the term "hyperreal" and argued that the hyperreal completely destroys anything "real" it touches. The souvenir shop was the kitsch of Historyland. The fake, the phony. And what a thrill it must have been. How great to go up North and find a genuine Mexican hammock. How convenient. What's wrong with that? In other words, exactly what real thing was being destroyed?

Both of these arguments were handed down from men writing from the exalted platform of high culture. These guys still hang around up there but their arguments have been hanging around even longer, since the mid-nineteenth century (Lears 1994). They reflect deeply felt fears about mass production and advertising, and an even deeper mistrust of consumption settings that seemingly seamlessly combine artifice and commerce in one place and thus allow "sinister motives to be concealed and misleading appearances created" (Lears 1994).

Journalists writing about Historyland shared the same mistrust. For example, the following 1959 article from the *Milwaukee Sentinel* opens by declaring that, "Some of the really worthwhile attractions in Wisconsin come under the head of profit making ventures. And among these are a few which are truly instructive as well as being entertaining and interesting."

Put another way, the author is saying that: (1) not all tourist attractions in Wisconsin are worthwhile; (2) of these worthwhile attractions, not all are nonprofit; and (3) of these worthwhile profit-making ventures, few are truly instructive, let alone entertaining and interesting. That Historyland managed to embody all of these mutually exclusive categories is quite an accomplishment.

Before Historyland could receive such praises, it had to pass the writer's test of historical authenticity. After introducing Historyland as "giving visitors a taste—for a price—of northern Wisconsin as it once was, when loggers and Indians held sway," the author describes Historyland:

The "old logging camp" dining room is most synthetic, of course. There are wood benches and tables and food is served "family style" [markers of authenticity] but an old lumberjack would have fainted at the sight of the stainless steel, electric gadgets and other modern equipment.

The extensive display of old-time photos and woodsmen's tools and utensils is very genuine, however, and eminently worth a half hour or so of anyone's time. One comes away amazed at the ingenuity of these men who pushed far from civilization to harvest the big timber under tremendous difficulty.

The writer closes by providing Historyland with a final stamp of approval: "As a profit-making tourist attraction, it is a credit to the state, the community and the operator." Despite its potentially nefarious melding of artifice and commerce, Historyland passed the test: "It is authentic as such a show could be nowadays."

Nowadays. That's the key word. "The past was more authentic when it was in the past," the author seems to say. "Nowadays, any representation of the past can't be authentic because we're in the present." It's a good logic, a no-duh kind of thing. Of course the past was more real than any attempt in the present to reconstruct it. So why did so many thinkers great and small spend so much time judging historical reenactments on the basis of how closely they resembled the "real" past? From 1959 to 1965, the search for historical authenticity propelled many narratives about Historyland. Journalists invariably sought the contrast between the "modern" and the past. For example the *Milwaukee Journal* writes: "In a model Indian village set up as a tourist attraction near Hayward, visitors can get an education in the ancient way of life of the first Americans. The sharp-eyed tourists sometimes chuckle, however, at the seemingly unavoidable way that anachronisms creep in. The Indians often use up-to-date touches in their village, for they are, after all, living in Wisconsin today rather than 100 or more years ago." Later, a caption under a photo declares, "Up the dirt road [of the Indian Village] run surprisingly modern auto tire tracks."

For these journalists, the anachronisms at Historyland symbolized exactly how far civilization had come. In other words, despite Historyland's best efforts (as illustrated by the fine collection of authentic equipment), it was innately incapable of being exactly like the past because society had progressed so far beyond where it was.

I think I know what made Boorstin and Baudrillard so nervous about reconstructions. To measure social progress, there must be some standard, some Greenwich Mean Time that serves as a point of comparison. There also needs to be an instrument. A linear conception of time is the instrument—no problem. But the standard is more difficult to manage. It has to be something of the past. In an ideal world it would *be* the past, but that is impossible so we take the next best thing: the leftovers. The problem is that leftovers leave more room for the imagination, and according to a long-standing belief, imagination is far removed from truth.

Furthermore, relics of the American past can be destroyed so easily (witness the quick demise of Historyland itself). When people like Tony Wise patch these ártifacts together to reconstruct the past, they create a fake standard, one that looks and feels like the "real" standard, except nobody can say whether it is or not. So places like Historyland offered a false basis for judging social progress. The quest for historical authenticity, then, is a quest for a stable standard. When an astute journalist discovers authentic history, it signals that we can now start measuring, we can start comparing and see just exactly where we stand relative to the past.

Social Progress and the Longing for Yesterday

But social progress also has its dark underbelly, because when we rely on a linear conception of history to measure just how far we've come, we also open ourselves up to considering exactly what we've lost. In the twentieth century, the processes of Modernization (with a capital M) promised to give a better life to all Americans. Progress (with a capital P) became the buzzword. Fueled by a belief in the inherently beneficial nature of industrialization, by faith in the power of organizations to create economic, social, and moral progress (Lears 1981), Americans frequently destroyed, or remade, traditional cultural elements: buildings, roads, farms, gender and race relations, consumption practices, and so on.

Modernization gave with one hand and took away with another. The realization of this double-edged sword brought forth a bunch of different forms of antimodernism, symbolic and often material rebellions against modernization. Nostalgia was one of them and this nostalgia was frequently embodied in open-air museums similar to Historyland. The first open-air museum was founded in 1891 in Sweden, shortly after the Industrial Revolution and sought to preserve a way of life that people feared was fading fast (Wallace 1986). This was the same kind of nostalgia that inspired the construction of Colonial Williamsburg and Greenfield Village. And Like John D. Rockefeller Jr. and Henry Ford, who founded Williamsburg and Greenfield Village, respectively, Wise hoped to create an environment in which people could relive a past that was better than the present.

There are almost as many theories about history and nostalgia as there are theorists. Marling (1984, p. 4) attributes the need to reconstruct the past to "an aching sense of loss—the sense of standing at a watershed where the values of the past were dying but the future was not yet clear." De Certeau (1988, p. 2) claims that, "History aims at calming the dead who still haunt the present and at offering them scriptural tombs." Henry Ford wanted to tell a story of the "saner and sweeter" way of life that existed prior to World War I (and, ironically, before the institution of Fordist production practices) (Wallace 1986). Wise wanted to tell a similar story, one that instructed people in the "pleasantness of small town life."

But there was one unusual difference. Ford and Rockefeller were key players in the rise of American industry. Wise wasn't even close to being in the same league. Furthermore, Ford and Rockefeller lamented the loss of a world they helped transform through their own economic successes. Wise, on the other hand, lamented the loss of a world transformed through economic failure. Deindustrialization (the type that eliminates various forms of work as well as the patterns of life that revolved around them) can also lead to a "tremendous sense of loss" (Urry 1995), coupled with a desire to reenact and preserve the past.

The logging industry—and the way of life it engendered—did die in northern Wisconsin. The charred stumps of felled trees stood among the new growth as reminders of a form of nature that may never exist again. For those familiar with logging as an industry, the stumps also stood as a reminder of a brief but vital way of life for men. Wise was aware of this loss and, beginning in the late 1950s, began to reenact parts of it through the staging of weekly logging shows at Historyland. "I am sorry you missed the logging show," Wise wrote to Howard Peddle, an "old timer" and history buff who had once hauled logs on the railroad. "I believe you would have really enjoyed seeing husky, agile men in action again." In this case, Wise sought to preserve a vanishing form of labor, but he also sought to enact a particular set of social relations.

He closed his letter to his friend by saying, "In the meantime, if you get down this way before the camp closes, be sure and let me know. We will always have a good meal on the stove for you." Never mind that the meal would have been prepared to serve to a tourist looking for some sights to see. Wise's reenactment of his perceived values of the past—masculine strength and a warm and welcoming neighborliness—overrode the blatantly commercial nature of Historyland. They represented the "pleasantness of small-town life" that Wise valued and sought to ensure stronger bonds between Wise and his friend in the future.

In return correspondence, his friend wrote, "I'll see if I can get the *Evening Telegram* to run some kind of small write-up in hopes that it can bring your Historyland some new customers."

Prosperity Lost, Prosperity Found

In 1965, Wise built "Old Hayward," by moving the eighty-year-old Hayward Hotel, eight retired Soo Line railroad cars, a brick train depot, and three smaller commercial buildings to Historyland. He then erected a peppermint-striped big top tent, booked live entertainment, and began an extensive promotional campaign. The expansion transformed Historyland. It quickly became a social center for many of the town's people, employing local youth who would have otherwise left the region to find jobs. No longer was Historyland simply an interesting way to learn about one's forefathers. Old Hayward allowed visitors to actually participate in old-fashioned activities, to play "as if" they were actually living in a bygone era. Instead of merely observing the simulated spectacle of Indian powwows and logging camps, tourists could actually participate in the full simulacrum (Firat and Venkatesh 1995).

Furthermore, Historyland now offered tourists a choice about how they wanted to imagine themselves living in the past. The Soo Line dining car offered a luxurious nine-course meal, "in the grand manner of railroad tradition." Just like in the old days, diners were required to fill out "meal checks furnished by the steward in charge," and ate off the same china and served by the same staff that worked the train before its decline. The Namakagon Queen allowed tourists to consume steak dinners as they "relived the past in the present." At the bar in the Hayward Hotel, refurbished and renamed Clark House, tourists could "have the kind of Gay '90s fun that made Hayward famous at the turn of the century" by singing along with Katie Hicks ("The Queen of Old Hayward") as she played honky tonk piano. And of course, visitors could imagine themselves to be hardy, hungry lumberjacks at the Cook Shanty Restaurant or at the new Wanigan Souvenir Shop erected on the Namakagon Queen boarding docks ("In the Old days, the Wanigan supplied all the personal needs of the lumberjack. Today the Souvenir Shop supplies the personal needs of our summer guests.").

Old Hayward was the place to be. Après ski in winter. Ice cream, teen dances, Indian powwows, seven-course meals served in a plush turn-of-the century dining car, Katie Hicks leading a sing-along in the Clark House saloon where tourists were asked to "Please! Keep the tabletops clean. Drop your peanut shells on the floor." Historyland and Hayward were so happening in the late 1960s that the pop music group The Monkees toured the place and even kissed a local girl on the cheek. Historyland had thoroughly blurred the line between museum, entertainment, and consumption site. Similar to Disneyland (which was founded the same year as Historyland), Old Hayward was structured as a "supermarket of fun" (Wallace 1989, p. 158).

If Historyland was a simulacrum, Hayward's success as a tourist destination was not. On a given summer day in Hayward in 1965, tourists couldn't find a place to park the family car. Hurley, Hayward's former sister city in sin, however, was languishing and the town's mayor had a plan to put an end to the city's woes. Silver Street, the town's "infamous sin strip of . . . saloons and girlie bars" was undergoing a face-lift. Six taverns were to be destroyed, "a feat," said the *Milwaukee Sentinel*, "that the state had been trying to accomplish for years through police raids." While decrying the vices that plagued Hurley, the *Sentinel* made an interesting comment about Historyland. One of the bars that was to be razed housed a "30-foot long bar of highly polished Philippine mahogany on top of pink Italian marble" with colored glass and mirrors behind it. Wise hoped to purchase it for Historyland, to (as the *Sentinel* said) "preserve the magnificent memento of bawdy lumbering and mining days . . . in his Historyland."

They key words here are "bawdy" and "sin strip of saloons and girlie bars." For all its historical accuracy, Historyland sanitized Hayward's most recent past—sort of. Instead of gambling and girlie bars, Old Hayward had Katie Hicks leading the gang in a sing-along. Instead of the spilled seed of rowdy hunters and fishermen, Clark House had peanut shells spilled on the floor. The spirit of decadence had prevailed, but the cost structure had changed. By celebrating the past, consumers were able to celebrate the present moment and support the future through spending tourist dollars throughout Hayward. It seemed one of the first journalists to write about Historyland was right: Hayward might indeed need the services of Paul Bunyan's old bookkeeper, Johnny Inkslinger, to record its newfound prosperity.

Conclusion

How nice to end the story here, just like the structure of a Hollywood movie: a man, a vision, hard work, and then boundless prosperity. The symbolic transformation of Hayward via Historyland leads to social and economic transformation. But we all know that's not the story. Tony Wise filed for bankruptcy in the early 1980s, and in 1989, two years after buying the bulk of Historyland's restaurants and buildings from Wise, the new owner fired Katie Hicks and all the Chippewa employees. Then he donated Old Hayward and the Indian Village to the town's volunteer fire department, who burned the place to the ground.

What happened between 1965 and 1989 provides insight into the complex ties between Hayward's history, tourism marketing, and economic resources. Wise had big plans for the future of Historyland: thirty-three buildings in all, hoisted off their foundations and carted to Old Hayward where they would form a miniature village, with a working, vintage train linking Old Hayward with Telemark, Wise's ski resort to the north. He also had big fears.

As Wise was fond of saying, "You've got to grow if you want to keep above in business." At the same time, he began to voice concern about the impact of tourism on the environment. When Wise founded the Voyageur Canoe Outfitter at Historyland, he marketed it using a narrative that combined antimodernist nostalgia with a growing awareness of environmental concerns. "Relive the Days of Early Voyageurs" was the theme: "Canoe Hayward's White Water Rivers." Wise's marketing suggested that by canoeing down the Namakagon, people could travel back in time to experience a more pristine world. Yet a person could not fully relive these days because the landscape surrounding Hayward had been vastly altered a mere sixty years earlier. Despite this, Historyland's promotional materials claimed that the Namakagon's "swift moving water flows through pioneer country unchanged since canoes were made of birch bark instead of aluminum."

Wise probably didn't believe his own promotional material. Concerned that the land around the Namakagon could be further altered by economic activities, he became an avid lobbyist for the National Scenic Riverway Bill, a federal bill that would prohibit further development along the Namakagon and St. Croix rivers. He also began arguing for the development of "more tasteful" tourism in Wisconsin. If this didn't happen, Wise said in a speech to statewide resort operators, "We deserve to be a depressed area and be called pulpwood savages."

The tension between preservation and progress was strong. And the hyperreal, actually, helped to ease the strain. For example, in the "real" past, Hayward's economy was supported by logging—a process that led to economic disaster. In Historyland, because the demonstrations were symbolic, the logging was preserved and so were the trees. Likewise, as modernization (and time) moved forward, the buildings and cultures of the past were destroyed. By moving these condemned buildings to Historyland, Wise prevented their destruction and also supported the new economy.

In 1965, a lengthy article in the *St. Paul Pioneer Press* gushed enthusiastically about Historyland's restaurants and attractions. After further elaborating about Wise's other developments (a ski hill near Hayward, sponsorship of the American Bierkebiner ski race, and the World Lumberjack Competition which bought thousands to Historyland every July) the author describes Wise as "the king of this leisure-time empire" and compares him to Frederick Weyerhaeuser, Anthony Judson Hayward, and Robert Laird McCormick, former kings of the Wisconsin lumber industry:

> They discovered this great stand of white pines and matched it with the demand for lumber to build America. What Tony is doing is taking the

> scenery, culture and recreational advantages of Hayward—the raw material —and matching it with the ever-growing demand for good leisure time resources.
>
> At the age of 44, Tony Wise has almost got his historic heroes shaded.

This quote suggests that the Hayward economy had moved into the postmodern era: Weyerhaeuser trafficked in lumber; Wise trafficked in signs, symbols, and simulations (Firat and Venkatesh 1995). MacCannell (1992) argues that historical simulacra provide a "mythical encounter" between tourists and their imagined heritage. What intrigues me is the processes that support this mythical encounter, the means through which the virtually invisible (Hayward history) becomes real and concrete enough to support economic exchange.

If I led you to believe that this happens only through the power of Discourse (with a capital D), I apologize. Discourse is only half the picture. The simulacra that was Historyland could have only existed with the support of hundreds of other people: employees, local businesses, and the local chamber of commerce, journalists, as well as the tourists who visited Historyland. Given that only a few Historyland attractions (primarily restaurants) were open year round, Historyland was a costly operation to maintain. These people frequently forgave bad debt because they supported Wise's efforts to develop tourism in the region.

In the early 1980s, Wise borrowed heavily to expand his ski resort (with the hopes of linking it via railroad to Historyland). This expansion was followed by several unprofitable ski seasons and Wise found himself in bankruptcy. "The man who had made so many friends . . . with his bold ventures still has admirers, but he picked up a long list of enemies, each representing an invoice that will never be paid," announced *Corporate Report Wisconsin* in 1988.

When Historyland was built, it was created out of scant resources: old junk, one man's vision, and a marketing narrative strong enough to generate collective enthusiasm and physical and financial support. In the mid-1980s, however, nobody in Hayward had the resources—discursive or financial—to maintain Historyland.

A "man from Illinois" (synonymous for "evil capitalist" in much of rural Wisconisin) bought Historyland in 1985. In 1989, when he decided to burn Old Hayward and the Indian Village, Hayward residents were hotly divided about whether to torch it. After all, Historyland was just old junk—cleaned up and organized to tell a story—but junk nonetheless. Yet for over twenty-five years, Historyland managed to be more than junk and it did so through a continuous, heart-felt process of discursive work—of naming something that had been either unnamed or differently named and giving it new meaning.

The problem is that meanings are ephemeral and change depending on context. For example, a nineteenth-century log loader took on one meaning when it was hauling timber out of the North Woods. After the timber dried up, the log loader became junk. In Historyland, however, the log loader took on a new meaning as a smiling man in a plaid flannel shirt explained its function to atomic-era tourists. By 1997, when I saw the same log loader, it was junk again: paint peeling, boards falling off, and a burnt-out television tossed in the grass behind it. Its meaning had changed entirely. Nobody would pay money to see it anymore. Its exchange value was gone.

Postscript

Or was it? What I mean is that I'm writing this essay and you've been kind enough to read it thus far. You undoubtedly exchanged something (for example, the price of the book, time, or the pleasure of doing something else) along the way. And you exchanged it for a story—something even less "real" than a broken down log loader. In other words, you exchanged something else to experience this simulacrum of a simulacrum of a logging camp up in northern Wisconsin.

Strange.

References

Baudrillard, Jean (1988), *America*, London, New York: Verso.

Boorstin, Daniel J. (1961), *The Image: A Guide to Pseudo-Events in America*, New York: Atheneum.

Clay, George R. (1960), "Do Museums Educate?" *Museum News*, October: 36–40.

de Certeau, Michel (1988), *The Writing of History*, New York: Columbia University Press.

Divine, Gene (1965), "Silver Street Will Never Be The Same," *Milwaukee Sentinel*, June 28, p. 1.

Firat, A. Fuat and Alladi Venkatesh (1995), "Liberatory Postmodernism and the Reenchantment of Consumption," *Journal of Consumer Research*, 22 (December): 239–67.

Fries, Robert F. (1951), *Empire in Pine: The Story of Lumbering in Wisconsin, 1830–1900*, Madison: State Historical Society of Wisconsin.

Holbrook, Morris B. (2001), *Some Radical Reflections of Axiological Axioms*, AMA Doctoral Consortium, Miami, June 2001.

Kaufmann, Donald L. (1980), "The Indian as Hand-Me-Down," in *The Pretend Indians: Images of Native Americans in the Movies*, ed. Gretchen M. Bataille and Charles L.P. Silet, Ames: Iowa State University Press, pp. 22–35.

Lears, T.J. Jackson (1004), *Fables of Abundance: A Cultural History of Advertising in America*, New York: Basic Books.

Loden, Connie (1997), "Iron County Tourism History Rooted in Forest Resources," in *Forest History's Impact on the Growth of Tourism in North Central Wisconsin*, Woodruff: Forest History Association of Wisconsin, pp. 24–32.

MacCannell, Dean (1976), *The Tourist*, New York: Schocken.

———— (1992), *Empty Meeting Grounds: The Tourist Papers*, London and New York: Routledge.

Marling, Karal Ann (1984), *The Colossus of Roads: Myth and Symbol Along the American Highway*, Minneapolis: University of Minnesota Press.

McDonald, J. Fred (1987), *Who Shot the Sheriff? The Rise and Fall of Television Westerns*, New York: Praeger.

Urry, John (1995), *Consuming Places*, London: Routledge.

Wallace, Michael (1986), "Visiting the Past: History Museums in the United States," in *Presenting the Past: Essays on History and the Public*, ed. Susan Porter Benson, Stephen Brier, and Roy Rosenzweig, Philadelphia: Temple University Press, pp. 137–61.

———— (1989), "Micky Mouse History: Portraying the Past at Disney World," in *History Museums in the United States: A Critical Assessment*, ed. Warren Leon and Roy Rosenzweig, Champagne-Urbana: University of Illinois Press, pp. 158–80.

Wilson, Alexander (1992), *Culture of Nature: North American Landscape from Disney to the Exxon Valdez*, Cambridge, MA: Blackwell.

Wilson, Pam (1996), "Disputable *Truths*," Ph.D. dissertation, University of Wisconsin, Madison.

8

Huntington Beach

The (Re?)Making of Surf City

Hope Jensen Schau

For those unfamiliar with California, I offer a brief geosocial preface. California is a large West Coast American state with arguably three distinct sociopolitical divisions: northern, central, and southern. Intense rivalry exists between northern and southern California, at times boiling into serious political discourse about state division. Northern California is urban, "European," and conveniently railed for public transportation like any proper metropolis. It is epitomized by San Francisco and the Bay Area, and its inhabitants believe they have created a viable West Coast alternative to New York City. At times, southern California residents have been known to abbreviate northern California as NoCal, as in "not California" or perhaps "not my California." However, no legitimate efforts to separate have ever surfaced, because, frankly, as a huge, highly populated, wealthy state, there is too much national political power at stake. Central (inland) California, is agricultural, "quaint," and removed from the northern-southern tension. Perhaps because it is outside of the great intrastate conflict, it is the site of the state capital and supporting government. Southern California, the regional context of the following analysis, is characterized by suburban sprawl. Beach-centric and car oriented, its most readily identifiable "city," Los Angeles, is often accused of lacking geophysical substance and I'm told, cultural depth.

Undeniably, cities in southern California (SoCal) do bleed into one another imperceptibly and indeed there is no center or proverbial heart to L.A. SoCal is a precarious mix of Mexican cultural influence, Spanglish (a combination of Spanish and English pejoratively referred to as "junk Spanish"), American commercialism, Hollywood realism, conspicuous personal and

Exhibit 8.1 **Beach scene in 1965**

corporate affluence, carefully disguised ethnic and economic class systems, and virtually perfect climate. In addition to the vague threats of state dissolution, violent outbreaks of social upheaval periodically emerge disrupting the otherwise ideal *Baywatch* image. Close scrutiny reveals the SoCal cultural conglomeration is as high maintenance as the pricey tri-colored blonde hair weaves adorning the heads of legions of both beautiful sun-kissed and leathery sun-smothered SoCal residents. Still, the oft-belittled beach mentality and the perpetual hum of the surf (heard even in the San Fernando Valley and further inland) unite the inhabitants in relative sun-soaked bliss.

I grew up in Huntington Beach, a surf town in SoCal between L.A. and San Diego (SanD). The locals call it Huntington, or most often simply HB. Jan and Dean immortalized it in the song "Surf City": "two girls for every boy." While undoubtedly the latter is a male fantasy, the name Surf City fits. HB boasts sweet year-round surf conditions, stretches of nearly pristine waterfront, and highly decorated life guard units that would make even David Hasslehoff proud. HB is the site of the International Surfing Museum, host to world-class surfing and beach volleyball competitions, and home of multiple ranked professional and amateur surfers. On the basis of the city's surf history and reputation, the HB officials opted to adopt a plan to formally brand the municipality Surf City and cash in on an international fascination with SoCal.

Exhibit 8.2   **Surf City and the Edison power plant in distance** *(Photo by Robert E. Ghysels, 2002)*

So what's not to like? As a marketing professor shouldn't I appreciate overt branding and elaborate marketspaces? I suppose I should and I often do, but there is something, dare I say sacred, about a hometown, my hometown. Beyond a facelift and economic boost, the prospect of branding HB involved replacing a low-key, multidimensional functioning community with an extravagant marketplace; or, what amounts to the sacrifice of a lifestyle in favor of commerce. Certainly even the most indoctrinated marketing professionals and b-school professors retain a legitimate sense of social responsibility. The Surf City endeavor is an ethical minefield and a by-product of commercial "progress" run amuck with manifest and disturbing consequences. The Surf City renovation, known as "the reno" by residents, was a substantial, ambitious, and dramatic plan which materially and socially altered the city.

A huge suburban renewal project took place where the entire HB beachfront area was transformed from beach kitsch to corporate chic. Using the Jan and Dean song, the nostalgia of the 1960s surf heyday, and a corporate dream of increased tourism and pay-to-play recreation, Surf City was conceived. At the dawn of the new millenium, the Surf City concept emerged from the "ruins" of the HB reality of mixed income residents, organically evolved architecture, locally owned and operated businesses, lived beach culture, and genuine community. The HB residents were initially lured into supporting the project by the promise of economic growth and city prosperity (i.e., better public facilities and schools). Unfortunately, they awoke to a harsh discovery: their landmarks, their businesses, and their public spaces had been co-opted by the corporate Surf City concept and most proceeds were tucked in the pockets of outside investors. To say the locals were deceived is a strong and tenable statement. The "retro paradise," Surf City, disenfranchised the long-term residents and in many cases displaced them completely.

Aesthetically, the pre-Surf City HB or Huntington BRR (before the retro renovation) was a horizontally oriented place, where the tallest building around was a modest two stories. The architecture reflected organic growth with buildings constructed in different time periods in various media (concrete, wood, brick, block, adobe) with numerous purposes (pharmacy, surf shop, restaurant, law office, piercing salon) coexisting on the same street. It lacked unity of form and purpose. It was endearingly unsophisticated and homey. Remnants of the hippies' rainbow walls, the seventies punk rebellion, and the eighties *Dynasty* fashions commingled with the nineties grunge anthems penned across cinder block walls ("subvert the dominant paradigm"). Not random graffiti, but personal and communal statements that reminded residents that the town existed before the present tense and would likely continue into the future. Hiding behind vague nostalgia décor and Spanish influenced designs, the new Surf City incarnation of HB does its very best to

Exhibit 8.3 **Waterfront Hilton, downtown Huntington Beach**
(*Photo by Robert E. Ghysels, 2002*)

disguise the temporality of life. Building high-rise beach view hotels and vast expanses of highbrow retail space, the Surf City HB became significantly more vertically oriented with man-made constructions encroaching on the surf landscape. Structures spanning several city blocks began to literally elbow one another for thumbnail ocean views.

Sound devastating? Well, it is . . . at least from my humble perspective. HB, my hometown, home of my folks and friends, geography of my childhood, and my favorite place on earth, vanished before my eyes, destroying any illusions of ever "going home" and lending credence to the folklore of California falling into the ocean. Beyond a great marketing coup, it was a disastrous blow to the locally grown economy and the committed residents who wanted to believe that the reno would live up to the promise and were powerless to stop the invasion by foreign interests. Like a machine set on autopilot, the reno maintained a steady pace and churned through the local raw materials generating a smaller scaled version of the overdeveloped Honolulu coastline.

Sure, the statistics show, the crime rates are down and tourism dollars are up courtesy of a "planned" downtown more reminiscent of a Disney interpretation of surf culture than the inspiration for Jan and Dean's song. An amalgam of recycled *Gidget* props, stale tropical shirt patterns, and island motifs replace the entire Main Street area and at turns confuse the retro surf vision with Hollywood's reimagined fifties era depicted in *Grease* and *Happy Days*. It seems one "retro" incarnation is almost indistinguishable from another. Sterile and California pink, the new beachfront development screams commercialism, detracts from the natural beauty of the ocean and sandy shoreline, and some argue even takes away from the carnal pleasure of enjoying bikini and trunk clad hotties prancing down the boardwalk. Obviously, the last claim is pure hyperbole as the HB boardwalk sports awesome eye candy that no gauche architecture can diminish. If you've never been there, that alone is worth a trip.

Still, the Surf City project that reinvented the beachfront property into a retro travel destination does not only disfigure the shoreline but permeates the entire city, imposing new zoning restrictions, unpopular citywide curfews, and increased patrols. These new impositions are apparently instituted to protect the coveted ocean tourists (and their dollars) from the HB residents. Given the current retail property rates and the new regulations, there is no chance for many local businesses to return to HB. This begs the question: who will sell the trappings of wave culture? The answer is overwhelmingly: inlanders, or what some die-hard surfers call "inlandies."

Similarly, the housing market is squeezing residents: sky rocketing rents and constricted supply. All appearances are that Surf City is an economic success, except that nagging fact that the asset winners are not the HB residents, but rather the renovation funding entities and other outside speculators that bought up properties, like Pac Man ate dots. The net result is that HB lifetime residents, or "lifers," are economically forced into a mass exodus inland. The irony is these are the very same people that built and lived the HB surf culture that is the foundation of the Surf City investors' enormous profits. Now, like many indigenous people before them, the HB lifers are relegated to less desirable and decidedly unfamiliar territories off the coast. These people must learn new modes of life, or create a new class of commuter beach culture.

The most serious wave riders have moved south to take up residence between Oceanside and SanD and then again between SanD and the Mexican border. Others still have cashed in their American citizenship in favor of Baja. All this migration will produce new cultures, some of which will be reminiscent of what I knew, but the surf lifestyle I lived is gone. My friends still in HB complain bitterly about the changes, but the new residents are blissfully unaware of any discontent; they live in three-quarters of a million (or better) dollar houses without yards and drive down Pacific Coast Highway (PCH) mistaking the slick bobbing heads of the surfers for dolphins in the ocean.

Exhibit 8.4 **Renovated pier** (*Photo by Robert E. Ghysels, 2002*)

I had the opportunity to chat with a recent immigrant to Huntington Beach. I recognized him in line at the HB post office as a guy I'd met at my best friend's wedding. After sharing the awkward epiphany that we attended the same wedding and dispensing with all the pleasantries that entails, like "did your fighting fish [centerpiece] survive?" Kevin told me he recently bought a house within walking distance of the beach for a mere $975,000. He was so excited about the Surf City renovation and his ability to buy into the corporate dream.

"So, what brought you to Huntington Beach?" I asked, sliding my sunglasses from my eyes to the top of my head and joining the post office queue directly behind Kevin.

"Oh, the new downtown I guess. Property values are rising and I think I got in on the ground floor of a terrific community. I was renting in Laguna [Beach], but when this project began and I realized I could grab a place like this for under a mil, I had to do it. My girlfriend and I think it's a great investment," Kevin was genuinely pleased with himself.

"Sure." I said, minding my native manners by avoiding any hint of conflict. "What do you think about the long-time residents' objections to Surf City?" I asked with natural, SoCal nonchalance.

"Objections, really? Why? The locals make money hand over fist off the tourists and the new downtown is beautiful . . . so much better than the mishmash of shacks and concrete that used to be there. And those ugly oil wells are gone. I think they're pretty happy. Plus the place is safer and the drug trade is almost nonexistent. Everybody wins. What's not to dig?" He was blatantly smug and simultaneously clueless about the locals' social and financial gains.

Exhibit 8.5 **Huntington Beach bungalow with oil storage next door**
(*Photo by Robert E. Ghysels, 2002*)

"Right," I said in an easy and obvious noncommittal tone. "I've heard there are some that wish it was a little more like old HB. You know, the surf culture and beach shops that sort of made HB famous," I offered him my argument for the asking.

"Really?" Kevin looked visibly shaken. Maybe he was having some postpurchase remorse for that overpriced tract box he just bragged about owning. He rapped his knuckles on his outbound package nervously and cast urgent glances at the bright white face of his shiny gold watch. I could tell by his demeanor that he had never known surf time, the rhythm of beach culture, and the anxiety release of passing burdens on to *mañana* (tomorrow).

"Yeah, there was a certain charm in the community that evolved in HB and the way the residents negotiated the balance of nature and commerce: ocean and oil." I tried not to preach the surf gospel, but it has a way of seeping out. HB has historically towed the line between ocean tourism and oil trade, juxtaposing wave worship and profit hunger in innovative and peculiar ways. For example, there was for years an oil field adjacent to a wetlands reserve and a toxic dump. The oil field was widely criticized for its industrial appearance. Likewise, beach goers frequently complained that the wetlands gave off noxious fumes. However, the toxic dump across the street from Edison High School (in the shadow of the imposing namesake powerplant) was commonly used as a picturesque backdrop for wedding photos. Strange, but absolutely true.

"Oh, all that is there; it's just cleaned up a bit. It was dicey just a few years ago: gangs and shit. I was nervous to hang out downtown after dark; sure as hell wouldn't leave my ride parked on PCH." Kevin crinkled his nose and wrinkled his forehead like kids do when offered unfamiliar foods. "The pier is really hoppin' now, almost like Newport's." His moment of insecurity passed. Kevin spit my argument back at me in chewed up morsels. "My girlfriend even shops on Main Street in all those great new places. Almost a beach Rodeo [Drive]. On the weekends, we bike down to that Starbuck's to grab a latte and then ride along the boardwalk. It's a whole new city." Kevin spoke the truth.

"Yeah, it is," I agreed and stifled a "$3 coffees, what more could you ask for?" knowing I'm quite guilty of hyping up on costly caffeine myself. Kevin's comments had betrayed his ignorance of beach culture and his nonverbals gave away his faltering confidence. I knew exactly how to discredit him, "Do you surf?"

"No, but I hang out at the beach on the weekends when it's warm. I drive home from work along the coast. Sometimes I catch the sunset. The place is awesome." Begrudgingly I had to admit Kevin demonstrated his own reverence for HB as the glossy marketscape it has become. Still, I walked away knowing I had the high ground.

Main Street sports the corporate retro dream with nostalgia diners and outlandishly expensive retailers sprinkled with Starbuck's and the ever-trendy microbreweries. The Huntington Beach pier that has collapsed spectacularly twice in my lifetime has been renovated yet again to sport the new and improved pier attraction: Ruby's Surf City Restaurant. Now you can eat greasy $7 burgers in a shiny red, white, and chrome atmosphere with the most fantastic view around. Hallelujah! How did we exist without it? Kevin was right that this once unique locale now bears a strong resemblance to the neighboring Newport Beach pier. Soon the entire region will be a homogenous corporately conceived marketplace. It's coming; if, as I argue, it's not already here.

Some might say that forcing the surfers out of Surf City isn't good for business and that the long-term will see justice prevail; I'm not so optimistic. I'm troubled that the Surf City project is no longer fastened to the HB surf lifestyle and reputation. I'm fearful that the hyperreal reigns, independent of the culturally and materially real wave culture. Or as many HB lifers lament: "they took the surf right out of the city." Worse yet, I'm terrified that the Surf City monster may in fact become a legitimate culture of its own, replacing what was with a cash cow investors crave. What if this is all that is left of the beach life, of the wave riding lifestyle, of hangin' ten and chillin' surfside? Dude, say it ain't so.

Exhibit 8.6 **Surf City in all its glory** (*Photo by Robert E. Ghysels, 2002*)

I spoke with a good friend and avid surfer, Chris, about Surf City over a packed lunch on the sand. Chris maintains a middle-management position in an Irvine-based company, drawing a decent salary. Last year in the wake of numerous tear down projects, he sold his bungalow just off PCH and Main. For economic reasons, he bought a place farther from the shore and hazardously inland. Chris shared my concerns and echoed the general rants of the lifers.

"Where do you shop these days?" I asked, remembering many late afternoons crawling the retail landscape of what I am tempted to call the "authentic" beach scene with Chris.

"For surf gear? Hell, I still go to Jack's on Main Street or Huntington Surf-n-Sport, but it just isn't the same. I mean [it's the] same name, but decidedly different folks. I don't know what arrangements they made with the SC [Surf City] project to stay on Main. Shit, Surf City, they took the surf so far outta this city you can't even smell it anymore. It's all sterile now. They make their money off our backs and shove us inland. We made this town and we're the ones paying to park. Fuck, it isn't fair. The government didn't even offer us a reservation." Chris was passionately indignant. I could almost see his BMW pulling onto reservation land.

"Paying to park?" I echoed as a question, knowing it would begin another rant.

"Yeah, you know, we used to live close enough to carry our boards, or pack them on our bikes. But then again, you could park along PCH back in the day. Now, they got this system [where] you gotta pay to park for the season or worse yet pay by the day. That's a huge tax on the regulars like me who are here early every morning. I think I built that damn building over there with my parking fees." He was quite serious as he motioned toward the new snack bar where Magnolia Avenue hits the beach.

"Hmmm. What about the Electric Chair where you used to get the coolest rags [clothes] and the hottest ink [tattoos]?" I asked.

"Right. They're up Main Street, but inside another shop and the clothes are pretty much Urban Outfitter, not surf stuff. You can get pierced and inked there, but just the basics. They'll punch the face and belly buttons and most of the ink has been replaced by henna painting. None of the artists there are any good. They all follow some pattern book you can buy at Michael's [craft store chain]. No surf tats [tattoos]. Nothing original. Really authentic HB, not! The real deal have moved either inland or south." Chris nodded longingly south.

"Tragic," I concluded and meant it.

"Lucky you're not still here, Babe. This place isn't home. It lost its soul the way ethnic restaurants do when they start making concessions for the locals and then become part of a huge chain. The perfect little secret gets blown to bits. HB was great. Now, its just one more SoCal chain community. Mi's well be Rancho Huntington these days. Damn Irvine Company Disneyfies the world in the name of progress." Chris looked more downtrodden than angry. He fingered the sand lovingly.

"Maybe we need to stage a coup," I said sarcastically.

"Man, if I thought it'd work." He shook his head sadly and I felt his emotional floor drop.

In the days BRR, the beachfront was a gathering spot and a place where oral traditions were handed down from one generation of wave riders to the next over thermoses of cocoa or beer. We bought our surfboards from weathered surfers with leather-like skin and names like Corky who knew all the best tweaks for your board and all the sweetest places to paddle out. We chose bikinis in shops where the sales staff could literally size you up and pull suits off the rack that fit just right and never slid during wear. We knew each other by name or at least by sight. We could get pierced, tattooed, or hennaed by local artists we used to know in school. We spent the evenings by fire rings talking late into the night in SoCal beach accents about everything under the sun. We blasted rock music with competing boom boxes and played volleyball and Frisbee up and down the shore for free. We drove cars and lived in houses with sand dust that could never be vacuumed away. We lived life with damp hair. It was an idyllic existence and one that won't be seen again.

Exhibit 8.7 **Lifer playing guitar on the boardwalk** (*Photo by Robert E. Ghysels, 2002*)

   In case you think this is entirely generational, I interviewed two surfers hangin' pierside early on a weekday morning. Aaron celebrated his sixtieth birthday last fall and Jake was newly thirteen. They were getting their gear together after a most excellent morning of surfing in wet suits.

   "Hey, could I ask you a few questions about the Surf City reno?" I asked in my authentic SoCal accent.

"Sure, big fuckin' mess if you ask me." Aaron said, as he spit sand and towel dried his thinning hair. "Who sings that song, you know 'pave paradise/put up a parkin' lot?' It's about like that. They come in and fix what clearly isn't broken and set up a Mickey town with all the Mouse House rules." Aaron was sun-dried and angry.

"It sure is different than when I grew up here," I agreed.

"Yep, and it happened almost overnight. Some [city] council vote and the investors came in and then the reno began. There was a definitive moment: BRR and SC living in the Mouse House." Aaron said bitterly, as he wiggled out of his wet suit and into his jeans. "Saddest thing is: this kid will never know what it was. He'll never know why this place is on the map." Aaron pointed to Jake with his right thumb.

"Yeah, when surf ruled!" Jake said, as if he were talking about a legend or reciting some line from an action flick. I marveled at his enthusiasm and his lack of SoCal-cool, even-tenored accent. A surfer without the unspoken "de nada" [it's nothing] in his speech? It seemed altogether unnatural. He was definitely a new breed of cat.

"It wasn't that long ago, man." I said, casually, but firmly. I'm not old yet and no poseur surfer punk can take me to past-cool without a fight.

"It's as good as a lifetime ago if you missed it." It was evident Aaron felt for this kid and on the strength of Aaron's Surf Guru status I softened. He continued, "I try to tell these kids about the fire ring nights, but it's all talk to them. The beach closes at 10:00 P.M. in the summer now and the rings are all taken by tourists. In the winter you're considered suspicious after dusk and they move you along like vagrants." Aaron mimicked the faces of paranoid policemen and Jake laughed openly. "All we have of 'gathering' is the time it takes to change and stow your gear. Damn shame."

"True that," I said, clicking off my tape recorder and nodding farewell.

Realizing I have presented a very biased perspective, I offer a competing minority lifer viewpoint for some semblance of balance. I phoned a friend, Megan, I used to know in high school who now works for the City of Huntington Beach. I asked her about Surf City.

"So, what can you tell me about the Surf City project?" I asked immediately following the five-minute recap of the ten years since I last saw her.

"Oh, you mean the marvelous Surf City renovation?" Megan replied, sounding more like an over-puffed commercial than the junior lifeguard I had known in school.

"Sure," I answered.

"Well, it is wildly successful and exceeded any of our expectations," she said proudly.

"Right," I said slowly, reminding myself of Brad Pitt's character in the

Exhibit 8.8 **Renovation protest** (*Photo by Robert E. Ghysels, 2002*)

film, *12 Monkeys*. "But where do the profits go? How come the public spaces are no longer public? Why haven't the schools been upgraded?" I asked.

"Things take time, Hope," Megan answered, almost annoyed that I had asked.

"But it's your hometown too. Don't you worry that all the local businesses have left and many of the lifers are relocating?" It was unfathomable to me that she expressed this position. I was aghast and I knew it showed.

"Renewal has casualties," she sounded a tad remorseful, but she was unyieldingly firm that the outcome is worth the price. My calculations didn't match hers. Everything in me demanded a recount and reclassification of any possible hanging chads.

"Easy for you to say as one of the few lifer Surf City insiders," I thought, but didn't utter it. "I suppose, but you know, my sister can barely afford the rent these days. Where is the gain?" I asked out loud. "When will she see it?" I thought about my sister working two nursing jobs trying to make rent and raise her kids alone. She is pure lifer to her core and so are her kids. Why should renewal see them displaced? Law abiding and unintimidating, I can't really see how tourists would benefit from their removal. I heard Aaron say again, "Damn shame," and decided it was so much more.

"It's already begun. We've cleaned up the place. Can't you tell? You can't score [drugs] downtown like you could back in the day. No one wanders nomadically along the shore living beneath the pilings. Nobody gets jumped for walking on the 'wrong' part of the beach. Cars don't get jacked up while you're out at night. The beach parks have greenbelts and the boardwalk has new concession stands so you don't have to bring your own food," she sounded almost convinced.

"OK, but where do the homeless go?" I thought of my sister's school friend, Mike, who rides his bike around town with a basket of his belongings on the handlebars. It would be easy for my sister to forget about him and look the other way, but instead she checks on him regularly and gives him money every time they meet "just in case." Mike is technically homeless and prefers it, but the community watches over him with understanding and respect far deeper than their breezy SoCal accents admit. Where else can he go? I continued, "Where are the dealers now?" Admittedly, HB must be better off without this element, but that kind survives like cockroaches. On which community did we dump these pests? I appealed to her sense of reason, "Real cities have these problems. I'd be the first to commend you if you solved poverty and drug dependence, but I think you've simply pushed them under one rug or another. Nobody gets jumped because the beach belongs to no one. The parking fee is almost a cover charge these days. Cars don't get jacked up because you built huge parking structures that displaced businesses and people and spoil the shoreline. And what's wrong with bringing your own food to the beach?" I tried to be respectful, but perhaps I missed my mark.

"Easy girl, you know as well as I do this was a rough town when we were growing up. I want better for my kids." Megan was emphatic. I envied her resolve, however misguided.

"I don't know. We grew up fine; you're an attorney and I'm a professor. All limbs are intact. No damage done," I tried to shake her, but it didn't work.

"That's not the point. We've seen a lot of things we probably shouldn't have," she pleaded with me.

"We've seen life. There's no harm in that," I responded. I knew it was one of those conundrums: protect your kids, but don't dupe them into denial about the world. "If we want our kids to be a part of the social solution, they need to know the problems."

"Maybe," she said, agreeing to disagree, and openly endorsing the Mouse House rules and social control, while pocketing the Surf City proceeds. Quisling.

We ended our conversation directly and I'm sorry to add haven't spoken again. I'm afraid I put her off with my discontent. It happens that people grow up and grow apart. I recall her as much more hip and fun. I remember her enjoying the beach scene, at times more than I did. Back in the day, we used to chill at the Golden Bear listening to live music in beach rags, knowing once upon a time Bob Dylan played there and never guessing Scott Weiland would be the rock star he turned out to be (Stone Temple Pilots). My, how things have changed. I read in the papers a few years back that Megan prosecuted a Huntington Harbor resident for having too much junk in her house. I should have seen the cheese she set for the Mouse then. I remembered Megan's overflowing school locker and how her crap sometimes fell on my head as I opened my own locker just beneath hers. Hypocrite.

Set aside a debate on cultural authenticity for now as I readily admit I favor a different retro HB that reigned from the seventies until the late nineties and reflected the aesthetic and functional diversity of the lifers. I can't prove my vision is more authentic beyond the fact that it was cocreated by residents and local businesses. Unlike Surf City, the HB I grew up with was not a corporately conceived concept developed in conference rooms with modular furnishings by people paid to design a profit machine. As a marketing professor I can appreciate the scale of the Surf City branding effort, the scope of the implementation plans that sought and achieved a tourist marvel, and the art of creating a solid, cohesive marketing strategy. As a homegirl, I feel the defilement of a landscape I knew intimately and the near annihilation of the community I called home. I long for a compromise between commercial success and protection of the land and people I love.

Okay, for argument's sake let's say this is just angst as I realize I'm now a grown-up and childhood is merely a happy set of memories. I don't think the Surf City renovation can be so easily dismissed. It was a corporate takeover and a well-documented, verifiable event. One day there was Huntington Beach, the inspiration for Jan and Dean's "Surf City," the next there was Surf City, the retro surf locale and profit machine. In making the commercial dream, the Surf City planners killed the HB cultural reality that made the dream possible. Imposing a stylized retro illusion, the investors destroyed the natural balance. There is a fine line between cleverly capitalizing on an organic phenomenon and bringing a culture to the brink of extinction for profit. Maybe as a marketing professional myself it's in poor taste to express this dissent, but I can't deny my homegirl perception. Surf City reminds me of Dr. Seuss's cautionary tale about respecting your environment. I worry about how many surf thneeds people need and I wonder what the Lorax will say as the last surfer leaves HB?

Maybe I'm nostalgic for a mythical past and looking through rose-colored sunglasses at a charming, harmlessly eccentric HB that never really was. Nah, I doubt it. Too many people inhabited this past with me and exhibit recollection convergence. Were we all suffering the same delusion? If so, what's wrong with our surf delusion? Where was the authenticity war? How did our vision get invalidated? Why wasn't it implemented? While we were out surfing or catching rays, a coup was stealthily staged. Without more than a whisper, Surf City was born; a gargantuan corporate baby that crushed old Huntington.

Nobody asked my opinion, but I give it just the same. If I were to remake HB, I'd play up the beach scene: hotties on the boardwalk, fresh music in downtown clubs alongside standard beach tunes, a pier to contemplate life upon, a shore so majestic you felt God, cool rags, hot tats, and waves that beckoned you to ride them. I'd erect a statue of Jan and Dean on Main Street and a fish taco joint along the boardwalk. I'd let the surfers park for free and have park rangers reenact famous moments in surf history. I'd dress the beach patrol in beach wear, have them scour the sand for garbage (a true menace), and give directions to tourists on sun protection and safe beach play. I'd sponsor more world-class surf competitions and head the campaign to make beach volleyball a permanent fixture in the Summer Olympic Games. My HB would be the best of what I remember and then some, loaded with lifers and sprinkled with local flavor and businesses. I'd foster the lived beach culture and (trite as it may sound) invite the tourists to catch a wave.

9

Travels in Retroreality

Aedh Aherne

A-well, a-well, a-well, a-huh. Tell me more, tell me more. Did you get very far? Tell me more, tell me more. Like, does he have a car? Uh-huh, uh-huh, uh-huh, uh-huh. . . .

Okay, okay, okay, I'll tell you more, tell you more. Give me a break, will you? I'm stuck in a rental car, en route to Wisconsin Dells and my three tweenage daughters have the *Grease* CD on perpetual play. I'm also having a flashback, a retro relapse of some kind or another. I'm not only heading to a retro holiday resort deep in the wilds of the Badger State, but I'm listening to a twenty-first century re-release of a 1970s movie soundtrack, set in the 1950s. While driving a Chrysler P.T. Cruiser.

What's more, I'm being transported back to the murky memoryscape of my own tweenagehood, because I too grew up to the do-wop wallop of *Grease.* Or, to be more specific, I grew up during the galvanic *Summer Nights* video, featuring Olivia Newton John in that unforgettable outfit. Black leather, skin-tight, sprayed-on and, all-in-all, much too much for a hitherto unsullied adolescent. Sullyhood beckoned and, suffice to say, it was downhill all the way thereafter.

However, that was many, many years ago and my raging, roiling hormones have since settled down into semirespectable middle age. They're not quite residents of Viagraville, you understand, but they're certainly checking out properties in the vicinity of that burgeoning community. Be that as it may, I don't think my innocent daughters should be listening to lyrics like: Did you get very far? Did she put up a fight? and so forth.

"I don't think the girls should be listening to that kind of stuff," I said to my stoical wife in the passenger seat beside me. "Why can't you put on something classical, something tasteful, something more appropriate. . . . Metallica, Motörhead, Mötley Crüe? Something with umlauts."

She looked at me. She didn't need to speak. Guess I'm stuck with *Grease*. Unless. . . .

"Well, I *really* don't think little girls should be listening to those lyrics," I announced pompously, with just a hint of petulance. I'm pretty good at pompous, if I say so myself, and my petulance is to die for.

"Don't be pompous," she said. "And don't even think of throwing a sulk, either. They've heard a lot worse. You're on holiday. Lighten up. Pretend you're enjoying yourself."

Did you notice the sly dig? Did you see how she put me in my place? Did you catch the one about them hearing a lot worse? She forgets nothing, that woman. She still refers to the incident eight years ago, when the kids were sent home in disgrace from kindergarten. For shouting abuse at the other kids. For shouting "Shut the fuck up," to be exact. Apparently, they picked up the expression from someone or other. Some cynics say they picked it up from their father, who was trying to write a book about postmodern marketing at the time and couldn't take any more of the incessant screeching, howling, and general yammering. Personally, I think they picked it up off a TV program or video. *Pingu the Penguin* probably, though it might have been that foul-mouthed fucker, Minnie Mouse. Regardless of where it came from, my wife has held the unfortunate incident against me for longer than is strictly necessary and, given her elephantine memory, I guess it'll be a few years yet before my debt is paid to civil society.

"Remember ladies, the driver gets to choose the music," I tried. "I've got an Iron Maiden CD somewhere," I joked. "Don't leave home without one," I quipped merrily. "Did I ever tell you about the reviewer of *Postmodern Marketing Two*, who entitled his piece 'Bring your Kotler to the Slaughter'?" I wheedled, even though wheedling isn't my strong suit.

That look again.

"How many times are you lot going to listen to that bloody CD?" I finally, and foolishly, asked.

"Until we get to Wisconsin Dells!" came the unanimous chorus from the back seat.

"I never wanted to go on holiday," I pouted, prior to resigning myself to not unappealing memories of *Summer Nights* past.

Nor did I. I'm afraid I'm not a happy-clappy holiday person. I'm not a pack-up-the-family-and-hit-the-highroad kinda guy. A Grinning Gaelic Griswold, as it were. I cleave to the chapter-to-finish, why-don't-you-go-without-me, sure-I'd-only-be-grumpy school of thought. It usually works. But Linda and the girls had flown out to join me for a few weeks during my sabbatical at Northwestern, and the delights of Evanston were beginning to pall. True, we'd done the Sweet Home Chicago thing: Buckingham Fountain (gust of wind, girls got soaked); American Girl Place (who needs a towel when you've got Mastercard); John Hancock Center (the most recognized building in the world, according to the commentary, presumably on a day when the Eiffel Tower, Sydney Opera House, and Empire State Building were shrouded in fog); the recently refurbished Navy Pier (where the girls completely ignored my minilecture on the Ferris Wheel and its antecedents in the Columbian Exhibition of 1892); and, of course, the peerless Art Institute (where Linda fell about laughing at the suggestion that we invest my royalties in a Monet—a Monet mouse mat, key ring, or fridge magnet, you must appreciate).

However, the city's oppressive humidity, my cramped apartment's serious shortcomings on the air conditioning front and, not least, the lack of a TV for our Simpsons-fixated threesome, dictated that we get out of town to somewhere with hot and cold running cable.

Well, if truth be told, the fact of the matter is that I was ambushed, bushwhacked, entrapped by a tenacious tweenage posse. I returned to the apartment one night, after slaving all day in Kellogg's air-conditioned confines, to discover that my darling daughters had staged a coup d'etat. Clearly, a lynching was in the offing—"How do you tie a hangman's noose, daddy?"—and despite my pompous protestations that (a) I am the pater familias around here, (b) you're on your holidays girls, now stop complaining, and (c) sure it's only 95 degrees and 100 per cent humidity, our sans culottes weren't prepared to brook any opposition. A tourist brochure was shoved under my nose.

"We're going to Wisconsin Dells, daddy. The biggest water park in the world is there. We can stay at the Great Wolf Lodge. It's got giant-screen TV. It's got air conditioning. It's got room service. It's got a talking moose."

"A talking moose," I reply, "now you're talking. Just set aside the lariat, girls, put away the electrodes, turn off the brazier, and release the ravenous rat. I'm sure we can sort this out amicably. The basic problem, dear hearts, is that it's four hours drive away, we'll have to rent a car and daddy has an issue with rentals. It's a Salt Lake City thing. I don't like to talk about it. All I can say is that if they try to rent us a red Chevy I'm not getting into it, let alone driving the thing to Wisconsin Dells."

"Mummy can drive."

"Mummy doesn't like driving in America, sweet peas. And, anyway, she doesn't want to stay in a tacky theme hotel."

"Actually, I'd like to see a bit of the country," Linda chipped in. "The water park looks quite nice. The moose sounds like fun. The resort has a retro flavor, moreover. There might be an article in it for you."

Waterpark and wannabe wapiti aside, that woman certainly knows how to press the right buttons. "An article, you say? It's retro, is it? Start packing, girls, we're on our way to Wisconsin Dells!"

Appearances to the contrary, fellow workaholics, you can rest assured that I struggled manfully all the way. In addition to the aforementioned *Grease* gambit, I tried the "You call this countryside?" routine, as we slid past serried ranks of Taco Bells, Motel Sixes, and telecommunications masts. I even attempted humor ("The cell phone crop must be doing well this year"), outrage ("What a rip off, toll booths every five miles!"), irony ("Flat, isn't it; there must be a hill here somewhere") and, when all else failed, a last-ditch appeal to their better natures ("Daddy's back is very sore and driving for four hours solid isn't good for him").

"Wisconsin Dells next exit," announced by ever-sympathetic companion of fifteen unforgettable years.

And, suddenly, there it was before us. In all its polystyrene splendor. UPVC as far as the eye could see. Here, the Camelot Hotel, a medieval fortress painstakingly constructed from the finest phony stone. There, an interwar gas station, with what looks like all too contemporary prices. Right over there, the Desert Star Cineplex, a retro rococo picture palace in the style of a Moorish citadel. Just beyond that, the Great Wolf Lodge—hey, that's us!—a magnificent monument to the local polypropylene logging industry.

Transfixed by this ersatz architectural abundance, I suggest to my accompanying aesthetes that we cruise through the town itself before checking in to our bogus arboreal abode. They agreed enthusiastically and we drive on into the deep dark heart of retrogeddon.

Well, what can I say? The only word to describe it is cheesy. Kraft Cheese Slices cheesy. Spray Can Cheese cheesy, with CFCs to go. Festering cheese at the back of the fridge cheesy. Cheese, I gather, is very big in Wisconsin and Wisconsin Dells is Cheeseville central. It is the beating, if sclerotic, heart of cheese country. The land that polyunsaturates forgot.

Actually, I'm very fond of cheese and cheesy holiday resorts are strangely compelling. Las Vegas, Atlantic City, Coney Island, Blackpool. Wherever. There's something sad, something shabby, something seen-better-days about them that appeals to you despite yourself. That's nostalgia, I suppose. Not personal nostalgia, obviously, since one has no experience of such places when they were in their pomp, if they ever were. It's more akin to collective nostalgia, a poignant sense that these are places where celebrities, shows, fads, fashions, and the canons of good taste come to die. The elephant's graveyard of the entertainments industry. The bottom rung of the showbiz ladder. Where stars fall to earth. Where the limelight finally fades. Where oblivion beckons.

Welcome to Wisconsin Dells!

The girls, as you can imagine, were on cloud nine by this stage. Stereotypical tweenagers, who seem to spend their entire allowances on cheap cosmetics and even cheaper costume jewelry, they were in raptures as tatopolis unfurled before them. Granted, this invites the somewhat unwelcome possibility that my existential angst has more to do with lost youth than the tackiness of the attractions. But I don't want to go there. I'm not too keen on plunging into the abyssal depths of Wisconsin Dells, either. However, a pop's gotta do. . . .

In a nutshell, me hearties, Wisconsin Dells is the full fathom nine of noisomeness, a fetid aquaretroscape of the first water. On your left, Noah's Ark, the largest waterpark in America (let me guess, the "guests" go in two-by-two?). On your right, a full-sized replica of the Trojan Horse surmounting an Ancient Greek go-cart circuit (Priam, presumably, provided the blueprints). Straight ahead, an almost Aztec watersplash and lazy river (so glad they've given up those gory human sacrifices). Next to that, a Jurassic themed crazy golf course (and they thought it was a comet that decimated the dinosaurs—evidently it was an errant nine iron). Coming right up, an historical triple-header: Tommy Bartlett's Robot World, a museum of the Space Program (experience the future as it used to be); H.H. Bennett's interactive photo studio (use space age technology to see the past in 3D); and, Paul's Famous Fossil Dig, where artifacts from all over the world can be unearthed for free. Includes real dinosaur bones (extracted, I'll be bound, from the tar pit hazards at Jurassic Crazy Golf).

Never let it be said, however, that Wisconsin Dells is lacking in class or ignores its aesthetic obligations. Apart from the world-renowned cuisine of Paul Bunyan's Cook Shanty and the Cheese Factory Pig Out, the resort boasts an authentic Mesoamerican temple complex (containing Ripley's *Believe It or Not*), a graceful, bougainvillea-garlanded neocolonial mansion (haunted, naturally), Wisconsin's very own Grand Ole Opry (with adjoining gift shop—sorry, "antique barn"), and a "genuine" Hibernian hotel, the Shamrock (does it give discounts to little people, I wonder). There's even an attraction entitled Adventures in Time—located immediately adjacent to Mass Panic—where one can experience the journey of ten lifetimes in ten minutes. But why bother? Driving through the retro resort is more than sufficient. It'll put years on you and takes a lot longer than the ride. Unfortunately.

Enraptured, the kids have already shortlisted the attractions they plan to patronize and it looks as though we'll be in residence for the next three months. Even though we've only got three days. Ever educational, I intimate that instead of wasting time on ersatz log flumes, we really ought to take in a boat trip around the Upper and Lower Dells, since that's what the resort is famous for. This suggestion, needless to say, had hardly set sail for itinerary harbor before it was scuttled by the submariners in the back seat. As the alternative uses of our precious time started to surface at a rate of knots and sibling rivalry kicked in, I was forced—in an unfortunate echo of that fateful day at the kindergarten—to insist on a spell of silent running until we checked in at the Great Wolf Lodge. So, we turned around and swam back against the tide of faux flotsam, gimcrack jetsam, and retroscaped attractions. The Fab Fifties, Live! (happy days, more *Grease*); Storybook Gardens (help Hiawatha find Bo Peep's sheep behind the Gingerbread House); and, of all things, a zoological themed crazy golf emporium (Tiger Woods the star attraction, perhaps?).

By the time our P.T. Cruiser had sidled under the *porte-cochère* of the inestimable Great Wolf Lodge, I was suffering from an aesthetic equivalent of the bends. However, my hopes for a period of gentle decompression were dashed by the monstrosity we'd booked ourselves into. The grandiloquent lobby was a full four stories of almost-aged sham-sequoia. Its fake field-stone-clad walls were judiciously sprinkled with phony trophies—stuffed wolf, stuffed moose, stuffed bison, stuffed beaver, stuffed taxidermist. The central area, moreover, was tastefully decorated with painted polyurethane totem poles, bronzealike statuettes of bald eagles, early Ikea sofas and armchairs, and, inevitably, a glass-sided high-speed elevator, as used for generations by the local Native Americans.

Happily, however, we arrived at the perfect moment—or so the check-in clerk told us—when the talking moose head was about to say a few words of welcome to bright-eyed guests and bushy-tailed employees alike. Keen to hear the ruminant's pearls of primeval wisdom, we joined the expectant throng and waited for the great antlered head to break the profound silence. Well, would you credit it, the critter addressed us in his native tongue! True, there was a touch of Elk in its inflections and I'm sure I detected some Bambi in his diphthongs, but it's gratifying to hear Moose spoken as it was in days of yore. Such traditions should be carefully maintained, I firmly believe. Warming to his welcoming task, the mighty mammal—the Oracle of Disney—then burst into song. My knowledge of the reindeer repertoire is somewhat limited, you understand. Nonetheless, I'm fairly sure the critter owed much to fellow Wisconsinite, Lawrence Welk, though there might've been a soupçon of off-key off-Broadway show tune in there as well. Still, it could have been a lot worse. An a cappella rendition of "There's a Moose Loose About the Hoose" would've been too much to bear.

After all the excitement, we repaired to our palatial suite with its breathtaking view over the raging I-90—listen to the thunder of 18–wheelers, thrill to the roar of SUVs—which was interrupted only by the mysterious undulations of the ancient ceremonial air conditioning plant. But at least it had the basics, room service and eighty channels of cable TV, which was more than enough to make the girls deliriously happy. I only wish I could say the same. Regrettably, our mattress was filled with particularly knotty offcuts of a giant redwood and a sleepless night ensued.

Next morning, still groggy from my night on the logs, I staggered around the lobby in search of a cup of coffee, while the kids were getting ready for Great Wolf's "70,000 sq ft of indoor and outdoor waterparks!" A swimming pool with plastic appendages, basically. Fortunately, a traditional Bear Trapper's Coffee Stand stood sentinel in the corner, complete with the comestibles that kept the mountain men going when the going got tough— donuts, bagels, muffins, cinnebuns, and an ice bucket brimming with sodas and fruit juices. With vittles like that, it's no wonder the West was won. Clearly, it rolled over and couldn't get up again. Now I know what put the middle into Middle America.

However, when in Rome. "A Howling Wolf double decaff and a Grizzly Cinnebun to go, my stout fellow," I requested politely. The attendant looked at me as if I had two heads and, to be honest, the way I felt I could well have had. Maybe I'm supposed to make my request in Moose. Maybe I've committed a terrible social gaffe by not ordering extra cheese on top. Maybe calling her a stout fellow wasn't a smart move. Maybe it's a self-service operation.

"It's self-service, sir," she said curtly. D'oh. I grabbed a plastic cup, opened the spigot and, while waiting for the fabulous fountain to fill my eco-friendly Styrofoam receptacle, I reached over for one of the frosted cinnebuns perched on top of the elaborate display. Not a good move in my groggy condition. I caught the edge of the platter and a cascade of cinnebuns, donuts, and muffins plunged into the half-melted ice bucket below. The attendant looked at me, aghast. Luckily, I have a quip for every occasion. "Dunkin donuts?" I ventured. Silence. "At least the bagels didn't take a bath." Not a flicker. "How much does all that come to?" Works every time.

Desperate for somewhere to hide my embarrassment, which was witnessed by a snickering line of holidaymakers waiting to be seated in the adjoining Loose Moose restaurant, I had no alternative but to make my way to the outdoor water park. Ordinarily, I don't participate in poolside activity of any kind, preferring to read a good book somewhere while the family splash around to their hearts' content. However, there was no alternative on this occasion. Taken aback, the girls erroneously assumed that daddy was coming to join them for the first time ever, but I explained that I was only planning to watch. You must appreciate that my legs haven't been exposed to sunlight for decades now, let alone revealed to innocent bystanders. Consequently, they have acquired a translucent hue—somewhat akin to an Aryan albino in a snowstorm—which might prove unsettling to unaccompanied minors. Anyway, I commandeered a lounger and, denied access to Derrida's *Of Grammatology* (which was back in the room, which necessitated a voyage through the lobby, which would be bulging with sated, still smirking, diners exiting the Loose Moose Restaurant), I decided to forgo the pleasure.

After about an hour or so of idle daydreaming in a cozy spot overlooking the torrential I-90, whilst listening to the dulcet tones of Van Morrison on the poolside PA, I came over all funny. It was a strange sensation I haven't felt since before going to college, when I bummed around the Greek Islands for a year, worked incessantly on my tan and generally did nothing except sell blood to keep body and soul together. I have a very rare blood group and plasma purchasers in the eastern Mediterranean went crazy for it. As I recall, I pretty much lived on a diet of iron tablets in order to maintain the requisite blood count. Every so often I'd make a well-paid deposit in the nearest plasma repository, hoping against hope that they wouldn't seize the opportunity to drain me completely and dispose of the empty vessel. Those were the days!

But what, I hear you ask, was the strange sensation that swept over me while sprawling beside the pool? Anemia? Constipation? Hepatitis B? All of the above? No, amigos, it was much, much stranger than that. I think they call it "relaxation." The affliction, admittedly, may have been anointed with a new, quasi-medical, media-friendly, politically correct name since last time I felt it. Activity Deficit Disorder, perhaps. However, I'm pretty sure it's what we old fogeys used to call relaxation. And, do you know something, I actually started to enjoy it, shameful though this is to confess. So much so, that I foolishly agreed to take Linda and the girls to Circus World Museum in nearby Baraboo. Apparently, there's a P.T. Barnum connection and, as this can be considered "work," I had no trouble justifying the side trip to myself. Pathetic, I know, but I was determined not to relax for a moment.

Well, we drove out along Highway 12, past the Dells Mining Company ("Mine for pleasure, take home a treasure"), the OK Corral Riding Stables (with its very own Boot Hill—for troublesome tenderfoots, no doubt), and the humongous Ho Chunk Native American owned casino (looks as though the Chippewa have come a long way since Historyland). After several wrong turns and a few kindly kindergartenesque words with my geographically challenged navigator, Circus World loomed before us. I was expecting a pathetic, fly-blown, down-at-heel exhibition—the circus, let's be honest, has seen better days—but the former winter quarters of Ringling Brothers Barnum and Bailey had obviously been refurbished at enormous expense. It boasted a brand new visitors' center, an impressive circus wagon restoration facility and a beautifully appointed research and development complex. The exhibit hall, a technicolor riot of chromolithographed circus posters and Ringling Bros memorabilia, was worth the entrance fee alone.

It couldn't last, of course, and the circus grounds themselves were as depressingly dilapidated as I'd feared. We caught the end of the majestic Street Parade, a pathetic procession of disgruntled elephants, gruntled giraffes, listless llamas, and next-stop-the-glue-factory Lippizaners, all ambling wearily around a time-grooved circuit to the enthusiastic, if incongruous, ululations of a circus pipe organ. They disappeared off in the general direction of the Big Top. Next performance in one hour! Videotaping of the show prohibited! Anticipation unbound!!

To quell the girls' mounting excitement, we filled them up with hotdogs and coke. There's nothing like carbonated MSG to calm the savage breast. The seating area, unfortunately, seemed to be the natural habitat of a gaggle of barnacle geese. Now, for all I know, barnacle geese may be a protected species and, given our surroundings, they might well have been a specially trained flock of the fuckers. But their principal talent, as far as I could make out, was shitting like it was going out of style. There was goose poop everywhere and, although the attendants hosed down the tables every fifteen minutes or so, that was more than enough time for a mountain of goose guano to accumulate on every conceivable surface. The girls, fortunately, decided to give the condiments a miss on this occasion.

We bolted down the wieners, made our way to the circus wagon pavilion (nice building, no display), checked out the "show train," which comprised the marketing epicenter of old-time traveling circuses (locked), worked our way through the animal menagerie (feed the camels, only $5 a bag!), peeped into the side shows of the imitation midway (hey, an exhibition of P.T. Barnum's greatest hits—General Tom Thumb, Chang and Eng, the Cardiff Giant et al.) and ended up in the Big Top just prior to the big show. The big audience must have numbered all of fifty people, some of whom had paid $10 extra for front row seats. I settled down for forty-five minutes of mortification. The ringmaster materialized and gave immediate notice that he couldn't carry a tune. This was going to be a nightmare.

How wrong can you be! The troupe had clearly graduated from the former state circuses of eastern Europe and were gradually working their way up to the dizzy heights of Siegfried and Roy. You gotta start somewhere, I guess. All things considered, they were brilliant, quite brilliant. The clowns were funny. The acrobats elastic. The trapeze artists daring. The bare back riders brave. The elephants unforgettable. The small but not so beautifully formed audience was ecstatic and even flinty-hearted skeptics such as myself were forced to admit afterwards that it was great fun. In fact, I almost bought a bunch of circus-themed collectibles in the gift shop—sorry, "antiques emporium"—on the way out. Fortunately, I resisted. I was working, you see.

Driving back to base camp, I suggested in another moment of weakness that we take in a late-evening trip around the lakes. According to the brochure, the "Original Wisconsin Ducks" circumnavigated the Upper and Lower Dells in reconditioned P45s, the wartime landing craft. We could squeeze through the steep canyon walls of Black Hawk Gorge; plunge down Roller Coaster Hill; rediscover the lost city of Newport; hide away in secluded Fern Dell; and finally splash down into the Wisconsin River. It was more than a tour. It was an expedition. It was the ultimate off road experience. It was one part boat, three parts time machine!

But my circus-sated prima donnas were having none of it, since the Simpsons were top of their nocturnal agenda, though I could always forage for chips, dips, sodas, and analogous necessities if I really wanted to do my bit. The Ducks were outlawed the next day, too, when our breakfast-time committee meeting in the flagrantly fake Loose Moose Bar and Grill unanimously decided that Noah's Ark was the afternoon's principal port of call. Linda, what's more, wanted to "take a trip back in time" on the Mid-Continent Railway, an old-fashioned steam train ride that plied a former branch of the Chicago and Northwestern Line. So that was that. Whatever happened to patriarchy?

The Railway Museum was situated in North Freedom, which necessitated another drive past the adobe-esque Ho Chunk casino. The parking lot was full, as before. Dells Bells! At this time of the morning?! Either Wisconsin-ites are addicted to gambling or the casino supplies complimentary cheese nibbles to its patrons. Then again, the owners might be playing that old commercial con trick from the early days of shopping centers, when employees' cars were parked out front to give the false impression that the place was buzzin. Retromarketing rides again.

Ho Chunk notwithstanding, the ten mile drive to North Freedom through the rolling countryside on a beautifully sunny morning was really rather blissful, I have to confess. It was spoiled only by the overhead telephone and electricity wires, which are sadly ubiquitous in the United States and detract considerably from the natural grandeur of the landscape. Haven't these people heard of underground cables? Are they some kind of retro signifier of the Great Depression? Yes folks, the rural electrification program has reached this neck of the woods. Yee-haw!

Still, North Freedom itself was pure *Last Picture Show*, a one-stop, one-horse, once-upon-a-time small town. Or designed to look that way, at least. The museum was on the other side of the tracks—appropriately enough—and, after purchasing our tickets at the "authentic" depot, taking in the "lovingly restored" tool house, watchtower, coach shed, and water tank, and contributing generously to the historical society's latest restoration project, an Art Nouveau passenger car designed by Edward Colonna, we were all fired up for our experience of "the sights, sounds, and cinders of a bygone era."

Except that the North Michigan Special turned out to be a diesel locomotive from the 1950s, the carriages needed quite a bit of work to get them back to the glory days of the golden age of rail, and the fifty minute round trip to Quartzite Lake involved a fearsome top speed of five miles per hour. To put it another way, it was all of two miles there and two miles back. It didn't even have a loop, since we had to dismount at the end of the line and wait patiently while the diesel performed a pirouette prior to recoupling.

Nevertheless, it was a nice day, they gave us the full "all aboard" treatment, threw in several excited blasts on the steam whistle and the constant clanging of the railroad crossing bells sounded like a herd of Alpine cattle had hit town and were ready to party. The uniformed attendants, what's more, swaggered through the cars, clicking tickets, disbursing safety instructions, and providing a wry running commentary on the passing countryside. "Hold tight, folks," cried Lou the engineer, "we're about to take a rickety wooden bridge over the roiling Swilley River!" which turned out to be a bone-dry drainage ditch. Okay, okay, it wasn't exactly Universal Studios. Lou's patter had clearly gone through a thousand and one iterations. But, it was enthusiastically delivered and highly enjoyable in an ironic, posttourist fashion. More enthusiastic still was his sales pitch for the authentic, the genuine, the original and best, the one and only Whistle Stop Ice Cream Shoppe in nearby North Freedom.

In lieu of lunch, we took Lou's advice and filled up at the Whistle Stop, an almost olde tyme soda fountain. I foolishly ordered a banana split, with all the trimmings. "We don't get much call for that," said the owner, Mrs. Lou. Having worked in catering, I suspect she means the ingredients haven't seen the light of day for several seasons now and have grown a bubonic beard in the meantime. Worse, as the show-stopping water slides of Noah's Ark were next on the agenda, I had a premonition that I'd be seeing the banana again before nightfall, to say nothing of the chocolate sauce topping. Silly boy. That's what happens when you relax your guard. Sloth costs.

Now, if you've ever read Umberto Eco's *Travels in Hyperreality*, you'll know he spent a lot of time traipsing up and down America's west coast in search of the perfect fake, the zenith of ersatz. Take it from me, fellow retronauts, he should have come to Wisconsin, Noah's Ark in particular. Far from being realer than real, as is normal with hyperreal environments, Noah's Ark is faker than fake. Horrorreality, so to speak. Apart from the names of the parking lots (Bear lot, Gator lot, Hippo lot, Ocelot) and occasional animal suited attendants, the theme park made virtually no attempt to embody its alleged Arkadian theme. It comprised, rather, a congeries of plastic tubes, some of which were open to the elements, some of which were completely enclosed, some of which were very steep, some of which were vertiginous, some of which were twisted, some of which were rock around the clock, and all of which were held together by a rickety spider's nest of scaffolding, supports, and staircases. Gulp.

At least the girls had found the promised land. They walked on water. They talked on water. They chewed gum on water. They even persuaded their pasty-legged pop to participate. The Flash Flood was first up, a 100-feet drop into a plunge pool, which sent a tsunami over those standing in line. I was soaked by the time we got on board, where we were joined by a bunch of heading-off-shift park employees, still in their animal costumes. Curiously absorbent animal costumes, it has to be said, since we had to help the sodden critters out of the car at the end. They weighed a ton! After that, I threw caution to the wind and, variously, floated gently along Adventure River, thundered down Black Thunder, lost myself in the curlicues of Bermuda Triangle, got swept up by Big Kahuna at the artificial beach and wave pool, and chickened out of the Point of No Return, a six-story plunge into what looked like a half-filled bucket of water. Shamefully, and much to my darling daughters' amusement, I screamed in the churning bowels of Dark Voyage, a happy family tube ride (screamed with excitement, I'll have you know). What's more, when the attendant at the top of Slidewinders asked if we were having fun yet, I was forced to reply in the affirmative. I even slept well that night, despite our lumpy, log-flumed mattress.

The fun continued next day at Denny's Classic Diner, where we break-fasted prior to driving back to Chicago. The restaurant was not only themed on fifties-style rock 'n' roll, but it was also themed on earlier incarnations of itself, Denny's restaurants from the 1950s. In addition to the classic cars parked outside—the P.T. Cruiser fit perfectly—and the polyplaster statues of Elvis, Marilyn, Marlon, and James Dean which guarded the chrome-paneled, neon-fringed entrance, every aspect of the interior was an hom-age to yesterdenny's. All sorts of corporate memorabilia, including framed menus, photographs, and newspaper clippings, adorned the walls. A Wurlitzer jukebox stood in the corner. Red leatherette banquettes lined the edge of the dining area. The serving staff were dressed in replica uniforms and the bill of fare was a throwback to the time before McDonald's be-strode the universe. Eggs over easy. All day breakfast. Gravy and potatoes. Hashbrowns . . . whatever they are.

It was completely fake, of course. The jukebox was a nonplaying imita-tion. The ambient rock 'n' roll was a Muzak Corporation compilation. The seating arrangements, catering equipment, and payment facilities were all fully computerized. The chrome-edged, neon-tipped interior bore no relationship whatsoever to any Denny's restaurant in existence heretofore. The framed memorabilia were probably manufactured all of six months previously in the firm's fake memorabilia factory. The uniformed waitresses were wearing pseudo polyester uniforms and, I presume, faux Corfam sneakers.

Yet for all that, it was a good fake, an unself-conscious fake, a marvelous metafake. The ultimate retroscape, in short, one that will no doubt serve as the model for Denny's Classic Classic Diner, a fast food format due to be rolled out during the forthcoming nostalgia boom of 2050, or thereabouts.

I sat there, sipping a bottomless cup of ordinary Joe, watching the girls tuck into archipelagos of pancakes and waffles set in a shimmering sea of syrup. They talked excitedly about the experiences of the past few days. Pop's shriek. Goose poop. Musical Moose. The Simpsons. Pop's yelp. I noticed they're starting to speak in American accents, just like they did several summers ago in California. A vision of retrosyntaxscapes loomed before me. But what the hell. This is nice. A great good place, of sorts. Derrida can wait. I'm a very lucky man. Ersatz or not, I'm glad I came.

"Okay, girls, it's time to go. Chicago here we come. Don't forget your seat belts. Hey, what about some music? All together now, "Summer lovin,' had me a blast. Summer lovin,' happened so fast. . . .""

10

Time Travels in Retrospace

Unpacking my Grandfather's Trunk—Some Introspective Recollections of Life on the Brule

Morris B. Holbrook

Sweet Dreams

Once upon a time, when I was a young boy, I had trouble falling asleep one night and asked my father what I could do to get some rest. Being a physician, my dad knew all sorts of pharmacological agents with potent soporific capabilities to invoke the powers of Morpheus. For example, he kept a supply of Phenobarbital on hand for service in such situations. But on this particular occasion, he was in a more holistic frame of mind. He told me that when he could not get to sleep, he would lie very still and think about something wonderful. He would fantasize and form mental images of some scene that he enjoyed tremendously, creating pictures in his mind of being in that place and doing something that made him very happy. So I asked my Dad, "What place should I think about that will help me feel like that." And he replied, "Well, I don't know what will work for you; but in my mind's eye, I envision a beautiful sunny day on the Brule River; and I'm in a canoe; and I'm casting a fly onto a dark pool under a tree; and I'm hoping to catch a big brook trout."

Brule, the Book

The Brule River—a seventy-mile stream in northern Wisconsin that begins thirty-five miles southeast of Duluth and winds its way northwest, via a series of rapids, still waters, and interspersed lakes, until it empties into Lake Superior—is the woodsy retreat where we spent three weeks every summer during the time allotted to my parents for exercising their privilege of using the family owned Gitche Gumee Lodge. If you look up the map of the Brule River State Forest on the Web site of the Wisconsin Department of Natural Resources (www.dnr.state.wi.us), you will find a constellation of geographic locations that, frankly, most people have never heard of—a thin black line that begins at Solon Springs, winds northward past Lake Nebagamon, passes the road to Iron River and then the town of Brule itself, and finally reaches Lake Superior somewhere east of Port Wing. The name Brule comes from the Chippewa word *Wis-a-ko-da*—meaning "burnt pines"—which the French explorers translated as *Bois Brulé*. These are not exactly household names for fancy locales on the fashionable resort scene. But, to us, Brule or Brulé (pronounced "Broolie" for those who want to be a bit pretentious) was the place where city worries ceased and summer adventures began—adventures in the forest and on the ineffably picturesque tree-lined stream itself.

My grandfather, Arthur Tenney Holbrook (ATH), presided over all this during most of the time I spent on the Brule. Born in 1870, he was an elderly gentleman of eighty by the time I first remember him, circa 1950. In these years, widowed and retired from his medical practice, he would move from Milwaukee to the river and stay for the entire summer—receiving visitors, like us, with an implicit understanding that we were blessed to enjoy the privilege of sharing the sacred territory over which he reigned with little official authority but with a whole lot of old-fashioned charisma.

ATH was a genuinely outgoing man—a great talker, a wonderful story-teller, a deliciously humorous raconteur—who commanded the attention of anyone within earshot. He always imbibed exactly one two-ounce shot of Old Crow eighty-six-proof bourbon just before dinner—no more, no less—and during this cocktail hour on the screened porch overlooking the water below, he would hold court and regale a porch full of fascinated listeners, who had often come from miles around, with his tales of earlier days on the Brule. Long ago, he had picked up the habit of "Fletcherizing" his food—that is, chewing each tiny mouthful a hundred times—a practice that routinely added hours to the meal at dinner time, all the more because his chewing was exceeded only by his talking. We listened politely—half enchanted, half aware that we were hearing history recounted firsthand.

This history involved an aura of respect and admiration for the river and everything in it—especially the rainbow, brook, and brown trout (well, not so much the browns, but that's a long story). Consistent with this ethos, each river-related object had a special name. The house was the "lodge." The surrounding yard was the "Gitche Gumee Camp Grounds." The living room was the "council room." A fishing pole was a "rod." A boat was a "canoe"; its oar, a "paddle"; its rear, the "stern"; its front, the "bow"; its sides, the "gunwales." You did not paddle up the river, you "poled upstream"—using a long, heavy, smooth wooden pole with a rounded metal pike at its end and standing in the stern of the canoe to practice a nearly balletic controlled strength of movement that few mortals have ever tried, let alone mastered. One false move and thé canoe would crash on a rock just below the water's surface. One slip and you would fall clumsily into the ice-cold waters of the spring-fed stream. How could one fail to be impressed by such ceremonious rituals and such liturgical jargon? How could one escape intimidation by the river's challenges? How could one not feel the soul-satisfying sense of mastery that came from catching the big rainbow trout or poling the canoe up one of the rapids or—gasp—The Falls? Yes, my grandfather loved the Brule.

So much did ATH love the Brule that he wrote a legendary book about it, self-published in 1949 and titled *From the Log of a Trout Fisherman*. As indicated by its title, this book describes my grandfather's love affair with the Brule River in general and portrays his fondness for fishing in particular. In the *Log*, ATH evinces an inextinguishable eye for detail—an inveterate habit of noting and reporting the most subtle nuances of what I would call "consumption experiences." And what fascinating consumption experiences they are. I have seen burly men grow tearful when reminiscing about the first time they read the *Log* and lamenting their inability to get a copy of this rare and long-out-of-print treasure. Finally—in 1983, a hundred years after my grandfather's first visit to the River—members of the Winneboujou Club at Brule reproduced an additional 250 copies so that many neighboring folks were able to read or reread ATH's recollections from long ago. Herein, they found the unforgettable poetry of ATH's limpid prose style, to which I referred at some length when I began my chapter on "The Log of a Consumer Researcher" for the book on the Consumer-Behavior Odyssey edited by Russ Belk under the title *Highways and Buyways*:

> Tucked into the top drawer of a large desk near the window of [the] council room, my family kept a book called *The Log*. Every day or so, my dad or grandfather would take pen in hand and, in a meticulous version of his best physician's scrawl, would enter a record in this logbook. Such entries contained the names of all guests and visitors, the number and sizes of trout caught on the river that day, the magnitudes and durations of significant storms, the dates and times of canoe-poling feats or sports-related accomplishments, and any other informational tidbits that he chose to immortalize in this fashion. Sometimes, lists of numbers would appear in the log; sometimes, passages of well-crafted prose. . . . One year, when I was about

ten, something extraordinary appeared under our Christmas tree. It was a book written by my grandfather, based on accounts he had entered into the log over a lifetime of trips to the Brule River and published at his own expense, complete with photographs. . . . His introspective, deeply personal narrative provided the first quasi-phenomenological portrayal of a lived world that I had ever read. Given that it came from a man who had studied under William James at Harvard, I ought not to have been surprised by its eloquence. But, in those days, I did not know such things. I only knew that it felt good to read and that, someday, I would like to try something similar.

The Photographs

After my father passed away in the early 1990s, my mom stayed for a couple of years at their house in Milwaukee and then decided to sell this home and move year-round to Sarasota. When the time came for this exodus to Florida, I helped clear out the attic and basement by claiming anything that I wanted to take back for storage at our already overcrowded apartment in New York City. Given our space constraints, I had to be very selective about what I kept. The number one things I refused to throw away—as is so often true of people who must make decisions about what material objects are worth keeping—were the family photographs in general and those taken by my grandfather ATH in particular.

It turns out that ATH began taking photos in roughly 1939 and continued until the mid-1950s, leaving behind one metal filing box of black-and-white negatives and several trays of Kodachrome slides, all meticulously labeled with details concerning dates, places, and people. Somehow, he had latched onto a thirty-five millimeter Leica circa 1939. I speculate that my father brought it back from his trip to Austria for medical studies in Vienna. For the next fifteen years, ATH went around snapping pictures of everything in sight that he happened to like. I would guess that there are about fifteen hundred black-and-white negatives and roughly half that many color transparencies. My first impulse was to get contact sheets made of the negatives, choose the best, and reproduce larger versions from the cream of the crop. However, one trial run with the "professional" services offered by our local camera center convinced me that such a strategy would lead to our immediate bankruptcy. I have therefore pursued the much slower route of personally scanning each precious negative, cropping-retouching-and-adjusting as needed, and transferring the resulting enormous data files to 650–MB CD-R discs. I have recently finished my first pass through the black-and-white negatives and have produced sixteen CDs—yes, Virginia, that's roughly ten gigabytes—containing over 700 black-and-white photos that will serve as a primary source of material for the present chapter.

Naturally, these photos represent many scenes that do not bear directly on the theme at hand—pictures of trips to North Carolina, shots of friends bowling on the green at Dunedin, photos of the fiftieth and sixtieth college reunions at Harvard, images of senior citizens playing golf, pictorial evocations of blizzards at the big house in Milwaukee, and such. I hope to be delving into these photographs for years to come, with little chance of reaching the end. But, for now, our story concerns the topic that appears most frequently in the ATH photos—namely, pictures of scenes, events, and people found at the Brule River in northern Wisconsin, a place that ATH created and re-created not only in his vivid prose but also on thirty-five millimeter film.

Method

Based on ATH's *Log* and his related photographs, this chapter presents a retrospective account of life on the Brule, viewed as a retroscape rich in the sorts of leisure-oriented consumption experiences of interest to those concerned with marketing theory. In this direction, I shall make use of an approach that I call *Subjective Personal Introspection* (SPI)—meaning that I ponder my own impressionistic apperceptions and appreciations of my life as a consumer participating in the consumption experiences that characterize the human condition and then tell the generally indifferent world what I have learned via this path of SPI-based self-discovery. In the present case I looked long and deeply at the ATH photographs, reread my grandfather's book, thought about this stuff, . . . a lot . . . , and dwelled on my most profound recollections of Life on the Brule River—recollections that I know to be accurate in the sense that they are evoked so strongly by the ATH-produced memorabilia and have the self-affirming property, philosophically speaking, of being identical by definition with what I recall.

Nonetheless, I do rely on two assumptions that provide methodological underpinnings for the introspections pursued here.

First, I assume that ATH took photographs primarily of what he liked, what made him happy, what brought him joy—the people, places, things, and activities he deeply cared about—specifically, the consumption experiences that mattered most to him. One often sees this in his manner of framing pictures. Many of his shots are either unusable or in need of heroic cropping because he had the habit of putting his target of admiration at dead center regardless of the effect this practice had on the pictorial composition. In other words, he appears to have cared little about the refinements of visual aesthetics in his photographs and far more about capturing consumption experiences that brought him pleasure. These he placed at the most central location, oblivious to the overall visual impact. For example, his love for my grandmother Bertha Andrews Holbrook (BAH or Bertie) manifests itself in his penchant for anchoring her in the middle of his photos, even if she was standing at the edge of a group of people, some of whom were chopped in half or omitted entirely in the off-balance array of bodies that ended up in the final lopsided image.

Second, I assume that my own introspections resonate so strongly with the prose and photos of my grandfather because ATH has, in effect, captured the essence of my own SPI-based recollections. This is true partly because he was there (shooting film) when I was there (as a young boy), during the most formative stages of my developing consciousness. And it is true partly because—as the figurative head of our family and impresario over our consumption experiences on the Brule—ATH instilled in me many of the same sensibilities that he himself brought to his enjoyment of the river. In short, I find such resonance in his prose and photos, I believe, because these artifacts reflect aspects of my own reconstructed memories that he had himself so strongly influenced.

Retroscaping the Brule-Based Consumption Experience: Ten Essay Pieces

If "landscaping" refers to the alteration of real estate to make it more aesthetically pleasing, then *retroscaping* might connote the re-creation of place-related memories to bring out their inner beauty. Such retroscapes hinge on consumption experiences and on the places—whether retail outlets, planned communities, tourist destinations, arenas for public events, resort hotels, or other consumer-populated venues—where such consumption experiences arise. In the case of the Brule River, we speak of tourism in general and of a travel destination—albeit a travel destination known to only a select handful of tourists—in particular.

This specific example of the tourism industry—to reduce its numinous nature to the crassest possible commercial language—did very little, if any, advertising for itself. Rather its mystique spread primarily by word of mouth, handed down as privileged information among the disparate members of just a few scattered families who came to the river from Minneapolis or St. Paul, from Duluth, from Ashland, from Milwaukee, from Detroit, and from various other locations spread around the Midwest. Once, President Calvin Coolidge had his Summer White House on the Brule. Presidents Ulysses S. Grant, Grover Cleveland, Herbert Hoover, and Dwight Eisenhower all fished there. But mostly, the river's existence remained a closely guarded secret.

ATH remarks that "It was our unwritten law that the Brule region was never to be advertised by us or indiscriminately recommended" (*Log*, p. 70).

Working with my grandfather's photographs and book, I have surveyed the consumption experiences associated with this secret place and have developed a list of what I believe are the *ten key themes* that characterize my most vivid SPI-based ATH-inspired recollections of river-related consumer behavior. These include: (1) canoeing; (2) fishing; (3) swimming; (4) eating and picnicking; (5) clothing; (6) cribbage; (7) music; (8) natural beauty; (9) smoking; and (10) photography. In what follows, I shall describe these ten key themes briefly—with occasional documentation from the *Log* and with a photograph to illustrate each.

Canoeing

When most people think of canoeing, they think of paddling a small aluminum boat at summer camp on Lake Cumangetwet when they were twelve years old. But on the Brule, canoes and canoeing have been raised to a high art capable of making strong, courageous, grown men cry. The current of the river varies from near zero in the lakes to warp speed in the most challenging rapids. And the only way to navigate the stream is to use a long pole to push a canoe up it and then float back down—or vice versa if you are the sort of foolish person who likes to play now and pay later.

But if hitting a curve ball is the hardest thing to do in sports—as journalists claim and as Michael Jordan appears to have demonstrated beyond reasonable doubt—then poling a canoe must have a secure grip on second place. You stand in the stern, hoist the long pole high in the air with one hand, throw it down vertically through the fingers of the other hand onto the river bottom, grab it in the middle, climb up it in a hand-over-hand motion, do the raise-throw-climb thing over and over again, and somehow try to keep the bow pointed up the center of a narrow channel between the sharp rocks on either side. You do not want to scrape the rocks because the eighteen-foot canoe has been meticulously hand-made out of lengthy cedar strips by a legendary local hero named Joe Lucius. It weighs hundreds of pounds, qualifies as an irreplaceable antique, and is worth considerably more than a used Volvo.

In the latter connection, I might mention that—one Christmas, during the mid-1950s, when I was about fourteen years old—my grandfather gave me one of his old canoes as a present. It was, at that time, fifty years old and had been bought from its builder Joe Lucius for thirty dollars in 1905 (*Log*, p. 81). My dad had it reconditioned, and we used it successfully for many years. Today, after subsequent refurbishings and now close to a hundred years in age, it is still in use on the river. My mother sold it recently for $5,000—167

Exhibit 10.1   Arthur Tenney Holbrook, in his late seventies, poling a canoe upstream

times what ATH paid Joe Lucius for it in 1905—about a 5.5 percent rate of return, compounded annually, and not too shabby a financial performance compared with that of (say) the typical dot.com company.

To repeat, the challenges of navigating the river in such a vessel are formidable. When I was a boy, only about nine people in the world could negotiate these navigational challenges with any degree of aplomb. Five of these were Indian guides from the Chippewa tribe. Three others were my grandfather, my father (the best there ever was), and me. Okay, so maybe I exaggerate. Maybe there were eleven people who could pole a canoe. But there are not so many Ojibwa guides around today; so the number has probably shrunk. And, okay, maybe I was not really all that talented at poling. But I have to make a place for myself in this particular retroscape, and I surely do remember my struggles to acquire this peculiarly recondite skill.

My father and a couple of the Native American guides could even pole up "The Falls"—so named because they put you in mind of Niagara. I did it once myself and lived to tell about it, but only because I had my dad in the bow to push us off every time I crashed the canoe into the riverbank—which was so often that it emerged looking as if a whale had been chewing on it. When I got to the top, I felt as if every fiber of my body had been put through a meat grinder.

Does this skill come in handy, you might be wondering, in facing the rest of life's challenges? Well, not really, I suppose. But I did triumph on one occasion when I went "punting" on the River Cam at Cambridge University and discovered that I was the only American who could propel a boat upstream without zigzagging from one side to the other or going around in circles. Tourism has its occasional minor victories. For me, this was one of the sweetest.

To capture all this, Exhibit 10.1 shows ATH at the stern of a canoe, expertly propelling the boat upstream. Even as a man approaching eighty years in age, he had not lost the form, learned as a boy from his own father, that he had subsequently passed on to his son, my dad, and from there to me.

Fishing

Further skills that every aspirant to the stature of River Rat on the Brule must acquire involve the art of fly fishing—any other mode of catching a trout being maligned by what ATH (neglecting to list worms, which are so far beneath contempt as literally to be unmentionable) describes as the "scorn of spinners, minnows, grasshoppers, chunks of meat, and any other lure but the fly" (*Log*, p. 57). Indeed, it is the ultimate put-down of President Calvin Coolidge when ATH recounts stories told about the chief executive by some of the Indian guides: "I have heard from them of his predilection for the 'Barnyard Hackle' or 'Hum Dinger,' as the lowly angle worm is locally yclept" (p. 105). (One does not encounter the word "yclept" very often, and what a wonderfully Chaucerian turn of phrase it doth provide.)

If poling a canoe is all about the carefully harnessed application of strength, casting a fly is all about a meticulously controlled delicacy of finesse. Even the appropriate knots for attaching fly to leader and leader to line are the subject for extended debate (p. 172): "I have a scrapbook collection of articles, clippings, diagrams, and pictures of knots recommended by anglers of note and amateurs, authors of books, writers in magazines, and pages from dealers' catalogues" and "have faithfully tried out practically all of them" (p. 172). And don't forget the sage advice on how one should care for one's snells (p. 175)—not to mention the glories of "good gut [never nylon] prop-

Exhibit 10.2   **Arthur Tenney Holbrook fishing from the bow of the Waboose, while Bertha Andrews Holbrook (BAH) watches and Ed Dennis holds the boat's position with the help of two snubbing poles**

erly cared for" (p. 176). In the *Log*, ATH goes into some detail on the retailers and brand names that supplied the equipment and tackle most favored by the serious fly fishers—names like Orvis, Weber, Spalding, Leonard, Hardy, or Ashaway (pp. 57–58, pp. 169 ff.)—many of them still around today.

But clearly, unlike this equipment and tackle for sale, the true art of fly fishing involves skills that cannot be bought for mere money but must instead be learned slowly and with infinite patience through long practice. Throw out the line as far as it will go (being careful not to get it caught on a branch, log, or other snag); slowly raise the tip while grabbing the line and pulling it in with your free hand in a sort of crab-like motion; when the tip gets to about eleven o'clock, flick it back, pause for a beat, and then throw it forward in such a way that the line runs out smoothly through your fingers, reaches full extension, and settles onto the water with not the tiniest hint of a perturbation. One could spend several lifetimes trying to master this particular craft, and my grandfather and father had achieved exalted levels of adroitness therein.

One could not possibly overemphasize the extent to which the ethos of fly fishing dominated Life on the Brule as we knew it. I could fish in this manner a little bit, but nowhere near so efficaciously as could my father, my grandfather before him, and my grandfather's father before that. And so I gradually gravitated toward preferring to guide the canoe, sitting in the stern and watching the incredibly skillful display unfolding before me. These men really knew how to catch trout—which is saying a lot because others of us could easily fish for an entire day or even for a week with nary a bite. It was all about understanding the mind of a fish, knowing where the creature would be hiding, and putting the fly in that exact location with optimal precision.

They did it with devout dedication. They did it with consummate artistry. But they did it for fun. Certainly, they caught innumerable fish—delicious brooks, leaping rainbows, slightly suspect German browns—that we all ate with great delectation. Sometimes the Brule fishermen threw back the trout they caught or fished with barbless hooks—the ultimate challenge to one's ability to land a big one. But statistics and numerical records also mattered to these sportsmen. During the summer of 1944, for example, ATH spent ninety-six days at Gitche Gumee, fished the river fifty-four times at an average of about seven hours per expedition, and caught 423 trout of legal size—263 brook, 114 brown, and 46 rainbows—for an average of 7.8 per day (pp. 178–79).

My grandfather fails to mention that during this long summer he fished for about 378 hours—roughly ten work weeks for the typical employee—pulling in about 1.1 fish per hour. We might add that—even making the generous assumptions that his catch averaged a half-pound per fish and that he paid his guide only ten dollars per day—inflating these expenses at the same rate that his canoes appreciated in value would place the cost of ATH's Brule trout in today's prices at $37.29 per pound. Some might find this a rather inefficient way to feed one's family.

I honestly think that nothing—I mean, nothing—made my male forebears happier than sitting in the bow of a canoe on a somewhat overcast and slightly windy day, inching upstream with an expert Chippewa guide in the stern, heading toward the picnic grounds in Big Lake where, with luck, we could enjoy a taste of the day's catch cooked to perfection as only an Ojibwa could cook it. Exhibit 10.2 captures ATH at such a moment, ensconced in the bow of his beloved Waboose, sitting comfortably but fishing intently, headed with all due deliberation toward a most agreeable lunch.

Swimming

The prevalent attitude toward swimming in the Brule River is: "Do it if you dare." The older residents—ATH, for example—considered the idea of vol-

Exhibit 10.3   **Two young boys splashing in the Brule River during the brief period before hypothermia sets in**

untarily immersing oneself in the Brule to verge on sheer madness. They knew that, spring fed, the river maintained a frigid temperature guaranteed to insure hypothermia after approximately seventeen seconds of exposure.

But some of us younger folks had not heard the news. Indeed, for some, submersion in the Brule constituted a sort of baptism—a trial not by fire but by freezing, a ritual dictated by the need to establish one's manhood and willingness to suffer for the sake of demonstrating masculine strength of character. Thus did I, as a child, get lured into the icy river waters—even before I knew how to swim—by a young woman from next door who held me up while I splashed around for a while but then inadvertently dropped me, after which I sank like a stone and endured a trauma from which I have never fully recovered. I subsequently learned to swim—required to graduate from my college, by the way—but never really enjoyed it very much after being nearly drowned by our well-intentioned but clumsy neighbor.

In short, the Brule was so chilly that the only incentive for going under water was to discourage the gigantic horseflies that would otherwise make a meal of your shoulder blades. My grandfather found great amusement in all this and liked to photograph the younger and crazier members of the family ashiver in the freezing water in front of our boathouse. In Exhibit 10.3, we see two such foolhardy swimmers—one of my cousins and a friend—timidly splashing in the river during that all-too-brief period between initial entry and hypothermia.

Eating and Picnicking

As already mentioned, mealtimes at the Gitche Gumee Lodge were occasions for great ritualistic ceremony, the most devout component of which involved attentively listening to my grandfather's stories. Never mind that some of these oft-told tales had appeared at the dinner table on hundreds of previous occasions. They gained with repeated retellings, acquiring new subtleties and nuances as they ripened into epic accounts of everyday events. One recounted the adventures of a young man who sent his father in Europe a telegram to let him know whether he had decided to propose marriage to Jane or to Mary: "Yes." "Yes, what?" inquired the irritated parent by return telegraph. Swiftly, the reply came back: "Yes, *Sir*!" Would you, could you believe that this story might take half an hour to tell? Perhaps not for you or me. But in the mouth of a master storyteller like ATH—one devoted to explaining every aspect of the father's occupation, the mother's home town, the son's exploits in boarding school, what kind of car the family drove, and where they went to church, not to mention the time of year and itinerary of the traveling parents, complete with details concerning the hotel they were staying at and how they had lost their luggage on the train from London to Brighton—a mere half hour would be quick work. Indeed, using props no more imposing than the back of a coffee spoon and a cup of espresso, ATH could happily spend an hour showing his fellow diners how to float heavy cream on the surface of the coffee and explaining the significance of such an accomplishment (a trick he had learned in the cafes while doing postgrad studies in Vienna). And, mostly, we would be fascinated. Thus did dinner drag on into the late hours of the evening while my grandfather—anticipating Garrison Keillor by several decades—told the most elegant imaginable stories, sipped his Vienna Roast through a thick layer of cream, and Fletcherized his food to oblivion.

Except, that is, on those occasions when we all went on picnics—an eagerly awaited and much enjoyed respite from the three-hour-dinner ritual. The picnics themselves also followed a ceremonial decorum that never varied: leaving the lodge, right after the post-lunchtime siesta, in canoes packed with food and fishermen; moving deliberately up the river while stopping by every bend in the brook to cast a fly or two; poling up rapids upon rapids and paddling through lake after lake; until eventually we arrived at one of the picnic grounds located on Big Lake, equipped with a grill, and waiting expectantly for the Chippewa guide Ed Dennis to cook the trout we had caught.

Exhibit 10.4   **Ed Dennis watching as Bertha Andrews Holbrook samples his freshly cooked trout at one of the picnic grounds upstream**

But sometimes, when no guide accompanied us to perform such deluxe gourmandian cooking services, my dad would build a big fire and prepare his woodsman's specialité in the form of egregiously burned-on-purpose canned corn and perniciously arteriosclerotic-by-design corned-beef hash. Though the latter culinary catastrophes literally took your breath away, by the time I had endured the cocktail hour, I usually felt so hungry that I would have eaten virtually anything placed on a plate, including the burned-corn-and-hash cardiovascular insult just mentioned.

At times like these, out came ATH's camera to snap a photo of the happy campers. Exhibit 10.4 shows Ed Dennis proudly watching as my grandmother Bertie enthusiastically samples his freshly cooked trout at one of the picnic grounds upstream.

Clothing

Now what would a person wear on a picnic such as I have just described—that is, for a full day of fishing and dining dangerously on greasy burnt stuff while sitting on a low bench, a rock, or even the floor of the forest sur-

Exhibit 10.5   **Bertha Andrews Holbrook dressed imposingly for a picnic in the wilderness**

rounded by woods in every direction as far as the eye could see on a river about seventy miles long with maybe twenty families living on it where your chances of encountering another human being would be smaller than finding an empty seat on the rush-hour subway in New York City? You might be thinking, maybe, blue jeans? Maybe a sweatshirt? Maybe an old baseball cap? Maybe some gear from L.L. Bean or Abercrombie & Fitch? Maybe a lot of insect repellent? Well, maybe, if you are normal. But certainly not if you are the Holbrook family at mid-century on a summer picnic in Big Lake.

For such people on such occasions, guess again. My dad kept a ratty closet full of old army uniforms and garishly striped shirts that he had worn in college. He would don this tribal costume and venture forth upon the river, looking as if he had embarked on a military mission in the jungles of the Philippine island where he had been stationed during World War II. My mom would wear a snappy costume from some upscale store such as Saks Fifth Avenue or Lord & Taylor, seeming less like a character in *Field & Stream* and more as if she had just stepped off the pages of *Vogue*.

Meanwhile, ATH himself honored an oft-repeated motto—"I don't have sports clothes; I just have old clothes"—meaning that he would embark upon a fishing expedition dressed in a white shirt, bow tie, tweed suit, and fedora, looking for all the world like the CEO of a Fortune 500 corporation. But my grandmother BAH took the prize for sartorial splendor on all-day picnics at the camping grounds upstream. I have grown to love Bertie, whom I never knew in person, just from gazing at the pictures that ATH so fondly took of her. She appears to have been a lovely person, with a handsome, calm, generous, and sweet countenance. She played the piano and collected alphabet books that ended up in a museum. She raised three fine sons and doubtless had all sorts of other wonderful qualities. But frankly—when setting forth into the forest in high-heel shoes, stockings, a dress, a scarf, jewelry, and an haute couture hat, often holding a dainty parasol—she looked just plain ridiculous. Where others would have carried a box with fishing tackle, she carried a purse with her cosmetics and a bag for her knitting. Her hats were preposterously flamboyant, sometimes with huge bunches of artificial grapes attached, making her look like a walking fruit basket.

Exhibit 10.5 catches Bertie at such a moment, standing on the dock at one of the picnic sites called Wheaton's Landing. The site itself—at the time Bertie poses for this photo—is knee-deep in tradition as "that beautiful little stream, where a landing, fireplace, and eating-shack had been set up at the place I hope will always be called 'Wheaton's'" (*Log*, p. 92). At this locally famous place, Bertie poses imposingly—heels, stockings, dress, scarf, hat, handbag—looking less like a woodsy camper and more like a person prepared to march in the Easter Parade down Fifth Avenue.

Cribbage

We had no television at the Brule—no hi-fi, no stereo, no VCR—not even a radio, on which in any case there would have been no station to audition. One year, I smuggled a tape recorder with me in the car. But when the swinging sounds of Paul Desmond and Art Farmer echoed through the woods near Gitche Gumee, I got such hostile responses from the other members of our clan—who felt that the hallowed tranquility of the forest had been desecrated—that I never made that mistake again.

Exhibit 10.6   **A game of cribbage on the front porch before lunch at Gitche Gumee**

This state of sensory deprivation meant that we were pretty much thrown back on our own devices to provide whatever entertainment we could extract from books, magazines, hobbies, or—especially—card games. If they could find a fourth adult to play with them, ATH and my parents sometimes dabbled at bridge. But the foremost card game among the campers at Gitche Gumee— perhaps because it could be played by two, three, or four people and was easy enough for a child but still tricky enough to amuse an adult—was cribbage.

Like everything else, ATH turned cribbage into a verbal adventure— leaning back in his chair, puffing on his inescapable cigar, staring at his cards, screwing up his face into a tangle of amazement, and muttering to himself, "Astounding, simply astounding." No small child with a lollypop or a choo-choo toy could have felt such simple joy as ATH experienced when he got a go for one point or hit thirty-one and pegged two. But the funny thing is that, though cribbage is undeniably a game that depends almost entirely on luck, *ATH always won.* He must have struck some sort of Faustian bargain with the gods of card games because when he needed a six of spades to improve an otherwise shabby count, a six of spades would inevitably turn up. If he had little of value in his hand, he would find a triple run of three in his crib. I can hear him triumphantly counting the points now: "Fifteen two, four, six; and a triple run of three, for fifteen; that makes twenty-one." Twenty-one is a lot of points for a crib, but ATH would do it every time.

I remember these cribbage games with bittersweet nostalgia. They were mindlessly entertaining—a way to kill time while accomplishing absolutely nothing useful whatsoever—yet they brought the family closer together. Exhibit 10.6 captures such a game in progress on the front porch—before lunch, judging from the position of the sun—with the pegs on the board indicating that my grandfather, as usual, is far ahead and with his friend looking somewhat dejectedly at his own cards after ATH has laid down a hand with a count of "fifteen two, four, six, and a pair is eight."

Music

As mentioned earlier—with no TV, stereo, or radio to provide media-based distractions—the Gitche Gumee campers relied pretty much on home-grown entertainment of the self-generated variety. This amateur amusement consisted largely of songs sung, sometimes around an evening campfire, to the accompaniment of an old guitar—songs with titles like "We Meet Again Tonight, Boys" or "Moonlight Bay" or "I've Been Workin' on the Railroad" or "Good Night, Ladies." These campfire sing-alongs were a gracious holdover from days of yore when the comforts of artificial lighting and other amenities had been even more primitive than in the years of my own youth: "It is a pleasant echo of the old days as now and then we gather at our lodge . . . and again sit about the campfire and . . . bring out the old guitar and sing many a song that those old trees must know by heart . . . and we have caught again some of the old campfire spirit, and are hoping that the youngsters in the circle will know something of what it all means" (*Log*, pp. 62–63). ATH forgets to mention the roasting of the marshmallows and the recital of "Casey at the Bat." And he does permit himself a bit of the "pathetic fallacy" in alluding to the memory of our old trees. But do not his words convey the depth of a most profoundly rich consumption experience?

Occasionally, with enough cajoling from his assembled fans, my grandfather would let loose with one of his finely crafted performances—perhaps his immortal version of "McNamara's Band" or the resoundingly jolly "Johnny Schmoker." Or my dad might do one of his own set pieces—maybe "The Irish Jubilee" or "A Cannibal Maid." Everybody joined in on these singalongs, mouthing the words they knew and faking the rest. And somewhere

Exhibit 10.7   **Arthur Tenney Holbrook performing a song with self-accompaniment from his guitar**

in the background, we could always hear the plucking of one or two guitars.

My grandfather and father each knew about four or five cowboy chords and played in a home-grown style that involved thumbing a bass note on one of the three lower strings followed by a chord plucked on the top strings with the first three digits of the right hand. This self-taught approach worked well for campfire songs and, now that I think about it, was actually a vague approximation of what a jazz pianist like Teddy Wilson used to do with his left hand—sometimes referred to as the "stride" style of pianism. Of course, it sounded a lot better at the Gitche Gumee Camp Grounds on the Brule River than it would have at a nightclub in Manhattan.

Pictures of musical activities seldom convey the essence of the relevant consumption experience. But, for me, Exhibit 10.7 comes close to capturing the *joie de vivre* that characterized my grandfather's approach to music on the Brule. I have heard guitar players with more technique and singers with better voices, but none who more fully express the essence of playfulness in music.

Natural Beauty

The breathtaking natural beauty of the river is an aspect of the Brule retroscape that shines forth in glorious color on ATH's Kodachrome slides but that proves more elusive in the black-and-white photos under consideration in the present chapter. Anyone who doubts my grandfather's depth of appreciation for natural beauty should contemplate his evocation of what he regards as a proper photographic subject: "When you reach Stone's Bridge, if you wish a bit of exercise, walk up the highway toward the east, and climb a pretty stiff hill to the bend of the road . . . turn and look down the road and unlimber your camera, for you will see a lovely picture of the roadway leading down hill between the high walls of dark pines and spruces, crossing the river and ascending the hill on the west side of the Brule Valley, until the gray ribbon of road loses itself in the forest" (*Log*, p. 106). Okay. Wind. Focus. Click!

Thus, everywhere on the Brule, especially when aided by the vision of a person blessed by such sensibilities, one finds magnificent scenes that unfold as one comes around a bend in the river and that confront one with a sense of nature in its most primeval splendor—untouched, uncontaminated, radiant, safe from human interference or pollution. These range from the quaint design of McDougall's Dam just below Joe's Lake, to the vast vista of Big Lake seen from the head of the Wild Cat Rapids, to the torrential fury of The Falls. Or perhaps we might find unsuspected beauties in the small details that everywhere give pleasure—the swirl of the river's current below a rock that juts up just above the surface, the proud splash of a rainbow trout as it rises to snatch an insect that floats on the water, the bubbling spring that invites every passerby to stop and have a deliciously cool drink. Or if we are extraordinarily lucky, we might find a chance to float in wonder beneath the star-filled nighttime sky that, from the middle of Big Lake, presents a 180-degree dome of unmatched beauty—free from the distraction of the city's glare, blazing with heavenly light, awesome in its majesty.

Newcomers to the Brule often return to the lodge in the evening with stories of amazed delight over how they have experienced for the first time a sense of what unspoiled nature must have been like before people came along to screw things up. Invariably, they have felt the powerful presence of the towering pine trees. Perhaps they have seen the beating wings of an eagle

Exhibit 10.8   **The Spring (aka, THE Spring)**

returning to its aerie high above Big Lake, or caught a fleeting glimpse of a rare white-tailed deer pausing timidly at one of the salt licks along the riverbank. Maybe they have marveled at the butterflies and dragonflies and—oh—the miraculous birds of every description that soar and circle and perch and sing in endless profusion.

One does not easily capture such moments with a camera from a canoe, especially not on black-and-white film. An exception appears in Exhibit 10.8 and depicts The Spring at the top of Spring Lake just below McDougall's Dam. ATH describes this as "a spot which has become almost a shrine to those who know and love the upper Brule" (p. 77). This lovely spring provides a place to pause for refreshment before beginning the exertions of poling first up the dam and then through the series of successively more difficult rapids that challenge the canoe's progress as it pokes its way upstream. Later, ATH describes a consumption ritual, centered on The Spring and deep with meaning for him and Bertie:

> As we come to The Spring and sing together the words of "Little Brown Jug," Ed slows down and sweeps under the overhanging cedars, for he knows from a hundred such trips that from the basket will come the leather case that carries the two silver traveling cups, which were a wedding gift, and which first went up the Brule River on the honeymoon, nearly fifty

years ago. There is not a spring from the Blue Springs at Stone's to the Co-op Park, where these beloved cups have not been filled, and although they have been around the world, and have been filled in the Arctic Circle and on the Cape of Good Hope in southernmost Africa, and have crossed the Atlantic twenty times, their first trip was to Gitche Gumee, and it is the springs along the Brule that they know the best. (p. 166)

Again, pathetic fallacies notwithstanding, it is a little difficult to escape being moved by these words—all the more because Bertie had died the year before they were written. The little silver cups come alive, respond to their role in the almost sacramental ceremony, and share in the joy of this elderly devoted couple as they pause for a refreshing drink at "THE Spring." (By the way, after reading this passage, my mother retrieved these silver cups from her collection of ATH memorabilia and put them under the tree as my 2001 Christmas present. They are very precious to me.)

Smoking

It might seem surprising that a household such as ours at the Brule—dominated by doctors in general and by my grandfather, a retired physician, in particular—would be a hotbed of tobacco consumption in all its forms: pipes, cigars, cigarettes, and even the occasional chew. Yet there it is. ATH was a confirmed devotee of tobacco and mighty proud of it—a cigarette or two at breakfast, several more during the morning's fishing, more at lunch and after, a pipe in the late afternoon, several additional cigarettes at the cocktail hour, another after dinner, followed by the inevitable cigar, always a Bering Straight, the merits of which could not be debated, at least not with my grandfather.

Worse, the habit seemed to be contagious because virtually everyone at the Gitche Gumee Lodge, except those under the age of about fifteen, considered smoking a full-time avocation. Thus, ATH pauses at one point in his narrative to comment that "everybody expectantly lights up for a fresh smoke" (p. 157)—by which he does emphatically mean "everybody." Even the Chippewa guide in the stern of the canoe always brought along "that indispensable round, brown, cardboard package that looks like a shoe-blacking box, and has a label reading 'Copenhagen Snuff,' and without which, to provide a wad of strong, black, powdered tobacco to slip under his upper lip, the guide would indeed face a glum day" (p. 167).

So the lodge—especially the council room—reeked of tobacco smoke. If I were to walk into such an environment today, I would have an instant asthma attack that, in the absence of a local hospital, would probably kill me on the

Exhibit 10.9   **ATH enjoying his afternoon pipe on a bench in front of the lodge**

spot. But in those days, I barely noticed it. It was just an inextricable part of the ambience of the place. Phew!

Further, ATH ran a continuous promotional campaign for the merits of smoking—regaling any and all who would listen with accounts of the incalculable pleasure that this habit had brought him over his lifetime and proclaiming his deep conviction that tobacco had helped immeasurably to prolong his life. If you gave him a Winston or a Marlborough, he would religiously break off the filter before smoking it. But, given his longevity, it would have been hard to argue with this formula for success. Since he lived to be ninety-seven years old, we must note that he appears to have been one of the lucky ones not adversely affected by tobacco. On the other hand, I did observe that the cigarettes he so profusely smoked—strong ones, namely, Camels—might have been less injurious to him than to others because *he did not inhale*. Rather, his technique of sipping at the weed and puffing smoke toward the ceiling lent itself especially to the consumption of cigars and pipes.

I conclude that ATH did not suffer from a nicotine addiction. He just liked to watch smoke curl up into the air and to have something to do with his hands—no doubt to the detriment of those around him breathing what we have now learned to call "secondhand smoke." In Exhibit 10.9, we find him sitting on a bench in the afternoon sun near the porch at the front of the lodge, enjoying his afternoon pipe and looking as contented as it is humanly possible to be.

Photography

To end on a reflexive note, another consumption experience found ubiquitously and insistently in recollections of Life on the Brule River involves the pervasive sense *not* of taking pictures, *not* of viewing images, but of *being photographed*. Apparently, my grandfather never went anywhere without his trusty camera, even places where extraordinary precautions were needed to keep it from getting wet, as when he ventured forth for a day's fishing in the canoe: "Under the bow is the paraffined bag with your extra clothing and the rain outfit; and the water-tight bag holding the cameras is there, too, in easy reach" (p. 164).

With ATH wandering around to snap his Leica at anything that pleased him and with my father following suit with his own omnipresent Stereo Realist camera, one could scarcely avoid spending a great deal of one's time . . . posing. Posing for action shots on the river. Posing for single portraits in a shaft of sunlight through the trees. Posing for group photos amidst cheerful attempts to persuade large numbers of subjects simultaneously to stand still and smile on the count of three.

So—when I go back and look at these pictures of my loved ones and, often, me myself as we appeared fifty years ago—I get that strong sense of retroscaped nostalgia that sweeps over us at moments like this, that sense of returning home via bittersweet memories of cherished people and places that we have lost in the sense that they can never be experienced in quite the same way again. Even though the lodge shown in the background of Exhibit 10.10 still stands, all of the people in the photograph have passed away. Viewing this picture, I experience the connection between this special place and so many of the people dearest to me. In this case, the people represent something of a family reunion and include (from left to right) my father Sandy, my grandmother Bertha, my uncle Herbert, my grandfather ATH, and my other uncle Matson. If there could have been a prize for who loved the Brule

Exhibit 10.10 **A family reunion of (from left to right) Sandy, Bertha, Herbie, Arthur, and Mat Holbrook**

the most, it would have been a close contest between these five core members of the family. But I'd bet on ATH.

Capstone

If forced to choose just one of my grandfather's photographs that encapsulates many of the themes discussed thus far, I would suffer mightily from the necessity of omitting so many pictures that I have come to cherish so dearly and to admire so much. But in the end, I would settle for the photo shown in Exhibit 10.11. This picture reminds me of a shot that might have been taken by, say, Alfred Stieglitz at his peak. It has the same sort of ethereal mist-on-the-water quality found in that master's pictures of Manhattan in the rain. But here, the subject is our boathouse on the Brule. The scene is shot from an

Exhibit 10.11 **The boathouse after heavy rains, with the dock flooded, lit
by a soft glow from the setting sun**

elevated position near the front porch of the Gitche Gumee Lodge, the porch
where so many sat together so often to watch the sun set on a lovely summer's
day. Here, we see the telltale signs of recent rain storms. The river has risen
until it covers the dock. The boathouse shines with a halo of light from the
sun setting behind it and diffusing the whole scene with a wondrously soft
glow. I remember this glowing retroscape even now, nostalgically, as I sit at
my desk in New York, gazing at the monotonous façade of the fifteen-story
nursing home across the street and longing for a whiff of the rain-soaked
pine-scented woods.

Finale

For I have lost the Brule. And with that loss comes . . . nostalgia. In discussing nostalgia at a recent consumer-research conference, Robert Schindler and I were asked whether one colleague's baby—who happens to like cucumbers— would be viewed as nostalgic if she still likes cucumbers when she is thirty years old. Our answer is negative because we believe that nostalgia refers to a liking or longing for some object (person, place, thing, event, idea) from the past that is no longer as common or accessible or easy to get as it once was. Presumably, cucumbers will still be available thirty years from now and, hence, not suitable targets for nostalgia. But . . . I have lost the Brule.

This loss came upon me gradually. It started when I moved first to Cambridge for college, then to New York for graduate school. After that, as the price of a plane ticket from New York to Duluth rose exponentially, we got to the point where it was far cheaper to travel to France or Italy than it would have been to visit the Brule River. Well, the river is nice, but France and Italy are nice too. So, for many years, our travels have taken us elsewhere. And I have lost the Brule.

But sometimes. . . .

Sometimes, when I'm worried and I can't sleep, instead of counting sheep, I let my mind drift back to those days, long ago, when as a young boy I would float down the Brule River in the stern of a canoe—paddle or snubbing pole in hand, gazing at the almost blindingly beautiful foliage around the glistening stream, listening to the chirping of the birds and the buzzing of the insects that are everywhere, guiding the boat into position for my father or grandfather to make an invariably perfect cast, watching the Royal Coachman or Grizzly King or Silver Doctor or Professor or Parmachene Belle settle effortlessly and without a ripple on the surface of a deep pool under a low-hanging branch, maybe humming a soft tune to myself or perhaps engaging in hushed conversation with the man in the bow, hearing the whoosh of his fly whizzing past my ear as he casts it with precision into yet another promising location, and waiting with eager anticipation for the magic moment when the waters bubble up around the lure and that expert fisherman deftly strikes his trout and lets out a joyous whoop as the battle to land the big fish begins.

Coda

I shall end with a photograph, shown in Exhibit 10.12, that sums up much of what I have said about Life on the Brule and—as an especially vivid retroscape—recapitulates my cherished memories of that place so full of

Exhibit 10.12 **Arthur Tenney Holbrook cradling a fawn in his arms**

meaningful consumption experiences recollected from long ago. My grandfather gave me this photograph when I was a young boy. For years, in Milwaukee, it sat on my desk where I would look at it whenever I grew bored with doing my homework—that is, very frequently indeed. I have clocked countless hours gazing at this image and know every subtlety of its composition by heart. It appeared in the *Log* (p. 116) and tends to make me catch my breath slightly as I look at it even today, after all these years. I could describe it at great length and in great detail concerning the theme of what the Brule River meant to me, but shall instead merely invite the reader to take a careful look. This picture, speaking way more than the proverbial thousand words, says it all.

11

The Moment of Infinite Fire

Robert V. Kozinets

Burning Man is a week-long event held every year in the Black Rock Desert near Gerlach, Nevada. It started in 1985, when Larry Harvey and Jerry James, two San Francisco natives, decided to bring a small group of their friends to San Francisco's Baker Beach and burn an eight-foot tall figure of a man they had made out of wood. At this first burning, an amazing thing happened. People gathered around the figure of the burning man and began to perform: singing, dancing, shouting, playing guitar. They commemorated the event by holding it on Baker Beach the next year. It attracted even more people. The added interest spurred Harvey and James to experiment with the event by holding it annually for several years. It attracted increasing numbers of people and more media and public attention each time. Eventually, after a near-riot ensuing from its originators rebelling and refusing to burn the man, the San Francisco police banned the event from Baker Beach. Picking up on some anarchist connection to San Francisco's Cacophony Society, the organizers moved their postmodern fire ritual to Nevada's Black Rock Desert in 1990. The event has grown exponentially ever since, and in 2002 it attracted almost 30,000 participants.

Burning Man is widely considered—by organizers, participants, media people, and other pundits participating within the event and commenting outside of it—to be about the creation of a primitive and sacred utopian space (see e.g., Pike 2001; Plunkett and Weiners 1997). This space is alleged to epitomize the leading edge of twenty-first century-community but also to manifest the retro power and psychic energy inherent in the primitive. While it is commonly described as an experimental social project that attempts to create a more or less lasting experience of renewed human caring and community contact, and a reinvigorating of the imaginative powers of society, the event also presents a useful site to explore and develop some of the implications of retroscapes. Burning Man is futuristic, but it is also undeniably a retroscape. Its status as sacred and relevant to both the past and the future confers upon the event considerable cultural cachet.

I have been studying the event since reading about it in 1997 in *Wired* magazine. I attended the event and conducted a detailed ethnography in 1999 and (with John Sherry as co-researcher) in 2000, pilgrimaging to and living at the event for six days out of the year, observing thousands of participants and interviewing and videotaping well over 200 of them. My first and strongest impressions of the event were subjective, experiential, emotional, and even spiritual. Although I have written several papers, chapters, and articles on the Burning Man experience, my favorite research presentation on the topic will likely be the videographic poem called *Desert Pilgrim* that I presented first at the 1999 Heretical Consumer Research conference in Denver. More than mere words on paper, the rhythm and the movement of that video poem capture some of a sense of the simultaneous quickening and slowing down that Burning Man's retroscape has on the enculturated being whose multiple selves interact to form the me-that-is-I. For me, the liquid effects that the future-anachronistic notion of "modern primitives" (as Burning Man's retrofuturistic inhabitants sometimes refer to themselves) and "time out of time" (Turner 1967) are captured in that poem. I quote a few pertinent lines here to set a subjective mood for this reflective paper (see Kozinets 2002a for the entire poem):

> Invitations to step away and
> look under the hood.
> You think.
> You believe.
> The moment.
> Is Here.
> In this place,
> Where life becomes art.

Let Me Stand Next to Your Fire

As an engaged participant in the event, I found that Burning Man contains multiple, momentary, and momentous invitations to move my way of thinking away from where it was, to break out of prior patterns, and to somehow lose the sense of the past following me around that otherwise and other-where seems

so inevitable. For certain, there are multiple, momentary, and momentous invocations of what psychologists call metacognition: thinking about how we
are thinking. I think, and reflect upon that I am thinking and what I am thinking much more at Burning Man. Second by second, with each passing strange
event and at each encounter with even stranger strangers, I question my own
beliefs, toss them up into the air to see, after the spinning is done, which side
they might come down on this time. It is metacognition, that results or at least
promises some kind of result in terms that neuroscientist and LSD/Ketamine
drug-guru John C. Lilly called "metaprogramming the human biocomputer"
(see Lilly 1976). But what it feels like is a stalemate, a sense of recursive
reasoning and logic loops that end in thought being temporarily stymied—just
as the sense of normal background animosity we feel toward our fellow anonymous human beings can be held back for a week, so too can a certain type of
thinking and certain thoughts. With enough exploded inhibitions and broken
tacit cultural rules packed into a single hour, belief systems start to fray around
the edges if not crumble. Overwhelmingly, creatively, as collective human
imagination turns the desert inside out, life becomes art. The subjective sensation I felt was a sense of timelessness grounded to a particular place: a sense of
sacred time, slower time, quicker time, precious-to-be-savored time: "The
moment is here, in this place."

Burning Man is perhaps as much about our sense of time as it is about any
collective or cultural sense of the primitive. It is about the transcendence of
our normal sense of time as much as it is about taking the time to transcend
our sense of what is normal. As Gleick (1999) notes, our sense of time passing gets ever more acute as our society gains more precision and our culture
becomes more saturated with things. "Sociologists in several countries have
found that increasing wealth and increasing education bring a sense of tension about time. We believe that we possess too little of it: that is a myth we
now live by. What is true is that we are awash in things, in information, in
news, in the old rubble of shiny new toys of our complex civilization, and—
strange, perhaps—stuff means speed" (Gleick 1999, p. 10).

Tied in with this sense of speed, this sense of overwhelmingness, yet unlike other retroscapes, Burning Man does not so much seek to echo the past
as to mock the present, but it does so using a vocabulary that is undeniably
spiced with the primitive. Indeed, much of Burning Man's metaphoric power
seems at first blush to come from its vital associations with the primitive. It
takes place in a remote desert location, over a hundred miles from Reno. The
area it is located within, the dry Pleistocene lakebed called the Black Rock
Desert, is considered to be one of the most desolate and lifeless areas on
Earth, 400 square miles of nothing. No sand dunes, no scrub, no vegetation,
no animals. Just a few hot springs and some insects.

People who enter into Black Rock's environment must undergo a pilgrimage to the distant location, and ready themselves for hardships that are imagined to be second only to Jesus's as he fasted forty days in the desert. Never mind that Burning Man has open bars, free ice cream and pancakes, espresso bars, and ice dispensers (but see Crace 1998). Never mind that the Reno Super K Kmart stocks the pilgrims up with everything from water, sleeping bags, disposable bicycles, and vodka to generators, ice cream, and disco lights. Burning Man's organizers' rule of Radical Self-Reliance infers and suggests that this will be a week filled with hardship, real or imagined.

That isn't to say it isn't tough for soft little city boys and girls. Frequently enough the wind blows up over forty or fifty miles an hour, the dust storms hit, the rain turns the ground impassable, the sun heats the air over 110 degrees, the desert cold drives the nighttime temperature near freezing levels. You're out and exposed in a very inhospitable environment. Like outer space, human beings would not last long in the Black Rock Desert if they did not have their technologies and stores of captured energy. This close to the Earth, to the land, to one another, to the frailties of our own bodies, life is primitive enough.

If this was not enough, much of the event is tailored to be intentionally ritualistic and primitive. One of the organizers' key injunctions is Radical Self-Expression. The way this self-expression expresses itself is of course culturally structured and bounded, coded to be decoded by others in the know. Differentiating yourself against the Black Rock Desert's blank canvas involves painting with cultural codes that draw heavily from the primitive.

Body painting is very popular. Red, green, and blue people are fairly common sights, sometimes travelling together as "rainbow people." Painted people are perfect fodder for the photographic habits of the many amateur anthropologists who populate Burning Man. Many tattoos and body piercings are proudly on display. In an interview, one young corporate chemist boasted to me that Burning Man was great because it gave her a proper place to display her matching twin nipple rings. Other participants I interviewed told me about the group use of ritual branding at the event. The metaphysical dimensions at Burning Man are such that some participants want to sear the event's significance into their flesh in the same way it has been etched into their hearts and psyches. A special Burning Man brand—male and female versions—was made for this purpose and used in late night rituals by dozen of attendees.

Costumes and body display are probably the most immediately defamiliarizing and destabilizing elements to Burning Man's retroscape. Costumes are common, and range from Mad Maxian retro-neo interpretations to shamanic feathers and wings to bondage culture's leather and all things in between. In addition, one of the commonest "costumes" is nudity. One of the most interesting aspects of Burning Man to outsiders, probably because of the Victorian era-remnants floating around in their own cultural unconscious and their concomitant need for self-titillation, is that some participants at Burning Man routinely peel it. They disrobe to various degrees, taking their clothes off, exposing their private parts, proceeding to hang out or parade around in their fleshy birthday suits. The sight of smooth and hairy naked bodies is again a cause for considerable photojournalism of the amateur and professional variety. Gawking, lewd comments, jeering, and grabbing are variously discouraged and prohibited by the organizers of the event (but exist to varying, mostly greatly reduced, degrees nonetheless). The organizers are trying to preserve the sanctity and legitimacy of various forms of self-expression, which rightly includes airing your sexual beefs and glorious gonads in front of thousands of strangers.

In the Heat of the Night

Let loose from the restraints of mundane life, people from our Thanatos-obsessed Western culture rather unsurprisingly feel the need to inject a bit more Eros into their day, to be free and expressive, to be the centerpieces rather than the cutlery on the table of daily life for a change, admired and attended to, turned on, and a source of anonymous others' arousal. Literalizing the Garden of Eden scenario, there is also often an innocence to the nudity that divorces it from sexuality. There is very little lewdness. It is more of a human potential movement kind of nudity, nudity for the sake of self-expression, for the sake of play, for the sake of intimacy, for the sake of freedom. An artsy, SoCal brand of nekkid: the kind of nekkid that Web-grocers and bankers promoted with their Shop Naked and Bank Naked Ads. It's probably an exaggeration to say that Burning Man's is a nudity oftentimes as chaste as Renaissance depictions of Adam and Eve. But it's certainly not a sex-shop naked. Not an offer, just a tease. More for the displayer than the displayee.

There's also a lot of tribe-talk within and about Burning Man, in the neotribe sense (see Maffesoli 1996; Muniz and O'Guinn 2001). As cyberphilosopher Kevin Kelly, writing in Plunkett and Wieners 1997, n.p.), notes, the Burning Man's gathering expresses a unique polyglot nature as "it commingles many strains of late 20th-century affinity tribes into a single seething meta-tribe." In Kelly's listing of these affinity tribes he includes: pyromaniacs, anarchists, "desert rats," high-technology wizards or "digerati," Deadheads, "wind surfers," gun and ammunition enthusiasts, "the rainbow family," ravers, art-car hobbyists and admirers, radio enthusiasts, "party hacks," New Age and alternative spirituality celebrants, neopagan "ritualists," and "modern primitives."

In addition, there are nationalist affinity tribes (e.g., camps with nationalist themes drawn from Israel, Switzerland, Canada), gay and lesbian tribes, environmental tribes, nudist tribes, feminist tribes, Satanists, bikers, and scores of others. Participants often emphasize the event's expansive social nature, tolerance of difference, and resultingly rich diversity of representation. They see in the gathering a culminating Stairway to Heaven in which All have come together as One. There's so much of everything, in fact, that clear demarcations of space and self become almost as malleable as the sense of time.

Burning Man's admixture of the unifying, the sacred, the utopian, and the primitive can be read into some of the key literatures circulating within consumer research: the admixtures of sacred and profane, structure and anti-structure, marketplaces and communities that were charted by Odysseans Belk, Wallendorf, and Sherry (1989), O'Guinn and Belk (1989), and Sherry (1990); the magical mystery tours of Arnould and Price (1993); the vibrant liberatory version of postmodern thought propounded by Firat and Venkatesh (1995) and the related "theaters of consumption" of Firat and Dholakia (1998); the tight knit idealism of skydiver culture described by Celsi, Rose, and Leigh (1993); the primitive out-on-the-edge machismo of Harley Davidson motorcycle riders as described by researcher-bikers Schouten and McAlexander (1995); the literalizing fundamentalist primitivism of modern mountain men as chronicled by Belk and Costa (1998), and the mass mediated technological utopianism of Kozinets's (2001) *Star Trek* fans. Utopia, the sacred, and primitivism coexists within the many multitudes and manifolds that make up Burning Man's affinity groupings.

Sacred, primitive utopias also exist within mainstream culture, in particular, within the flow of marketing images and communications. Brown, Maclaren, and Stevens (1996) are not wrong when they point out that marketing is among the world's greatest utopian enterprises, the contemporary keeper of the utopian flame. Rather than grand visions of a better world of peace and understanding, marketers are generally marketing little utopias of clear skin, minty fresh breath, close shaves, positive attention and adoration, and instant credit. But consider the source and semblance of these daily desires. Was there ever a time in humanity's past when we smelled good, were automatically shaven, instantly loved, and had access to every material thing our little hearts could desire? Again, the Garden of Eden springs to mind. But more tellingly than that even, these private youtopias are retro in orientation: in our pampered civilized world we—many of us, perhaps each of us— once smelled of talcum and baby-freshness, were gorgeous and fabulous, had all the attention and love and toys we could handle. Our own childhood was, to varying degrees and at various times and for various people in various ways, an idealized state to which many of us long to return.

Primitive Love

Yet the primitive is often not nearly so childlike, innocent, or harmless. The primitive contains within it hints of deep dark danger. As noted scholar of the primitive Marianna Torgovnick (1996) notes in her book *Primitive Passions*, the metaphorical power of primitive peoples comes from the fact that they are culturally coded as radically Other (see also Belk and Costa's [1998] insightful work on the modern mountain men enclave in the American West). The primitive contains within it all that we have shut out from civilization. It is coded with the animal within, the savage beast, the dark emotional desires we seek, often for very good reason, to suppress. In everyday parlance, to call someone primitive is to call them ignorant, unmannered, unsophisticated, or worse.

The former, more romantic, notion of the primitive is at once ancient and modern. In master historian Jacques Barzun's (2000, pp. xv–xvi) history of Western cultural life from 1500 to 2000, he states that

> the longing to shuffle off the complex arrangements of an advanced culture recurs again and again. It is a main motive of the Protestant Reformation, it reappears as the cult of the Noble Savage, long before Rousseau, its supposed inventor. The savage with his simple creed is healthy, highly moral, and serene, a worthier being than the civilized man, who must intrigue and deceive to prosper. The late 18C returns to this utopian hope; the late 19C voices it in Edward Carpenter's *Civilization: Its Cause and Cure*, and the 1960s of the 20C experience it in the revolt of the young, who seek the simple life in communes, or who as "Flower People" are convinced that love is an all-sufficient social bond.

As Barzun suggests, not only is the modern notion of the primitive the repository of our deepest animal desires, it also contains our loftiest aspirations. Primitives came from a time of miracles, of shamanism, animism, and prophets who heard the beloved voice of God, witnessed God's miracles firsthand. The primitive connects the Earth with the sky, bridges our most grounded reality—animalistic being—with our dreams of practical, material transcendence. This is the source of the primitive's mythic and ritual potency, the reason primitive peoples serve as the sources of so many utopian dreams. The foundational European Eutopian novels of the past (Barzun 2000), and George Lucas's powerful fictions are similarly peopled by fascinating and mysterious beings who are fascinating and mysterious precisely because of their great distance from us—they come from far, far away.

Writing for her paradigm, Torgovnick (1996) may be putting an unnecessarily feminist spin on the primitive when she states that it is coded meta-phorically as "feminine, collective, and ecstatic" while the current modern civilization is coded as "masculine, individualistic, and devoted to the quotidian businesses of the family, city, or state" (p. 14). Yet many of the female participants I interviewed at Burning Man would agree wholeheartedly with her. They experienced Burning Man's conjuring up of primitive spirits as a freedom from the artificiality and inhibitions of the everyday. They found the role of the primitive female to be one that resonated deeply within them, allowing them to express sides of their identity they normally had to repress. Wild women and savage girls in hiding secretly roam the streets of San Francisco, it seems.

Hunting Freedom

Yet freedom is a double-edged sword, and so is Burning Man. Its attraction comes from its promise of danger, the hint that, by attending, you will some-how surprise yourself. Surprising yourself may be a necessary prerequisite to finding yourself, or at least to self-transformation. But transformation is change, and change is dangerous to the ego. The primitive qualities of ec-stasy, collectivity, and femininity have acquired "a double valence—both violent and spiritual" (Torgovnick 1996, p. 14). Cannibalism was regarded like this, a sacred rite and a violent act. Potlatches were similarly Janus-faced: the way to power, wealth, or ruin. So were the sexual appetites, primitive signs of erotic life force and sources of excess and violence. At Burning Man, people play with their own inner fires—religion, spirit, the erotic, beliefs, histories, the communal, the ecstatic—and with real fire—psychoactive agents, desert conditions, trance dance, real fire. Burning Man is, for one week a year, a place to draw close to the flame, with all of the endless dance of rich associations and threats that this metaphor suggests. And all of the time travel—the freezing of time, its quickening, its condensation into a se-ries of moments, its evaporation in the frenzy of trance—that it propels.

Could something like this burn for more than a week? Could it continue as a way of life? For a culture to live in a state of perpetual celebration seems unlikely and impractical. Release of inhibitions is only possible where there are inhibitions to escape.

Ecstasy must be followed by return to the body. To live in a perpetual state of ecstatic Bacchanalian revelry would reduce any city, like Black Rock City's central art piece, to ashes. Unbridled ecstasy is primitive and dangerous. Yet, as Turner (1967) originally, and Torgovnick (1996) more recently, argued, the release of the ecstatic and transcendent urge seems essential to many, perhaps every, culture. Occasionally transcending self may be the road to a healthier self. Frequently transcending self may lead to dysfunction, violence, and a death wish.

These are the tensions that Burning Man rides, represents, and reveals. It rides the razor's edge of ecstasy, of community, of creative destruction so well, I believe, because of its temporary nature. The primitive, the ecstatic, the bacchanalian, may be vital in occasional doses, but toxic or at the very least unsustainable on a constant basis.

This Magic Moment

Primal Scream

Currently, as the 2002 Super Bowl and Winter Olympics readily attest, retro is stylish, trendy, and in. And what could be more retro than primitivism? As the trend-setting and trend-spotted, feminine, ecstatic, wild, sexy, mysterious, rodent-eating eponymous street-dweller in Alex Shakar's (2001) wonderful book, *The Savage Girl*, exemplifies it, primitive is hotly marketable and endlessly cool. So, unsurprisingly, again, retroprimitivism is everywhere.

The fact that the primitive is everywhere is kind of a necessary corollary to the notion that everything is related to everything else—the shared cosmology and intuition of the mystic, the theoretical physicist, and the wise statistician all (see Tipler 1994). But, Bell's theorem aside, there are inevitably distances between the strands of cultural meaningfulness that comprise Indra's net. And where there's distance, there's cultural polarity. The opportunity to bring those points together is a critical source of ritual potency. Uniting thematic contradictions is the cultural equivalent of tapping together the negative and positive on a battery. It sparks. That's the power of Burning Man's ritual. How does it feel? Like time stops. Like life speeds up. Like we don't have words and even thought must surrender to sensations.

Burning Man is unabashedly after Oneness, the When All Is One Stairway to Heaven sentiment to which I alluded earlier. The tribes of mankind united. Heaven and Earth conjoined. Past and present reconciled. Present and future meshed. Machines and people combined. Male and female linked. And in that it is a very prototypically modern or tribal experience (Torgovnick 1996). It is about seeking the transcendent, expansive, or—if you've a Freudian bent—oceanic experiences, wherever they can be had. Much of Burning Man's experience is primordially physical: sleeplessness, thirst and constant drinking, fecal encounters of the port-a-pottie kind, incessant drumming, inescapable dancing, drinking, drugs and contact highs, bright lights in the darkness, endless walking and watching and talking. In keeping with the pattern, the event's drug of choice is called Ecstasy.

Get Back

The Burning Man experience is a way of getting away from much that we avoid facing in life (Where does the stuff go that we throw or flush away? What am I afraid of? What do I need? Who am I when I'm away from all the usual things in my life?). It means being true to the body, to the organic self, to the animal that calls itself human. It's felt as an untangling of Cartesian knots, even a science meets religion mystical Omega point where out of abstracted roles, jobs, knowledge bases, and circumstance we become material beings once more, made flesh. A culmination. A resurrection. A cleansing. All wrapped into a timeless week that each participant deeply values because it is so limited, so temporary, and will be over so soon. Burning with the passion of the moment becomes the order of the day. This is death row in reverse. We know that soon the party will be over, that the time of free-living will soon cease and we will have to return to our little boxes, our caves, our cages.

Yet the very notions of the primitive embodied in Burning Man's embodiment experience are inescapably Western notions. Burning Man's organizers and other promoters (see Plunkett and Wieners 1997) partake ideologically in many of the primitive utopian streams that Torgovnick (1996), Barzun (2000), and Kozinets (2002b) mention: the noble savage cult, the wild woman and men's human potential movements, paganism and Native American styles of New Age spiritual belief, the idealizing communal primitivism of Marxists and Situationists, the hippie movement of the sixties, the various art and performance art subcultures that incorporate and play with all of these elements.

The power of primitivism as it occurs in multiple manifestations at Burning Man—or within any other notions of the primitive—is the power it yields in juxtaposition with other things. Going primitive becomes interpreted as license to do that which civilized people do not, and it thereby reveals a culture's notions of civilization. For Burning Man, there are conceptions of markets and money, passivity and distance, individualism and selfishness, sexual repression and constriction, artificiality and mass culture, big corporations and oppressive religions to resist. The ritual power of the primitive is particularly useful and interesting at Burning Man because it is juxtaposed so vividly and so consistently with the modern, the postmodern, the digital, the futuristic, the high tech. Many of Burning Man's participants live in the Bay Area, and are involved in Silicon Valleyesque high technology businesses and services of one sort or another. In Burning Man, it is as if their real lives floating on the future's edge must be counterbalanced by occasionally being grounded down into the past. The abstract made physical. The soaring bird latched onto the slithering snake.

Back to the Present

In the end, the distant past and the future (and in contemporary America, while the latter is privileged over the former, it's sometimes hard to remember that *both* are amazingly distant) end up being hopelessly romanticized and utopianized because of their very distance from us. Blobs, cloud shapes, collective dreams, Rorschachs. Our own limits, our own possibilities: that's what we see in the past and the future. In all of the science-fictional daydreaming about Internet worlds, virtual realities, and space travel, all of it is about limits and transcendence, ecstatic principles as easily attributed to the advanced dream quests of ostensibly primitive people. In *The Dream of Spaceflight*, space writer Wyn Wachhorst (2000, p. 54) wonderfully captures this sense that past and present are united in possibilities carrying within them a mystical promise that is, in the end, ecstatic, primitive, dark, and mysteriously feminine:

> Men once looked out over the melancholy wilderness of water as we now look to the stars, knowing it to veil some great mystery of unknown size and origin. Though the sea no longer bounds the universe, it remains a vast, inscrutable presence, growing darker and deeper in the distance, the darkness of a world before man, unchanged through eons of continual evolution, yet ever restless. . . . And out beyond the breakers abides the silent face of the Great Mother, an effervescence of light, flashing like countless suns.

The stars, the sky. At Burning Man, the desert is the sea. A cultural *tabula rasa*, a social palette for combining the infinite shades of human conception and experience. Wachhorst's feminized notion of primitive creativity is endlessly interesting. Surrender means transformation. Transformation means creation. Creation means production. Production means reproduction, expression, and art. Gifts, art, femininity, ecstasy, community: these are the cultural code words of Burning Man and the primitive. They manifest in and through the rituals and practices used to enact them, be they gifts of nudity, barter, candy, body painting, sand painting, sand sculpting, branding, wrestling, desert dream questing, alcoholic beverages, musical performances, meditation and yoga lessons, ecstatic trance dancing, elaborate rave facilities, drumming circles, whooping and hollering, fire-twirling, or ritual explosions. There's no limit to the numbers of practices and rituals that can simultaneously express the primitive and the modern, that can mix the two together in potent semiotic combination, then conjure up and dispel the deepest darkest desires.

As scholars, it is probably not necessary for us to inscribe or analyze exactly what people did at Burning Man, or even the cultural codes they used. The point that is far more important is how they cracked their own cultural codes, and manifested them. Introspection becomes a most powerful tool here. For so much of Burning Man's ritual power comes not from a purist's reinterpretive attempts to relive the primitive past—as do the literalizing mountain man adherents of Belk and Costa (1998) or some of Torgovnick's (1996) informants—but from participants' openness to an experimentation that blends past, present, and future. Opening the door to play with these cultural contradictions releases much cultural power.

Burning Man is *A.I.*'s Flesh Fair, *Star Trek*'s Planet Eden or Genesis Planet, *Mad Max*'s Thunderdome, and *The Planet of the Apes*—a future that returns to the primitive, but twists it, turns it, tweaks it in unexpected ways. Although it contains trees made of cow bones, and corporate biochemists wearing animal skins and bone splinters through their nose, it never claims to be an exclusively primitive or primal event, or any other kind of event for that matter. It is described again and again by participants who believe in such things as "modern primitive." But its organizers unerringly insist it can be everything, anything, and nothing. Drawing on the emancipatory "theatres of consumption" of Firat and Dholakia (1998; see also Firat and Venkatesh 1995) it could as easily be termed postmodern primitive. Or, because we were never modern, or never postmodern (see Latour 1993), perhaps, answering George Marcus's (1994) intriguing question, it is post-postmodern primitive.

Sub-Liminal

What is most important about Burning Man is what Burning Man is not. That there is a primitive to escape to, a Black Rock City to construct, is due to the reality that we feel we need to escape from something, to some place, for some time to have time away from our other time. Experientially, it is other-when at least as much as it is elsewhere. Why do we need to construct this place for a time? What is it this place is resisting? What are we afraid of? Who are we? What is it we need to give ourselves permission to do? The answers to these questions will map out our society, our civilization, our selves, our passions, our constraints, our contradictions: the cultural polarities that define our existence.

Are people of the late twentieth and early twenty-first centuries "empty selves" (Cushman 1990) who need to be filled to the rim with Brim, fulfilled by empty commercial promises, which might include the chimerical postmodern primitive promises of para-spiritual events such as Burning Man?

As someone who has found Burning Man personally transformative, I find that a very incomplete way to pose the question. We are all half-empty and half-full most of the time, fully empty and fully full some of the time.

Have we lost of "a life of engagement," a state of affairs brought about by the presence of what Borgmann (2000) calls "paradigmatic consumption"? Have we completely split up on so many social levels that we need to be brought together, the person with their creation, the role with the self, the me with the us? According to Situationist Sufi philosopher Hakim Bey, "the intervention of Capital always signals a further degree of mediation" (Bey 1994, p. 7) and so Burning Man might be thought to be dispensing with capitalism and therefore also doing away with mediation (see also Borgmann's (2000, p. 422) related contention that paradigmatic consumption and the culture of technology are intertwined).

Somehow, I think the hungers we feel for connection are far more pervasive than this, built into the very acts of communication and conception that allow us both to self-identify and to differentiate from one another. High technology may have exacerbated some of the prickly problems of social being that were already there, but it didn't create them out of the ether, or the ethernet.

All of this suggests that the primitivism of social gatherings and movements should be conceptualized as more connected to a micropolitics of utopia, ecstasy, and the desire for timelessness than it previously has been. Utopias technological, social, and postmodern primitive are all sung in the key of Other. They suggest the importance of ecstasy, release, culmination, transformation, creative destruction, temporariness, simultaneity, danger, and mystery in these conceptions.

Holidays, festivals, wild parties, and other gatherings of many sorts might not be political movements we can easily recognize as such, but they may be youtopian moments. Moments, not movements. Movements through time as much as place.

Our attention can shift, should shift, from the calendar to the clock, from the block to the blip, from decades to days. Utopias and primitive potentialities may not need to be classified dichotomously as either reformist or revolutionary but as odd hybrids that don't seek Social Change but instead savor moments of change on a very small and local level. As the days of our lives tick away, we seek our moment of truth at the watering hole, the salt lick of culture, in the middle of the desert, surrounded by the world.

And When the Music's Over

Burning Man is definitely, unequivocally, a ritual of consumer resistance, even a cathartic ritual of rebellion (Gluckman 1954) that leaves society mostly unchanged, although more wryly amused, by its annual passing. Modern and primitive, postmodern and digital, stone age spiritual hothouse, outdoor desert revival meeting and high-tech futuristic idea exchange, it is a time out of time that uniquely represents its time even while it changes it (see Pike 2001). It resists American hegemony, late capitalism, monopolistic powerful markets, heavy-handed and unidirectional persuasion, impositions of bitter morality and sexual propriety, governmental invasions, overly sanctimonious interpretations of spirituality, and the power of industries and the mass media (Kozinets, 2002b).

Why? Because these are the powerful forces of our day, manifestations of a world still throwing off the skin of old fixations, machine age inequities, colonial repressions, and Victorian age perversions as we step out into a world of intensely new technological powers and global connectedness without any guidemaps about how to dispel old notions of exclusion and inclusion, in-group and out-group, right and wrong, reality and unreality.

The future may have the same problems, mounted onto other problems, different problems. What Burning Man's utopian spirit may say to you and to all times, if I can for the moment be so bold as to interpret it, is that we need to try to address these problems at times in a way that playfully, openly, experimentally, and with a sense of freedom suspends the rules. It is productive to occasionally untie ourselves from the past and from anyone else's definition of what the future is going to be, or the current situation is. This is the value of time out of time. Suspending time means, for a moment, freeing ourselves of the Sisyphean burden of hauling the past around with us, dragging our old patterns, our feeble little frameworks and problem-hammers with us wherever we go. Think for yourself, and for your immediate clan. Express what's within, and act from it as your foundation. It sounds flaky and New Agey. Don't forget that Burning Man is distinctly San Fran, as Californian as alfalfa sprouts, granola, and Zen Buddhism. So maybe Burning Man is odd. Perhaps it is a lesson, too.

The Youtopian Moment

Burning Man changes radically with each movement of the sun across the sundial sky, within each day, within each ever-beckoning and distinctive night, within each theme camp, within each blazing heart. A mutable metropolis, far more insubstantial in the end than the shifting sands it was built upon. And perhaps that insubstantiality is its greatest gift and its biggest lesson. Watching the city rise on a Sunday and collapse the following Monday allows us a god's eye peek at the way things really are, at every city, at every civilization. We bonded together in intense closeness because the sense of

Being in all the hyperactivity, the burning and mortality was simply so intense. We were watchers at the world's end, dwellers for a time in a city on the edge of forever, compatriots in chaos, reveling in it all because it was utterly clear to us that, past and future combined within it, this moment is all we've got. There is no going back.

We may try in our explanations or our exploration to try to breathe academic life into Burning Man's rituals as they are described on the printed page, but they'll probably seem as stale, boring, lifeless, and irrelevant as the descriptions of religious rituals, or spiritual incantations do when reduced to words. Ever read about meditative insights? It is not exactly akin to having them. The vibrancy of Burning Man isn't in what we think or do out on the scorched earth of Black Rock City—which wasn't really all that remarkable, after all—but it lies in the spirit of the place. It is alive—so alive—with the presence of the moment. That's what the chief difference is. The art, the decorations, the drumming. Those were all props. On the main stage, the play was devoted to concentrating our collective energies on the ever-fragmenting presence of present moments, making the most of every second by actually being within it, being here now, watching the ineffable butterfly for a moment as it flits behind your eyeballs, catching it, and then gently setting it free, aware of the experience's every instant.

There is no utopia. Really there's only now. We want Utopia and we want it . . . now. Ken Wilber perhaps said it best, in his wonderful New Age Hindu Freudian book *The Atman Project*. Interpreting the meaning of *Bardo Thotrol* (the Tibetan Book of the Dead), Wilber (1980, p. 175) wrote:

> In this moment and this and this and this, an individual *is* Buddha, is Atman, is the Dharmakaya—*but*, in this moment and this moment and this, he ends up as John Doe, as a separate self, as an isolated body apparently bounded by other isolated bodies. At the beginning of *this* and every moment, each individual *is* God as the Clear Light; but by the end of the same moment—in a flash, in the twinkling of an eye—he winds up as an isolated ego.

The process of getting out of this cycle is one of anamnesis, forgetting how to forget your true self, remembering that you've remembered what you always were: that clear light. It's in all the great books, Hindu, Buddhist, Kabbalic, Sufi, Platonic, Christian. It fascinated so many great minds, among them Philip K. Dick, one of the greatest science fiction authors, modern mystics, and ontological philosophers of our time (see Sutin 1991).

Anamnesis, the reincarnation of the moment, the self's remembering of the self: ultimately, I think that's what Burning Man really teaches us. Surrounded by the carnival, the endless promenade, the colors and smells and smoke and sun and bodies, you are drawn back into your own sense, your own body. Surrounded by hundreds of silly ideologies, you feel freed from the bullying ideologies that drive your own life, your petty hungers and wants. Almost against your will, you are trapped again in your body and forced to experience the now. Not some TV set reality, not some marketized mall. But right here, right now. Encouraged to burn the things you don't need, you realize just how very much you don't need. Toss it all in the fire. Good bye, good bye. That's the utopia, I think. The youtopia. The place of freedom, where it's just you and a clan and the land and the sky, in cozy close communion.

Primitive retroscapes. They're Rorschach. They're real only in our imagi- nation. Everything in the past is an interpretation, a projection of our imagi- nation. History's history. For now, for you, I am words on a page. To me, I'm long gone. This is an echo, a shadow; it's barely even a memory.

Sure, we have remnants, shards, junk that's left behind, scattered around. But what made the past moment precious wasn't that it was in the past. It was that it was in the moment. This desperate thirst for the perfect past. It's only a way of avoiding the perfection of the present. A way of avoiding saying our true names.

There's only the moment. This moment. This one (stop and savour it). You don't have to go to Burning Man to realize that. Certainly, there's always time to realize that there's always time to realize it. But somehow, the quality of time in particular places seems different. The moments at Burning Man seem to stretch on, a chain, almost as infinite as the clear blue sky, almost as majestic as the sunset-pinkened mountains, almost as open as the fire, the drumming, the smiles and throaty laughs. It tells us how we should process time. Resets our biological clock to the stars, our cultural clock to some realm of ancients, Giants, imagination and Other. Filled with distractions, momentarily freed from some of its most commonplace distortions, time just is, and in it as we somehow should be, were meant to be, we just are. Infinite.

References

Arnould, Eric J. and Linda L. Price (1993), "River Magic: Hedonic Consumption and the Extended Service Encounter," *Journal of Consumer Research*, 20 (June): 24– 45.

Barzun, Jacques (2000), *From Dawn to Decadence: 500 Years of Western Cultural Life*, New York: HarperCollins.

Belk, Russell W. and Janeen Arnold Costa (1998), "The Mountain Man Myth: A Contemporary Consuming Fantasy," *Journal of Consumer Research*, 25 (Decem- ber): 218–40.

Belk, Russell W., Melanie Wallendorf, and John F. Sherry, Jr. (1989), "The Sacred and the Profane: Theodicy on the Odyssey," *Journal of Consumer Research*, 16 (June): 1–38.

Bey, Hakim (1994), *Immediatism*, San Francisco, CA: Zone Books.

Borgmann, Albert (2000), "The Moral Complexion of Consumption," *Journal of Consumer Research*, 26 (March): 418–22.

Brown, Stephen, Pauline Maclaren, and Lorna Stevens (1996), "Marcadia Postponed: Marketing, Utopia and the Millennium," *Journal of Marketing Management*, 12 (October): 671–83.

Celsi, Richard L., Randall L. Rose, and Thomas W. Leigh (1993), "An Exploration of High-Risk Consumption through Skydiving," *Journal of Consumer Research*, 20 (June): 1–23.

Crace, Jim (1998), *Quarantine*, New York: Picador USA.

Cushman, Philip (1990), "Why the Self Is Empty: Toward a Historically Situated Psychology," *American Psychologist*, 45 (May): 599–611.

Firat, A. Fuat and Nikolesh Dholakia (1998), *Consuming People: From Political Economy to Theaters of Consumption*, London: Routledge.

Firat, A. Fuat and Alladi Venkatesh (1995), "Liberatory Postmodernism and the Reenchantment of Consumption," *Journal of Consumer Research*, 22 (December): 239–67.

Gleick, James (1999), *Faster: The Acceleration of Just about Everything*, New York: Pantheon.

Gluckman, Max (1954), *Rituals of Rebellion in South-East Africa*, Manchester, UK: Manchester University Press.

Kozinets, Robert V. (2001), "Utopian Enterprise: Articulating the Meanings of *Star Trek*'s Culture of Consumption," *Journal of Consumer Research*, 28 (June): 67–88.

——— (2002a), "Desert Pilgrim," *Consumption, Markets and Culture*, 5 (September): 171–86.

——— (2002b), "Can Consumers Escape the Market? Emancipatory Illuminations from Burning Man," *Journal of Consumer Research*, 29 (June): 20–38.

Latour, Bruno (1993), *We Have Never Been Modern*, trans. Catherine Porter, Cambridge, MA: Harvard University Press.

Lilly, John C. (1976), *Simulations of God: The Science of Belief*, New York: Bantam.

Maffesoli, Michel (1996 [1988]), *The Time of the Tribes*, trans. Don Smith, London: Sage.

Marcus, George E. (1994), "What Comes (Just) after 'Post'?: The Case of Ethnography," in *Handbook of Qualitative Research*, ed. Norman K. Denzin and Yvonna S. Lincoln, Thousand Oaks, CA: Sage, pp. 563–74.

Muniz, Albert, Jr. and Thomas C. O'Guinn (2001), "Brand Community," *Journal of Consumer Research*, 27 (March): 412–32.

O'Guinn, Thomas C. and Russell W. Belk (1989), "Heaven on Earth: Consumption at Heritage Village, USA," *Journal of Consumer Research*, 16 (September): 227–38.

Pike, Sarah M. (2001), "Desert Gods, Apocalyptic Art, and the Making of Sacred Space at the Burning Man Festival," in *God in the Details: American Religion in Everyday Life*, ed. Katherine McCarthy and Eric Mazur, New York: Routledge, pp. 155–76.

Plunkett, John and Brad Wieners (eds.) (1997), *Burning Man*, San Francisco, CA: HardWired.

Schouten, John W. and James H. McAlexander (1995), "Subcultures of Consumption: An Ethnography of the New Bikers," *Journal of Consumer Research*, 22 (June): 43–61.

Shakar, Alex (2001), *The Savage Girl*, New York: HarperCollins.

Sherry, John F., Jr. (1990), "A Sociocultural Analysis of a Midwestern American Flea Market," *Journal of Consumer Research*, 17 (June): 13–30.

Sutin, Lawrence (1991), *Divine Invasions: A Life of Philip K. Dick*, New York: Carol Publishing Group.

Tipler, Frank J. (1994), *The Physics of Immortality: Modern Cosmology, God and the Resurrection of the Dead*, New York: Doubleday.

Torgovnick, Marianna (1996), *Primitive Passions: Men, Women, and the Quest for Ecstasy*, Chicago: University of Chicago Press.

Turner, Victor (1967), *The Forest of Symbols: Aspects of Ndembu Ritual*, Ithaca, NY and London: Cornell University.

Wachhorst, Wyn (2000), *The Dream of Spaceflight: Essays on the Near Edge of Infinity*, New York: Basic Books.

Wilber, Ken (1980), *The Atman Project: A Transpersonal View of Human Development*, Wheaton, IL: The Theosophical Publishing House.

Part III

Macro Retroscapes

12

The Lure of Paradise

Marketing the Retro-Escape of Hawaii

Janet Borgerson and Jonathan Schroeder

Indoor and outdoor, walled and boundary-blurring, retroscapes have been explored in many forms, from high-tech, highstim Niketown to the pseudo-quaint country stores of heritage park mainstreets. The mobilization of uto-pian and paradisal discourse in marketing research contexts has evoked visions of nostalgic futures, futuristic pasts, and an expulsion from the Garden of Eden as Adam and Eve succumb to carnal knowledge of the banana (Brown 2000). In theological terms, paradise is the ideal state. In marketing terms, Hawaii might be considered the ideal state. Through the lens of paradise, the relationship between retroscapes and the ideal state of Hawaii becomes clear.

Paradise has enjoyed high brand equity for as long as humans can remember. Only recently has marketing entered the scene, adding value to the basic concept, offering paradise a week at a time to weary workers in search of . . . paradise. This pedestrian version of paradise seems to require a few key at-tributes: palm trees, tropical breezes, exotic fruits, and premodern peoples—especially females, preferably someone seductive, like Eve. In this way, paradise has been packaged as a retropia—a place permanently in the past that reminds us of, well, it reminds us of the paradise that we lost when we learned too much marketing theory.

In the realm of retropian representation, Hawaii has arisen from oceanic depths as a Garden of Eden variety paradise offering premoral, before the fall, guiltless existence. Hawaii, a group of isolated volcanic islands in the Pacific, emerged from precolonial history as a geographical, political, and conceptual resource, and, of course, as a brand. Airlines, travel agencies, the Kodak Film Company, and the U.S. government support of the *Hawaii Calls* radio show worked to develop her brand recognition; hi-fi stereo and photographic information technology helped frame the retro image. Moonlit beach, palm trees swaying, and a flora-bedecked female from a pagan civilization—seen most commonly through the viewfinder of the1950s—definitively capture the Hawaiian retro-escape.

Many tourist-marketing campaigns not only relied upon a visual representation of Hawaii, but also defined a Hawaiian sound. In fact, one of the most powerful background features of this tropical island state has been the soft and lilting, sometimes fast and primitive, sounds that have come to be known the world over as "Hawaiian music." Hawaiian music calls forth an earlier era, and invokes a complex legacy of culture and history. The Hawaiian music genre captures the retro, the paradise, and the escape of Hawaii's marketed image—perhaps vibrating through strings of a steel guitar or a ukulele, or from coconut shell bongos on famous favorites "Little Brown Gal" or "Lovely Hula Hands." The hula girl and her musical accompaniment have for decades formed the foundation of a strongly appealing and attractive Hawaiian identity, helping make Hawaii instantly recognizable the world over (e.g., Desmond 1999). This image, specifically designed for consumption, has been reflected in and transmitted through familiar easy-listening music created mostly by white mainland songwriters with little or no connection to the islands. Hawaii, as a sound, a repertoire of songs, and a musical identity, provides a performative example of what has been called "sonic branding."

The present image for consumption remains steeped in fifties kitsch: hula girls, luaus, easy-listening island music, aloha shirts, Trader Vic's style pupu platters and fruity rum drinks (see e.g., Brown 2001; Costa 1998; Kirsten 2000; Sturma 1999); and continues to be filmed through this era that consists of a strong style, and forms a basic retro-trope in itself. This double dose of retro—mythical Paradise and modern paradise of the fifties—contributes to the captivating concoction. Exotica music, lounge culture, *Temptation Island*, ClubMed, hedonism, and many other current marketing trends and consumer destinations rely on the retro paradigm of packaged Hawaii.

Retroscapes are not limited to product designs, retail environments, or heritage parks. An entire geographical location, such as the fiftieth state, can serve as a vast retroscape, complete—and at no extra cost—with the sights, sounds, and sensuous tropical breezes of a relaxing retro lifestyle. In this essay, we explore the retro of packaged paradise escape, the packaged escape of a retro paradise, and the paradise of packaged retroscape: Hawaii—soft, warm, vibratingly fertile—and her undulating call lure us to the ultimate retro-escape. We unpack the Hawaiian presence via an analysis of the retro-escape, a visit to our growing archive of Hawaiiana, and a nod to recent

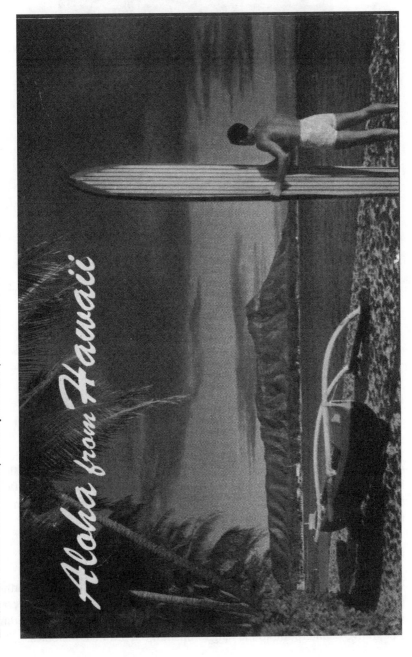

Exhibit 12.1 **Aloha from Hawaii, 1940s postcard** (*From authors' collection*)

Exhibit 12.2 **Hawaiian woman, 1950s postcard** (*From authors' collection*)

developments in marketing thought, such as sonic branding (Barnet 2001; Hirsch and Schneider 2001) and visual consumption (Schroeder 2002; Schroeder and Borgerson 1999b; 2002a). Our journey invokes our own experience of retro and provokes some broader retro reflections.

Analysis in the Retroscape

The harmonic strains and sensory hues of retro, packaged "escape," and earthly paradise have become intimately entangled. We have found it helpful to consider the elements one at a time and observe the interconnections, providing a cognitive counterpoint to the languorous lull of Hawaiian melodies.

The Retro of Packaged Paradise Escape

An escape paradise, the ideal of a true remove from the modern world, a place untouched that remains completely separate and unaffected by the world and reality "out there" emerges as an essentially retro ideal. As irrefutable evidence of how nuclear clouds from one country decimate animal herds and poison soil in countries far beyond single national borders, and further, as well-recognized and long-standing practices and strategies of cultural domination reveal, such an escape is an ideal of a world long disappeared. Yet, the appeal of the ideal paradise remains, carrying with it the ring of retro.

The Packaged Escape of a Retro Paradise

Lessons on the packaging of a retro paradise, from the treasure trove of kitsch hula girls and bright flowered dresses, to promises of safe and sensual nature, and the ease of an easy preindustrial precivilization, lure us to the islands of Hawaii. In the wake of anxious interconnections, whether economic, environmental, or cultural, to find oneself in a land of roughly cut coconut cups and sizzling roasted pig turning on an outdoor spit, tended by a scantily clad and smiling "native" far from urban urgency and information clutter perhaps provokes a sigh, a deep breath, a moment of calm. The musical accompaniment cannot be pounding symphonic complexities or heavy metal chords amidst the tropical breeze. Rather, melodies and instrumentation are formulated to evoke an innocence and simplicity, the ease and saunter of a guilt-free consciousness that is also a thing of the past.

Unlike the permanently unknowable, uninhabitable, untouchable stage of human evolution that is Paradise, packaged paradise has been imagined as an unspoiled, unpolluted playground. Metaphorically, connections to the primitive, pagan, and virginal have inspired visions of exotic young females, sensual, sexually available, and ready to frolic. What better escape than the postcoital sigh, the fall into slumber, and a tasty luau meal upon awakening?

The Paradise of a Packaged Retro-Escape

Paradise remains unalterable in its essence, hence free from care and responsibility. The constructed unreality of a past time, perhaps just far enough back that no one remembers what really happened, how life really might have been lived, attracts with its unrecoverable opportunities. The risks taken and choices made lay behind us, not looming. Paradise has always been a retro-escape. Paradise could never be modern, never circumnavigate the temporal and spatial divide between Now and the mythical Then. Paradise has *always* been a Then. A retroized Hawaiian paradise that consists in style, stereotype, and authenticized falsities emerges as the ultimate postmodern paradise. Paradise, once caught forever in the past of a modern historical conception can, through postmodern historical sensibility, be present for guilt-free retro consumption. Paradise made possible again, soundtrack included.

Soundtrack to the Summer

For a couple of summers in the mid 1990s this chapter's authors stayed at a family cottage in northern Michigan. Our summer home was a cozy and time-warped log cabin called "Loon Lookout." On one of the thousands of freshwater lakes in the Great Lake State and steeped in unrefurbished "up north" appeal, Loon Lookout evoked the lifestyle of our grandparents' generation. We found many reminders of past summers, family get-togethers, and the fabled fifties—the rustic cabin's décor had not changed much since it was built in 1951. A Fiestaware bud vase, heavy brown Hall coffee mugs, and worn wooden fishing lures lay forgotten in the back of kitchen cupboards and musty drawers. We pulled them out, dusted them off, and displayed our finds as retro treasures.

We added a few of our own touches, gathered from a growing number of antique shops in the area: olive and turquoise decorated Temporama dishes from the late fifties, vintage murder mysteries with lurid covers, and an old-fashioned hi-fi set. We also exhibited items from one of our collecting crazes, record albums from the 1950s. Cheap and colorful, these vinyl artifacts fit right in with the cabin's pine paneling, bamboo furniture, and original appliances. After a while we noticed that we favored one record album theme above all others—the Hawaiian album. Soon, we found our living room overflowing with Hawaiian images—hula girls, Hawaiian beaches, steel guitars, Tikis, wave-riding dugout canoes, and surfboards on the sand at Waikiki. We liked the campy and kitschy covers—they added some brightness to the somewhat dark cabin, built before floor to ceiling windows and designer lighting became popular.

Being academics, we began to discuss the images we encountered in our daily admiration of the cabin's new motif. We began to think about how marketing, tourism, music, and stereotypes combined to "package paradise" and how powerful these visions remained fifty years later. We recognized several emergent themes. Hawaii was portrayed as magic, as paradise, and as female, seducing visitors to the tropical resort. Despite the disturbing racist and sexist stereotypes, we were struck by how appealing the album covers were—as they were intended to be. What began as an ironic, yet playful stance, turned more complex as we interacted with the images—and of course the music—which occupied our living space.

Exhibit 12.3 **Hawaiian record album** (*From authors' collection*)

What became known worldwide as Hawaiian music provides a soothing soundtrack for the retro-journey. A Hawaiian craze swept the United States after World War II, fanned by airlines, hotels, and the Hawaiian Chamber of Commerce. Hula dancing, backyard luaus, and tiki-lights became the rage. The marketing of Hawaiian popular music through radio shows and record albums aided in Hawaii's transformation from a "primitive" paradise into the fiftieth state. The marriage of stereo technology and so-called authentic music was a potent force in the acoustic branding of Hawaiian paradise. By capturing the tropical sounds of Hawaii on the latest hi-fi advanced recording equipment, the recording industry offered up Hawaiian music as part of the latest achievement of modern technology, promoting paradise as a sound as well as a place to visit (Schroeder and Borgerson 1999a).

What struck us first in collecting retro Hawaiian records was the stereotypical and often campy images of Hawaii and Hawaiians in the music and on the album covers. We liked the tacky renderings of music recorded under the guise of "Hawaiian" and found the album covers visually stunning. Our collection led us to think about how Hawaii was portrayed through music and album cover art. We learned that most of the popular songs were written by white tunesmiths and were produced by mainlanders, though the liner notes attempt to represent the music as authentically Hawaiian by focusing on the use of Hawaiian instruments, musicians, and song lyrics that invoke the natural qualities of an island paradise.

With titles such as "Island Paradise," "The Lure of Paradise," and "Paradise Found," many of our records promise the listener a substitute for the actual journey to Hawaii—listen and be transported to paradise. In this way, records offered an inexpensive alternative to a Hawaiian vacation, and served as an important element in the tourist industry's campaign to attract visitors (e.g., Tatar 1987). Now, the songs and images from the albums are retro reminders of both the heady days of Hawaii's impending statehood and of our summers in the cabin by the lake. Here we describe some highs and lows from our collection.

"In your heart lives your dream of an island," begins the liner notes of *Paradise Found* featuring "the fantastic strings" of Felix Slatkin (Liberty), an especially hyperbolic album of Hawaiian standards performed in syrupy sameness by yet another string orchestra in something called "Visual Sound Stereo." What makes this LP interesting is the effort that went into the elaborate packaging, which includes a gatefold sleeve, extensive liner notes, and an informative thirty-page color booklet about Hawaii. Great importance is given to the claim "Recorded in Hawaii." The liner notes inform us that: "Felix Slatkin, one of Hollywood's most brilliant conductors, is an ardent enthusiast of the Islands and Island music. It was during one of his recent trips through the Pacific Islands that this revolutionary musical idea was conceived: real Hawaiian music with lush string backgrounds." This is the kind of album that made Hawaiian music synonymous with elevator music in which authenticity seems to rest on a melodic steel guitar.

A young Polynesian-looking woman with orchids in her hair, posed in front of a cascading waterfall beckons us with flowers on the cover of *Hawaii: Nearer Than You Think, Lovelier Than You Dreamed.* One of the more elaborate album packages we have seen—in any genre—this set, packaged by TradeWind Tours, was meant to be a souvenir of a trip to Hawaii. The album contains a record—"Honeymoon in Hawaii" by the HiLo Hawaiians (Hawaii Hosts)—and a forty-page color booklet featuring pictures of the tour limousine, tour guides, and vacationing couples as well as a history of Hawaii, a shopping guide, and an island by island description of Hawaii. We are told that "the music in this album helps tell a part of the story of the happy, carefree experience awaiting you in Hawaii." Upon returning home, Hawaiian vacationers can create an album of their own; there are places for writing in personal notes and affixing keepsake photos. The enclosed album is fairly typical and includes the favorites "Hawaiian War Chant" and "Hawaiian Wedding Song."

Webley Edwards created *Hawaii Calls*, the most successful radio show of its kind. Partially funded by the legislature, and broadcast weekly for almost forty years, *Hawaii Calls* was perhaps the most influential force in making mainlanders Hawaii-conscious. Webley Edwards reached a worldwide audience with a carefully constructed image of Hawaiian music. In the liner notes of the *Hawaii Calls*, Mr. Edwards (who was from Oregon) insists that his show is the real Hawaii featuring real Hawaiian music Hawaiian style. Oddly, though, he says a song written yesterday in Peoria is as Hawaiian as something written a hundred years ago by a native "if it has that certain something," and is sung by a Hawaiian. This latter requirement soon faded away, and many of the most well-known purveyors of Hawaiian music are mainlanders. Of course, also at work were copyright laws and royalty payments. Most of the songs on the *Hawaii Calls* shows were written, or at least copyrighted, by whites. Edwards did much to promote Hawaii via his brand of Hawaiian music, but it wasn't particularly authentic.

Webley Edwards Presents Hawaii Calls: Fire Goddess with music by Al Kealoha Perry (Capitol) plays on the Pele theme depicting a rendition of the mythical fire goddess of the islands who inhabits the many active volcanoes in the island chain. An exotic looking woman—naked above her lowslung native cloth—with heavy lipstick, eyeliner, and accentuated eyebrows glares hypnotically, handing us two glowing gold bowls of fire that both cover and stand in for her breasts. Snake bracelets wrap around her upper arms. The liner notes explain that "here for the first time in modern fidelity are the unusual sounds of instruments that the Hawaiians devised long before the islands were discovered by Captain James Cook in 1778." Included on the back cover is a glossary explaining the featured instruments and the materials—such as, sharkskin, coconuts, gourds, split bamboo, and lava rock—from which they are constructed. "Fire Goddess Pelé," a supposedly traditional song, begins with sounds of a furious storm and a chant. We find that drumming and chanting attempts to capture our sense of an earlier Hawaiian culture in contrast to the homogenized music played for tourists.

Martin Denny, of course, is well-known for his highly collectible musical "exotica." He released several specifically Hawaiian themed albums for Liberty Records; including *Hawaii Tattoo*, *20 Golden Hawaiian Hits*, and *Hawaii Goes a Go-Go*. Songs are often repeated, and some reappear on his hit record, *Quiet Village*. *Hawaii Goes a Go-Go* represents Denny's attempts to remain hip into the late 1960s. The cover shows a blond go-go girl, sporting sixties staples—shag haircut, tight top, and checked capri pants—and that essential Hawaiian element, a lei. This album's version of "Pearly Shells" is up-tempo with tambourine and stand-up bass set to a rocking beat. The liner notes brag that "Denny swings and rocks through some of the top Hawaiian hits associated with his name to give you the beat of the frug, monkey, watusi, etc." This is a strange artifact of the dance crazed sixties, whereas Denny's other Hawaiian titles *Golden Hawaiian Hits* and *Hawaii Tattoo* represent retro lounge music par excellence.

Bing Crosby's *Blue Hawaii* (Decca) presents a tourist brochure shot of an endless sand beach, an outrigger canoe, a lone palm tree, and famed geographical feature Diamond Head. A small note printed along the bottom of the front cover reminds us that Hawaii is 2,394 miles from the United States via Pan American World Airways. One of the first big stars to release a Hawaiian album, Bing started a massive trend. As the liner notes attest, Bing sings the standard Tin Pan Alley penned Hawaiian tunes such as "Blue Hawaii," "Sweet Leilani," and "Tradewinds." Dick and Lannie McIntire's Hawaiian choruses back Bing's crooning. His versions of the Hawaiian classics are haunting and slow, and stand up well to the test of time.

The familiar face of Elvis Presley adorns one of the most well-known Hawaii albums, the soundtrack of Hal Wallis's film *Blue Hawaii* (RCA Victor). This hit record introduced the big hit ballad "I Can't Help Falling in Love" as well as hiccuping versions of the Hawaiian standards "Blue Hawaii," "Aloha oe," and "Hawaiian Wedding Song." Also featured is "Rock-A-Hula Baby," a game attempt to blend the Hawaiian sensibility with Rock and Roll. Less successful are the film soundtracks *Gidget Goes Hawaiian* and *Diamond Head.* Both seem to rely on the slightest of Hawaiian touches to make their humdrum music sound Polynesian. Great covers, though.

Hawaiian Favorites (Tops) features a sleazy cover and a disturbingly cynical appropriation of Hawaiian music. Danny K. Stewart and his Aloha Boys play "Knock-kneed Napua." A slide guitar over a typical lilting Hawaiian beat plays the melody from "Lovely Hula Hands." "There's a Yellow Rose in Hilo" is a barely disguised version of "A Yellow Rose of Texas." The lyrics point out that a dancing female tourist "didn't learn that movement behind an office desk." The appalling lyrics and overall effect reveal an apparently unintended parody of "Hawaiian" music.

"Texas Has a Hula Sister Now" on Harry Hoomele and His Orchestra's *Come to Hawaii* (Grand Award Recordings) also uses the yellow rose melody, and is one of our favorite song titles. The confluence of statehood, womanhood, and kinship is spectacularly suggestive. Texas, of course, was a state; the Lone Star State, a big brawny braggart of a state. Hawaii is dubbed a "hula sister," thus feminizing this distant, rather small tropical new state. By linking hula—an exotic, alluring dance—with sister, a familial relation, the songwriter captures much of the fascination of Hawaiian music. At once exotic and familiar, distant yet belonging, Hawaii stirs up issues of attraction and taboo (see also Schroeder and Borgerson 2002b).

Our archive of Hawaiian records has grown to include several hundred examples. What a surprise to observe the recent retro renaissance of exotica, lounge music, and tiki culture that features many images recycled from albums like those in our burgeoning collection. Our Hawaii project has become one of our greatest hits, sparking reflections on paradisal promises and retro representations.

Sensing Paradise

> From my earliest recollection of the Biblical description of the Garden of Eden I have retained a vivid picture of a Paradise in my mind's eye and have often compared it to the Hawaiian Islands . . . the verdant foliage—balmy climate—gentle breezes—extravagant colors from the abundant tropical flowers with their delicate shades of lavender, pink and yellow—the everchanging ice-blue-greens of the ocean . . . a perfect setting for a tempo of life that defies tension and strife . . . this is Paradise! We can see it and we can also hear it.
>
> (Ralph Carmichael, liner notes to *Hawaiian Paradise*
> on the Sacred Productions label, Waco, Texas)

Hawaii is stoked by sensations. The color, scent, and sound of Hawaii contribute to an all-encompassing, retro-escape branding campaign. We catch the perfume of roasting luau pig, freshly cut pineapple, or sun warmed coconut oil. Color photography—in films such as *South Pacific, Diamond Head*, and *Blue Hawaii* and on tourist brochures, record albums, and travelogues—worked to market Hawaii as a fantastic paradise, and continues to represent Hawaii as a kind of timeless, but vibrant resort (e.g., Farrell 1982; Slater 1991). Hawaiian tourist stops like the Polynesian Cultural Center, Sea Life Park, and the International Marketplace made available and manageable the stylized sights and sounds of Hawaii. The legendary Kodak Hula Show is our favorite. This retroscape, a packaged photo opportunity and outlet for the company's film, purportedly represented the essence of Hawaii. Kodak film, designed to accentuate tropical reds, greens, and yellows, allows tourists to capture old Hawaii's scenes and sensuality, spectacularly supporting the "dominant tourist-industry myth of Hawai'i as an accessible paradise, one that promises and delivers more than beautiful beaches and balmy weather—'more' being the human element of a culture and the *'aloha spirit'* that make Hawai'i something special" (Buck 1993, p. 2). Such a well-established attraction provides a comfortable familiarity for anxious visitors who have already planned the experiences they themselves will have and seen the pictures they will take. Hula-dancing natives on display for camera-toting tourists follow a retro-recipe, reproduced in travel brochures, magazine articles, Hollywood film soundtracks, and now on the Internet. We treasure our Kodak Hula Show album from 1956, complete with tips on how to best photograph the show.

Though an authentic 1950s picture of Hawaii, one that carried through on an almost ethnographic interest in the "natives," would presumably be shot in black and white, here, color—used to evoke the musical and fantastic—documented the "real" Hawaii. That an escape from the everyday could be signaled through the color of fantasy and the fantasy of color was well understood as advertisers, using early forms of color photography, held out promises in vivid hues. However, an authentic Hawaii captured in color is something of a contradiction, or at least a signifying coup of the inauthentically authentic island paradise retroscape. Black and white signifies news, seriousness, documentation. Filmmakers separated themselves from the black and white documentary world, shooting into the realm of the hypercolored hyperreal. Thus, we can speak of a semiotics of film color; one that relates to paradisal escape from reality (Goldman and Papson 1996). Color became synonymous with fantasy, escape, and exoticism. Just remember Dorothy who opens the door of her cyclone-transported weary gray house to find a glowing yellow road, singing munchkins, and an entire world of Ozified color. Kodak, in a fine example of pushing the consumer to become a producer, has aided decades of photographers in capturing and creating the fantasy life of retro paradise.

The striking colors of particular places and the ability to reproduce certain kinds of light have supported the mythos of twisting red bougainvillea in bright island sun or the glowing calm of Tuscany's landscapes seen through the brush of Renaissance master Piero della Francesca. But for the most part, the Western past has been badly lit, especially in places where long dark winters emphasized shadowy dark corners in gloomy windowless interiors. The sunny places where people lived without walls in a sense of warm freedom—dreamed of without sickness-infected insects, dangerous animals, or deadly winds—this was paradise.

Retro Representations: Packaging Paradise

The retro appeal of Hawaii easily transcends national boundaries. In September of 2001, we are asked to contribute to an art show in Berlin. In November, we carefully wrap, pack, and ship our exhibit with sketched and written instructions—we'll be arriving after everything is hung for the show. In December, we expectantly enter the exhibition and search for our contribution. Issues of representation and identity occupy this part of the gallery. Gold-framed photographs set out on a white cloth-covered table create a domestic atmosphere and evoke moments of another artist's intimate history. Yet, we are told, the images emerged from a discarded roll of film found in an abandoned house in former East Berlin. The artist knows none of the young men and women pictured. Against the other wall, a writer has re-created his studio workspace. We know him and recognize the single bed with white cover, the typing table that swings over the bed, the chair piled with books.

A smallish transparent greenhouse set in the middle of the showroom catches our attention. Attracting the eye with brilliant yellow banana décor and paraphernalia—a furry banana chair, slippers with small bunches of plastic fruit adorning the toes, a banana welcome mat, and a sign that reads, "If you like bananas come right in"—the plexiglas building also emits the smell of overripe bananas. There they are. We can see them through the walls—lined up along a shelf within the greenhouse, the darkening, softening fruit, maybe eight of them. Recognition of the smell's effect only comes after the initial attraction and desire to enter the banana house, which clearly would have been more enjoyable before the fruit became so ripe. We wonder whether the artist will just let the bananas rot, leaking their juices, molding. The eight or so blackening examples in the warm gallery are clotting the air with an increasingly sickening stench.

Despite the smell, the bright yellows and the festive exotic associations of the greenhouse exhibit evoke a mirage of other warm climate fruits: coconuts, mangoes, and pineapples. In Jane Austen's *Northanger Abbey*, a greenhouse designed to allow the growing of pineapples in Great Britain's northern climate provides a curious detail in the description of Northanger's gardens. The pineapple, harkening from tropical colonies, is clearly unusual, a high status novelty that might, if properly cultivated, prove a smart agricultural investment on home turf. Also a welcome gift from seafaring captains, pineapples became an icon of hospitality. On the U.S. mainland, Hawaiian pineapples are consumed with a certain national pride, and symbolize Hawaii's warm lands, commercial development, and fertile potential.

Packaging Paradise, our contribution to the show, has been installed in an alcove just past the banana house—the cloying scent follows us. On a low pedestal rests a worn Kodak slide carousel box. The presence of the box emphasizes the Kodak company's role in picturing and packaging Hawaii as tourist paradise and ultimate escape. Huge poster sized versions of record album covers that had at one time adorned the walls of our Michigan cabin

Exhibit 12.4 *Packaging Paradise* exhibit; Haus am Lützowplatz Gallery, Berlin, December 2001 (*Photo by Jonathan Schroeder*)

hang on the wall. Stars from the Kodak Hula Show figure in one poster, the female dancers dressed in brilliant green grass skirts with glowing yellow flower leis around their necks and pulsating red feather pom-poms in their hands. Six smaller identical posters display varying saturations of green, red, and yellow emphasizing the Kodak company's chromatic focus in the color capabilities of its film. We have tried to emphasize how Hawaii and her people have been carefully constructed through the visual impact of information technologies.

Incantations: Living, Loving, and Listening in the Retroscape

> I thought Hawaii precisely as advertised—a dandy paradise with all the comforts of home.
>
> (Carson, 1960, p. 86)

The project of collecting Hawaiian records and the accompanying images that began as we ironically decorated our northern Michigan cabin has allowed us to study Hawaii as a retroscape and to reflect upon the work of creating our own retro-escape. We have found that in our own attempts to shape an environment in which to entertain friends, love, and write we surrounded ourselves with images, sounds, and performative and reflexive identities that provided the foundation for analytic and scholarly work, as passion turned into professional pursuit. In this sense our ritual performance of domesticity produced and formed our personal retroscape—complete with soundtrack—the fruits of which we have spun out in the proceeding narrative.

We have argued that paradise is a retro construction and that Hawaii—a packaged paradise—provides a productive paradigm of a retro paradise escape, an ultimate retroscape. Further, the retro packaging of Hawaii offers a useful model to understand the rise of retroscapes. Retroscapes are not restricted to heritage parks, product designs, or retail environments. An entire geographical location can function as a huge retroscape via representation. As such, retroscapes are assemblages of memory, fantasy, and sensation—sights, sounds, scents, and perhaps, dreams.

Retro-escapes fill the senses. Nostalgic smells, like a musty cabin just opened up for summer, album covers damp from basement storage, or the luscious luxury of island hibiscus, scent the retro. The simple steel guitar strains of "Lovely Hula Hands" instantly evoke white sand, blue ocean, palm trees blowing in a warm breeze, and the hula girl. Marketing research has suggested that music, color, scent, and of course, sex, can function as "background features" or "peripheral cues" in influencing consumer preferences. Reaching an audience "through emotionally arousing background features may make the difference between their choosing and not choosing a brand" (Gorn 1991, p. 152). The representations of Hawaii and Hawaiians found in our record albums are an integral part of Hawaii's brand image that include sensations and memories of places, peoples, and particular eras.

Hawaiian music invokes the nostalgic nirvana of a time when jet travel was still glamorous, tiki culture was the rage, and aloha shirts were in style. Hawaii is no longer very exotic, yet current marketing efforts resemble the classics from mid-century (Buck 1993). These tourism campaigns recycle vintage ads without looking dated or odd—not many industries can match Hawaii's consistent image over the decades. Although Kodak no longer sponsors the hula show, the classic name of this renowned tourist attraction remains. The retro-escape of Hawaii provides a consumption arena in which visitors in loose, loud shirts go barefoot like pre-Nike natives. This escape from work routines, dress codes, and cold climes embraces hanging out on the beach, learning to surf, and photographing friends and family doing the hula. Thus, Hawaii is visually, acoustically, and sensually consumed. Hawaii is also literally consumed; what people take to be significant about places like Hawaii—its link to retro paradise—is over time depleted, devoured, and damaged (cf. Borgerson and Schroeder 2002b; Urry 1995). Hawaii's unspoiled setting, its indigenous peoples, and its cultural traditions are all en-

Exhibit 12.5 **United Airlines retro advertisement, c. 1999**

Exhibit 12.6 **Tauck Tours, Hawaii travel brochure, 2001**

dangered by the cultural transformations of Hawaii's bounty into consumption sites (cf. Brown, Hirschman, and Maclaren 2000; Löfgren 1999). The allure of the Hawaiian retro-escape lives on, and on, and on. We only worry that having plucked the exotic fruits, expulsion is immanent.

Coda

As human beings we engage in an intricate and intimate interplay of relations and sensations, including feelings of love and connections with others. There is no reason to think that one of the features of this complexity could not consist in multiple time frames coming together, creating sensations that merge the desires, needs, and comforts of those diverse times and time sequences—what, currently, they meant in the past, what they mean at present, and may mean in the future. We join together elements of human experience and reflection, sounds and colors and smells to create combinations that suit us. Perfumes, for example, contain many levels—from dank, musky base notes to light, flowery top notes. Why should we, then, conclude that retroscapes are so different? Retroscapes, far from being a space of no then, become time/space saturated realms, combining thens and now and future visions, as well, in which we struggle not to fall into isolation, but to build opportunities for interaction and community.

References

Barnet, Kim (2001), "Sonic Branding Finds Its Voice," brandchannel.com, www.interbrand.com.start.asp.

Borgerson, Janet L. and Jonathan E. Schroeder (2002), "Ethical Issues of Global Marketing: Avoiding Bad Faith in Visual Representation," *European Journal of Marketing*, 36 (516): 570–94.

Brown, Stephen (2000), "Going Bananas in Paradise: From McDonaldization to Fyffefication" *Marketing Intelligence and Planning,* 18 (6/7): 356–67.

———— (2001), *Marketing—The Retro Revolution*, London: Sage.

Brown, Stephen, Elizabeth C. Hirschman, and Pauline Maclaran (2000), "Presenting the Past: On Marketing's Re-production Orientation," in *Imagining Marketing: Art, Aesthetics and the Avant-Garde*, ed. Stephen Brown and Anthony Patterson, London and New York: Routledge, pp.145–92.

Buck, Elizabeth (1993), *Paradise Remade: The Politics of Culture and History in Hawai'i*, Philadelphia: Temple University Press.

Carson, Robert (1960), "Hawaii—Can Paradise Change and Still Be Paradise?" *Holiday*, 27 (July): 34–86.

Costa, Janeen A. (1998), "Paradisal Discourse: A Critical Analysis of Marketing and Consuming Hawaii," *Consumption, Markets and Culture*, 1: 303–46.

Desmond, James (1999), *Staging Tourism: Bodies on Display from Waikiki to Sea World*, Chicago: University of Chicago Press.

Farrell, Bryan H. (1982), *Hawaii, the Legend That Sells*, Honolulu: University Press of Hawaii.

Goldman, Robert and Stephen Papson (1996), *Sign Wars: The Cluttered Landscape of Advertising*, New York: Guilford.

Gorn, Gerald J. (1991), "The Effects of Music in Advertising on Choice Behavior: A Classical Conditioning Approach," in *Perspectives in Consumer Behavior*, ed. Harold H. Kassarjian and Thomas S. Robertson, 4th ed. Upper Saddle River, NJ: Prentice Hall, pp. 144–53.

Hawaii [Tauck World Discovery brochure] (2001).

Hirsch, Wilber and Michael Schneider (2001), "Brand Aesthetics and Acoustic Branding," Audio Consulting Group paper, www.interbrand.com.

Kirsten, Sven A. (2000), *The Book of Tiki*, Cologne and London: Taschen.

Löfgren, Orvar (1999), *On Holiday: A History of Vacationing*, Berkeley: University of California Press.

Schroeder, Jonathan E. (2002), *Visual Consumption*, London and New York: Routledge.

Schroeder, Jonathan E. and Janet L. Borgerson (1999a) "Music from Paradise," *Cool and Strange Music.*

———— (1999b), "Packaging Paradise: Consuming Hawaiian Music," *Advances in Consumer Research*, 26: 46–50.

———— (2002a), "Innovations in Information Technology: Insights from Italian Renaissance Art," *Consumption, Markets and Culture*, 5(2): 153–69.

———— (2002b), "Dark Desires: Fetishism, Ontology and Representation in Contemporary Advertising," in *Sex in Advertising: Perspectives on the Erotic Appeal*, ed. Tom Reichert and Jacqueline Lambiase, Mahwah, NJ: Lawrence Erlbaum Associates, 65–89.

Slater, Don R. (1991), "Consuming Kodak," in *Family Snaps: The Meaning of Domestic Photography*, ed. Jo Spence and Pat Holland, London: Virago, pp. 49–59.

Sturma, Mark (1999), "Packaging Polynesia's Image," *Annals of Tourism Research*, 26: 712–15.

Tatar, Elizabeth (1987), *Strains of Change: The Impact of Tourism on Hawaiian Music*, Honolulu: Bishop Museum Press.

Urry, John (1995), *Consuming Places*, Routledge: London.

13

Contemporary Haute Cuisine in France

When French Chefs Are Paying Their Tributes to the Past

Patrick L. Hetzel

Authors such as Firat and Venkatesh (1993), and Brown (1995) have noted that postmodernity is prevailing in contemporary consumption. This means that aestheticism, eclecticism, and individualism are becoming more and more important. If we consider that these characterizations of contemporary consumption are true, and that in order to attract new customers or keep their clientele, French chefs have to respond by creating new offers or modifying their existing offer, it can be interesting to study the evolution of this offer system over a period of time. Such an analysis can help us discover how "haute cuisine" has been kept (which is probably the specificity of haute cuisine versus non–haute cuisine) and what has been changed over the years (which is probably the adaptation of the chef's offer to the sociological change of the society). We will argue that the whole haute cuisine offer system changed a lot over the years but also went more and more back to references coming from the past. Such a situation in which the codes of the present and the past are more and more brought together by the chefs is, with no doubt, an indication of postmodernity. The restaurants of a lot of Michelin three-stars chefs are presenting a way of life that no longer exists (the best examples are the restaurants of Alain Ducasse). But whether the way of life is remembered via the interior design and the dishes, or simply imagined via the linguistic and historical references of the menu, it nevertheless signifies a widely held nostalgia (Holbrook 1990; Rybczinski 1986). The simple fact that the word haute cuisine is used very often, establishing a linguistic parallel with haute couture signifies that the chef is an artist and who is not only doing "cuisine" but something very distinctive that is signified by the adjective "haute." And like in the artistic system, there is a strong opposition between two visions of the world: the artist has to create something or the artist has to talk about what is created (the product versus the discourse). These two visions coexist in the French haute cuisine system, but what is interesting is that both lead to the fact that the focus is on the experience of the customer on one hand (by stimulating the five senses), and that the past is strongly romanced in order to be a powerful tool of sense making on the other hand. The dominant factor of customer stimulation moved from the supremacy of the gustative dimension to the preeminence of the visual dimension with on overall stimulation of the five senses, and haute cuisine is not only an organoleptic experience but also an intellectual experience (like going to the theater or a museum). Eating becomes a pretext for experiencing something unique: destroying a piece of art through incorporation. This phenomenon of incorporation of the creation means that the customer, through a magical process, gains some power. Only she/he knows it . . . until the experience is described to friends, relatives, and so on. Constructing and maintaining a sense of the past for their customers allows French chefs to give even more consistency to their offer system. Such a perspective with a strong emphasis on the past is not new in analyzing consumption systems (Havlena and Holak 1991; Holak and Havlena 1992) but has not yet been extended to the specific case of haute cuisine. This is our major objective in the present chapter.

As a System of Distinction, Haute Cuisine Develops Its Reference to the Past

One of the best examples of a chef who is strongly developing the reference to the past in his work but also tries to become a chef who will have his own place in the history of cuisine is Alain Ducasse. His relationship to the past is very particular: on one hand he talks about what other big chefs did in the past (going even back to the Renaissance) and on the other hand he tries very hard to become a name that will never be forgotten by the history of cuisine and gastronomy. Not only is he the first French chef to obtain three Michelin stars for two different restaurants at the same time (one in Paris at the Plaza-Athénée Hotel and one in Monaco), which will give him a place in the history of gastronomy, but he also recently published an encyclopedia of cuisine (Ducasse 2001). What is so special here is that since 1902 every chef in

France used another encyclopedia as a guide: the famous "Guide culinaire" of Auguste Escoffier (Escoffier 1902). Even chefs like Blanc, Bocuse, Chapel, Jung, Loiseau, Pic, Point, Robuchon, Senderens, Troisgros, or Westermann never published a book that tried to be the equivalent of what Escoffier did. Ducasse's encyclopedia contained 1,056 pages, more than 700 recipes, and a huge thematic index. The book was launched in November 2001 at a high price (€220), and within six weeks had already sold 20,000 copies, which is very unusual on the market.

But this is only anecdotal, because the entire career of Ducasse has to do with strong references to the past. He was an apprentice of Alain Chapel in Myonnay who himself was an apprentice of Alexandre Dumaine in Saulieu and Fernand Point in Vienne (Dumaine and Point were the two most famous chefs in France of the middle of the twentieth century). In this way, Ducasse is perpetuating a tradition: his knowledge has been transmitted to him by the older chefs, who themselves received it from their ancestors. Such a chain can bring us back to very ancient times. Ducasse never forgets to mention that haute cuisine is the perpetuation of a tradition that takes its roots in the past and has a very famous history.

Another way in which Ducasse insists on the past and tradition is that his best restaurants have to be located in palace hotels that were renovated recently but have a history going back to the nineteenth century. This allows him to develop the luxurious dimension of the restaurant. Palace surroundings are very impressive and the interior designs maintain a strong reference to the past while also reinforcing the status of the place. The architectural style is "Louis XV" (which is, by the way, the name of his restaurant in Monaco). Ducasse bridges the present with ancient times. Customers at his restaurants are invited to get in touch with the "good old days" when France was still one of the most powerful countries in the world: all this is very "grand siècle." The service place is one element in an offer strategy in which the overall rhetoric is to sell something unique: a piece of ephemeral "eternity." Strong references to the past are used to materialize the notion of temporal "thickness" established via the bridge of time between the past and the present. As if haute cuisine would be a combination of a physical and intellectual approach to allow customers to touch and experience, in a very ephemeral way, what immortality is. . . . Should this be the case, as Zola said about department stores, haute cuisine restaurants would than be cathedrals of our postmodern times.

A Short History of French Haute Cuisine

One cannot understand contemporary cuisine in France without having an overview of what happened in the country over the centuries. France has a long tradition of gastronomy going back at least to the Middle Ages and the Renaissance period with King Henry IV and the famous "poule au pot" dish he liked so much (a recipe with poultry). The first well-known chef was a man called Taillevent who lived in the fourteenth century. He became famous not only because he worked for King Charles V, but also because he wrote a book titled "Le Viandier," about different ways of preparing meat, in which he formalized most of the culinary knowledge of his time. The book traveled around the country and became a reference for those who cooked for the aristocracy. During the middle of the fifteenth century, a distinction clearly appeared between two kinds of cuisine: the cuisine for the aristocracy and the cuisine for the bourgeoisie.

Published in 1543, *Grand Cuisinier, Fleur de Toute Cuisine* (Big cook, flower of every cuisine), strongly insisted that a chef working for the aristocracy had to respect very specific rules, and that it was fundamental to differentiate between the "noble" and the "ordinary." The contemporary distinction made in the sixties (around 1962) about haute cuisine clearly finds its roots in this very ancient rhetoric. It has to do with a kind of nostalgia about those ancient times (but we will come back to this somewhat later in our text). During the Renaissance period and because of the strong relationships between France and Italy, brought about by the likes of Queen Catherine de Medici, French chefs influenced Italian chefs who developed more and more "alla francese" recipes in their own culinary practices, as can be attested by *Libro Novo*, written by the Italian chef Messisburgo.

François Pierre, also called La Varenne, who became the cook of Louvois (a well-known French statesman), edited a book in 1651 titled *Le Cuisinier François* (The French Cook), which is a real manifesto of the cuisine of the "grand siècle": for the first time recipes about fishes prepared "à la bleu" and very sophisticated stuffing preparations and methods are conceptualized. During the seventeenth century, the very famous "grande cuisine française" starts its development, strongly encouraged by the extravagance of the court of King Louis XIV. His cook, Vatel, also became famous for his strong quest of harmony between wines and culinary recipes: everything had to be perfect. Ironically, Vatel decided to commit suicide because the fresh food he had ordered for the king did not arrive in due time. It finally arrived five minutes after he died and the dinner was still a strong success for the great pleasure of the king. . . .

A foreign influence appeared in French gastronomy during the eighteenth century, as attested by the book *Le Cuisinier Moderne* (The Modern Cook) by Vincent La Chapelle. He was the first well-known French chef hired by the English statesman Lord Chesterfield before becoming the cook of William IV, Prince of Nassau. La Chapelle even mentioned a very exotic "tea cream" and ways to make huge progresses in the science of sauces and other complementary preparations. At the same time, during the reign of Louis XV, a very powerful aristocrat, Louis-Auguste de Bourbon, Prince of Dombes, wrote a culinary book in which he developed the whole concept of a culinary feast.

The beginning of the nineteenth century became a time for all those who liked good food to use books to theorize their impressions. Some famous French authors elevated the art of gastronomy to the ranks of nobility, while French gourmet chefs spread the refinement of cuisine throughout France and beyond its borders. One of those authors was Grimod de la Reynière, heir in a famous family of bankers, who was encouraged by the development of gastronomy during the Empire period. Alexandre Balthazar Grimod de la Reynière (1803, 1808) invented gastronomical critique. As Parienté and de Fernant (1994), historians of French cuisine, explain it, two other individuals also had a tremendous impact on cuisine in France during the beginning of the nineteenth century: Charles de Talleyrand and Anthelme Brillat-Savarin. Talleyrand, a French statesman who survived all the regimes from the French Revolution to the Restoration and was one of the major participants of the so-called Congress of Vienna, determined very precisely want he wanted to eat each day and made suggestions to his personal chef. He was lucky enough to employ the best chef in Paris: Antonin Carême. Before traveling abroad, he was making sure that the places he would visit would allow him to eat according to his very high standards, and he carried with him huge quantities of exclusive wines. When he was in Vienna, the French embassy had to import wines from France for him and his guests. When Talleyrand died, Carême was immediately hired by the court of England and then the Tsar of Russia made him the biggest financial offer ever made to a cook. He finished his career, working for the famous Baron Rothschild. No doubt, employing a famous cook was a sign of power. Brillat-Savarin became famous with his book, *Physiologie du Goût* (Physiology of Taste), in which he conceptualized taste and how culinary preparations can stimulate gustative and organoleptic sensations (Brillat-Savarin 1825). Others who helped to transform cooking into art and tasting into a science include the Marquis of Cussy who wrote: *Art Culinaire*, Colnet who poetized *L'art de Dîner en Ville* in 1810, and Berchoux who, in 1801, wrote *Gastronomie* in verse. One of his famous alexandrines "Un poète jamais ne valut un dîner" (a poet is never worth a dinner) is often used by French chefs who want to insist on the fact that cuisine is art.

The Gradual Triumph of French Chefs

The modern system of the chefs began in the early nineteenth century when great restaurants opened one after the other amidst a huge flurry of impressive advertising in Paris. It was, however, a strange combination of circumstances. First of all, many cooks had found themselves out of work following the departure abroad (or elsewhere . . .) of their aristocratic employers in the wake of the French Revolution. Second, new opportunities were beginning to emerge in the capital, attracting more and more people from the provinces who, after all, had to eat somewhere. It was a time that saw the prodigious rise to fame of chefs suddenly able to go freely about their delectable trade. They reconciled a taste for perfection with sound business sense. That period was to last until the end of the Second Empire and the fall of Emperor Napoleon III. Thereafter, in France, the prestige of restaurant chefs was to wane once again. During the interwar period, the best chefs took up office at leading hotels, which began to develop along with travel and the *Michelin Guide*.

But the real boom as we know it began at the end of the fifties. Economic growth was soaring and consumption was in full swing. After the end of World War II, Europe took a huge step forward and eradicated the problem of malnutrition. A new right, the right to food, was emerging both in principle and in habit. At the same time, a new target group was gradually appearing out of the social fabric: business executives. Halfway between the capital for which they had power of authority and the work that gave them a salaried status, they were to modify the economic and cultural landscape across Europe. As the prime beneficiaries of the general upward trend, they were to fashion for themselves a system of epicurean symbols. Good food and good living were available on demand. Slowly, yet irresistibly promoted by affluent society, to live well and to fare sumptuously became synonymous with a comfortable existence. In France in 1960, two journalists, Gault and Millau, compiled the editorial content of the magazine page for Paris-Presse; each week they featured the "in" stores for shopping and the restaurants that catered to the new, up-and-coming middle-class society. It was the beginning of the triumph of the chef-cum-restaurant proprietor. It is interesting to note that this triumph is linked to the popularity of automobiles, TV sets, refrigerators, and washing machines, among others. Very soon consumers were everywhere and, consequently, they were in the big restaurants, too.

As of 1960, the restaurant chef attained a reputation to which he would never have dared lay claim at the height of his past glory in the nineteenth century. The excesses of the media and consumerism transformed his profession and talent into a legend. Gradually, like any show business celebrity, he became a star and traveled from Paris to Tokyo, from Lyons to New York. Less and less present in their own establishments, the great chefs became heads of cultural establishments and even theaters. They wrote books on anything and everything (rather than just about recipes) and were the representatives of a new star system: they are celebrity chefs. Take, for instance, the above mentioned example of Alain Ducasse, the first chef to be the head of two restaurants simultaneously awarded three stars by the famous *Michelin Guide*, one in Monaco, the other in Paris (formerly chef Joël Robuchon's establishment). Robuchon has launched a new career for himself as a hybrid between a chef, a business dealer, and a stage director, constantly transforming the experience of eating out into a staged performance by arranging the lighting; choosing the decor, the tableware, and the wines; handling his staff like actors and his customers like spectators/actors (not unlike characters in a play by Bertold Brecht); and orchestrating the products like a carefully scored passage of which he is the sole conductor. But the first signs of a counterculture are beginning to emerge. The employees of those we mention often prefer to remain more modest and to stay discreetly at their stoves. Only the difference, it seems, makes sense.

The Contemporary Chef as Artist: From the Sense of Taste to all the Five Senses and Sense Creation

The transmutation from cook to artist chef has been gradual. It is based on a phenomenon of imitation with regard to fashion designers. Indeed, just as the great couturiers have in the past decided to set up the Committee of French Haute Couture, France's great chefs have, over the two last decades or so, founded the Committee of French Haute Cuisine to give recognition to their recipes as creative output. As with the sector of haute couture studied by Bourdieu (1979), the value of the object lies not in the scarcity of the product but in the scarcity of the person producing it. That person possesses a symbolic capital, a capital of authority in the sector concerned. Thus a chef can authenticate food preparations even if he is rarely directly responsible for it (yet another point in common with the great couturiers). Indeed, the chef neither prepares nor in some cases even creates the dishes on offer. The busy chef's caps we catch a glimpse of in front of the kitchens may well be merely the virtual image of those talented creators we know as chefs. We are therefore dealing with an "invisible creator" consisting of the entire kitchen and dining room staff. The chef stage-manages the *grande cuisine* offer and, in doing so, conceals the repetitive act of preparation, the organization of the kitchens, the expertise on the gas ranges, the fragrances, and the orchestration of dining room duties. There is something of a magical borderline that separates the head chef from the other members of his team. This is exactly what a chef like Vatel was doing at the court of King Louis XIV in Versailles. Everyone in a big restaurant puts himself at the disposal of the chef and his project, seeking to understand his concept and to implement it in their own area. The acknowledgment of the chef's team members is based on their participation in the work of art that is the meal of which the composer and conductor is the head chef. Only he appears as the author of the entire performance in the eyes of his customers. He can then do the rounds of the tables, sign a customer's menu, and thus bear witness to his creative and artistic act. Haute cuisine, like other areas of consumption, is becoming very spectacular (Peñaloza 1999).

Passeron (1989), for example, who studied the activities of artistic creation that precede the work itself, mentions that there are several interesting criteria to study: the artist's credentials, the critiques made about the work, its inclusion in the history of art, the attestation of the artist's success by his economic capital, and his relationship with the system of recognition and commercialization. These variables are entirely relevant when we talk today about a great chef. Indeed, his professional credentials are a guarantee first and foremost of the quality of the work. The critiques given about the work of chefs influence the relationship between the chef and his work. Fame, for its part, is based on longevity. It is only after many years of good ratings that a chef can put some distance between himself and the food critics (a current example is Paul Bocuse, who over the past few years has even gone so far as to appraise his own peers by organizing an international competition known as the famous "Bocuse d'Or" in Lyons). Another element that very strongly has contributed to the success of a chef like Bocuse is that he insists on tradition: he worked with the famous chef Fernand Point in Vienna, who was one of the best, if not the best, just after World War II in France. Bocuse insists that a chef has to keep the "tradition" of the profession. To maintain this tradition, most of the French chefs belong to an association called "Maîtres Cuisiniers de France" (Robuchon 1995), which has rules that are very similar to those of Fellowcraft Lodges during the Middle Ages. These organizations, structured by professionals, were crucial for the edification of cathedrals.

The Restaurant as a Stage: The Spectacular Dimension of Haute Cuisine

As mentioned in a significant number of works on the design of an environment (Augé 1995; Brown and Patterson 2000; Gottdiener 1997; Sherry 2000; Sorkin 1992), venues in the services sector have become stages, more and more. In shops, not only are products staged but it is the role of the interior designer in our postmodern era to work on the staging of the venue itself. This is particularly true of big restaurants. In a very rich and well-documented sociology paper, Terence (1996 shows for example that the staging begins outside the restaurant. Indeed, to use the terminology of Guy Debord, high-class restaurants like many other consumer sectors have entered a veritable "society of showmanship" (Debord 1971). The façades of individual country mansions and the ground floors of private townhouses in cities have many entrances protected by curtaining. The curtains act as screens and serve to exclude the noncustomer. In other instances, the façade bears the chef's logo or trademark: his initials or name identify the chef, thereby authenticating the premises. Near the entrance, the signed menu, under glass, also contributes toward constructing the image of the restaurant. As for the interior space, it is often divided into a "front office," accessible and ostentatious, and a "back office," inaccessible and intended as the area of creative output. Here, too, it is interesting to note that this separation between the accessible and the inaccessible, between the public space and the private space, is gradually fading.

Richard Normann (1984) cites for example the case of the Troisgros hotel-restaurant in Roanne, near Lyons:

> Welcome to the world of Troisgros. You will be very satisfied with your room. . . . Open the shutters and you discover the view into the courtyard. Opposite and to the right, behind a large window, silhouettes dressed in white begin to assemble, getting to work with commitment and dedication but without hurry. You are looking straight into the kitchens, where all is open and nothing is concealed. Suddenly, a small Citroën drives into the courtyard and towards the kitchen entrance. Someone, undoubtedly a member of the Troisgros family, comes out to meet the driver, who takes out a crate containing some splendid-looking salmon. The fish is examined, turned over, pressed on all sides; those that are chosen are taken into the kitchens, where they are immediately rinsed and put into the refrigerator. As the Citroën rumbles off, the entire procedure is repeated yet again, this time for a delivery of duck or vegetables. In the kitchens, you can see the staff, who have just finished eating, gathered around a table in a pleasant-looking atmosphere. . . . Other customers are also watching from their open windows. From time to time, one of the chefs looks up towards you—they know they are being watched; evidently, they are "on stage" and keen to give a good performance. You then realize that each one of them is aware of belonging to a team that is unique, that the show is well worth the detour, and that they are proud of it. (p. 46)

For a long time, there was a clear separation between what was shown and what was not shown, between the public space and the private space. That distinction has changed a lot with time. At Georges Blanc's in Vonnas, for example, to get to your table you walk along the kitchen, the inside of which is visible. The wine cellar, too, has been designed with walls made of brown-tinted yet transparent glass. More and more, there is an interplay between the public and the private. Here again, it is a characteristic of our postmodern age. Ralph Lauren's stores, a shrine of the postmodern age if ever there was one, operate by re-creating the interior of a private home. There is no doubt that the store is a public place but the aesthetic codes shown there are those of a private space (Rybczynski 1986). At Troisgros and Blanc's, the markers between the public and the private sphere have also been blurred. The emphasis is on the fact that the customer is about to discover things he cannot discover elsewhere. The particular care and attention given to the staging is an integral part of the world of luxury that is *haute gastronomy*. The underlying statement runs along the lines of "we make the inaccessible accessible, just for you." This way the customer's participation becomes central to the process. His experience is precisely that: an experience. The offer system presented is not limited to the culinary preparation; the staging goes much further.

But one must also be aware of the fact that this generalized staging and this increasingly frequent mix of public and private space does pose a number of problems. Indeed, in the great tradition of *restaurateurs* trained to the precepts of Escoffier, the separation between kitchen and dining room was clear-cut. Indeed, the chef never appeared in person and remained in his kitchens. The workspace was diametrically opposite the ostentatious space of the dining room. The kitchen was a place for doing while the dining room was a place for appearing. The hustle and bustle of the kitchens was not to be perceived by the customer. This was also the case since the Renaissance in the aristocratic world: the kitchen was separated from the place in which food was enjoyed. In some cases, the distance between the kitchen and the dining room was so long that it was almost impossible to keep the dishes warm. A few historians, for example, mention that King Louis XIV never could eat his meals warm. Nowadays, when the customer gains access, if only visually, to the kitchens, it alters the profession, the show becomes a general one and all the personnel must adopt the appear mode. And that, for a long time, had been the exclusive prerogative of the dining room staff.

This notion of show is so present in the mind of certain chefs nowadays that they no longer hesitate to say that they experience it as such. Another example that speaks volumes on this subject is that of Paul Bocuse, probably the best-known French chef of all. For him, everything is a show. Near his Michelin three-star restaurant he has even opened a second establishment designed to accommodate large parties (of up to 350 people). There he has designed a show. He took his inspiration from what was happening in Versailles at the court of King Louis XIV: a dinner there is like an aristocratic feast. Indeed, the meal is not just an occasion to discover his cuisine; the entire procedure involved in the meal has been designed so that the waiting staff parades down a giant staircase with each new dish served. All this to the accompaniment of a very impressive musical score performed on a giant barrel organ. The show also provides for the chef to pass through in person to greet his guests (and, naturally, he does so in full regalia with a *tricolore* collar to indicate that he is a *meilleur ouvrier de France*, with his name embroidered on his white tunic). And, as if to cement the cult of showmanship and of his own personality, the restaurant dining room contains a wax model that is an exact replica made by the famous workshops of the Musée Grévin in Paris. So, evidently, people go to Bocuse not just to eat but also for the entertainment value. In any case, the chef has certainly realized that, just like in a good play at a theater, his role is to do everything to make the time spent at his restaurant unforgettable. And what if his customers remember the experience for the rest of their lives and tell everyone about it? What of it? Isn't word of mouth one of the oldest media in the world?

How Chefs Create Experiential Phenomena for Their Customers

To say that the search for organoleptic elements other than the flavor of a dish in cooking is a recent phenomenon would be an oversimplification. Indeed, since the end of the Middle Ages (Fischler 1990), gourmets have looked for more than just delicacies and how food actually tastes. They also want dishes that are nice to look at. A new form of cooking developed throughout the West, where spices are used less for adding flavor than to color food, and where sugar is there to imitate the beauty of the fruits supplied by divine nature. Nonetheless, the systematic work carried out on the senses has been perfected during our postmodern era by the great chefs, as we have seen above. Therefore, luxury cuisine has two predominant stakes. First, an event-like, ritualized character: a haute cuisine luncheon or dinner requires a set of actions, words, and objects that are strictly codified, usually a result of the historical dimension of cuisine. Second, a sensationalist component: the customer must experience a number of sensations, and this is a key aspect for the success of the operation. Luxury restaurant dining can exist only if the customer is able to benefit from a local receptivity (that is why everything is organized around the customer in order to stimulate all his senses).

In fact, Pierre Bourdieu (1982) has stated that "it is in the relationship between playing and the sense of play that stakes are created and that values are formed which, although they do not exist outside that relationship, impose themselves within it, with an absolute necessity and obviousness." "Haute cuisine" is therefore inconceivable without a coded sign language, without the observance of a procedure (the ceremonial of the dinner table layout for example). For us, this section is highly representative of all the complexity involved in an act of consumerism. All the most rational factors of choice occur in it (quality, originality, etc.) as well as all the most irrational (the search for distinction, the love of rare objects, the quest for the sublime, etc.). Without an intellectual approach, haute cuisine becomes difficult to understand.

The rules that prevail most of the time when establishing the culinary offer in French haute cuisine were formally set out in 1973 by Gault and Millau through their Ten Commandments (with the subtitle: "Never the same, always the same"): a sort of manifesto of *"nouvelle haute cuisine,"*; they still apply in part today:

1. Thou shalt not overcook.
2. Thou shalt use fresh, quality produce.
3. Thou shalt lighten thy menu.
4. Thou shalt not be systematically modernistic.
5. Thou shalt seek out what the new techniques can bring you.
6. Thou shalt eliminate brown and white sauces.
7. Thou shalt not ignore dietetics.
8. Thou shalt not cheat on thy presentations.
9. Thou shalt be inventive.
10. Thou shalt not be prejudiced. (p. 24)

This shows how haute cuisine depends on its history, especially because these rules are very similar to the suggestions made by Brillat-Savarin and Grimaud de la Reynière in the nineteenth century. Of course, the content is somewhat different, for example dietetics were not an issue at that time, but even if some elements of the content are different, it is obvious that haute cuisine only exists via a reference to specific concepts and rules.

It is interesting to study these rules as it was a matter, at the time, of calling into question certain so-called common practices in the "old" cuisine. Cooking times must be reduced, produce must be fresh and of an extremely high quality. Faked presentations must be discarded. There is a refusal of sophistication in the sense of falsification; in other words, one has to cook fresh from the market, to use the terminology of Paul Bocuse. The new chefs discovered the virtues of light dishes (and no longer ignored dietetics) and thereby contributed toward complying with the change in attitude. Likewise, the emphasis is on authenticity and the respect of the product: this trend is confirmed with new cooking techniques such as steam cookers and the like. Thus, the nutritional qualities of food are preserved and all fats and rich foods are virtually banished. The chefs in the *"nouvelle cuisine"* trend prefer to "cook pink," which, it is thought, preserves the taste and the structure of the food, and use shorter cooking times for vegetables. Thus, the body, its appearance, and its well-being are present in the consciousness and concerns of the new chefs: the cuisine prepared by the new chefs must no longer be fortifying.

The cuisine of the "almost raw" and of "less is more" is a cuisine in which spiritual enjoyment is as important as physical enjoyment: it is subtle and delicate. Another recommendation is to steer clear of excessively stereotyped accompaniments. Old habits are called into question. The chef's invention and creation therefore consists of experimenting with new ingredients, new cooking methods, and new presentations. And the creative process can even involve the rehabilitation of simple things such as tuna and boiled eggs. Joël Robuchon is a case in point for this trend, for instance, reintroducing cod and potatoes on his menus but accommodating both in a surprising way. It is an unerring quest for flavors, blends, and quality of dishes at the expense of fake look-alikes, conventions, and arbitrary social habits. In "nouvelle haute cuisine" particular attention is paid to the small, the fragmented (cutting up foods into fine strips, dicing, etc.), and the young and tender. We enter the register of the miniaturized. In this new order, the diminutive becomes the superlative, with such terms as "*lapereau.*" Its originality resides in the inversely proportional ratio it establishes between the actual size of the dishes and the importance of their designation. The name of the dish alone should allow the diner to construct his desire for it and to understand, when it comes to the bill, that he is paying for the nobleness of the signification rather than the abundance of the significans. The precious language must be as much of a surprise as the taste and its skillfully executed contrasts. The humbleness of the product does not prevent it in any way from acceding to the ranks of culinary nobility. The taste for transgressive contrast and ostentatious simplicity is readily combined in a studied dissonance, between the noble and the humble, the precious and the rustic.

More and more, we have also witnessed the spread of the poetic turn of phrase in the use of the language, which consists of replacing the prepositions "au" or "à la" by "de" in the designations used for dishes. For example, the designation "*vinaigre de framboise*" is nowadays preferred to the older "*vinaigre à la framboise.*" In this particular case, the raspberry passes from the stage of condiment ingredient to that of essential component. The trend is still and always toward lighter dishes but today it is no longer irreconcilable with a return to authenticity. Like a painter, a chef may go through various periods, and the genuine cuisine is one that does not resemble any other.

Conclusion

With this work we have sought to demonstrate that to look at a consumer system, whatever it may be, is to obtain an awareness of the complexity of the phenomena we are interested in. In the present case of haute cuisine, a world of luxury and distinction *par excellence*, it is important to note that we are dealing with a very subtle phenomenon. We need to take account of physical dimensions (the location for example) as well as psychological, cultural, social, and even anthropological dimensions. Obviously, we do not pretend to have addressed them all in-depth in this chapter. Nonetheless, interpreting the world is beneficial for research into consumer behavior as it provides some elements of understanding of the constant interaction between the system of offer and demand. This interdependence is easily discernible here as, on one hand, we have the great chefs seeking to adapt to the ways in which their clientele has changed and, in doing so, take account of the demand (i.e., less fatty dishes more and more sought after by customers); on the other hand, they are also seeking to innovate and to surprise their customers by offering them new and original recipes. We may even say that chefs are in fact sociologists unbeknownst to them, just as in the *Bourgeois Gentilhomme* by Molière, Monsieur Jourdain, unbeknownst to himself, was a great writer of prose. . . . As Bourdieu (1979) already said it about distinctive consumption practices, haute cuisine is an act of "social magic." The reference to the past has then a very specific meaning: it gives the whole system some temporal "thickness." What customers of three star restaurants are buying is not only an immediate consumption experience but also something very intangible: letters of nobility. This is probably one of the reasons why Paris still is a place where people want to go to make this very specific consuming experience: for some tourists it is not only a travel into a space but also a travel into a different time. What our contemporary chefs are doing is constructing symbolic bridges between the past and the present. This is, at least, a selling argument that is used by French chefs to show the difference between them and their colleagues who may master the art as well as them, but do not have the chance to practice their job in the historical country of gastronomy. . . .

References

Augé, Marc (1995), *Non-Places: Introduction to an Anthropology of Supermodernity,* London: Verso.

Bourdieu, Pierre (1979), *La distinction: Critique sociale du goût,* Paris: Editions de Minuit.

——— (1982), *Leçon sur la leçon,* Paris: Editions de Minuit.

Brillat-Savarin, Jean-Anthelme (1825), *Physiologie du goût,* Paris.

Brown, Stephen (1995), *Postmodern Marketing,* London: Routledge.

Brown, Stephen and Anthony Patterson (2000), "Knick-knack Paddy-whack, Give a Pub a Theme," *Journal of Marketing Management,* 16 (6) : 647–62.

Colnet (1810), *L'art de dîner en ville*, Paris, Bibliothèque Nationale Française.

Cussy (1805), *Art culinaire*, Paris: Bibliothèque Nationale Française.

Debord, Guy (1971), La société du spectacle, Paris: Editions Champ Libre.

Ducasse, Alain (2001), *Grand livre de cuisine d'Alain Ducasse*, Paris: ADF.

Escoffier, Auguste (1902), *Le guide culinaire*, Paris: Flammarion.

Firat, A. Fuat and Alladi Venkatesh (1993), Postmodernity: The Age of Marketing," *International Journal of Research in Marketing*, 10: 227–49.

Fischler, Claude (1990), *L'homnivore*, Paris: Odile Jacob.

Gault and Millau (1973), *Guide culinére France*, Paris: Editions Gault et Millau, p. 24.

Gottdiener, Mark (1997), *The Theming of America: Dreams, Visions and Commercial Spaces*, Boulder, CO: Westview.

Grimod de la Reynière, Alexandre Balthazar (1803), *Almanach des gourmands*, Paris: Bibliothèque Nationale Française.

———— (1805), *Manuel des Amphitryons*, Paris: Bibliothèque Nationale Française.

Havlena, William J. and Susan L. Holak (1991), "The Good Old Days: Observation on Nostalgia and Its Role in Consumer Behavior," in *Advances in Consumer Research*, vol. 18, ed. Donna J. Hoffman and Michael R. Solomon, Provo, UT: Association for Consumer Research, pp. 323–29.

Holak, Susan L. and William J. Havlena (1992), "Nostalgia: An Exploratory Study of Themes and Emotions in the Nostalgic Experience," in *Advances in Consumer Research*, vol. 19, ed. John F. Sherry, Jr. and Brian Sternthal, Provo, UT: Association for Consumer Research, pp. 380–87.

Holbrook, Morris B. (1990), "Nostalgic Consumption: On the Reliability and Validity of a New Nostalgia Index," working paper, New York: Columbia University.

Normann, Richard (1984), *Service Management: Strategy and Leadership in Service Business*, Chichester: John Wiley, p. 46.

Parienté, Henriette and Geneviève de Fernant (1994), *Histoire de la cuisine française*, Paris: Editions de La Martinière.

Passeron, René (1989), *Pour une philosophie de la création*, Paris: Klincksieck.

Peñaloza, Lisa (1999), "Just Doing It: A Visual Ethnographic Study of Spectacular Consumption Behavior at Nike Town," *Consumption, Markets and Culture*, 2 (4): 337–400.

Robuchon, Joël (1995), *Le carnet de route d'un compagnon cuisinier*, Paris: Payot.

Rybczynski, Witold (1986), *Home: A Short History of an Idea*, London: Penguin Books.

Sherry, John F., Jr. (2000), "Place, Technology and Representation," *Journal of Consumer Research*, 27 (September): 273–78.

Sorkin, Michael (ed.) (1992), *Variations on a Theme Park: The New American City and the End of Public Space*, New York: Hill and Wang.

Terence, Isabelle (1996), *Le monde de la grande restauration en France: La réussite est-elle dans l'assiette?*, Paris: L'Harmattan.

14

Retrospecting Retroscapes

Form and Function, Content and Context

Janeen Arnold Costa and Gary J. Bamossy

From Disneyland to Le Parc Disney, from Las Vegas to the Tivoli Gardens, scholars have been consumed conceptually by "conspicuous consumption," particularly in the context of postmodernism, hyperreality, and hedonism. Recently, the Disney/Vegas phenomenon has expanded exponentially, and space and place seem to have become more relevant to consumers, marketers, and intellectuals. In this context, we and the other authors represented in this book seek to understand the "rise of retroscapes," where the sense of place is "reanimated . . . through evocations of times past" (Brown 2001).

We suggest, however, that human social phenomena resembling what we now term "retroscapes" have been part and parcel of the human condition for some time. Thus, while the specific form and number of "retroscapes" are currently changing, our examination indicates this is most likely a response to aspects of twenty-first-century capitalism, including the First World postmodern consumer and marketing to entice him/her. While the world has indeed seen the rise of retroscape-like events, these experiences, places, and performances are actually spatially broad and temporally deep.

In this essay, we move beyond an emphasis on spectacular and profit-motivated spaces of advanced industrial and postindustrial capitalist countries or enclaves within other societies. From passion plays and ritual reenactments to traveling shows, vaudeville, and Buffalo Bill; from circuses to folkloric displays; from the contrived "authenticity" of Irish theme pubs to the feng shui–informed Hong Kong Disney, retro places, spaces, performances, experiences, and events all fit a broad conceptualization of retroscape. Spanning time, space, and culture, the retroscape has been a part of human history and geography since the recording of human activities began (and presumably before that!). The retroscape, intensively and extensively, *exemplifies itself.*

Thus, the "recent rise" and exemplification of the "postmodern moment" applies most to the particular form retroscapes typically take in advanced capital societies or through the spread of consumer culture from the United States and Europe to the "rest of the world." To illustrate our point, we show that forms of, and reasons for, retroscapes vary. In addition, retroscapes occur in specific places in ways that are identifiably related to the societies in which they occur. Along these lines, we will investigate several forms of retrospace and suggest where and why such forms appear. In the end, we conclude that retroscapes are panhuman and culturally universal, and we will suggest some reasons why this is the case.

Forms and Functions

Retroscapes take many forms. For our purposes here, we will investigate the types of retroscapes or spaces, the places in which they are likely to occur, and possible reasons for their existence in each case. The following four varieties are among those we will consider: spectacular constructed hyperrealities and themed spaces typically created for the purpose of profit; costumed actors/dancers, props and mobile stage sets; ritual reenactments (which may overlap with the previous category); and "natural" landscape or viewed human constructions deemed to be retroscapes from the perspective of the consumer.

For each of these retroscapes, we will consider the general character of the societies in which they are likely to occur and provide specific examples that describe the retroscape and the society. Some of these forms are found in all societies, we believe, at least at some point in time, while others may be unique to certain types of society. Closely related to this discussion is the posited function or reason underlying the prevalence of certain retroscapes in given societies. We believe that variations in time, place, and form may be explained by understanding the needs, wants, and behaviors of consumers in different societies, as well as the historical and economic circumstances of the societies in question (see Exhibit 14.1).

The Rise of Retroscapes

As we have suggested, the "growing popularity of retroscapes" may refer primarily to retroscapes that characterize advanced capitalist societies, particularly the United States and Western Europe but also portions of, or places in, Asia and South America. Here we find such themed spaces as Niketown (e.g., Sherry 1998), foreign country as theme parks (Hendry 2000), and Disneyland/World in its various manifestations (e.g., Costa and Bamossy 2001; King 1981; Moore 1980), as well as various sites in Las Vegas, representing both specific time and place (Belk 1998; Gottdiener 1997, 2001; Ritzer 1999; Sorkin 1992). Themed eating and drinking establishments are also represented here (e.g., Brown and Patterson 2000; Lego et al. 2002), as are hotels and resorts (Belk 1998). These places are constructed realities, often representing significant financial outlay and with an eye toward attracting the fickle consumer, and generating a return on a commercial investment.

Precisely *because* of the large numbers of fickle consumers in advanced capitalist societies, retroscapes are highly visible and are the subject of scrutiny by scholars in anthropology, sociology, marketing, and consumer behavior. Offering a multisensory, nostalgic atmosphere, a temporary escape in time and/or space, a chance to play, and the prospect of allowing consumers to confirm their own expectations, companies construct or evoke retroscapes for consumers, much like tourist destinations who lure tourists to a constructed and commodified destination. Within this category of Exhibit 14.1, retroscapes are analogous to Redfoot's "first-order tourist," who travels with family, tour groups or friends (almost never alone) bearing cameras, visiting sites, and comfortably avoiding "real" contact with the surrounding environment (Redfoot 1984, p. 293).

Like Redfoot's first-order tourists, the retroscape consumer comes with a past and leaves with a future full of memories. With expectations molded by glossy brochures, picture postcards, travel agents' catalogues, and shaped by past experiences (often from the media and not direct, firsthand experiences), expectations are well-formed in advance as to just what one is "supposed" to experience at the retroscape. Personal, idiosyncratic memories of times and places may play a role, but the design of commercial retroscape does its best to shape those recollections as well. The 'scape's goal is to assure that the experiences approximate the consumer's expectations, and the consumer measures his/her satisfaction by the degree to which the 'scape conforms to its prebilled attributes. Even those consumers who want to avoid the staged retroscapes of our first category will have trouble in doing so as they seek out other 'scapes, such as natural landscapes, or viewed human constructions. We will return to this point in our upcoming discussion of the American West.

Actors and Mobile Stages

In general, the retroscapes and themed spaces of the type we have just discussed are immobile. The "sets" are so elaborate, substantial, comprehen-

256

Exhibit 14.1

Types of Retroscapes

Retroscape type	Examples	Typical Reasons for Existence		Type of society
		Producer	Consumer	
Category I: hyperreality and themed places	Disney Parks (USA, Europe, and Japan)	Revenues	Need to look back	Consumer cultures
	Restaurants	Product differentiation societies	Escape	Advanced capitalistic societies
	"This-is-the-Place" Heritage Park (Utah)	Competition for consumers' resources (time and money)	Play	
	Films (*Lord of the Rings*; *Ben Hur*)		Explore and understand self vs. other	
			Hedonic consumption	
Category II: costumed actors and mobile stages	Buffalo Bill's Wild West Show	Revenues	Entertainment	Historical USA and Europe
	Circuses	Preservation of art form or lifestyle	Otherness	First to Third World travel destinations
	Vaudeville		Education	Most societies at some point in time
	Hotel tourist bubbles		Reinforcement of history, values	

Category III: ritual reenactments	Bali drama dances Hopi home dances Passion plays, Thanksgiving	Revenues Preservation of art form or lifestyle	Ritual responsibility Preservation Entertainment Education Renewal Ethical and spiritual motives	Smaller "traditional" societies Segments of larger industrial societies
Category IV: natural landscapes or "viewed human constructions"	The American West Hawaii and Alaska Mythical Irish countryside	Commercial co-opting of spaces/icons for associative values, and revenues	Consumer perceptions and expectations serve to form a unique (or popularly held) discourse	Takes on different forms in different societies

sive, and complete, that they actually *create* a place, a retroscape, in and of themselves. Retroscapes of this second category do not accomplish the experiential totality such complicated construction implies. Nevertheless, the mind of the consumer in this category is bent toward the past through costumes and sets that are often complex and extensive, albeit to a degree definitively less so than the hyperreal 'scapes discussed above. Because—or perhaps as a result—of the less bulky sets and scenes, many of the retroscapes in this category are/were "traveling shows."

It is important to note that, at the time these types of performances developed in various settings, they may not have fit the description of "retro." For example, when the combination of equestrian feats, acrobats, and wild animal exhibits that became known as "the circus" began in 1768, the entertainment was new and exciting. The addition of sensational costumes added to the enthusiastic audience response (May 1963; Saxon 1978). Similarly, American vaudeville is an entertainment form that developed in the nineteenth century. Comedy, musical acts, and dancing were performed in theatres and on the streets for the amusement of working people (Stein 1984). Despite an occasional reference to the past, vaudeville was at first considered more avant-garde than retro, primarily because of the nearly revolutionary organization, timing, and combination of the various forms of entertainment. The French cabaret also costumed actors singing and dancing with portable sets as background. Again, this entertainment was considered avant-garde, even futuristic (Senelick 1989–1990).

However, when these specific forms of entertainment are performed, encountered, and consumed *now*, they are, in fact, retroscapes. The traditional circus, vaudeville, and cabaret acts, as well as minstrel shows, British music hall entertainment, traveling medicine shows, and others, are all distinctive in terms of artistic style, managed performance, costuming, and sets. As such, they evoke nostalgia for times and events of the past; they represent not only the art forms themselves but the social and political times when they developed and were first presented. Thus, despite their not being anchored to a particular place, retroscapes involving costumed actors and mobile sets create a consumption experience that involves times that have gone before.

Retroscapes that fall within this category are not confined to those we have just discussed, however. When people from a given society or cultural group, including subcultures, perform dances or engage in plays and "skits" exemplifying their cultural background, and when such performances are based upon the past, they also can be said to be retroscapes. Within the subcultural arena of complex societies, they often serve to "preserve the past." For example, the Greek-American folk dancers in various communities throughout the United States perform dances that are no longer found in

Greece. In addition to display, entertainment, and profit-making, the Mexican Folklorico Ballet similarly maintains choreography and costumes that are not a part of Mexican culture at this time. These types of retroscapes are found throughout the world.

Tourist productions, both inside and outside the "hotel bubble" are also excellent examples of this type of retroscape (Edensor 2001; MacCannell 1973; Redfoot 1984). Marketers assess which performances and created stage scenery are likely to be most entertaining for visitors, most profitable for the producers, and most amenable to production. Thus, at the Polynesian Cultural Center in Oahu, Hawaii, dances and scenes from all over the Pacific Islands are performed, yet the dancers themselves typically do not originate in the island from which the scene is created. Here, the viewing desires of the audience, the profit motive, and the production scheme—whereby it has been deemed unnecessary to have the "original" natives perform the dances—have combined to create an actor-stage retroscape. Of course, given that this is also a "themed place," we may wish to place this in the first category. However, the emphasis on dancers, actors, costumes, and stages, makes it a good fit for this category as well.

The tourist productions that are found in this category of retroscape are typical of "cultural tourism," primarily from the First World to Third World destinations. Here, tourists seek the cultural "authenticity" their own presence indicates is disappearing (Desmond 1999; MacCannell 1973; Redfoot 1984; Urry 1990a, 1990b, 1992). Of course, the typical tourist would be inconvenienced by the necessity of traveling around the countryside, hoping to view actual cultural events, which they are unlikely to find in most cases. As the First World intrudes in various ways, "hosts" or "natives" sometimes wish to keep their cultural performances intact and away from the prying eyes of camera-carrying visitors. Nevertheless, whether in public or private, these types of retroscapes exist both to please and simultaneously to preserve.

Ritual Reenactments

The events that fall into the category of "ritual reenactments" sometimes overlap in character and form with the traveling shows and other actor/stage retroscapes discussed above. Nevertheless, the motivations of the consumer, the societal and individual functions such enactments may be said to serve, and the types of society in which ritual reenactments predominate vary substantially from those of other retroscapes. Like the circus, vaudeville, and folk dance displays, the "actors" in ritual reenactments are playing a dramatic part, are often costumed, and perform in the context of props and mobile sets. Here, however, in addition to entertainment and education, the retroscape displays aspects of the past related to the supernatural. Therefore, these retroscapes may fulfill functions such as societal questioning, rebellion and reinforcement, responsibility, and renewal.

Within the anthropological tradition, British structural-functionalism is most well-known for analysis and explanation of various social traits and behaviors on the basis of the role these play in a given society. Since our purpose here is to provide descriptions and examples of retroscapes in other times and places, we will ignore for the moment the appropriate criticism leveled at the British school for its adynamic qualities. Among the social structures most studied by the British are religious systems (e.g., Malinowski 1922/1950, 1935, 1948; Radcliffe-Brown 1948, 1952; Turner 1952, 1963, 1969), and we provide here a few examples of the retro form that rituals often take and of the social systemic functions they have been said to perform.

Focusing on the ritual responsibility of various individuals in a society, Fortes has written about the duty of Tallensi (Africa) chiefs and Earth-priests in terms of their "due performance of ritual obligations" (p. 73). In an annual ritual, the Tallensi construct a retroscape, which "consists in dramatizing salient episodes in the myths of the founding ancestors" (p. 75). The point of the ritual is not only to reaffirm the role of the officials, the chiefs and Earth-priests, in terms of ritual responsibility, but also to cement the relationship between the two Tallensi clans. Thus, according to Fortes, "it is not only a dramatization of the myth of the origin of the politico-ritual relations of the two clan groups; it is also a rite of renewal of the chief's office" (1962, p. 78).

Durkheim, often referred to as a founder of modern sociology, was similarly interested in the social nature of religion and ritual. Focusing specifically on Australian aboriginal groups whose practices he felt would be closest to forms of the distant human past, Durkheim described totemic rites emphasizing the deification of society and origin myths. For example, among the Warramunga, the "mythical history of the ancestor Thalaualla, from the moment he emerged from the group up to his definite return thither" is reenacted (1915/1965, p. 416). Details such as the ancestor's journeys and places of residence and his activities are reenacted:

> The myth says that in each of the localities where he sojourned, he celebrated totemic ceremonies; they now repeat them in the same order in which they are supposed to have taken place originally. The movement, which is acted the most frequently, consists in twisting the entire body about rhythmically and violently; this is because the ancestor did the same thing to make the germs of life which were in him come out. The actors have their bodies covered with down, which is detached and flies away

during these movements; this is a way of representing the flight of these mystic germs and their dispersion into space. (pp. 416–17)

According to Durkheim, "The rite consists solely in recollecting the past and, in a way, making it present by means of a veritable dramatic representation" (p. 416).

Death, burial, and rejuvenation are common themes in ritual reenactment retroscapes. In what is perhaps the greatest compendium of religious beliefs and rituals in existence, Frazer's *Golden Bough* (1922/1963) provides descriptions of rites throughout the world, including Europe. Frazer presents myths and rituals, comparing and contrasting them to one another, and often relating the construction of retroscapes. For example, reenacting the myth of Adonis, Frazer indicates:

At the festivals of Adonis, which were held in Western Asia and in Greek lands, the death of the god was annually mourned, with a bitter wailing, chiefly by women; images of him, dressed to resemble corpses, were carried out as to burial and then thrown into the sea or into springs. (pp. 389–90)

Of particular interest is the myth of Balder and its reenactment in the fire-festivals of Europe. The Norse god Balder was a "good and beautiful god, the son of the great god Odin, and himself the wisest, mildest, best beloved of all the immortals" (Frazer 1922/1963, pp. 703–4). The myth proceeds with the contention that all the gods so loved Balder, that they made a pact not to use their weapons and magic to kill him. However, Loki, a mischief-maker, found that Balder could be killed with mistletoe, after which Balder's body and all of his things were placed upon his ship and were burned. Frazer contends that virtually all of the European bonfires, from the Lenten fires of France, Belgium, and Germany, to the Easter fires in most Catholic countries, to the Beltane fires of the Scottish highlands, the midsummer and midwinter fires, and the Hallowe'en fires throughout Europe at the time of Frazer's research in the early twentieth century are in some ways reenactments of the death of Balder, with an expansion of their purpose and meaning to include warding off evil in general.

The retroscapes in the ritual reenactment category occur *primarily* in what we term smaller, "traditional" societies; the separation between those who produce the retroscape, those who participate in it, and those who observe or consume it is much less rigid and may not actually exist. For example, in the context of trance dancing in Bali, members of the "audience" may at any time feel the urge to dance and enter into trance as part of reenacting the perpetual conflict between good and evil expressed in dramatic form and ritual (Mead and Bateson 1951).

However, examples of ritual reenactment retroscapes are also found in segments of larger, complex societies. Many of Frazer's European, as well as some of his Middle Eastern and Eastern, examples represent these "larger" societies, albeit from nearly a century ago, but instances of ritual reenactments abound in these societies today as well. For example, Orthodox Christian Easter rites are reenactments of the last period of Christ's life. Found in Russia, Greece, the United States, and elsewhere, these religious ceremonies are clear examples of retroscapes within the category of ritual reenactments. The following description and symbolic account is offered, based on one of the authors' research in Greece (Costa 1983) and in the Greek-American community of Salt Lake City, Utah (Costa 1995), as well as on personal experiences in Russia and in Greek-American communities in California, New York, and Washington, D.C.

The Orthodox Christian rites begin with the Lenten period forty days prior to Easter Sunday and intensify with the reenactment of Christ's entering Jerusalem on Palm Sunday, when church organizers lay palm fronds in the aisles of the church and provide palm leafs folded in the shape of a cross to each participant. As "Holy Week" proceeds, each lengthy service revisits in symbolic form the activities, events, trauma, and drama of Christ and his followers in the days leading up to Easter Sunday and Christ's resurrection. Perhaps the most clear retroscape is apparent in the Good Friday service, when a large wooden or metal frame is covered entirely with fresh flowers, a tapestry or fabric with the image of Christ is laid inside the structure, and the celebrants carry this construction around the church and then around the village (in Greece or in Russia) or city block (in larger settlements and in the United States). Referred to as the *epitaphio*, the Greek word for the structure literally translates as "very tomb" or simply "tomb." The journey of the epitaphio symbolically reenacts the carrying of Christ's body from Mount Olivet, the site of crucifixion, to the cave where Christ's body was entombed. In the reenactment, several men carry the epitaphio, followed by priests and other church officials, as well as lay worshippers, all of whom carry lit candles to symbolize Christ as "the light of the world."

It is worth noting that these celebrations do not take place at the same time as Easter is celebrated elsewhere around the globe. True to attempts to replicate faithfully the events of Christ's death, the rituals are scheduled differently each year, based on a specific formula. In particular, the phase of the moon, the spring equinox, the day of the week, and the date of the Jewish Passover are all taken into account, so that the Orthodox Easter is celebrated *as if it were taking place now, this year*, instead of 2,000 years ago.

In the cases of retroscapes constructed through ritual reenactments, symbols of the supernatural abound, including references to myths, to gods/goddesses, to specific mystical events, and so on. The reenactments are precisely that—reenacting, replaying, reaffirming events, stories, and images that are said to have occurred before, in the past. However, it would be superficial to assess these rituals as mere copies of the past, with no present purpose. Clearly, the topics are somehow significant enough to warrant the attention of participants in these elaborate performances. Can we accept the approach of the British social anthropologists and focus on the societal functions of unity, cohesion, and renewal? Perhaps, but within the context of these rites individuals also express devotion, intention, and participation, the latter often intense. In the perspective of theorists such as Durkheim, this individual passion would equate with the societal deification and unity. We suspect, on the other hand, that individual vehemence has more to do with nostalgia, the supernatural, and the "meaning of life" in a religious context.

Retro-Landscapes

In this category of retroscape, the perceptions of the viewer, and the interpretation of the consumer become particularly active, *defining* the space as place, and explicitly giving meaning to observed surroundings. Unlike the other three retroscape forms that we have already discussed, retro-landscapes are not typically constructed by marketers or producers, or even co-produced as in ritual reenactments. Thus, the meaning of the retro-landscape is not usually provided overtly through constructions where the retro intentions are clear. Instead, retro-landscapes are contextualized, most often by the consumer and in the absence of a marketer, in a discourse that is socially and historically embedded, but is not explicitly communicated. This type of retroscape, therefore, calls for consumer "action" and participation, perhaps in ways that the other retroscapes do not.

Humans ascribe significance to their physical surroundings; Hirsch (1995, p. 1) claims this is one of the anthropological senses of "landscape," referring to "the meaning imputed by local people to their cultural and physical surroundings (i.e., how a particular landscape 'looks' to its inhabitants)." This meaning is often based on the past, particularly with respect to a group's ancestors and relevant social organizational features and systems. For example, Keesing differentiated between the local scenery as seen by "outsiders" and that seen by the Kwaio (Pacific):

> The landscape of the Kwaio interior appears, to the alien eye, as a sea of green, a dense forest broken periodically by gardens and recent secondary

growth, and an occasional tiny settlement. . . . To the Kwaio eye, this land-scape is not only divided by invisible lines into named land tracts and settle-ment sites; it is seen as structured by history. (Keesing 1982, p. 76, quoted in Hirsch 1995, pp. 1–2)

Similarly, Morphy (1995) describes the Yolngu (Australian) view of their land as linked to the past and to the supernatural in ways not experienced by outsiders:

> They recognize the existence of ancestral forces in the land, and they feel the spirits of generations of the dead in the surrounding land . . . so that the possibility of avoiding spiritually powerful or dangerous places can be re-covered, thereby enabling them to act properly. (pp. 185–86)

Local inhabitants *see* the countryside, the vista, the human incursions in ways that are frequently retro, inscribing the landscape with events, activities, and details of the past.

However, one does not have to be indigenous to a landscape to ascribe meaning to that 'scape. Rather, while the discourse of the past provides mean-ing of a specific type for local residents, a different discourse may (or may not) impart another interpretation, perhaps also based in the past, but quite unlike that developed and held locally. The "local version" tends to be more detailed, to include both recent and past events, and to incorporate specific known humans and behaviors attached to them. This may or may not be the case with visitors' interpretations of the retro-landscape, where meaning tends to be drawn from a larger discourse.

Let's take a hypothetical example. Mount St. Helens, a volcano in the northwest region of the United States, erupted with a fury in 1980. The image of the explosion and the devastation to the surrounding landscape was communicated around the globe via photographs in newspapers, maga-zines, and on the television screen. Visitors to this site now may well re-member the exact images of the blast, perhaps comparing it to what they see currently. Their interpretive consumption is based on visions of the past as provided through the media. Contrast this with the experience and memories of the "locals," those who lived nearby and "lived through" the disaster. Not only did they see the media-constructed representations, but they also saw the event as it transpired, the dramatic alterations to the landscape. Most importantly it is likely that they associate humans with various facets of the catastrophe—friends who were lost, formerly lived-in homes washed away or abandoned, rescue attempts, successes and fail-ures. In a microcosm, the visitors bring with them the "discourse of 1980," the photographs, the commentary, the film, the "created reality" that has become a retro-landscape through focus on this calamity that took place in the past. But the local residents are likely to have a somewhat different discourse, one that not only includes the mediated visions of the explosion, but also goes beyond it to include more details and occurrences unknown to the visitor.

The world is replete with retro-landscapes, and the discourse in which their retro-perspective is embedded is not always as obvious, recent, or accessible as Mount St. Helens from 1980. For instance, many consumers see the Hawaiian landscape as colorful, bountiful, and suggestive of unfettered nature and humanity. Costa (1998) assesses this consumption perspective as embedded within paradisiacal discourse, which is itself a form of primitivist discourse. Here, the consumers draw upon a discourse thousands of years old, embedded in social perspectives and European and American history, that gives meaning to the Hawaiian landscape as an Edenic paradise. The dry, barren desert of the American West is given significance and substance through a discourse that embraces individualism and isolation, battle with the elements and with indigenous peoples (cowboys vs. Indians!), and struggles for survival through taming the land and animals that feed upon it. Movies featuring cultural icons such as John Wayne, Henry Fonda, and Clark Gable perpetuated the discourse through vivid imagery and scripts consistently featuring the rugged, independent male of the American West (Murray 2000). Now a well-integrated part of the discourse, early entrepreneurs literally invented the Western American tourist experience of Santa Fe and the Southwest (Thomas 1978). Today, visitors to the American West may see stores with Western facades, participate in cattle drives, or eat dutch oven and barbecued meals brought to their campsites with horses and wagons. But we argue that these are just further reinforcements of a retro-landscape interpretation that consumers already see and expect, one in which strange and magnificent stone shapes, aridity and stark sunlight, harsh winds, stunted and struggling flora and fauna remind them of the appropriate discourse. Perhaps without ever having seen or experienced the marketers' efforts and entertainments available on a local basis, consumers of the American West see a retroscape, specifically a retro-landscape, replete with meaning provided by a discourse of which they may not be fully conscious.

Thus, retro-landscapes are examples of retroscapes that may not even require the intervention of "modern" or "postmodern" marketers. The creation of meaning is a long and complex process. Again, we suggest that retro-perspectives that imbue a 'scape with retro-meaning are not merely a feature of the complex societies many marketers and consumer behavior scholars study. The forms we have discussed, including retro-landscapes, suggest a much broader and deeper (in time) prevalence of retroscapes, or at least retroscape-like phenomena, which brings us to the most interesting part of our discussion—why are they so widespread, and what does this pervasiveness mean?

Understanding Retroscapes

Numerous theorists have been fascinated by the creation and proliferation of spaces that emphasize and/or exemplify the hyperreal and spectacular. Many of these constructed spaces are retroscapes, erected as exemplars of the past, evoking nostalgia, assembled to enhance experiences of escape within the context of things that have gone before. Having recognized that such places exist, our intellectual focus as cross-cultural researchers was directed toward issues of cultural context, universality, and specificity.

We believe we have argued persuasively that retroscapes exist in many, if not all, societies, but that they take varying forms and serve diverse functions across time, place, and culture. The retroscapes with which many of our colleagues have been concerned are mostly a component of postindustrial, service economies based on capitalism. A section of the population large enough to support consumption of expensive experiences directed solely toward "fun" must also exist. However, the fact that retroscapes of a different form exist in other societies than these leads us to question what motivates consumers to seek and/or construct retroscapes in general. People in these other societies, noted as examples in the various categories analyzed above, do not conform to the features of the societies where the hyperreal spectacle predominates. Thus, we have several things to consider as we seek to understand the "why" of retro.

The Mind of the Consumer

Focusing on the mutual construction of experience, this dialectical interaction of producer and consumer has been considered to be a critical part of the postmodern position (Brown 2001; Firat and Venkatesh 1995). We believe, however, that the consumer as observer, as witness, and as spectator may be a much more accurate and realistic assessment of consumption in this context. If we look at the other forms of retroscape that we have described and considered, the amount of overt, visible detail that is given, that comes from the producer to the consumer, actually seems to lessen as one proceeds through the categories. By the time we consider retro-landscapes, it is clear that a retroscape does not have to be a literal construction at all—not a building or props or costumes or lights—but can be assembled *within the mind* of the consumer, drawing upon social and historical discourse.

It has been suggested that the sense of a place is dependent upon the basis of what "it is made with" (Basso 1996, p. 84). In this sense, it is the mind of the consumer, of the observer, that is most critical, and it is the image, the impression, even the aura that a space evokes that makes it a place of one type or another. According to Basso:

> Disquisitions on wisdom, and cautionary stories of thirst-crazed women and puffed-up medicine men do not "add up" to a Western Apache sense of place. But they can be used to construct one. . . . They give us, in short, a sense of the Apache sense. (pp. 84–85)

The elements that are used to construct a space must be added to one another, pulled together, most often in the context of an elaborate discourse, then interpreted and understood by the consumer.

As a further note, it would appear that, in all other categories save the hyperreal and themed places associated with the postmodern West, the provided imagery calls for more interpretation and animation on the part of the consumer. If this is so, then perhaps this leads us back to Baudrillard (1983). Our work suggests that, by being more literal and specific, providing a 'scape that is more fully constructed by the marketer, the hyperreal retroscape actually becomes more real and less imagined, providing fewer degrees of freedom in interpretation on the part of the consumer. Thus, the reading of the past as presented in postmodern hyperreal and themed retroscapes is more determined, more stable, and less open to interpretation.

The Social Sense and Retroscapes' Permanence

Theorists who have considered the origins and content of sense of place have observed that "places gather" and are, therefore, inherently social. According to Casey, places "gather experiences and histories, even languages and thoughts. . . . The power belongs to place itself, and it is a power of gathering" (1996, pp. 24–25). Perhaps, herein lies the popular attraction and longevity of retroscapes. The strong social context stemming from a shared past provides a sense of belonging for consumers. The production and consumption of nostalgic feelings and memories with friends and family during the active participation at retroscapes, and the leaving of retroscapes to a future "daily life" of shared meanings, are the fabrics that allow retroscapes to endure across eras. In our postmodern times, retroscapes, particularly those in our Category I, seem to be relegated to a lower ontological status—a "pseudo" experience (Boorstin 1961) wherein capitalism is able to convert experience into a "lesser" commodity to be consumed within the confines of a constructed retroscape. This perspective ignores the argument that the meanings evoked by retroscapes are not frivolous, superficial, or "inauthentic"; in fact, they represent the shared memories of the private sphere that serve as an important anchor for the modern consumer. Across eras and cultures, there always have been retroscapes. Whether they appear to be commercial, ritualistic, constructed, or imagined, there has always been then, there.

References

Basso, Keith H. (1996), "Wisdom Sits in Places: Notes on a Western Apache Landscape," in *Senses of Place,* ed. Steven Feld and Keith H. Basson, Santa Fe, NM: School of American Research Press, pp. 53–90.

Baudrillard, Jean (1983), *Simulations*, New York: Semiotext(e).

Belk, Russell W. (1998), "Three Coins in a Caesar's Palace Fountain: Interpreting Las Vegas," in *Advances in Consumer Research*, vol. 25, Provo, UT: Association for Consumer Research, pp. 7–9.

Boorstin, Daniel J. (1961), *The Image: A Guide to Pseudo-Events in America*, New York: Atheneum.

Brown, Stephen (2001), *Marketing—The Retro Revolution*, London: Sage Publications.

Brown, Stephen and Anthony Patterson (2000), Knick-knack Paddy-whack, Give a Pub a Theme," *Journal of Marketing Management*, 16 (6): 647–62.

Casey, Edward S. (1996), "How to Get from Space to Place in a Fairly Short Stretch of Time: Phenomenological Prolegomena," in *Senses of Place*, ed. Steven Feld and Keith H. Basso, Santa Fe, NM: School of American Research, pp. 13–52.

Costa, Janeen Arnold (1983), "Migration and Economic History in Rural Greece: A Case Study," dissertation Stanford University, Department of Anthropology.

———— (1995), "The Social Organization of Consumer Behavior," in *Contemporary Marketing and Consumer Behavior: An Anthropological Sourcebook*, ed. John F. Sherry, Jr., Newbury Park, CA: Sage Publications, pp. 213–44.

———— (1998), "Paradisal Discourse: A Critical Analysis of Marketing and Consuming Hawaii," *Consumption, Markets and Culture*, 1: 309–46.

Costa, Janeen Arnold and Gary J. Bamossy (2001), "Le Parc Disney: Creating an Authentic: American Experience," in *Advances in Consumer Research*, vol. 28, Valdosta, GA: Association for Consumer Research, pp. 398–402.

Desmond, Jane C. (1999), *Staging Tourism: Bodies on Display from Waikiki to Sea World*, Chicago: University of Chicago Press.

Durkheim, Emile (1915/1965), *The Elementary Forms of the Religious Life*, New York: Free Press.

Edensor, Tim (2001), "Performance Tourism, Staging Tourism: (Re)Producing Tourist Space and Practice," *Tourist Studies*, 1 (1): 59–82.

Firat, A. Fuat and Alladi Venkatesh (1995), "Liberatory Postmodernism and the Reenchantment of Consumption," *Journal of Consumer Research*, 22 (December): 239–67.

Fortes, Meyer (1962), "Ritual and Office in Tribal Society," in *Essays on the Ritual of*

Social Relations, ed. Max Gluckman, Manchester, UK: Manchester University Press, pp. 53–88.

Frazer, Sir James George (1922/1963), *The Golden Bough*, New York: MacMillan Publishing Company.

Gottdiener, Mark (1997), *The Theming of America: Dreams, Visions and Commercial Spaces*, Boulder, CO: Westview.

——— (2001), *The Theming of America: Dreams, Media Fantasies, and Themed Environments*, Boulder, CO: Westview.

Hirsch, Eric (1995), "Landscape: Between Place and Space," in *The Anthropology of Landscape: Perspectives on Place and Space*, ed. Eric Hirsch and Michael O'Hanlon, Oxford, UK: Clarendon Press, pp. 1–30.

Hendry, Joy (2000), "Foreign Country Theme Parks: A New Theme or an Old Japanese Pattern," *Social Science Japan Journal*, 3(2): 207–20.

Keesing, Roger (1982), *Kwaio Religion: The Living and the Dead in a Solomon Island Society*, New York: Columbia University Press.

King, Margaret J. (1981), "Disneyland and Walt Disney World: Traditional Values in Futuristic Forms," *Journal of Popular Culture*, 15(1): 116–40.

Lego, Caroline, Natalie Wood, Michael R. Solomon, and Darach Turley (2002), *Real or Replica? Deciphering Authenticity in Irish Pubs*, Valdosta, GA: Association for Consumer Research.

MacCannell, Dean (1973), "Staged Authenticity: Arrangements of Social Space in Tourist Settings," *American Journal of Sociology*, 79(3): 589–603.

Malinowski, Bronislaw (1922/1950), *Argonauts of the Western Pacific*, New York: E.P. Dutton.

——— (1935), *Coral Gardens and Their Magic*, New York: American Book.

——— (1948), *Magic, Science and Religion*, Boston: Beacon Press.

May, Earl Chapin (1963), *The Circus from Rome to Ringling*, New York: Dover.

Mead, Margaret and Gregory Bateson (1951/1991), *Trance and Dance in Bali* (film), video distributed by Audio-Visual Services, University of Pennsylvania, Philadelhia.

Moore, A. (1980), "Walt Disney World: Bounded Ritual Space and the Playful Pilgrimage Center," *Anthropological Quarterly*, 53: 207–18.

Morphy, Howard (1995), "Landscape and the Reproduction of the Ancestral Past," in *The Anthropology of Landscape: Perspectives on Place and Space*, ed. Eric Hirsch and Michael O'Hanlon, Oxford, UK: Clarendon Press, pp. 184–209.

Murray, John A. (2000), *Cinema Southwest*, Flagstaff, AZ: Northland Publishing.

Radcliffe-Brown, Alfred R. (1948), *The Andaman Islanders*, Glencoe, IL: Free Press.

——— (1952), *Structure and Function in Primitive Society*, Glencoe, IL: Free Press.

Redfoot, Donald L. (1984), "Touristic Authenticity, Touristic Angst, and Modern Reality" *Qualitative Sociology*, 7 (4): 291–307.

Ritzer, George (1999), *Enchanting a Disenchanted World: Revolutionizing the Means of Consumption*, Thousand Oaks, CA: Pine Forge Press.

Saxon, Arthur H. (1978), *The Life and Art of Andrew Ducrow and the Romantic Age of the English Circus*, Hamden, CT: Archon Books.

Senelick, Laurence (1989–1990), *Cabaret Performance: Sketches, Songs, Monologues, Memoirs* (2 volumes), New York: PAJ Publications.

Sorkin, Michael (ed.) (1992), *Variations on a Theme Park: The New American City and the End of Public Space*, New York: Hill and Wang.

Stein, Charles W. (1984), *American Vaudeville as Seen by Its Contemporaries,* New York: Knopf.

Thomas, Diane H. (1978), *The Southwestern Indian Detours*, Phoenix, AZ: Hunter Publishing.

Turner, Victor W. (1952), *The Lozi People of North-Western Rhodesia*, London: International African Institute.

————— (1963), *Ndembu Divination, Its Symbolism and Techniques*, Manchester, UK: Manchester University Press.

————— (1969), *The Ritual Process: Structure and Anti-Structure*, Chicago: Aldine Press.

Urry, John (1990a), *The Tourist Gaze: Leisure and Travel in Contemporary Societies*, London: Sage.

————— (1990b), "The 'Consumption' of Tourism," *Sociology*, 24 (February): 23–35.

————— (1992), *"The Tourist Gaze* 'Revisited,'" *American Behavioral Scientist*, 36 (2): 172–86.

15

The Catalog and the Web Page

An Existential Tension?

Alladi Venkatesh

This is the story of the return of the printed catalog via the dreamy, reflective, and hypertextual surface of the Web page. It is almost as if we failed to notice the aesthetic and dramatic quality of the catalog until the Web started looking like one—albeit an electronic one. In this chapter, I attempt to capture the retro nature of the catalog. It is not clear if the Web page signifies the last hurrah for the catalog or whether it announces its resurrection in electronic guise. I can picture the Web page in two ways—one is to view it in opposition to the catalog, as a new kid on the block poking fun at its ageing ancestor whose days are numbered, and the other is to see the Web as the next catalogic (pardon my neologism) incarnation paying homage to its long-lasting, never-say-die friend that has inspired the Web to be what it is now. Perhaps the truth lies somewhere in between, as they say. To verify my point I went to the Web sites of Lands' End and Victoria's Secret, both successful as catalog companies selling clothes to the unsuspecting public. One sells clothes that are wholesome, the other sells garments that bare the sculpted body. I also managed to get copies of their printed catalogs. In my aesthetic judgment, the printed catalog has a slight edge. To hear the rest of the story, please read the remainder of the chapter.

The intellectual roots of this chapter can be traced to several sources. In a series of articles culminating in a recently published book titled, *Visual Consumption*, Jonathan Schroeder (2002) has demonstrated in a compelling fashion that one competing paradigm for examining consumption is through market visualization and the aesthetic experience of the consumers in modernity. It is in the context of visuality and aestheticization (but not exclusively) that I discuss the current chapter. The chapter is a philosophical and cultural journey that takes us from the catalog to the Web page, a journey that is as technological as it is visual. More generally, it is a transition from the printed matter to virtual (non)matter.

Brown, Doherty, and Clarke (1998) compare our present postmodern age to the late eighteenth century and early nineteenth century when Romanticism in art and literature began to supplant the rationalism of the Enlightenment period only to be challenged by the functionalism of the Industrial Age in reference to arts and technology. The industrialization of Europe and North America also saw the birth of modern marketing and advertising (Fullerton 1988), the rise of retail industry, and the entry of the modern catalog into the marketing scene. Rather questionably, if somewhat regrettably, by being relegated to the background, the catalog as an epistemological source (or for that matter as an aesthetic text) never made it into the mainstream marketing literature although its preeminent position in marketing practice was never in doubt. The catalog became the backbone of mail order marketing as told to us by Emmet and Jeuck (1950) in their historical account of Sears, Roebuck and Company. One objective of this chapter is to reinscribe the catalog into the marketing discourse as a way to give meaning to the emerging visual/virtual paradigm in our field.

In this chapter, I treat the traditional printed catalog as an aesthetic document as well as an instrument of marketing knowledge and promotional culture whose critical position is being both emulated and challenged by the electronic Web page as the next technological frontier. The emulation of the printed catalog by the electronic Web page clearly tells the story of "retroscapes" that is the theme of this book. Instead of viewing the catalog merely as a marketing medium, which it certainly is, I will also look at it as an epistemological construction.

This chapter is divided into five sections: first, I provide a brief historical background to the modern consumption system whose origins can be traced to as early as the fifteenth century (Mukherji 1983). I then proceed to examine the history of printing and the role of catalog as part of the contemporary marketing practice. This is followed by a discussion of the philosophical and cultural basis of the catalog. In the next section I introduce the concept of virtuality and the relationship between virtuality as an emerging concept and the catalog as an embodiment of its own virtuality. In the last section, I elaborate on the idea of catalog-based representation and contrast it with virtual representation forms.

The Modern Consumption System Is Not Very New

According to Chandra Mukherji (1983), the modern consumption system showed its early signs of arrival in the fifteenth and sixteenth centuries, when "the markets were filled with silks, pottery, woolens, spices, potatoes and other stuffs, and woods, both exotic ones for inlays in fine furniture and lumber for building ships. . . . Homes of wealthy merchants and aristocrats began to fill with painted portraits, oriental rugs, tea services, and upholstered chairs. . ." (p. 1). Mukherji attempts to relate the birth of the consumption system to the rising hedonism and patterns of materialism both of which have found resurgence in the recent works of Hirschman and Holbrook (1982) and Belk (1985), respectively. Mukherji's main thesis points to the growing tension between asceticism of the Weberian type and hedonism/materialism, as we know it today and offers the view that the "so-called capitalist man was not transformed overnight with the industrial revolution" but evolved over a period of two centuries. In addition, "[T]he hedonistic culture of mass consumption was probably as crucial in shaping early patterns of capitalist development in Europe as the asceticism usually associated with this era" (1983, p. 10).

We hear a similar refrain in the works of McKendrick, Brewer, and Plumb (1982) and Campbell (1987) although both are referring to a later period, and specifically to the English experience in the late eighteenth and early nineteenth centuries. McKendrick, Brewer, and Plumb (1982, p. 1) begin their book with some dramatic statements lest there should be any doubt:

> There was a consumer boom in England in eighteenth century. More men and women than ever before in human history enjoyed the experience of acquiring material possessions. In the third quarter of the century that boom reached revolutionary proportions.

They then go on to establish that the Industrial Revolution and the consumer revolution were concomitant events in history (or, two sides of the same coin, as it were), which developed side by side although consumerism never received the attention or prominence it deserved in historical writings or in public discourse. Thus consumerism unfolded as a silent revolution. To emphasize their point of view, McKendrick, Brewer, and Plumb use such colorful terminology as the "orgy of spending," the cultural/economic forces of "envy, emulation, vanity and fashion," "the doctrine of beneficial luxury," and the like, to describe the rising consumer boom in the English society. The trend toward consumerism, they propose, began even earlier but did not reach great heights until the late eighteenth century. The products that contributed to this revolution are many and varied, "blankets, linens, pillows, rugs, curtains and cloths, pewter, glass and china, and brass, copper and ironware, fashionable mahogany, new novels, tobacco, soap and spirits, candles and printed fabrics,"—all products of consumption ideology. One of the conclusions of the authors is that "the intellectual justification of materialism was matched by a recognition that the democratization of consumption was actually taking place" (p. 25). To further prove their point, the authors spend considerable space in their book on the role of Joshua Wedgwood in the commercialization of potteries and George Packwood on the commercialization of shaving, two contrasting styles of consumer marketing, both very much of historical significance.

What is generally overlooked by readers of this book, however, is one of the later chapters (pp. 265–85) which focuses on the role of printing in the history of consumerism. This is a key development and of particular relevance to the topic of this chapter. The phenomenon of printing is directly related to the growth of educated populace and the diffusion of printed material as a triggering process in the history of commercial communication. Clearly, the practice of advertising as we know it today could not have flourished in the absence of printing (Fullerton 1988). For our purposes, the history of consumption combined with the developments in printmaking point to the rise of the catalog as a very important visual marker in the history of consumption.

The History of the Catalog

The Rise of Printing Technology

In the 700 years between the fall of Rome and the twelfth century, it was the monasteries and the ecclesiastical establishments who held the monopoly of the book culture (Clair 1976). This period is also known as the monastic age. The monastic age was followed by what is generally regarded as the secular age. Many social and technological changes were occurring in the thirteenth, fourteenth, and fifteenth centuries, considered to be the early period of Renaissance, that had a major impact on social, cultural, and political developments in the subsequent periods. This is also the period when many guilds and industrial crafts began to sprout. Of particular interest to us is the production of paper and the emergence of the book culture and book trade. As the industrial guilds began to take root, paper making and book production increased in intensity.

As the demand for learning began to grow, so did the demand for books.

The cost of book production was still high and began to drop only gradually. Along with the book production came the booksellers. To promote the book culture more widely, people began to write more in the vernacular and less and less in the classic languages, an important development in the history of mass culture and the catalog. With paper being abundantly available, multiple copies of books became a possibility. The notion of mechanical production was becoming a reality.

The major revolution in the book industry was the invention of the printing press by Gutenberg and his associates. The invention of printing 500 years ago based on movable type heralded a major revolution that has impacted all aspects of social and economic life. We place the catalog as a central by-product of this revolution although the catalog itself did not appear until the middle of the nineteenth century.

Specifically, the history of the catalog can be placed in a series of events that mark the features of associated history.

- 1880s lead generation, John Patterson, NCR
- 1900s Richard Sears—mail to list of railroad agents, gold watches, Sears, and Aaron Montgomery Ward—mail order catalog, farmers
- 1910 Sears credit card—finance farmers
- 1940s Book-of-the-Month Club
- 1950s Diners Club, American Express cards, Fingerhut—computer letter, seat covers
- 1960s 1–800– telemarketing, ZIP codes—segmentation
- 1970s upscale catalogs—Horchow, Neiman-Marcus
- 1980s VCR, Cable TV, Fax, home shopping TV, PC, on-line information services
- 1995 Creation of Web site

Catalog Marketing

Some Conventional Perspectives

Catalog marketing is a multibillion dollar enterprise and the mainstay of direct marketing. It is a very popular method of conducting business relating to consumer and industrial products. Catalogs began to appear in the mid to late nineteenth century as an instrument of direct marketing, or direct mail marketing, which expanded into telemarketing when the telephone became a common feature of home and industrial life (Kotler 2000). The technology of catalog production and distribution is at the heart of marketing practice and its institutional ethos. Although direct marketing is a pervasive feature of marketing and has existed for over a century, it has never been a subject of serious scholarship. Ironically, with the advent of the Internet it has assumed greater importance among marketing scholars, as a recent article by Mathwick, Malhotra, and Rigdon (2001) suggests, where they compare consumer perceptions of the catalog with their perceptions of the Web page on certain key dimensions.

Web-based Marketing

As Web technology began to diffuse, many companies embarked on both paper-based offline catalogs and online catalogs (e.g., Lands' End, Victoria's Secret). Of course, in the last few decades, there has been a tendency for numerous marketing channels to appear either in conjunction with the catalog or in direct competition with it. The best-known example is the toll free 800 number, now expanded to 888. The converse of the toll free ordering is telemarketing where companies employ sales people to directly call on consumers in their homes using the fixed telephone line. Consumers can also shop via the TV using the Home Shopping Network. In this chapter, the focus is on a particular version of the paper-based marketing channel, that is, the catalog, and its comparison with the Internet marketing.

An Implied Model of the Catalog

The literature on catalog marketing is rather sparse. There are some practitioner-oriented books that are very rudimentary and provide very little critical analysis (Muldoon 1995). From this rather sparse literature, one notices that the catalog is a specialized marketing tool that occupies the lower echelons of promotional culture as compared to advertising. However, one can argue that catalogs can be considered part of a company's image system in the same way company logos are (Marchand 1998). Although Marchand does not discuss catalogs in any specific detail, some of his arguments regarding the creation of corporate images are very applicable here. Generally speaking, the corporate image is synonymous with the brand image and is at the heart of brand marketing. One of its chief aims is to inscribe the brand in the minds of the consumers as a corporate icon. The catalog is no less an instrument of permanent visual inscription in the consciousness of the consumer. In a recent article, Stern, Zinkhan, and Jaju (2001) have proposed how marketing images are created and disseminated. Some of their arguments regarding how companies manage their controllable symbols to create the right or most desirable "corporate image" in the minds of stakeholders is quite relevant here. Their chronological account of how marketing images have become the ultimate significatory system of marketing practice can easily be extended to the catalog.

Catalogs not only represent a complexity of corporate images, but they are a means to legitimize company business practices and a periodic reminder to its collective audience that the company is a live entity, and it is surviving and growing. The fact that the catalog arrives at the door of the customer through mail every few months is a reminder that the company is alive and ready to serve its clientele. Thus in the language of Marchand (1998) the catalog becomes the corporate soul. Through the catalog, the corporation represents itself in corporeal terms, as an embodiment of company persona through its products. The fact that the corporation makes entry into the homes of thousands and millions of its customers is a statement of moral and social legitimacy. The corporation cannot prevent the customer from dropping the catalog into the wastebasket the moment it arrives. However, many catalogs are preserved for days and weeks on end for future consultation until the next edition arrives. This is the power of communication through the catalog.

Thus the catalog is at once the soul and the identity of the corporation and a friend of the customer. It does not impose itself like a telephone call, it blends with other magazines and friendly reading material in the home. One discards the catalog in the same way one discards the magazines, when its time expires.

Many catalogs supposedly provide an uplifting experience for the customers. There are pretty pictures and prettier models. Homes look beautiful when decorated by the furniture printed in the catalog. Social life is accentuated when you use the wine glasses pictured in the catalog. There are catalogs that promote health related products and exercise machines. Bosoms can be expanded, muscles can be tightened, executive suites can be conquered, friends can be won, children will be happy, dogs will look friendly and ferocious, and for those who wish to escape the harsh realities of modern life, Tahiti cannot be very far and holidays can be spent in an exciting fashion. Money can be saved if you buy two instead of one, doctors can be avoided if you imbibe the vitamin pills, burglars can be turned away if you use the alarm, gardens will look beautiful and princely if you use the recommended fertilizer, bodies can look flatteringly shapely, teeth will look white, and lost hair can grow back.

The catalog is thus a combination of marketing statement and magic cure, an unfolding of the corporate presence, an irrepressible invitation, a bewildering cornucopia of pleasurable objects, and a treasure trove.

A catalog is both an image and an object. You can look at it, pick it up, and touch it. Since the most highly recommended way to experience objects is by touching them, catalogs provide this touch when the material is printed on glossy paper.

The catalog is a record and a harbinger of change, a change in consumer tastes and preferences. It embodies the prevailing fashion in clothes, home decorations, and various products where aesthetic experience is the sine qua non of good and happy life.

The Catalog as a Cultural Text

Having descried the functionalities and aesthetics of the catalog, we are now ready to move beyond the standard image formulations of the above types into a philosophical interpretation of the catalog as the embodiment of modernist textual episteme, and contrast it with the postmodernist hypertextual interfaces.

Our reference point of departure is cultural studies and emerging critical discourse on media and the language of new media. We argue that the catalog is the basic iconic form of the print paradigm whose origins can be traced to the fifteenth century, and its existence and continuous development over the last century and a half are not an epiphenomenon but a major expression of marketing practice, ignored by scholars but ever present in its ubiquity, and challenged if not threatened by the arrival of the Internet. Because of its longevity, the catalog represents a permanent member of the corporate sign system and must be taken seriously by scholars of marketing.

A Conceptual Scheme

We propose Exhibit 15.1 as the starting point of our philosophical/cultural narrative. We divide the relationship between the virtual and the real spaces in three parts: marketing imaginary; marketing reality; and, connecting the two, the symbolic world of marketing. The symbolic world refers to marketing images as found in the world of advertising and other forms of communication. The intersection of the symbolic and the real is where we situate the conventional catalog. The epistemology of the virtual world is the emerging paradigm.

A Philosophical Representation of the Catalog

We refer to Pierre Levy's (1997) work in providing a philosophical representation of the catalog. In his recent work, Levy uses two fundamental concepts, hierarchy of epistemologies and collective intelligence. In a rather provocative demonstration of how epistemologies have developed during the

Exhibit 15.1 **The Three Worlds of Marketing**

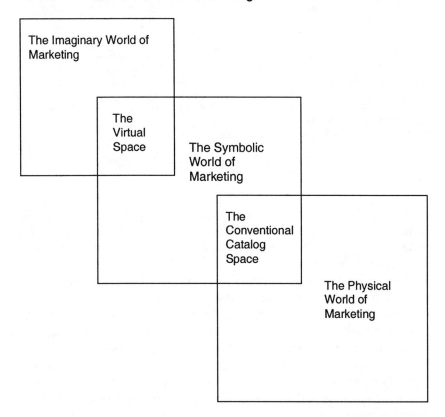

history of human civilization, he argues that there has been a hierarchy of concepts from the stage of orality to the stage of cyberspace. This development is shown in Exhibit 15.2. Each stage of development represents certain social and epistemological conditions. Thus in his hierarchy there are five stages: orality, writing, alphabet, printing (paper), and cyberspace (virtuality or electronic space). We are at the advanced stage of printing and at the early stages of virtuality. Each stage represents a certain human condition as shown in Exhibit 15.1. The printing stage, which is the stage from which we are poised to move into the virtual stage, also coincides with the development of experimental science, realism, and perspectivalism in art, the rise of individualism and modern democracies, and the rise of capitalism and market economy and the industrial revolution. The printing stage is also the stage of paper currency. The printed document is a record of individual, social, and economic transactions and the stage of collective intelligence which is shared both privately and publicly. Thus in this sharing process, science becomes a

Exhibit 15.2 **Phases of Collective Intelligence** (techniques of communication)

Type of Technology	Emerging Social Order
Cyberspace (twentieth century A.D.)	omnivision, economy of knowledge, artificial life, artificial intelligence, cyber democracy
Printing press (fifteenth century A.D.)	experimental science, capitalism, human rights, modern democracy
Alphabet (fifth century B.C.)	monotheism, money, commerce, citizenship
Writing (fifteenth century B.C.)	agriculture, livestock
Orality (pre-fifteenth century B.C.)	technique, art, images

Source: Pierre Levy (2002), presentation to the Critical Theory Institute, University of California, Irvine, February.

public discipline, technology becomes a public artifact, art becomes a public aesthetic enterprise, and the private individual becomes a public figure. It is this public nature of art, science, and knowledge that makes the printed material a condition of democracy.

Using the terminology of Pierre Levy (2002), a catalog is an embodiment of collective intelligence. The collectivity we are referring to is the marketing firm which produces the catalog, the customer to whom it is directed, and the competitor against whom the catalog is positioned. The catalog is not a secret or private document between two parties or a mere internal document of the company. A catalog exists for everybody to see. The catalog is at a very minimal level an information source. Over the years, the catalog has assumed many roles. It is also an aesthetic representation of the company's image. At a meta level it is also the company's manifesto. The production of the catalog begins as a representation of world of objects. The production of the catalog and its reproduction are an act of engaging in the manipulation of collective intelligence.

The catalog is not subject to erasure. Once printed, it cannot be written over. Thus it transcends orality. As part of the written communication culture, the catalog can survive the person who communicates orally. Written communication can be disseminated geographically to distant places. Oral communication needs emissaries (e.g., the spread of Christianity, Budhism, Islam, etc.). The catalog is indeed the product of the history of the last 500 years, which is also the history of print. Print appears on a piece of paper, assumes a quality of permanence, and an invulnerability to rapid change. Anything not contained in the original print is considered a copy or a counterfeit.

In examining what the printed matter denotes, we must go through a long period of representation based on a "signifier-signified" relationship. The print became both the signifier and the signified. It also became its own signifier. Although print was supposed to represent something else, it also represented itself. For example, a royal decree or a court judgment written on a piece of paper not only represents the intentionality of the signer, but the document becomes the document of record. The document attains an aura of authority displacing the individual's authority that caused it to happen in the first place. It is this sense of documentary record that has made the written instrument a powerful symbol in the history of human transactions.

The more orchestrated the printed document is the greater its power. If the print appears on special paper, uses special color, is stamped with a special seal or limited to fewer copies, is signed by the author, or is specially bound, its auratic value increases. In other words, one could do a lot of things with print to augment its material and symbolic value. Here are some examples that illustrate this point.

- Ordinary paper versus glossy paper/embossed paper
- Ordinary print versus specialized print
- Ordinary binding versus specialized binding (leather bound)
- Unsigned book versus autographed book
- Mass printing versus limited edition

Print processes involve the management of value creation through the above dichotomies. For example, a colorfully printed glossy catalog has a greater value for the same product than a typed document. In one sense, form begins to dominate content. In another sense form becomes its own content.

The Catalog and the Web Page

Catalogs as Works of Cultural Production

One of the effects of industrialization is the popularization and commodification of artistic products. With the growth of mechanical reproduction, artistic material has become accessible to the average citizen at low costs. What was considered the exclusive domain of the aristocratic elite has now become a commonplace occurrence. In addition, some artistic material deteriorates in value within a short period of time. Just consider the picture calendars with beautiful sceneries, reproductions of classical paintings, and attractive models that are sold at a fraction of their original price within weeks of the coming of the new year. Varnadoe and Gopnik (1990) explain this phenomenon in their exposition of high-low culture, which represents extraordinary interactions between fine art and popular cultural apparatus. As opposed to the duality of high and low cultures, Walker (2001) goes one step further to include a middle category and divides cultural objects and practices into three categories: high, medium, and low. Walker expands the typology where cultural production can be discussed in terms of particular media and art forms—painting, photography, graphic design—as well as some broader groupings that include industrial design, crafts, and electronic media. The catalog can be considered a visual artifact belonging to the same cultural milieu with a certain aesthetic, functional, and commercial value. In terms of cultural production, the catalog serves a combination of ideological, symbolic, and decorative functions.

Artistically speaking, the catalog is at the intersection of high art and the popular culture. No doubt, the primary motivation for the catalog is its ability to produce sales, a mundane prospect at best. But within this broad focus, it cuts across social boundaries by making itself accessible to a large audience. Warhol demonstrated this effect more than any one else (Schroeder 2002). The catalog is an icon of the media-saturated environment and yet provides a value for the consumer. The consumer does not dismiss the catalog as a piece of low art but recognizes its artistic merits in the context of her personal consumption system. How does this compare to the artistic merits of the Web site? The clever mixture of high and low art, artistic elitism, and popular culture that the catalog represents are not as easily available on the Web site—at least not yet. The catalog has a 500-year history of printing behind it. This sense of history gives an edge to the catalog. The Web simply is not backed up by a wealth of history. Nor does it have the backing of creative artists who are trained in this genre. Most people working on the Web are programmers, or early experimenters, and fusion artists. Sure, in the years to come, things might change when the technical medium and artistic genius draw on each other synergistically. Besides, the average user of the Intenet has not developed the artistic consciousness that is appropriate to the Web images. Currently, Web sites cannot be differentiated easily based on commonly understood artistic forms and expressions. The consumer has no basis to form the opinion that a particular Web site is more artistic and therefore has a greater brand image. All Web sites look alike while all catalogs do not. Paradoxically, the printed catalog is both an equalizer and a discriminator. What Warhol has to say about business art applies to the catalog more than it does to the Web site:

> Business art is the step that comes after art. I started as a commercial artist and I want to finish as a business artist. . . . Being good in business is the most fascinating kind of art. . . . Making money is art and working is art and good business is the best art. (Warhol 1976, p. 88, cited in Walker 2001)

The Representational System

The catalog represents a Cartesian subject-object world. When one looks at the catalog there is no object behind the catalog, except the maker of the catalog. The catalog is not a malleable surface, it is not connected to another concrete object. If it is connected, this connection is a physical link that can be easily discerned. One cannot expand or shrink the catalog dynamically. The catalog is a closed system, bound in a temporal and spatial world with well-defined parameters. On the other hand, the Web page is within a network of connected elements and is only an entry point to different nodes. There is no way to tell beforehand just by looking at the Web site what lies behind or how deep is the system. While this may appear to be a technological artifact, it is also at the heart of the Web.

The representational system in the catalog makes the reader a passive recipient of the information content. The search process, to the extent possible, is limited by the surface depth of the catalog, or the number of pages. When we move from the physical to the virtual space, the linearity of the catalog is replaced by the "web" like character of the virtual space. The logic of the catalog is that it is bound in a system of mechanical reproduction. A company has to decide in advance how many copies to produce before establishing a contact with its customer base. The cost of production of a catalog is different from the cost of its distribution. The Web is neither created nor maintained by the logic of reproduction. That is the reason why the Web has a register of visitors. In a sense the Web site is the only copy that is accessed dynamically by thousands of company customers. This has an important implication for spatial and temporal relationships between the customer and the organization. In one case (i.e., the catalog), the organization visits the customer and in the other case (i.e., the Web) the customer is the visitor.

The catalog uses media techniques with which the average consumer is familiar from an artistic standpoint if not with its technical details. For example, people understand what an oil painting is, what a color photograph means. Such a common level of understanding does not exist in the computer-produced images, at least not yet, for pixels do not seem to count much. Computer images are understood as technical representations. Until the average consumer understands the meaning of the computer screen (notwithstanding Sherry Turkle's [1995] well-intended exhortations) in the same way as the print photograph or any other form of printing, the Web designer has to experiment with various methods to produce both an intuitive and explicit understanding of the medium. This poses an interesting challenge to the Web-based marketers whose business model includes copying and mimicking the catalog on the Web site.

While the Web-page is made to mirror the catalog, Brottman (1997) uses an interesting metaphor to describe Covent Garden as a spatial text and one can walk through it as if one is browsing through a large catalog. It is a very graphic account of how one can navigate through Covent Garden as both an architectural space and a spatial text. The imagery here is that Covent Garden is a spatial catalog of shops, products, and people, and thus in representational terms, it is a catalog of space. We invoke this imagery only to compare it with the virtual catalogs, which are representational systems of a special kind.

Cannibalization of the Catalog Through Emulation

While the Web site is different from a print catalog in many respects, it behaves like a catalog. It incorporates many features of the catalog and thus cannibalizes it. This is both the power and weakness of the medium, power because it attempts to displace the existing medium by emulating it and weakness because it has not developed its own tools of a commonly understood aesthetic appeal.

For example, the typical marketing researcher uses the same criteria to assess the attractiveness of the catalog and the Web site. In a recent consumer study (Mathwick, Malhotra, and Ridgon 2001, cited earlier) the two were compared on the following factors: visual appeal, entertainment value, escapism, enjoyment, efficiency, excellence, and economic value. The fact that they were compared at all shows the substitution of the one by the other. More important, we should note that the similarity also extends to the common criteria used. Many studies seem to rely on similar measures which can be collapsed into experience and search factors (Hoffman and Novak 1996). The assumption here is that both interfaces can be compared on similar value bases or criteria. But this hardly pleases the creators of Web technology who want to radicalize the significatory system and take it into a different realm of possibility. In fact, recent indications are that the semantic Web is not too far off and once it arrives things will look totally different.

The Catalog/Website as Text

In recent years, consumer scholars have shed some important light on textual analysis in the context of advertising that we take note of here (Scott 1994; Stern 1996, 1998). If we imagine the text to have a beginning, middle, and an end, the printed catalog certainly represents this linear sequence in many ways. A reader generally does not wander through a catalog although it is conceivable that a reader can go to the middle and skip a few pages and go back and forth. At least the catalog is not constructed with that kind of reader in mind.

However, if a text were to permit the reader to pursue alternate paths within the text, searching for material that are not linearly arranged, we will call that kind of text a "hypertext." This is the central idea behind the Web page.

Thus no two readers will follow the exact path in a hypertext. The permutations and combinations vary. The multiple branching outs in a textual experience is what makes the Web a postmodern document and the consumer a postmodern consumer. Usually, this is defended in the name of customer empowerment because each customer decides for herself how to go through the Web-based catalog.

While the virtual text seems to be very accessible, it is, in reality, mediated by several intervening technologies. (See Appendix for an elaborate system of technical details that produce the text.) Writing long before the dawn of the Internet, Barthes (1974/1970, pp. 5–6) gave an indication of what he called the writerly text: "In this ideal text, the networks are many and interact, without any one of them being able to surpass the rest; this text is a galaxy of signifiers, not a structure of signifieds; it has no beginning; it is reversible; we gain access to it by several entrances, none of them can be authoritatively declared to be the main one; the codes it mobilizes extend as far as the eye can reach, they are indeterminable."

The Role of Technology

The Concept of Space

In an earlier paper, we developed some fundamental notions of the virtual space (Venkatesh, Meamber, and Firat 1998). The question we raised is, how is cyberspace/virtual space different from the physical space? We ask a similar question here with respect to the catalog, which is the product of physical space, yet is quasi-virtual in its own right (not cyber) in the sense that it is a representational system of products that exist in a physical space, which is the store. The question is easier to answer at the level of technology. Catalogs are printed on paper. Virtual space is created through digital technologies. Catalogs are mailed. Virtual space material can be transmitted through telephone lines, cable lines, or wireless. Virtual catalogs are based on multimedia technologies, and include animation and video/audio. Print catalogs are not created in video or audio environments and therefore represent limited sensory capabilities. Because they are products of physical space, one envisions that catalogs are easy to handle and to carry from one place to another, can be put in a bag, and can be enjoyed while relaxing in a chair. It is faster to leaf through a catalog than it is to go from page to page on a computer. Catalogs, however, are limited in terms of how much information can be stored or printed. The contents of the catalog cannot be changed once it is printed. Any changes have to wait until the next edition is printed, which may be months. Even if there are small changes, they cannot be included until a new version appears. Since the information cannot be changed easily, it will have to remain current a little longer. On the other hand, virtual catalogs can be changed dynamically on a real-time basis. Updated information can be inserted at frequent intervals and at an instant notice.

Probably the most important difference is that virtual spaces are interactive. That is, the user can interact with virtual technologies and receive and exchange information in real time as if the user is talking to another human being. The machine comes to life as it were and begins to respond to the user.

Many of the changes just mentioned are technological and may be considered matters of tedious detail. Or, one can look at the differences more closely and argue that the differences are very fundamental.

The Virtual Catalog and Its Relationship to the Physical

In marketing, until very recently, that is, until the dawn of the Internet, there has not been much discussion of alternate spaces in marketing (for post-Internet discussion, see Venkatesh, Meamber, and Firat 1998). We can think of the printed catalog as coming close to being an alternate space but nothing in the literature suggests that it was discussed or analyzed as such. We can now raise the question for the purpose of argumentation: if a customer uses catalogs for shopping instead of buying a product from a physical store, can we say that the catalogs are virtual. The catalog was considered an alternate medium for shopping or a complementary medium but never an alternate "space." Catalogs have existed for more than a century and their history is as old as the modern departmental store. Catalogs are a way to do shopping for those who do not have the time to go to the store but can still enjoy the convenience of ordering goods from their home or work locations. In fact, for a variety of products, a main method to order is via the catalog. And for a number of customers who live in remote geographical locations, the catalog is the only way to acquire goods.

Before we go any further, let us address the question of what is the relationship between the catalog and the physical store?

Partial Representation

A physical store may use a catalog to facilitate the sale of its products. For example, the catalog lists various products that are available in the store. In this case, the catalog usually contains a reasonably exhaustive set of offerings but may not list everything in the physical store.

Total Representation

In other instances, catalogs contain all the products that are currently available. Catalogs in this case are the only means of access to a company's products and customers place their orders based on the information in the catalog. In this case, there may be no physical store as such—there could be—but all orders are placed with the aid of the catalog. Typically, in such instances, the company maintains a large inventory of products in a single warehouse location or in different locations and as soon as orders are received they are processed and the products are shipped to the destination. In this example, the catalog is the only link between the customer and the marketer.

The Essence of Retroscape

A quote from Walker (2001, p. 71) is an appropriate beginning for this section:

> Because the medium of diffusion tended to take precedence over direct experience of the object, art was being changed retroactively. For example, color reproductions and prints fostered a rawness of vision, a crudity of taste, which influenced the way original works or art were received. Viewers who become familiar with a painting via inaccurate, garish color reproductions may well find that when they finally encounter the original, they experience a sense of anti-climax because the original appears dull in comparison.

The reproduction of art was a central theme of John Berger's (1972) four-part television series *Ways of Seeing*. As Berger argued, reproductions distance the viewer from the original, and remove all the shortcomings of the original. As a consequence the reproduction becomes a retroscape.

Catalogs function as retroscapes in many respects. Objects are glamorized beyond their original content. Artistic productions need not be perfect in a catalog, but must tell the story in a credible fashion. That is, the key is the translation possibilities in the medium of catalog. It is this translation into another medium and not simply its reproducibility that enhances the value of the object. The question is, is the Web a better or more powerful medium for such translations? Technologically speaking, yes.

The Web page does not mean the death of the catalog in much the same way that the television did not lead to the death of the newspaper or the radio. On the other hand, the catalog can undergo even greater transformation or perfection in light of what the Web page can and cannot do. In the age of photography, the machine-made pictures were considered inferior to the actual paintings and prints from the paintings. This meant that not only did photography have to compete with painting, but also it took many of the qualities of painting and incorporated them into photography. Thus photography borrowed from painting painterly characteristics. In the same fashion, painting began to borrow from photography certain technical elements that were not well known earlier.

Some Final Remarks

The electronic word is a renegotiation of the communication contract, and more broadly the textual, visual, and the symbolic contract. At this point in the history of media, print is considered serious, electronic text is playful, frivolous, transient and changing. A catalog as a printed document represents order, the Web page is made to order. A catalog is a modernist representation, its legacy is the legacy of modernity while the Web page with its hypertextual formation is postmodern. The business world as we understand is modern, the tools of conventional business are inscribed in the rational world. The Web is anything but rational. You *look* at the catalog and *examine* it, you *look through* the Web site and *navigate* it. The Web creates its own reality just as the catalog created its own virtuality.

Appendix : The World Wide Web

History and Development

> The dream behind the Web is of a common information space in which we communicate by sharing information. Its universality is essential: the fact that a hypertext link can point to anything, be it personal, local or global, be it draft or highly polished. There was a second part of the dream, too, dependent on the Web being so generally used that it became a realistic mirror (or in fact the primary embodiment) of the ways in which we work and play and socialize. That was that once the state of our interactions was on line, we could then use computers to help us analyze it, make sense of what we are doing, where we individually fit in, and how we can better work together. (Tim Berners-Lee in www.w3.org)

Tim Berners-Lee, a physicist at CERN, an international scientific organization based in Geneva, Switzerland, began the development of the World Wide Web in 1989. He and his colleagues created hypertext transfer protocol (HTTP), which is a communication protocol between computers and is the underlying basis for the Web along the TCP/IP protocol for the client-server model of computing. He later developed a text-based Web browser that was released in January 1992.

Description / Definition

The World Wide Web (WWW, also called the Web) is a universal, seamless network of computers and is a part of the Internet, which is used to access different forms of information (data, text, graphics, images, voice/audio, and video) on the Internet, in a manner transparent to the user. The basic idea of the Web is the marriage of technologies of computer networking and "hyperlink technology" into a gigantic and easy-to-use global information retrieval system. The Web is the biggest network on the Internet. The WWW is the reason why the Internet has transformed from being merely used by specialists and scientists to gaining popularity among the masses, because of its graphical interface, multimedia capabilities, and end-user friendliness.

Hyperlinks

Hyperlinks are shortcuts to related documents/locations. They are electronic links that connect related pieces of information to enable easy access to the users. Hypertext enables the user to choose a word/text and thereby access other documents that contain related information pertaining to that text; hypermedia files feature links to graphic images, audio sounds, videos, and animations. The hyperlink technology is not a new invention. Hyperlinks are similar to references in a scientific paper or cross-references in a dictionary. In electronic documents, these cross-references can be followed by a mouse-click, and with the pervasiveness of the Internet, these documents can be anywhere in the world. A document could contain various links to other documents on different computers anywhere on the Internet. As more and more documents are created linking to each other, the "map" of the documents would look like a spider web, hence the phrase *World Wide Web*. This navigation which permits roaming from one page to another is called "browsing."

Hypertext

Hypertext is a method for exploring the visual and conceptual writing space presented to us via the World Wide Web. Writing is always spatial, and each technology in the history of writing has presented writers and readers with a different space to exploit. The goal of conventional writing (including word processing) is to create perfect linearity and hierarchy. Hypertext is simply a nonlinear way of presenting information. Rather than reading or learning about things in the order that an author, or editor, or publisher sets out for us, readers of hypertext may follow their own path and create their own order—their own meaning out of the material. This is accomplished by creating "links" between information. These links are provided so that readers may "jump" to further information about a specific topic being discussed (which may have more links, leading each reader off into a different direction). For instance, this medium is not limited simply to text. It can incorporate pictures, sound, even video. So it presents a multimedia approach to gaining information—hypermedia.

WWW and Its Purpose

The World Wide Web was created with the intention of making the Internet more widely accessible; easier to retrieve information to browse, and to navigate; and more informative than some earlier Internet services such as gopher, FTP, or telnet. The principal technology behind the Web, HTTP is a protocol that understands and transmits the documents containing hyperlinks. One of the early languages used to create these documents is called HTML (hypertext markup language). Such a language enables creation of documents, which can include text, graphics, and hyperlinks to other documents. A hypertext document is written using this language and is assigned an Internet address called a uniform (or universal) resource locator (URL). The computer application, which was used to view the hypertext documents, is called the *Web browser*. The documents which are viewed using the browser on the WWW are themselves are called *Web pages*.

Web and the Internet

The word Internet means "interconnected networks." A computer network is formed when two or more computers are linked together to share information. The Internet (with a capital "I") is the largest computer network in the world, and literally spans the globe. The Internet allows for the transfer of data from one computer to another. The data may be a simple text message, such as those sent via electronic mail, or the data can be more sophisticated such as a digital picture, a digitized sound bite, or even computer software. Without the Internet, the World Wide Web could not exist.

What Can We Do on the Web?

- Create forms for transactions and data collection.
- Perform searches on a database or on a particular Web site.

- Create counters and track the domain names of visitors.
- Customize Web pages to meet individual user preferences.
- Create dynamic Web pages on the fly.
- Create interactive Web sites.

References

Barthes, Roland (1974 [1970]), *S/Z*, trans. Richard Miller, New York: Hill and Wang.

Belk, Russell W. (1985), "Materialism: Trait Aspects of Living in the Material World," *Journal of Consumer Research*, 12 (3): 265–79.

Berger, John (1972), *Ways of Seeing*, London: Penguin/BBC.

Brottman, Mikita (1997), "'The Last Drop of Desire' Covent Garden and the Spatial Text of Consumerism," *Consumption, Markets and Culture*, 1(1): 45–80.

Brown, Stephen, Anne Marie Doherty, and Bill Clarke (1998), "Stoning the Romance: On Marketing's Mind-forg'd Manacles," in *Romancing the Market*, ed. Stephen Brown, Anne Marie Doherty and Bill Clarke, London: Routledge, pp. 1–22.

Campbell, Colin (1987), *The Romantic Ethic and the Spirit of Modern Consumerism*, Oxford, UK: Basil Blackwell.

Clair, Colin (1976), *A History of European Printing*, New York: Academic Press.

Delaney, Paul and George P. Landow (eds.) (1994), *Hypermedia and Literary Studies*, Cambridge, MA: MIT Press.

Emmet, Boris and John E. Jeuck (1950), *Catalogs and Counters: A History of Sears, Roebuck and Company*, Chicago: University of Chicago Press.

Fullerton, Ronald (1988), "How Modern Is Modern Marketing? Marketing's Evolution and the Myth of the 'Production Era,'" *Journal of Marketing*, 52 (1): 108–15.

Hirschman, Elizabeth C. and Morris B. Holbrook (1982), "Hedonic Consumption: Emerging Concepts, Methods and Propositions," *Journal of Marketing*, 46 (Summer): 92–101.

Hoffman, Donna L. and Thomas P. Novak (1996), "Marketing in Hypermedia Computer-Mediated Environments: Conceptual Foundations," *Journal of Marketing*, 60 (3): 50–68.

Kotler, Philip (2000), *Marketing Management*, Englewood Cliffs, NJ: Prentice Hall.

Levy, Pierre (1997) *Collective Intelligence*, New York: Plenum Trade.

——— (2002), Presentation to the Critical Theory Institute, University of California, Irvine, February.

Marchand, Roland (1998), *Creating the Corporate Soul: The Rise of Public Relations and Corporate Imagery in American Business*, Berkeley: University of California Press.

Mathwick, Charla, Naresh Malhotra, and Edward Rigdon (2001), "Experiential Value: Conceptualization, Measurement and Application in the Catalog and Internet Shopping Environment," *Journal of Retailing*, 77 (1): 29–56.

McKendrick, Neil, John Brewer, and J.H. Plumb (eds.), (1982), *The Birth of Consumer Society: The Commercialization of Eighteenth-Century England*, London: Europa Publications.

Mukherji, Chandra (1983), *From Graven Images: Patterns of Modern Materialism*, New York: Columbia University Press.

Muldoon, Katie (1995), *Catalog Marketing: The Complete Guide to Profitability in Catalog Business*, New York: American Management Association.

Schroeder, Jonathan (2002), *Visual Consumption*, London: Routledge.

Scott, Linda M. (1994), "Images in Advertising: The Need for a Theory of Visual Rhetoric," *Journal of Consumer Research*, 21 (2): 252–73.

Stern, Barbara B. (1996), "Textual Analysis in Advertising Research: Construction and Deconstruction of Meanings," *Journal of Advertising*, 25 (3): 61–73.

——— (1998), "Introduction: The Problematics of Representation," in *Representing Consumers: Voices, Views, and Visions*, ed. Barbara B. Stern, London: Routledge, pp. 1–23.

Stern, Barbara B., George M. Zinkhan, and Anupam Jaju (2001), "Marketing Images, Construct Definition, Measurement Issues, and Theory Development," *Marketing Theory*, 1 (2): 201–24.

Turkle, Sherry (1995), *Life on the Screen*, New York: Simon and Schuster.

Varnadoe, Kirk and Adam Gopnik (1990), *High and Low: Modern Art and Popular Culture*, New York: Museum of Modern Art.

Venkatesh, Alladi, Laurie Meamber, and A. Fuat Firat (1998), "Cyberspace: The Next Marketing Frontier?" in *Consumer Research: Postcards from the Edge*, ed. Stephen Brown and Darach Turley, London: Routledge, pp. 300–21.

Walker, John A. (2001), *Art in the Age of Mass Media*, London: Pluto Press.

16

Once Upon a Marketplace

Stephen Brown

Memories, according to the imperishable humorist P.G. Wodehouse, are like mulligatawny soup in a cheap restaurant. Best left unstirred. This may be so, but in keeping with F. Scott Fitzgerald's (1926, p. 188) equally imperishable assertion that "we are boats against the current, borne back ceaselessly into the past," I am obliged to break into the boathouse of recollection, select a suitably rose-tinted skiff, and set off across the mulligatawny soup of memory to the dim 'n' distant shore of yesteryear (pausing only to spit in the face of mixed metaphors—and not for the first time).

It was one of those early fall days in Evanston, Illinois. Perfect blue sky. Perfect 75 degrees. Perfect humiditylessness, if there is such a word. Perfect for walking to work, in short. I strolled toward Kellogg School of Management, a modernist outcrop in the center of Northwestern's lake-side campus, where I had a 10:30 A.M. meeting with Philip Kotler, the capo-di-capo of marketing thought. I was writing an article about the great man and, notwithstanding his extremely busy schedule, he had kindly agreed to set aside a few hours so that I could interview him about his life, his work, his beliefs, his background, his intellectual influences. His scholarly retroscape, so to speak.

I got to the marketing department with fifteen minutes to spare and nipped across the hall to check my mailbox. Passing through the reception area, I said good morning to Azra, the secretary on duty. Instead of the usual cheery greeting, however, I was met with a strange salutation, "You're very appropriately dressed, Stephen."

Bemused by this inappropriate use of "appropriately," I asked her what she meant.

"Black jacket, black T-shirt, black jeans, black shoes," she replied. "Very appropriate."

Even more confused by now, I inquired what's appropriate about them, meanwhile wondering if my ensemble was a bit too retro, too pseudo, too Goth for my own good.

"Well, in light of what's happening in New York."

"Why, what's happening in New York?"

She pointed to the television set in an adjacent office, where a group of faculty and ancillary staff were glued to the screen. It was Tuesday, September 11, 2001.

I ran into Philip a few minutes later and, naturally, my first thought was to cancel the interview. Sagely, he suggested otherwise, since talking about something else might take our minds off the unspeakable events unfolding on the East Coast. He was right. A consummate professional, first and last, Phil gave me a few uninterrupted hours of his valuable time. He reminisced about his upbringing (hard, Kotler's father was a Russian immigrant who made his way in the retail trade during the Great Depression), his education (incredibly, he was once a research assistant for Donald Reisman, of *The Lonely Crowd* fame), his artistic inclinations (he's a collector of antique glass and sits on the board of Chicago's Art Institute), and his working methods (he never stops, frankly, Phil'll publish till he perishes . . . be afraid, be very afraid). In retrospect, I realize that I was asking the kind of questions he'd answered dozens, possibly hundreds, of times before. But he was politeness itself, the perfect tour guide through the landscape of autobiographical memory, the topography of time was.

Time was up before long and, although I'd have been perfectly happy to continue chewing the fat in Phil's corner office, he suggested we chew the fat over lunch in Evanston. As we dandered downtown, the great man regaled me with stories about Northwestern in the late sixties, when the streets were a war zone of antiwar protest, and expatiated engagingly on the historical development of the central business district. He then started interviewing me.

I'd been told that Phil has a remarkable ability to extract information from people. And so it proved. Before long, I was reminiscing about my own admittedly modest academic career. So much so, that I even told him my best-kept marketing secret; something that precipitated my methodological mid-life crisis; something that catapulted me into the deconstructive embrace of postpositivism; something directly related to the book you're currently reading; something that involves memories of marketplaces, memories of memory, and memories of memory and marketplaces.

Ah, I remember it well. It was going to be the research project that made my academic name. It was the one that would transport me to scholarly superstar status. It was an all-singing, all-dancing, bells-and-whistles study that combined elements of retail location, consumer behavior, and market research methodology. As a student of retail location, I was interested in shopping center layout and the minutiae of consumer movement within the mall itself. As a student of consumer behavior, I was fascinated by the copious literature on "prepurchase information seeking," which concurred that people gathered very little information before they bought things, even extremely expensive items like autos, appliances, and apparel. As a marketing researcher, I was curious about the methodological implications of memory, the fact that these prepurchase studies required respondents to recall the fine details of their shopping behavior, sometimes months after the event. How, I asked myself, could they possibly remember such trivia? Maybe the apparent lack of prepurchase information gathering had more to do with methodological shortcomings than actual consumer behavior. Maybe shoppers gather lots of information but can't remember the details when cornered by a questionnaire-wielding marketing researcher. Maybe.

So, fired up with the ambition and arrogance of youth, I set out to tackle time, space, and the market. I decided to conduct a comprehensive survey of consumer behavior in the Abbeycentre, a seen-better-days shopping complex approximately five miles from the university. The aim of the study was twofold. First, to unobtrusively observe the behavior of shoppers in the shopping environment (shops entered, purchases made, time spent, browsing activities, group behavior, and so on). Second, to conduct face-to-face interviews with the self-same shoppers about the intracenter activities just observed. Ergo, a wonderful comparison between observed and reported consumer behavior. Eat your heart out prepurchase researchers. Prepare to be amazed. Just give me the Maynard Award now and be done with it. How could it possibly fail?

Well, as sophisticated marketing researchers, you can doubtless think of all sorts of ways in which it could possibly fail or, indeed, the sorts of alternative approaches I really should've considered. But I was pretty naïve at the time (still am, sad to say); it took place before the postmodern "turn" in marketing and consumer research (Sherry 1991; Hirschman and Holbrook 1992); and many of the techniques that are now commonplace, such as CCTV cameras to automatically record people's behavior (Underhill 1999), simply weren't available to me. What I lacked in methodological sophistication, however, I made up for in enthusiasm. Indeed, looking back on it, I think my instincts were correct, inasmuch as many cutting-edge marketing behemoths, most notably P&G, have latterly eschewed questionnaire-based surveys in favor of unobtrusive observation (Khermouch 2001; Nelson 2001). Consumer recollections can't really be relied upon, you see.

Or can they? That's what I was trying to find out and, boy, was I determined. An exploratory, week-long pilot survey soon ensued, just to see if it were possible to unobtrusively observe consumer behavior in a busy shopping mall. And the answer was a resounding yes! True, the observed occasionally catch the eye of the observer, who immediately surmises, "Oh God, they've spotted me. . . . Hell, I'm in heap big trouble. . . . He looks like a gorilla and a pretty ornery one at that." But, in the vast majority of cases, it's simply a sideways look or fleeting glance, an accidental optical contact. Most shoppers have no idea whatsoever that they're under observation. You can literally walk at their shoulder, listening in on the conversation, and they haven't a clue. Trust me.

Having determined that large-scale unobtrusive observation exercises were possible and having worked out the details of the consumer behavior notation system (essentially, this involved maps of the center, on which shopper movements were traced, coupled with written records of outlets entered, time expended, etc.), the next preparatory task prior to my pre-postmodernist survey of time, space, and the market was questionnaire design. Well, if ever a questionnaire were carefully designed, that one was. It was pilot tested to death. And then some.

That said, the single most important question on the questionnaire referred to respondents' recollection of their shopping behavior and I went to great lengths to get it right. I read everything there was to read about memory—short-term, long-term, primacy effect, recency effect, the Ebbinghaus curve, episodic memory, semantic memory, echoic memory, and on and on and on. Hell, I even have a flashbulb memory about flashbulb memory. I remember to this day where I was when I first read Brown and Kulik's (1977) article on memories of the Kennedy assassination. Naturally, I had no idea what I was getting into. The literature on memory is enormous (e.g., Baddeley 1986, 1990; Cohen 1989; Conway 1990; Harris and Morris 1984; Neisser and Winograd 1988). Still, it was really interesting stuff and, better yet, the field was moving in the direction of "ecological validity." That is, real world as opposed to experimental research. Jeez, I was going to hit the psych journals as well. There'd be no stopping me.

Be that as it may, my less than prodigious powers of synthesis were indicating that the best way to maximize consumer recall was to: (1) interview them as soon as possible after the observed shopping episode, before the wretches had time to forget; (2) ask them about their behavior in the same physical setting as the activities took place, since situational variables can adversely affect recall; and, (3) get them to recount the events in sequence rather than in an higgledy-piggledy, off-the-top-of-the-head fashion, which would help counter any tendency to remember only the first and last stores they entered. Anyway, and if memory serves, the final wording of the key question went something like this. . . .

> As part of our study we are looking at how people actually shop in the Abbeycentre. I would like you to relive your shopping trip today by telling me the *first* store you went into, the *second* store you went into, the *third* store and so on. Please tell me all the stores you *went into*, not just the ones where you bought something.[1]

Needless to say, this question was extensively pretested, as was its position in the overall questionnaire. Not too early, not too late. The memory literature also suggested that reading the answer back to the respondent, thereby giving them an opportunity to reflect on and alter their initial response, would increase the overall accuracy of consumer recall. So that tactic was adopted, too. Boy, was this going to be a killer survey.

Well, the bright day eventually dawned—okay, okay, it wasn't so bright, we're talking Ireland, remember—and my super-duper, extra-large, mega-maxi marketing survey was ready to roll. It was scheduled for a full trading week, from 9:00 A.M. Monday morning to 5:30 P.M. Saturday afternoon, including three late nights. The time of year was carefully selected in order to capture "normal," "average," "everyday," shopping patterns, preferably unaffected by promotional factors and seasonal variations (early November I think it was, just after Halloween and before the Christmas shopping surge kicked in). The management of the center was also on board—very much so—since they had some concerns about the extant tenant mix and, accordingly, were mad keen to see the shopper circulation patterns. I promised them a report. They let me do my thing. Everyone's a winner.

As these things go, it went. I think I can honestly say that I've never worked as hard as I did that week. Come Saturday night, I was completely wiped out. It was worth it, however, because all things considered the survey went exceptionally well. There were quite a few unanticipated problems, of course. One of the women I observed turned out to be a shoplifter! Apparently, Belfast boasts the highest shoplifting rate in Britain and, given the principles of random sampling, I suppose I should've expected one or two to show up. However, I was completely taken aback when I saw her stealing all sorts of goodies in the health and beauty store. In case you're wondering; no, I didn't report her to security. I simply stopped her outside the center and demanded a share of the loot. Not that the pink eye shadow and black fishnet tights did an awful lot for me.

Shoplifters aside, there was another significant problem with the interview procedure. This didn't involve refusals, strangely enough, though whenever refusals occurred they were something else. On one unforgettable occasion, I tracked a shopper for two and a half painstaking hours and, just as she was leaving, I stepped forward to conduct the interview:

"Good afternoon, madam." Smirk, smirk. Simper, simper. Smarm, smarm. "I'm from the University of Ulster and I'm doing a survey on shopping in the Abbeycentre. Would you mind answering a few ques. . . ."

"You're a bit old to be a student!" she barked. And marched straight out of the center.

A Merry Christmas to you too, madam.

No, the real problem with the interview was getting into position. Think about it. After following the victim—sorry, shopper—around the center for some considerable time, you have to get ahead of them in order to conduct the interview. It has to appear like an ordinary, everyday, mall-intercept encounter between researcher and consumer. You can't grab people by the shoulder as they're leaving the center (shoplifters excepted) and expect them to answer your questions. It's not going to happen. Remember, the would-be respondent has no idea that they've been under observation and at no time during the interview was this revealed to them. As far as the shopper's concerned, they were selected purely by chance as they leave the center. However, you have to get in front of them in order to convey this "accidental" impression. But, and this is a big but, shoppers speed up as they're leaving a center, a bit like water in the vicinity of a waterfall. So it's not unusual to find yourself sprinting past fast-moving shoppers, whilst trying to look casual, only to discover that they've turned around and are heading back the way they came.

When *are* they going to build a better trap for mall rats, that's what I want to know.

At this point in the proceedings, some of you are no doubt deeply affronted by the author's egregiously unethical activities and are mentally composing a stern letter to marketing's governing bodies. Before you report me to various standards standing committees or have me dishonorably discharged from the AMA—not that I'm a member—I should perhaps point out that the study was conducted in accordance with Market Research Society guidelines, which state that unobtrusive observation is permissible provided the subjects are in an environment where they can reasonably expect to be observed. That is, in public places like department stores, airports, museums, bowling alleys, and—wait for it—shopping centers. What's more, the center management posted notices informing customers that a market research study was taking place under their auspices. Phew, that was a close one. My AMA epaulettes are safe, for the time being.

Anyway, I could entertain you with all sorts of stories about that particular study. The time I was mistaken for a mannequin, for example, or the bickering couple I tracked for a couple of hours whilst trying to keep a straight face (hey, I didn't want to listen in on their hate-you, hate-you-too conversation, but a scholar's gotta do. . .). However, as rigorous marketing scientists, you don't want to be bothered with that kind of narrative nonsense. Cut to the chase, Stephen, I hear you say. Fair enough, then. The bottom line is that, over the week-long survey period, the intracenter activities of 250 shoppers were recorded. I know that doesn't sound like much, but it's a big sample for unobtrusive surveys of that type. Bear in mind that each observed shopping episode averaged fifty minutes and ranged from five minutes to three and three quarters hours. Of the 250 observees, the vast majority were successfully interviewed about their intracenter behavior. Some were lost (yes, it happens), some turned out to be nonshoppers (staff on lunch breaks, sales reps, etc.) and some were straightforward refusals. (The bitch! I don't look that old. I could easily pass for a student. It was the harsh lighting in the center, I tell you. It came at the end of a long week. I was tired.)

When all is said and done, and the data are suitably sifted (who said massaged?), the final figure shows that some 90 percent of those "eligible," about 200 shoppers in all, were observed and interviewed. So, what did I find out? Well, the unobtrusive observation element revealed all sorts of high-traffic, low-traffic, hot-spot, cold-spot, overperforming and underperforming parts of the center. The management loved it. Some of the most interesting findings, what's more, weren't actually part of the formal study. They just came out in the wash, as it were. Things like the sheer amount of socializing that goes on (shoppers spend more time in the malls, talking to or watching other people, than they do in the stores), the importance of center atmospherics (consumers are drawn to natural light and repelled by "dead frontage," as retail location lore suggests), the functioning of shopper groups and the division of labor therein (men guard the shopping cart, or supervise the children, or read the newspaper, while women do all the work).

The big one, however, the one about memory, the one that set the whole study in motion, the one you've forgotten about on account of my self-indulgent digressions . . . was . . . was . . . was . . . really quite remarkable. Really! Only 40 percent of those interviewed had *total* recall of the stores they'd entered and, while there were all sorts of variations on this basic pattern (depending on age, sex, mood, time expended, situational factors, total number of stores visited, phases of the moon, and so forth), the fundamental fact of the matter is that consumers can't remember their intracenter shopping behavior. Bearing in mind that every effort was made to maximize recall and that the interview took place immediately after the shopping episode concerned—before the memories had time to fade, before they'd even left the center—these findings were quite worrying for marketing researchers. In truth, some of the lapses were nothing less than mind-boggling. One woman bought an ice cream in the final store she visited. She was licking the ice cream during the interview and forgot to mention the ice cream outlet. Another shopper, with a small child in tow, had spent some time in a footwear retailer, but again omitted to mention the fact. Her little boy started tugging on her skirt, "Mummy, mummy, we were in the shoe shop." She looked down at him, shouted "Shut up, Peter, your mother's trying to think!" and gave him a swift cuff around the ear for his trouble. It's also amazing how many people "forgot" to mention that they'd been in the liquor store, even as the bottles and cans were clinking and clanking in their carrier bags.

Still, I had concrete proof that consumers couldn't remember their behavior, that they were unreliable narrators, that accepted market research methods needed to be reexamined (just think how many questionnaire surveys rely on human memory), that the prepurchase information seeking literature was questionable at best and complete rubbish at worst. What's more, I had tons of stuff on shopper circulation patterns, sequences, and ancillary activities. Hallelujah. I'd be milking this material for decades.

And then I realized where I'd gone wrong. It suddenly dawned on me that I'd been wasting my time. Far from being a passport to the marketing big time, the Abbeycentre study was revealed as fatally flawed, a foolish foray into memory research, an amateurish and misplaced attempt to make an academic killing out of time, space, and the market.

No doubt you've already identified numerous shortcomings in the study just described. If you're using this chapter for class discussion, feel free to work out ways in which it could've been improved. But no letters please. The memory's painful enough as it is. As I see it, the principal problem was the single word "store." The memory question asked people to recollect all the "stores" they'd been into, whether or not they bought anything. The word "store," however, may have meant different things to different people. What, after all, is a "store"? As far as I was concerned, it referred to every establishment in the shopping center, but the respondents might not have interpreted the word that way. Take the woman licking the ice cream. The ice cream "store" is a small kiosk—a serving counter, in effect—at the side of the mall. Perhaps she didn't consider it a "store." Likewise the liquor store. Maybe people don't mentally place liquor retailers in the "store" category. What about the bank, or the dry cleaners, or the optician? When does a store become a store? Then again, what exactly constitutes going "into" a store? From my perspective going "into" meant crossing the threshold. But the respondents may not have seen it like that. Going "into" might mean handling the merchandise, or talking to sales clerks, or actually making a purchase. Who knows? I certainly didn't.

Now, in fairness to my pre-postmodern endeavors, I suspect that most of the respondents had a reasonable idea of what was meant by the question. It seemed to work well enough at the time. Indeed, it's a problem that still besets almost every marketing research questionnaire, where received wisdom is that you clarify the meaning of a word or concept, if it's likely to cause confusion ("by 'store,' I mean every establishment in the center"; "by going 'into,' I mean crossing the threshold," etc.). This is no solution, however, since it simply adds another layer of interpretive possibilities (what is an "establishment"?; what does "threshold" mean?). The unfortunate fact is that we can't be sure our words—even the most "obvious" words—mean the same thing to everyone and, if that is the case, then the scientific integrity of the study is compromised. True, this interpretive issue is an interesting research topic in itself, as I discovered in my subsequent studies of the expression "I Hate Shopping!" which is often spontaneously uttered by interviewees, men in particular. However, when you ask what they mean when they say "I hate shopping," it transpires that for most men the word "shopping" refers to items like groceries, apparel, or anything to do with women. Buying books, CDs, gadgets, computer games, and audio equipment, on the other hand, do not constitute "shopping," as such. They are mentally recoded as "hobbies," "pastimes," "work" or, my favorite, "an investment."

There's much more to this issue, however, than clarifying consumer understanding of constructs like "stores," "shopping," "buying," or whatever. It raises the specter of postmodernism in general and Derrida's deconstruction in particular. Derrida has his critics, I grant you, most of whom fail to appreciate *frère* Jacques's sense of humor. Nevertheless, his insights into the inherent instability of language are very astute. For Derrida, linguistic meaning is not fixed or firmly established, but fluid, contingent, suspended, postponed, and influenced by the specific use, context, or occasion. Meaning cannot be nailed down, no matter how hard we try. Every attempt to "clarify" matters merely adds to the confusion. Meaning is a hall of mirrors, distorted, disorientating, difficult to escape from. There is nothing outside the text. The real world cannot be accessed except through language, or analogous sign systems, which are inherently unstable, ultimately indefinable, and beyond our capacity to control.

If this sounds pretty nihilistic, it should, because deconstruction is an exercise in negativity. It takes things apart and puts nothing back in their place. In Derrida's dexterous hands it demonstrates how the Western literary and philosophical canon is predicated on the false promise of meaningfulness. Indeed, if Derrida ever turned his attention to marketing matters, he would probably seize on something as inconsequential as the multiple meanings of "store" and use it to bring Western capitalism to its knees. Begging for mercy.

As indeed was Professor Kotler. If you recall, he'd asked me a simple question about my career path, only to receive a blow-by-blow account of retailing research gone awry and a philological philippic about Derridean deconstruction. That would be enough to give anyone pause, or at least ask for the check. Pronto! But Philip K is made of sterner stuff. Changing the subject, he asked what I thought of the restaurant, a retro diner tastefully decked out in nearly-nugahide, bogus-bakelite, faux-formica, pseudo-polypro-pylene, and quasi-chromestique. Big mistake. I immediately launched into a ramble on retro, about how in the tear-stained aftermath of the Abbeycentre study I'd written a book on postmodern marketing containing a section on retrospection (Brown 1995) and how that subsequently led to a book about retromarketing containing a chapter on retroscapes (Brown 2001), such as the one we were sitting in. I'm paraphrasing, you understand.

Well, as you can imagine, Kotler couldn't get out of the diner quick enough. He'd been cornered and given an ear-bashing by a less than scholarly (let alone saintly) Irishman, who was clearly several waffles short of a serving. There's only so much of the gift of the gab that one can take before grabbing the tab and paying the ransom money.

Actually, I do a disservice to Professor Kotler. He was kindness personi-fied. True, he may well dine out on his cautionary tale of the prattling paddy, a shopping center stalker with a memory fixation who worried about words while disbursing them with gusto. However, he was never less than helpful to someone who had poured scorn on his work in the past. Ah, the impetuos-ity of youth. What can I say?

Our interview at an end, I popped into a friendly neighborhood mega-bookstore. Not for a postprandial browse, you understand, but because I vaguely remembered from my previous visit that a book on memory was on special offer. Given the personal confession just concluded and the painful marketplace memories it stirred up, buying an apt book seemed like the sen-sible thing—the scholarly thing—to do. Not that I'm a pathetic bibliophile, or anything. The numberless books that line the walls of my study are neces-sary for work, I tell you. They're an investment.

Well, I searched high and low for the thing. Couldn't remember where I'd seen it. Couldn't remember the name of the author. Couldn't remember the title, for Christ's sake. There was no point pestering a sales clerk, since those people can spot an imbecile from miles off.

"So, you can't remember the title, sir, but it has something to do with memory?"

"Erm . . . well . . . um . . . sort of . . . ahem . . . you know."

"Security to information desk."

"Ah, maybe it was in Barnes and Noble."

Clearly, the clerk was not an option. It was once more into the bookish breach, a final assault on the magazine-mounted, page-protected, tome-tiered battlements. Shopping is hell. What did you do in the war, daddy? Borders patrol, son. Just as I was leaving, armed to the teeth with hard and soft cover supplies—well, I had to stock up in case rationing was introduced—I spotted the enemy dug in on a display table close by the entrance. Ordinarily, I avoid such blatant promotional attempts to tempt the book-buying masses into impulse purchases, but he'd fought a good fight and deserved to be borne out in triumph. When I clocked the title, moreover, I just knew it had to be acquired, irrespective of the book-seller's wiles. It was called—get this— *Searching for Memory*. Searching for *Searching for Memory*, more like.

Written by a renegade called Daniel Schacter, *Searching for Memory* was exactly what I'd been searching for, an accessible account of latter-day developments in memory research. And, would you believe it, boys and girls, the field has advanced somewhat since the days when I was toiling in the forget-me-not trenches. More pertinently perhaps, memory research has taken a retro turn! When I was filching stuff from the repository of memory, it was all about information processing. The dominant metaphor was the computer. Input and output were where it was at. Parallel processing was hot to trot. Articles were chock-a-block with references to storage, retention, and retrieval of memories, which were held on cerebral hard disks like a complex assemblage of system files, access routines and backup operations.

But that's all come crashing down.

As Schacter (1996) explains, there has been a retro turn in memory research. It is now recognized that memories are reconstructions not recollections of an event. It's not about retrieving the past, exactly as it was. It's about re-creating the past in the present. Past and present combine to produce our memories. Memories are not passive or literal recordings of reality, akin to mental photo albums or home movie archives:

> It was once believed that remembering a past experience is merely a matter of bringing to mind a stored record of the event, but recent research has overturned this persisting myth . . . even the seemingly simple act of calling to mind a memory of a particular past experience—what you did last Saturday night or where you went on your first date—is constructed from influences operating in the present as well as from information you have stored about the past. (p. 8)

Another recent trend in the study of memory is researchers' heightened appreciation of the subjective side of things. Memories, so it seems, are emotional, experiential, deeply meaningful, highly individual. Now, this does not mean that a postmodern coup has taken place in the body politic of psychology. Hell no. What it *does* mean, is that the hard, objective, mechanistic model of memory has been supplemented by a softer, subjective, essentially aesthetic perspective. Memory researchers are increasingly turning to poets, painters, performers, philosophers, and the like for their nonscientific but nonetheless significant insights into remembrance of things past:

> In Ridley Scott's movie *Blade Runner*, computer technology and bioengineering conspire to produce a species of "replicants" that seem human in virtually all respects. Rachel is a newly developed experimental replicant that has been implanted with a rich set of memories that provide her with a personal past, a past so compelling that she is unaware of her nonhuman status. Deckard, whose job is to . . . weed out wayward replicants, awakens her to reality by reeling off a series of Rachel's most personal childhood memories and informing her that "those aren't your memories; they're somebody else's." But Rachel's emotional reactions to these memories, as indicated by her tears, facial expression, and tone of voice, are intense. Deckard is thus convinced that the memories do in some sense belong to her, and so concludes that she should be allowed to live as a human. . . . Deckard cannot distinguish this replicant's subjective response to her memories from that as a person because Rachel shows the full subjective force of memory's power. The depth of subjective experience Rachel displays is the hallmark of explicit remembering in people. Because this is such an integral part of human remembering, compelling evidence of intense subjective experience is what it would take for most of us to be convinced that a computer does indeed remember in the same sense that we do. (Schacter 1996, p. 36)

Above and beyond *Blade Runner*, Schacter's book is suffused with references to movies, novels, and artworks of all kinds—several specialist volumes have also been published (e.g., Fara and Patterson 1998; McConkey 1996)—and he notes how the subjective, essentially aesthetic process of introspection, once the procedure non grata in behavioral and cognitive psychology, is back with a bang:

> Artistic depictions of the rememberer are suggestive and even provocative. But scientists who study memory have only lately begun to study subjective experiences of remembering. For much of this century, the study of memory—like that of other areas of psychology—adhered to the tenets of behaviorism, which held that subjective mental experience is not a proper domain for scientific study. Then came the rise of cognitive psychology during the 1960s and 1970s, driven by an information processing meta-

phor in which subjective experiences of remembering had no place. Philosophers offered eloquent introspective accounts of what remembering is like but scientists generally ignored them. . . . Now, accumulating scientific research is starting to tell a surprising story about the inner world of the rememberer. (Schacter 1996, p. 18)

These days, it seems that "the inner world of the rememberer" is considered a research topic of vital scholarly significance.

Alongside the rise of retro and the advent of introspection, contemporary memory research is deeply reflexive. That is to say, it is increasingly prone to reflect on itself, its assumptions, its beliefs, its ground rules, and, not least, the root metaphors that have accompanied the development of the field (Draaisma 2000). This striking self-consciousness is no doubt attributable to the demise of the hitherto dominant memory-as-computer conceit. The disadvantages of the information processing analogy—rather than its productive parallels—are increasingly the subject of discussion and debate. Regardless of the reasons for this reflexive perspective, the upshot is a growing appreciation of prior attempts to metaphorically encapsulate memory's elusive essence. Famous examples include Freud's "mystic writing pad," Sherrington's "enchanted loom," Draper's "photographic plates," Descartes's "homunculi," and Plato's "wax tablet."

Yet, despite the waxing and waning, as it were, of the dominant metaphor, spatial similes have always figured prominently among memory's figurative favorites. Whether it be Simonides's concept of *loci* (a still used mnemonic device in which the items to be memorized are consigned to specific mental locations), medieval "memory theatres" (a later version of the same, used for memorizing religious tracts), Carus's "vast labyrinth" (an effulgent offshoot of the German Romantic movement), William James's "rooms in a private house" (Simonides domesticated), postwar preoccupation with "depth of processing" (deeper is better), or latter-day experiments with brain-scanning technology (which show that remembering occurs in localized parts of the cerebellum), space and place are integral to our understanding of memory. From time immemorial.

But, what does it all mean for the study of retroscapes? Well, apart from the fact that I'll be digging out my Abbeycentre dataset—hey, it's ten years old now; that makes it retro, right?—it reinforces almost everything that has been contended in this book thus far. The first and most obvious point of concurrence is that it suggests retroscapes are worthy of academic investigation. Granted, their very ubiquity in our turn-of-the-century times is enough in itself to warrant scholarly scrutiny. Marketing researchers, moreover, have been very active of late in their attempts to recuperate the fourth "P" of place and some of these studies refer to retroscapes, unbeknownst to the authors concerned. Analogous analyses are also appearing in the wider sociological/ cultural studies sphere. One thinks, for example, of Goss's (1996) study of festival shopping facilities and his concerns about the commodification of heritage. DeLyser (2001) contends that a specter is hovering over the ghost towns of eastern California, a pretty unhappy specter at that, since the authenticity of the original settlement has been compromised to cater for cheap thrill-seeking customers. Beardsworth and Bryman (1999), meanwhile, have spent many a long hour in retro themed "eatertainment" venues in order to inwardly digest the mendacious machinations of multinational corporations. Fries with that?

The literature on memory, however, indicates that it's more than a matter of "authenticity," or "commodification," or "eatertainment," or the last languishing legume in marketing's P-piled pantry. Retroscapes are repositories of memory, of meaning, of feeling, of passion, of the collective unconscious, of how we got here, and where we're going next. The emotional side of space and place needs must be addressed by marketing and consumer researchers. Facts may speak for themselves but they do so *sotto voce*. As this volume has endeavored to demonstrate, it's time to make a racket about retroscapes.

A second consonant matter arising from latter-day trends in memory research pertains to the pertinent scholarly palette. The emotional side of reminiscence has encouraged recollection researchers to engage with aesthetic issues, to turn to the artistic superstructure for academic inspiration. Within marketing and consumer research, admittedly, there is a long and distinguished tradition of tapping into the arts, both high and low (Brown and Patterson 2000). This culling of the artistic canon, however, rarely involves servicescapes, let alone retroscapes. But the spatial insights that are available from creative writers simply can't be ignored. As the contributors to *Time, Space, and the Market* have convincingly demonstrated, everything from peripatetic comedians and album covers to computer games and not so grand pianos can set the retro pulse racing.

The third congruent issue arising from latter-day developments in memory research is a hoary methodological chestnut, the Marley's Ghost of marketing and consumer research. Introspection, as we have seen, is back on the psychological agenda, but it remains a contentious issue in marketing. Subjective personal introspection, as it is generally known, has received a hammering from the defenders of the marketing faith (Wallendorf and Brucks 1993), notwithstanding the closely argued rebuttals of Gould (1995), Levy (1996), Sherry (1998), Holbrook (1995), and several others. So contentious is the topic, that it might be better to abandon the "introspection" tag completely, especially as the term doesn't quite capture what our introspectionists are up to. Yes, they may be making withdrawals from their recollective memory banks, but they are also disbursing their autobiographical fortunes in a creative fashion. They are storytellers, first and foremost, not white-coated lab workers. They are engaged in artistic acts, not the pursuit of science, social or otherwise. They aren't so much introspectors as retrospectors. It is surely no accident that almost every published introspection in marketing and consumer research, be it Morris Holbrook's (1984) paean to Charlie Parker, John Sherry's (1998) classic essay on Niketown, or Russ Belk's (2000) cultural biography of his Groucho Glasses, is an exercise in retrospection.

The present book, then, has refused to engage in marketing's introspection "debate." It is unproductive so to do, since the technique is well established in adjacent academic disciplines, albeit the nomenclature varies considerably from domain to domain. Anthropology, for example, has witnessed the rise of "mystories" (Denzin 1997); sociologists are urged to embrace New Literary Forms (Banks and Banks 1998); cultural studies is deep into its anecdotage (Simpson 1995); literary theorists are getting in touch with their inner storyteller, as the advent of autobiographical criticism attests (Brown 1998); and, of late, our colleagues in organizational behavior have taken to narrative like the proverbial duck to water (Boje 2001). Regardless of what it is called, the key point is that introspection provides depths of insight that are unobtainable from more conventional methods.

In this regard, it is the editors' belief that the qualitative side of retroscapes—their innate *genius loci*—can't be captured in dry and dusty academese or a standard, all-too-standard research report. It requires, rather, a reflexive mode of academic discourse. That it to say, it requires researchers to reflect on their retroscape experiences, to reflect on their reflections on their retroscape experiences, and to reflect on their reflections on their reflections on their retroscape experiences, as our contributors have shown. At first blush, admittedly, this sounds like scholarly solipsism of the highest order. Reflexivity, however, involves much more than mere academic self-absorption (Alvesson and Skoldberg 2000; Steier 1991; Woolgar 1988). In a series of powerful volumes, the literary theorist Frederick Turner (1986, 1991, 1995) maintains that aesthetic appreciation—our love of beauty—is not only hard-wired into the mammalian cerebellum, but it is also reinforced by reflexivity, a cultural feedback loop that leads to increasingly successful actions, choices, and decisions, all of which have helped humankind become better adapted to its environment. Aesthetic appreciation, in other words, is a superior form of cognition that enables its possessors to appraise a situation with greater efficiency. Better yet, it is in tune with "the deepest theme or tendency" in the cosmos itself, where "the smaller parts of the universe often resemble in shape and structure the larger parts of which they are components, and those larger parts in turn resemble the still larger systems that contain them" (Turner 1999, p. 127). Just as the three-line stanza of Dante's *Divine Comedy* parallels the tripartite structure of the poem as a whole, so too snowflakes, ferns, and the fractal geometry of coral reefs echo the natural world's most elemental theme. And this, Turner concludes, is *reflexivity*, the self-reflecting feedback loop of extant behavior systems, be they natural or cultural, historical or spatial.

Reflexivity, then, is the essence of retroscapes. They aren't so much replicas or reproductions of prior retail environments, as self-conscious representations of marketing-implanted memories of times past. They are the false memory syndrome of late capitalism. That's what Philip Kotler told me. Honest.

Note

1. I should perhaps point out that I've "translated" the question for an American readership. The actual question, in keeping with standard British/Irish practice, used the word "shop" instead of "store." In retrospect, however, it is interesting that the word requiring translation is the word that caused all the trouble at the time.

References

Alvesson, Mats and Kaj Skoldberg (2000), *Reflexive Methodology: New Vistas for Qualitative Research,* London: Sage.

Baddeley, Alan (1986), *Your Memory: A User's Guide,* Harmondsworth, UK: Penguin.

——— (1990), *Human Memory: Theory and Practice,* London: Lawrence Erlbaum.

Banks, Anna and Stephen P. Banks (1998), *Fiction and Social Research: By Ice or Fire,* Walnut Creek, CA: Altimira.

Beardsworth, Alan and Alan Bryman, (1999), "Late Modernity and the Dynamics of Quasification: The Case of the Themed Restaurant," *The Sociological Review,* 47 (2): 228–57.

Belk, Russell, W. (2000), "A Cultural Biography of my Groucho Glasses," in *Imagining Marketing: Art, Aesthetics and the Avant-Garde,* ed. Stephen Brown and Anthony Patterson, London: Routledge, pp. 249–59.

Boje, David M. (2001), *Narrative Methods for Organizational and Communication Research,* Thousand Oaks, CA: Sage.

Brown, R. and J. Kulik (1977), "Flashbulb Memories," Cognition, 5: 73–99.

Brown, Stephen (1995), *Postmodern Marketing,* London: Routledge.

——— (1998), "The Wind in the Wallows: Literary Theory, Autobiographical Criticism and Subjective Personal Introspection," in *Advances in Consumer Research,* vol. XXV, ed. Joseph W. Alba and J. Wesley Hutchinson, Provo, UT: Association for Consumer Research, pp. 25–30.

——— (2001), *Marketing—The Retro Revolution,* London: Sage.

Brown, Stephen and Anthony Patterson (eds.) (2000), *Imagining Marketing: Art, Aesthetics and the Avant-Garde,* London: Routledge.

Cohen, Gillian (1989), *Memory in the Real World,* London: Lawrence Erlbaum.

Conway, Martin A. (1990), *Autobiographical Memory: An Introduction,* Milton Keynes, UK: Open University Press.

DeLyser, Dydia (2001), "When Less Is More: Absence and Landscape in a California Ghost Town," in *Textures of Place: Exploring Humanist Geographies,* ed. Paul C. Adams, Steven Hoelscher and Karen E. Till, Minneapolis: University of Minnesota Press, pp. 24–40.

Denzin, Norman K. (1997), *Interpretive Ethnography,* Thousand Oaks, CA: Sage.

Draaisma, Douwe (2000), *Metaphors of Memory: A History of Ideas about the Mind,* Cambridge, UK: Cambridge University Press.

Fara, Patricia and Karalyn Patterson (1998), *Memory,* Cambridge: Cambridge University Press.

Fitzgerald, F. Scott (1926), *The Great Gatsby,* Harmondsworth, UK: Penguin.

Goss, Jon (1996), "Disquiet on the Waterfront: Reflections on Nostalgia and Utopia in the Urban Archetypes of Festival Marketplaces," *Urban Geography,* 17 (3): 221–47.

Gould, Stephen J. (1995), "Researcher Introspection as a Method in Consumer Research: Applications, Issues and Implications," *Journal of Consumer Research,* 21 (March): 719–22.

Harris, John E. and Peter E. Morris (1984), *Everyday Memory, Actions and Absent-Mindedness,* London: Academic Press.

Hirschman, Elizabeth C. and Morris B. Holbrook (1992), *Postmodern Consumer Research: The Study of Consumption as Text,* Newbury Park, CA: Sage.

Holbrook, Morris, B. (1984), "Theory Development Is a Jazz Solo: Bird Lives," in *Proceedings of the 1984 AMA Winter Educators' Conference,* ed. Paul F. Anderson and Michael J. Ryan, Chicago: American Marketing Association, pp. 48–52.

—— (1995), *Consumer Research: Introspective Essays on the Study of Consumption,* Thousand Oaks, CA: Sage.

Khermouch, Gerry (2001), "Consumers in the Mist: Mad Ave.'s Anthropologists Are Unearthing Our Secrets," *Business Week,* February 26: 77–78.

Levy, Sidney J. (1996), "Stalking the Amphisbaena," *Journal of Consumer Research,* 23 (3): 163–76.

McConkey, James (1996), *The Anatomy of Memory,* Oxford, UK: Oxford University Press.

Neisser, Ulric and Eugene Winograd (eds.) (1988), *Remembering Reconsidered: Ecological and Traditional Approaches to the Study of Memory,* Cambridge, UK: Cambridge University Press.

Nelson, Emily (2001), "P&G Plans to Visit People's Homes to Record (Almost) All Their Habits," *The Wall Street Journal,* May 17.

Schacter, Daniel L. (1996), *Searching for Memory: The Brain, the Mind, and the Past,* New York: Basic Books.

Sherry, John F., Jr. (1991), "Postmodern Alternatives: The Interpretive Turn in Consumer Research," in *Handbook of Consumer Research,* ed. Thomas S. Robertson and Harold H. Kassarjian, Englewood Cliffs, NJ: Prentice Hall, pp. 548–91.

—— (1998), "The Soul of the Company Store: Nike Town Chicago and the Emplaced Brandscape," in *Servicescapes: The Concept of Place in Contemporary Markets,* ed. John F. Sherry, Jr., Chicago: NTC Books, pp. 109–46.

Simpson, David (1995), *The Academic Postmodern and the Rule of Literature,* Chicago: University of Chicago Press.

Steier, Frederick (1991), *Research and Reflexivity,* London: Sage.

Turner, Frederick (1986), *Natural Classicism: Essays on Literature and Science,* New York: Paragon.

———— (1991), *Beauty: The Value of Values,* Charlottesville: University of Virginia Press.

———— (1995), *The Culture of Hope: A New Birth of the Classical Spirit,* New York: Free Press.

———— (1999), "An Ecopoetics of Beauty and Meaning," in *Biopoetics: Evolutionary Explorations in the Arts,* ed. Brett Cooke and Frederick Turner, Lexington, KY: ICUS, pp. 119–37.

Underhill, Paco (1999), *Why We Buy: The Science of Shopping,* London: Orion.

Wallendorf, Melanie and Merrie Brucks (1993), "Introspection in Consumer Research: Implementation and Implications," *Journal of Consumer Research,* 20 (December): 339–59.

Woolgar, Steve (1988), *Knowledge and Reflexivity: New Frontiers in the Sociology of Knowledge.* London: Sage.

Conclusion

What Time Is This Place?

17

What's Past Is Prologue

Retroscapes in Retrospect

John F. Sherry, Jr.

It was one of those late winter days in Evanston, Illinois. Overcast grey sky. Overcold windchilled thirty-something degrees. Overly humid lake effect dreariness. A fitting day for my quarter grading finally to be over. Donning my overcoat, I got into my car and sped to the airport, there to collect my collaborator on this retroscapes project, Stephen Brown, on the last leg of his jaunt across the pond. While the coming vernal equinox portended the kind of light-and-shadows balance I hoped our partnership would bring to the project, I couldn't have orchestrated a more fitting climatic embrace.

Not only would this weather welcome remind him of the damp charm of his native Belfast, it would also ease his transition into Chicagoland culture, well in advance of my weaning him off Ulster fries and hooking him up to deep dish pizza and wet beef sandwiches. Best of all, it was St. Patrick's Day in the Windy City, an alignment of adjectives so appropriate to the occasion a more auspicious augury could not be imagined.

Stephen debarked upon the adventure this present volume represents with a foot-wiping on the antiseptic astroturf carpet our customs inspectors required of U.K. visitors. Back in the day, hoof-and-mouth and mad cow disease seemed our principal threat of foreign invasion. We were oblivious to plastic explosive shoe soles. In the postapocalyptic aftermath of 9/11, we are transformed udderly, and we in the midwestern heartland have experienced this bovine reversal as our personal *Tain*. I was to return Stephen to this same airport six months later, in much better weather, but in a martial climate far more similar to that of his hometown than anyone might ever have predicted. A brave new world for me, back to the future for Stephen, is what I imagined then.

This project has continued to unfold in a retro-atmospherics of meteorological palpability. Our brandscapes were once alive with totems and fetishes, bracketed by Barbarism and Kenosis. They are now pervaded by a new set of Ps—patriotism, parochialism, profit, and prophecy—as world systems recollide, reconfigure, and recombine, and they are wrapped in a polysemous package of public paranoia. Marketing, consumption, and state ideology have become more interpenetrating than ever before. Advertisers are now our official diplomats. America's most recent premiere annual secular ritual, its perennial paean to civil religion, Super Bowl XXXVI, is a testament to this perfusion. The event comprised a retroscape of spectacular proportion, replete with stirring performances of tribal militarism, culture nationalism, and pluralistic solidarity. Warrior sodalities and vestal virgins, high priests and sacred harlots, Americana reprised in genuflecting Clydesdales and Pepsi pastiche, a focal contest with an underdog yet predestined protagonist, and countless other strands of retropageanty were woven together by marketers in the warp of everyday heroism and the weft of quiet desperation. It is against this conservative-to-reactionary mythological backdrop of a return to Eden through enlightened consumption that the retroscaping of America, if not the Western world, will accelerate for the foreseeable future.

As I complete the draft of this chapter, it is St. Patrick's Day once again. This is dramatic unity on an anthropological scale, the year being the ethnographer's ritual equivalent to the psychoanalyst's fifty-minute hour. There is a satisfyingly calendrical correctness to the feel of a yearlong immersion in a project, and of emerging from the overwhelming welter of the mundane exotic into the relative clarity of written accounting. The effort has allowed me, as a consumer ethnographer—a deep hanger-out, a loiterer with intent—to illustrate the portion of my life project that is unfolding among fanatics, cultural transvestites, and hermenauts. So also have my colleagues revealed something of themselves in their own accounts of their encounters with retroscapes. Like some melancholic Nipper® before the gramophone, I strive to hear disaster's voice in the revolving grooves of my informants' enthusiasms, but fail miserably in the attempt, managing simply to chronicle my own willing descent into the vortices of retrotopia. I offer my own abjection to the forces of the retroscape as a warning to critical thinkers and liberation theologists, and toss conventional canons of programmatic closure to the winds, in offering these concluding remarks.

In his trenchant lampoon of marketing practice (in particular, the coolhunting of trend analysts) Alex Shakar (2001) describes a "post-ironic" culture so saturated with ironic doubt that it comes to doubt its own mode of doubting, causing its members to blur the boundaries between irony and earnestness; thus does schizophrenia, if not multiphrenia, become a characteristic mode of apprehending, as opposites are suspended. He coins the term "paradessence" to capture the paradoxical essence of products that fosters their mystical relationship with consumers, when opposites are suspended. In keeping with the vampiric models of marketplace behavior afloat in cultural studies today, we can appropriate Shakar's criticism and harness it to our understanding of the dynamics of the retroscape's appeal. Designers exploit our Mobius-strip grasp of time, and our human groundedness in place (whether we are nomadic or sedentary), while consumers willingly suspend their disbelief and collaborate in creating an illusion of authentic time travel, in the realization of the retroscape. When we experience the present as a disconnected series of fragments of immediacy, and exist primarily (and perhaps, more accurately, simultaneously) in the past and the future, we have succumbed to the retroscape's aura.

Our contributing authors have variously storied the topography of the retroscape, providing us with what the punning an-trope-ologist, Roy Wagner, might call both "near-life" and "near-depth" experiences of this nominally retail world. According to Wagner:

> Time is always the *beginning* of space, wherever it may be and whatever the circumstances, so that space is the only part of it still left around to tell us what it *was*. (2001, p. 187)

He understands styles of architecture and ritual to be temporal phenomena, but their defining moment to be a spatial one. Whether the retroscape occurs in cyberia or suburbia, in the desert or at dessert, in hestial or hermetic surroundings, on fields or screens, among Lincoln logs or catalogs, or in paradise or the mind's eye, it manages to collapse our sense of a spatiotemporal continuum inward upon itself. Our authors ground us in a land where time stands still, even as we pay attention to the man behind the curtain, helping him sustain the illusion of progressive conservatism. We are natives in a familiar land, our hosts having tamed the exotic appeal of "there" and harnessed it in such a way as to refresh or renew our identities through our dwelling in that "then." Everything old is new again; *plus ça change, plus c'est la même chose*. Marketers strive mightily to keep the product life circle turning (Brown, Kozinets, and Sherry 2002).

When it comes to charting retroscapes in the cartography of moral geography, clearly one critic's "architecture of reassurance" (Marling 1997) is another's "anthropological recrudescence" (McMurtry 1999). Our volume's authors have displayed emotions ranging from a nativist disdain worthy of a

Carl Hiaasen to a childlike enthusiasm characteristic of a Joseph Pine. They have told realist, confessional, and impressionist tales (Van Maanen 1988), making full use of introspection and exteroception (Sherry 2000). Evocation of place requires representation that encourages the reader to vibrate with the same resonance the author has achieved when he or she held up the turning fork of intraceptive intuition to the retroscape of interest (Bochner and Ellis 2002; Sherry and Schouten 2002). Further, our authors have generally grounded their interpretations in encounters with consumers who are actually engaged in cocreating these retroscapes, providing an empirical cast to their critical commentary, a kind of countercultural studies tack that incorporates emics into etics, and interdisciplinary insight into complex phenomena, a vigilance and holism missing from otherwise often exemplary accounts of servicescapes from thinkers such as Gottdeiner (2000, 2001), Satterthwaite (2001), and Ritzer (1999), and just beginning to appear in work by Miller (2001) and Twitchell (2002).

From the flamboyant opulence of the ersatz ancient Roman mall that is the Las Vegas Forum Shops, to the hauntingly evocative verisimilar starkness of the U.S. Holocaust Memorial Museum in Washington, D.C., the retroscape acts as a vehicle of cultural memory that encourages its dwellers to reflect upon the impact that time continues to have on his or her life project. Memory is selectively stored in and retrieved from such sites, affecting the shapes our futures assume; history is remade upon each successive visit. Our identities are also (re)constructed in transit through these places (Ben-Amos and Weissberg 1999; Brown 2001). Further, the invented traditions (Hobsbawm and Ranger 1983) embodied and emplaced in many retroscapes suggest just how contingent our identities are upon the careful positioning of temporally bounded cocreation or coproduction of the consumption experience. This is as true for such ideologically freighted consumption as the "Americanizing" of the Holocaust (Cole 1999) as it is the romanticized consumption of cowboy culture at stock shows and rodeos (Peñaloza 2001). This marketing mythopoeia, this retrofuturistic revisionism, is equal parts découpage and bricolage, and seems as emancipatory as repressive. But how best to calculate the net present value of nostalgia?

I have heard my futurist colleagues cackle with pencil-headed glee at a notion they label "aiglatson," a condition they describe as a romantic attachment to the future. This is the figurative (and virtually literal) mirror-image of nostalgia, and is a culture-bound syndrome most U.S. (if not European) consumers will recognize. Grosz (2001, p. 145) understands this syndrome as the essence of the utopian: "the projection of a past or present as if it were the future":

> The utopian is in fact a freezing of the indeterminable moment from the past through the future that the present is unable to directly control. . . . The utopian mode seeks a future in which time will cease to be a relevant factor, and movement, change, and becoming remain impossible.

This timelessness, however, is ultimately antithetical to the aura of the retroscape, as the dweller must continually renegotiate a relationship with time while on the premises, and the marketer must constantly refresh the ambience of the site.

Describing the "ultimate homelessness" that is part of our human condition, and the penchant for revivalism that is "quintessentially American," Tuan (1996, pp. 93, 188) anticipates the rise of retroscapes we have experienced in the United States. Consumers are spatiotemporal nomads who can be enticed to dwell in the "there and then" by the inherently exotic and romantic nature of retrospace. The utopian cast of this space is not lost on Tuan (p. 181), who cites the philosopher Kolakowski on cosmopolitanism:

> When I am asked where I would like to live, my standard answer is: deep in the virgin mountain forest on a lakeshore at the corner or Madison Avenue in Manhattan and Champs-Elysees, in a small tidy town.

This archetypical longing for a no-place animated by a dialectic of regression/progression, purity/turpitude, serenity/turbulence, hestial/hermetic, aboriginal/modern . . . is enflamed by the retroscape, which promises momentary satisfaction to its dwellers-in-transit. As the American apotheosis of retail theatre proliferates around the globe via the thematization (Gottdiener 1997) of both the so-called new means of consumption (Ritzer 1999) and new forms of consumption (Gottdiener 2000), and as the experience and entertainment economies (Pine and Gilmore 1999; Wolf 1999) widen their theatres of influence, pattern-standardized retroscapes smoothe the transition of consumer diasporas parsing through customs.

The culture of memory that has diffused through Euro American societies since the late 1970s has both a global register and local manifestations (Huyssen 2001). Extending the philosopher Lubbe's concept of "musealization" in accounting for modernism's inevitable shrinking of the lived experience of the cutting-edge present, Huyssen (pp. 70–71) describes the way in which

> the present of advanced consumer capitalism prevails over past and future, sucking both into an expanding synchronomous space [and weakening] its grip on itself [providing] less stability . . . for contemporary subjects.

Memory culture advances as a form of "historicizing restoration" and "self-musealization"; its spread is accelerated by the new media (Huyssen 2001, pp. 61, 66), among which we must include marketing, which is ultimately charged (*pace* Benjamin) with the reauratization of what amounts to a cocreated or coproduced "original."

As commercial utopianism rushes to fill the gap created by collapsing ideological and scientific utopianisms (Bindé 2001), the retroscape is in the vanguard. As suggested in Stephen's introduction to this volume, the mystic chords of memory resonating in the retroscape are not nostalgic in the stripped down American sense of that term, but rather in the more evocative Greek etymological sense. Nostalgia is

> the desire or longing with burning pain to journey [home]. It also evokes the sensory dimension of memory in exile and estrangement; it mixes bodily and emotional pain and ties painful experiences of spiritual and somatic exile to the notion of maturation and ripening. . . . [Finally, it] evokes the transformative impact of the part as unreconciled historical experience. (Seremetakis 1994, p. 4)

Marketers as often blunt as sharpen the pain of nostalgia, converting the neuralgia of exile to the ataraxia of homecoming, but they strive to craft the retroscape in such a way that the past commingles intimately with the future. This retrofuturism is as palpable in the technoutopias of cyberspace (Barbrook and Cameron 2001) as it is in the paraprimitive precincts of the Black Rock Desert (Finkel 2000, Hamrah et al. 2000). Our contributing authors are bent on recovering the meanings consumers generate in encounters with the retroscape, irrespective of the marketer's intention. Such meanings have generally been lost to conventional marketing research (Maclaran and Brown 2000). Some seem subversive of the marketer's intention, others affirming. Whether critical or complimentary, we have tried to pin them to the board.

I'm reminded of a prospecting trip I made with Jim Twitchell last autumn, to the Willow Creek Community Church, of Harvard Business School case study fame, an institution that can fairly be described as a postmodern chautauqua enterprise creolizing such secular venues as the mall, food court, rock concert, theatrical performance, sporting event, community college, day care center, cinema, and living room in its liturgy. Two knaves (naifs?) in the nave, we prowled the grounds, attending services, talking with "seekers" and "believers," observing the activities of a host of ministries, browsing the bookstore, and roaming backstage to the degree propriety allowed, marveling at the ways in which high technology and secular rhetoric were imagineered to produce contemporary communities of biblical proportions.

The sanctuary we experienced flowed as much from the spigots of Starbucks' coffee urns and state-of-the-art audio systems as it did from the vernacular commentary on the Good Book, delivered in street clothes by a minister onstage and amplified on two enormous viewing screens. Pomo-proselytizing, e-evangelizing, and retro-recruiting appeal to contemporary consumers of religions, whose flagging brand loyalties have left them unchurched, if not all together unhoused. We felt unthreatened, unchallenged, and comfortable as we were led back to the source (at which point we balked, bugged out, and debriefed at a local deli).

Retroscapes share precisely this utopian essence, their managers eager to immure consumers within a total institution, their residents willing to suspend disbelief and collude in the staging of the eternal return to Never/Always-land. Our resurrection, our salvific consumption, requires, in the words of John Denver's song, going home to a place we've never been before. Paradoxically, that place is always Kansas, for, as Dorothy discovered (and as heroes from Odysseus through Col. George Taylor always do), there's no place like home. On behalf of the authors in this volume, "Welcome home" and as T.S. Eliot might wish, may you know the place for the first time.

References

Barbrook, Richard and Andy Cameron (2001), "Californian Ideology," in *Crypto Anarchy, Cyberstates, and Pirate Utopias*, ed. Peter Ludlow, Cambridge, MA: MIT Press, pp. 363–87.

Ben-Amos, Dan and Liliane Weissberg (eds.) (1999), *Cultural Memory and the Construction of Identity*, Detroit, MI: Wayne State University Press.

Bindé, Jérôme (2001), "Toward an Ethics of the Future," in *Globalization*, ed. Arjun Appradurai, Durham, NC: Duke University Press, pp. 90–113.

Bochner, Arthur and Carolyn Ellis (eds.) (2002), *Ethnographically Speaking: Autoethnography, Literature and Aesthetics*, New York: Altamira Press.

Brown, Stephen (2001), *Marketing—The Retro Revolution*, Thousand Oaks, CA: Sage.

Brown, Stephen, Robert Kozinets, and John F. Sherry, Jr. (2002), "Still Ahead, A Look Back: Reconnoitering Retromarketing," unpublished working paper, Kellogg School of Management, Northwestern University, Evanston, IL 60208.

Cole, Tim (1999), *Selling the Holocaust*, New York: Routledge.

Finkel, Michael (2000), "Burning Man," *Hooked on the Outdoors*, 2 (3): 132–37.

Gottdiener, Mark (1997), *The Theming of America*, Boulder, CO: Westview Press.

——— (2000), *New Forms of Consumption: Consumers, Culture and Commodification*, New York: Rowman and Littlefield.

——— (2001), *Life in the Air: Surviving the New Culture of Air Travel*, Boulder, CO: Rowman and Littlefield.

Grosz, Elizabeth (2001), *Architecture from the Outside: Essays on Virtual and Real Space*, Cambridge, MA: MIT Press.

Hamrah, A.S. et al. (2000), "Dunking Booth at Burning Man," *Hermenaut*, 16 (Winter): 140–47.

Hobsbawm, Eric and Terence Ranger (eds.) (1983), *The Invention of Tradition*, Cambridge, MA: Cambridge University Press.

Huyssen, Andreas (2001), "Present Pasts: Media, Politics, Amnesia," in *Globalization*, ed. Arjun Appadurai, Durham, NC: Duke University Press, pp. 55–77.

Maclaran, Pauline and Stephen Brown (2000), "The Future Perfect Declined: Utopian Studies and Consumer Research," *Journal of Marketing Management*, 17 (2–3): 367–90.

Marling, Karal Ann (1997), *Designing Disney's Theme Parks: The Architecture of Reassurance*, New York: Flammarion.

McMurtry, Larry (1999), *Walter Benjamin at the Dairy Queen: Reflections at Sixty and Beyond*, New York: Touchstone.

Miller, Daniel (2001), *The Dialectics of Shopping*, Chicago: University of Chicago Press.

Peñaloza, Lisa (2001), "Consuming the American West: Animating Cultural Meaning and Memory at a Stock Show and Rodeo," *Journal of Consumer Research*, 29 (2): 369–98.

Pine, Joseph and James Gilmore (1999), *The Experience Economy*, Boston, MA: Harvard Business School Press.

Ritzer, George (1999), *Enchanting a Disenchanted World: Revolutionizing the Means of Consumption*, Thousand Oaks, CA: Pine Forge Press.

Satterthwaite, Ann (2001), *Going Shopping: Consumer Choices and Community Consequences*, New Haven, CT: Yale University Press.

Serematakis, C. Nadia (1994), "The Memory of the Senses, Part I: Masks of the Transitory," in *The Senses Still: Perception and Memory as Material Culture in Modernity*, ed. C. Nadia Serematakis, Boulder, CO: Westview Press, pp. 1–18.

Shakar, Alex (2001), *The Savage Girl*, New York: HarperCollins.

Sherry, John F., Jr. (2000), "Place, Technology and Representation," *Journal of Consumer Research*, 27 (2): 273–78.

Sherry, John F., Jr. and John Schouten (2002), "A Role for Poetry in Consumer Research," *Journal of Consumer Research*, 29 (1): 218–34.

Tuan, Yi-Fu (1996), *Cosmos and Hearth: A Cosmopolite's Viewpoint*, Minneapolis: University of Minnesota Press.

Twitchell, James (2002), *Living It Up: Our Love Affair with Luxury*, New York: Columbia University Press.

Van Maanen, John (1998), *Tales of the Field*, Chicago: University of Chicago Press.

Wagner, Roy (2001), *An Anthropology of the Subject*, Berkeley: University of California Press.

Wolf, Michael (1999), *The Entertainment Economy*, New York: Random House.

About the Editors and Contributors

Aedh Aherne is professor of marketing aesthetics at Coole Community College of Commerce, Ireland. After completing his Ph.D. on the marketing acumen of W.B. Yeats, he spent several years as a versifier for the Hallmark Corporation. Like most Hallmark trainees, he started off composing verses for the "Family and Friends" suite, was quickly promoted to "Christmas and Mother's Day," and, despite an unsettling secondment to the "In Loving Memory" division, eventually attained the greeting cards' pinnacle of "Blank Inside for Special Messages." Academically, Aherne is best known for his books *Postmodern Marketing* and *Postmodern Marketing Two*, both of which were written under pseudonyms.

Gary J. Bamossy is visiting professor, and director of the Global Business Program at the David Eccles School of Business, University of Utah. He is also part-time professor of marketing at the Vrije Universiteit, Amsterdam, and research fellow of the Tinbergen Institute, Amsterdam. Bamossy is coauthor of *Consumer Behavior: A European Perspective* (2002), and coeditor with Janeen Costa of *Marketing in a Multicultural World: Ethnicity, Nationalism, and Cultural Identity* (1995). His research focuses on topics of international marketing, and cross-cultural consumer behavior.

Russell W. Belk is N. Eldon Tanner Professor in the David Eccles School of Business at the University of Utah. He is past president of the Association for Consumer Research, and is a fellow in the American Psychological Association and the Association for Consumer Research. Belk is past recipient of the University of Utah Distinguished Research Professorship and two Fulbright fellowships. He currently edits *Research in Consumer Behavior*, has served on the editorial review boards of 25 journals, has written or edited 15 books or monographs, and has published over 250 articles and papers. His research primarily involves the meanings of possessions and materialism and his methods have been increasingly qualitative and cross-cultural.

Janet Borgerson is philosopher in residence at the School of Business at Stockholm University, and a research affiliate with the European Center for Art and Management in Stockholm. One of her current projects focuses on agency, desire, and the infinite, and how they function in the marketplace. She has published many papers at the intersection of marketing, philosophy, and culture, with a particular emphasis on ethical issues surrounding identity and ontology.

Stephen Brown eked out a living on the edges of the entertainment industry prior to entering academic life. He variously worked as The Sex Pistols' interpersonal skills consultant, played one of the exploding drummers in *This Is Spinal Tap*, and served as Dave Lee Roth's body double in several Van Halen videos. Since taking up an academic position, Brown has written extensively. He has written lots of other words as well, but "extensively" remains his favorite. He uses extensively extensively in *Time, Space, and the Market*, though, prominently, figures prominently as well.

Janeen Arnold Costa is associate professor of marketing and adjunct associate professor of anthropology, University of Utah. She received her doctorate in cultural anthropology from Stanford University and undertook postdoctoral training in marketing. Her research focuses on the sociocultural and historical dimensions of consumption and marketing, published in the *Journal of Consumer Research*; *Journal of Marketing*; *Journal of Macromarketing*; *Consumption, Markets and Culture*; *Advances in Consumer Research* and numerous other books and conference proceedings. She edited *Gender Issues and Consumer Behavior* (1994), and coedited *Research in Consumer Behavior* (1993, 2000) and *Marketing in a Multicultural World* (1995). Costa founded the gender, marketing, and consumer behavior conferences sponsored by the Association for Consumer Research, and chaired and edited the proceedings of the first three conferences (1991, 1993, and 1996). She serves on the Policy Review Board of the *Journal of Consumer Research* and has been on numerous editorial review boards.

Christina Goulding is a professor of marketing at the Business School, University of Wolverhampton. Her research interests include issues of identity and consumption, subcultures of consumption, and nostalgic consumption. She has published her work in a number of journals including *Psychology and Marketing, European Journal of Marketing, Journal of Marketing Management*, and *Advances in Consumer Research*.

Patrick L. Hetzel (MBA from Université Robert Schuman, Strasbourg and Ph.D. from Université Jean Moulin, Lyon) is chaired professor of marketing at the Université Panthéon-Assas, Paris, France. His current research interests include: semiotics, hedonic consumption, fashion, design management, sales area design, postmodernism, and history of consumption. Hetzel has published many journal articles and book chapters and a book about consumption (*Planète Conso*, 2002). He is also editor in chief of *Decisions Marketing* (the Journal of the French Marketing Association).

Morris B. Holbrook is the W.T. Dillard Professor of Marketing in the Graduate School of Business at Columbia University, New York. Holbrook graduated from Harvard College with a B.A. degree in English (1965) and received his MBA (1967) and Ph.D. (1975) degrees in marketing from Columbia University. Since 1975, he has taught courses at the Columbia Business School in such areas as marketing strategy, sales management, research methods, consumer behavior, and commercial communication in the culture of consumption. His research has covered a wide variety of topics in marketing and consumer behavior, with a special focus on issues related to communication in general and to aesthetics, semiotics, hermeneutics, art, entertainment, nostalgia, and stereography in particular. Holbrook pursues such hobbies as playing the piano, attending jazz and classical concerts, going to movies and the theater, collecting musical recordings, taking stereographic photos, and being kind to cats.

Robert V. Kozinets is an assistant professor of marketing at Northwestern University's Kellogg School of Management. A marketer and anthropologist by training, he has consulted with a range of companies. His research encompasses high-technology consumption, subcultures, communities (online and off), media and entertainment, videography, consumer activism, and consumer resistance. Kozinets has written and published articles on *Star Trek*, the *X-Files*, coffee connoisseurs, Wal-Mart, ESPN Zone, and the Burning Man festival for journals such as the *Journal of Consumer Research*, the *Journal of Marketing Research*, the *Journal of Contemporary Ethnography*, and the *Journal of Retailing*. He can be reached at r-kozinets@kellogg.northwestern.edu.

Pauline Maclaran is professor of marketing at De Montfort University, Leicester. Her research has two main strands: gender issues in marketing and consumer behavior; and the experiential dimensions of contemporary consumption, particularly in relation to utopia and the festival marketplace. Much of this work draws on the tools and techniques of literary theory to gain insights into the symbolic aspects of consumer behavior.

Anthony Patterson is a marketing lecturer in the School of Management at the University of Liverpool. Coeditor of *Imagining Marketing: Art, Aesthetics and the Avant-Garde* (2000), his teaching and research interests include consumer behavior and marketing communications.

Hope Jensen Schau had an idyllic childhood in SoCal with sand in her hair and sandals on her feet. She is a newly minted Ph.D. from UCI and recently relocated to the "other" coast to be an assistant professor of marketing at Temple University in Pennsylvania. To distract herself from chronic homesickness and in an effort to achieve the ever-elusive tenure goal, she is diligently attempting to publish her research in respectable academic outlets. She also writes fiction and poetry that seem to find their way to publication, but ultimately "don't count" toward anything tangible. Such is life.

Jonathan Schroeder is senior lecturer and director of marketing in the Department of Industrial Economics and Management at the Royal Institute of Technology in Stockholm. He is also a visiting professor at Bocconi University in Milan. His research is focused on articulating how images work— clarification, communication, and conceptualization of brand image, product image, and images of identity.

John F. Sherry, Jr. joined the Kellogg marketing faculty in 1984. He is an anthropologist (Ph.D. University of Illinois, 1983) who studies both the sociocultural and symbolic dimensions of consumption, and the cultural ecology of marketing. He has researched, taught, and lectured around the globe. He is a fellow of both the American Anthropological Association and the Society for Applied Anthropology. Sherry is a past president of the Association for Consumer Research, and a former associate editor of the *Journal of Consumer Research*. He has edited *Contemporary Marketing and Consumer Behavior: An Anthropological Sourcebook* and *Servicescapes: The Concept of Place in Contemporary Markets*; he is coeditor of *Advances in Consumer Research, Vol. 19*. He has won awards for his scholarly work and poetry. Time permitting, he is an avid flatwater paddler, and is still trying to perfect his fifteen-foot jumpshot.

Maura Troester, a Ph.D. candidate at the University of Wisconsin–Madison, studies the volatile romance between marketing and culture. This particular chapter is indebted to the ideas of Michel Foucault, Michel de Certeau, John Urry, Rob Shields, Craig Thompson, and the generous people of Hayward, Wisconsin. Primary archival material for this essay can be found in the Anthony Wise Collection at the State Historical Society of Wisconsin.

Alladi Venkatesh is professor of management and computer science at the University of California, Irvine. He is very much interested in postmodern theory and is one of the few left on the planet who still believe in it, as the more sensible are returning to safer pastures. Venkatesh's other interests include the social impacts of information technology (IT) and in particular how IT has diffused into homes and among children. His various publications are available at his Web site, www.crito.uci.edu/noah.

Index